NAOKI URASAWA'S

MONSTER

volume **10**

Naoki Urasawa's
Monster
Volume 10
VIZ Signature Edition

STORY AND ART BY NAOKI URASAWA

English Adaptation/Agnes Yoshida
Translation/Sumiko Katsura
Touch-up Art & Lettering/Steve Dutro
Cover & Interior Design/Courtney Utt
Editor/Kit Fox

VP, Production/Alvin Lu
VP, Publishing Licensing/Rika Inouye
VP, Sales & Product Marketing/Gonzalo Ferreyra
VP, Creative/Linda Espinosa
Publisher/Hyoe Narita

Printed in the U.S.A.

Published by VIZ Media, LLC
P.O. Box 77010
San Francisco, CA 94107

VIZ Signature Edition
10 9 8 7 6 5 4 3 2
First printing, August 2007
Second printing, February 2009

www.viz.com
store.viz.com

PARENTAL ADVISORY
NAOKI URASAWA'S MONSTER is rated T+ for Older
Teen and is recommended for ages 16 and up. This
volume contains realistic and graphic violence.

ratings.viz.com

Naoki Urasawa's
Monster
Volume 10
Picnic

Story and Art by Naoki Urasawa

Chapter 1 Grimmer

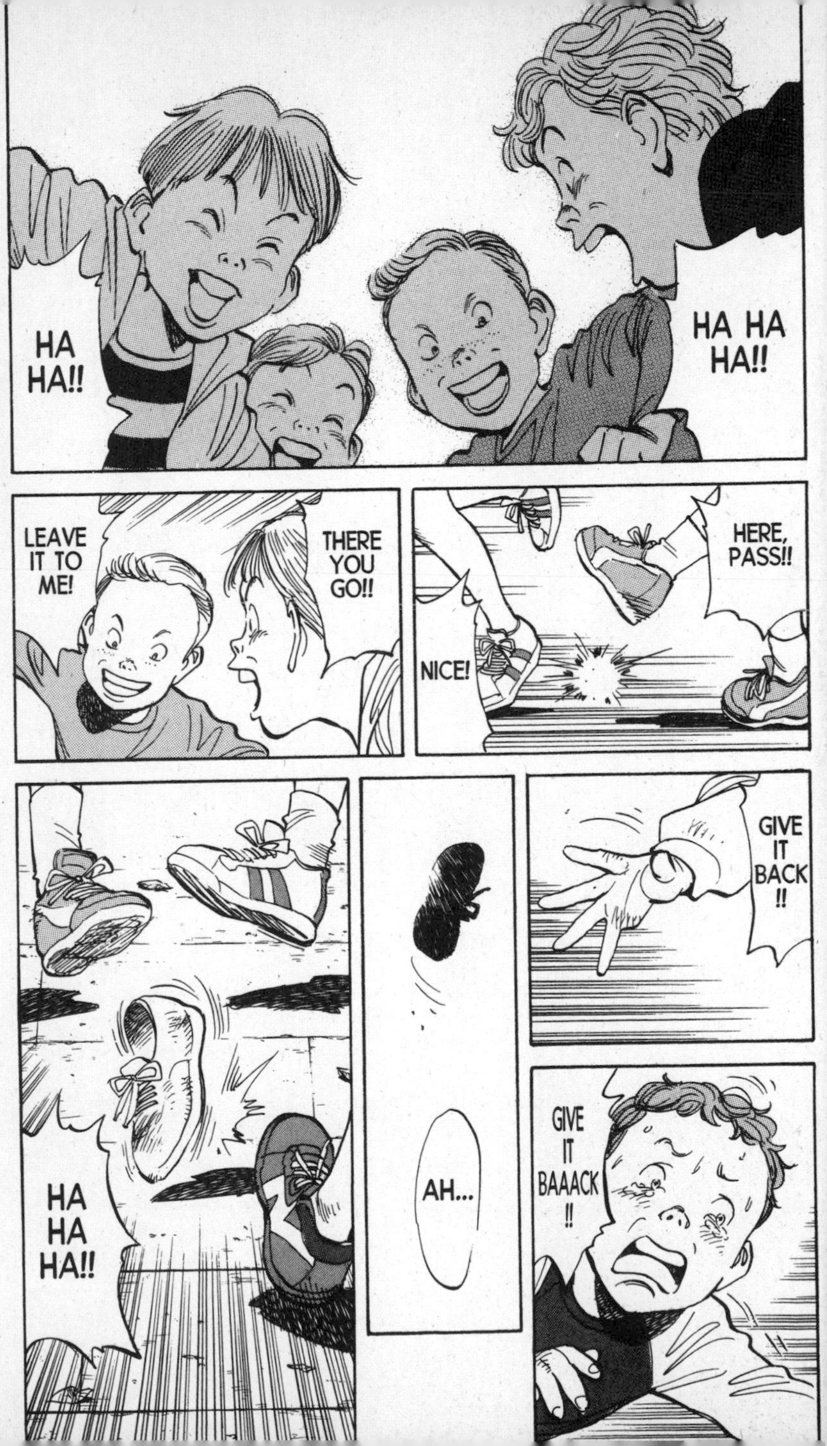
HA HA HA!!
HA HA!!
HERE, PASS!!
NICE!
THERE YOU GO!!
LEAVE IT TO ME!
GIVE IT BACK !!
GIVE IT BAAACK !!
AH...
HA HA HA!!

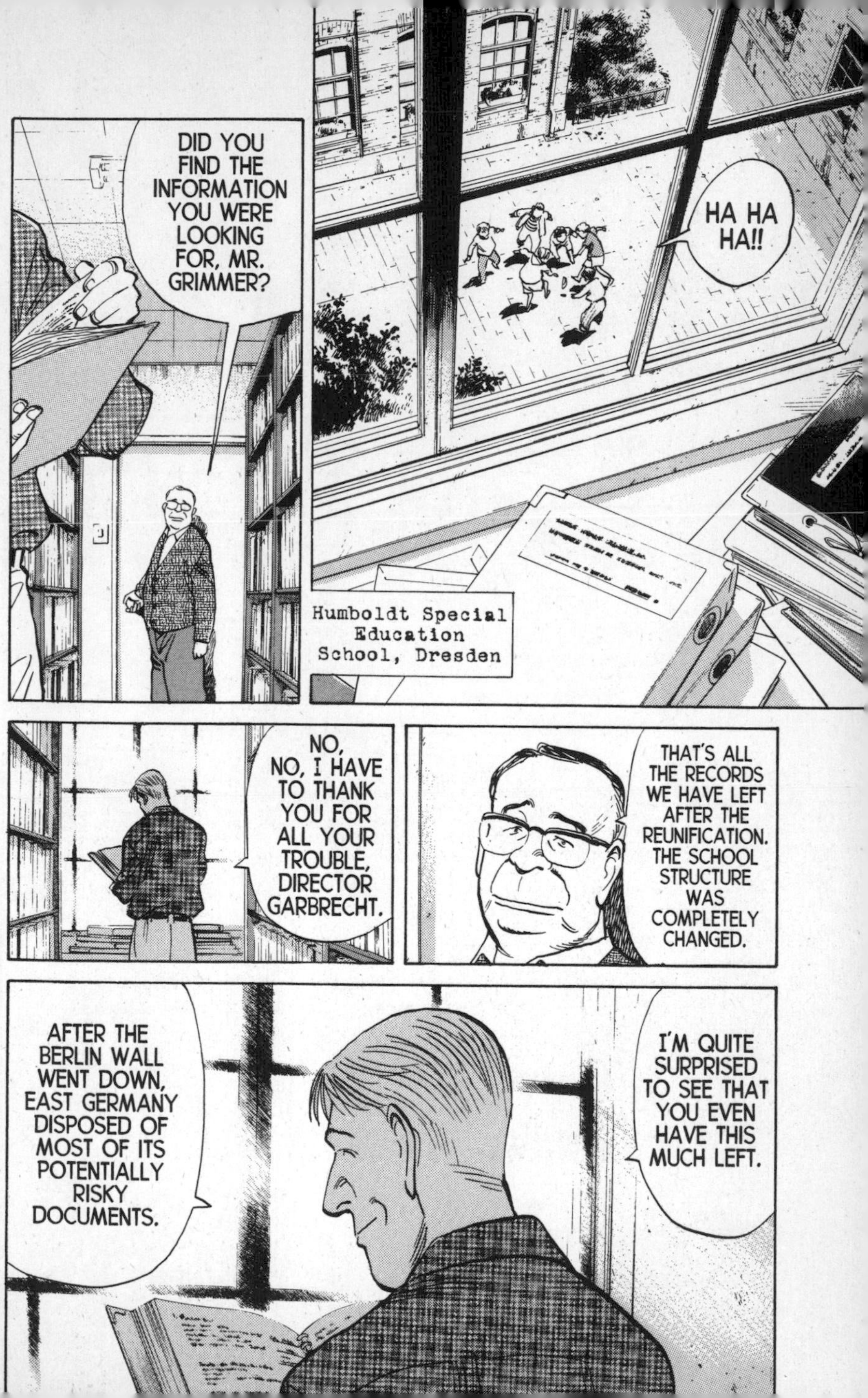
HA HA HA!!
Humboldt Special Education School, Dresden
DID YOU FIND THE INFORMATION YOU WERE LOOKING FOR, MR. GRIMMER?
THAT'S ALL THE RECORDS WE HAVE LEFT AFTER THE REUNIFICATION. THE SCHOOL STRUCTURE WAS COMPLETELY CHANGED.
NO, NO, I HAVE TO THANK YOU FOR ALL YOUR TROUBLE, DIRECTOR GARBRECHT.
I'M QUITE SURPRISED TO SEE THAT YOU EVEN HAVE THIS MUCH LEFT.
AFTER THE BERLIN WALL WENT DOWN, EAST GERMANY DISPOSED OF MOST OF ITS POTENTIALLY RISKY DOCUMENTS.

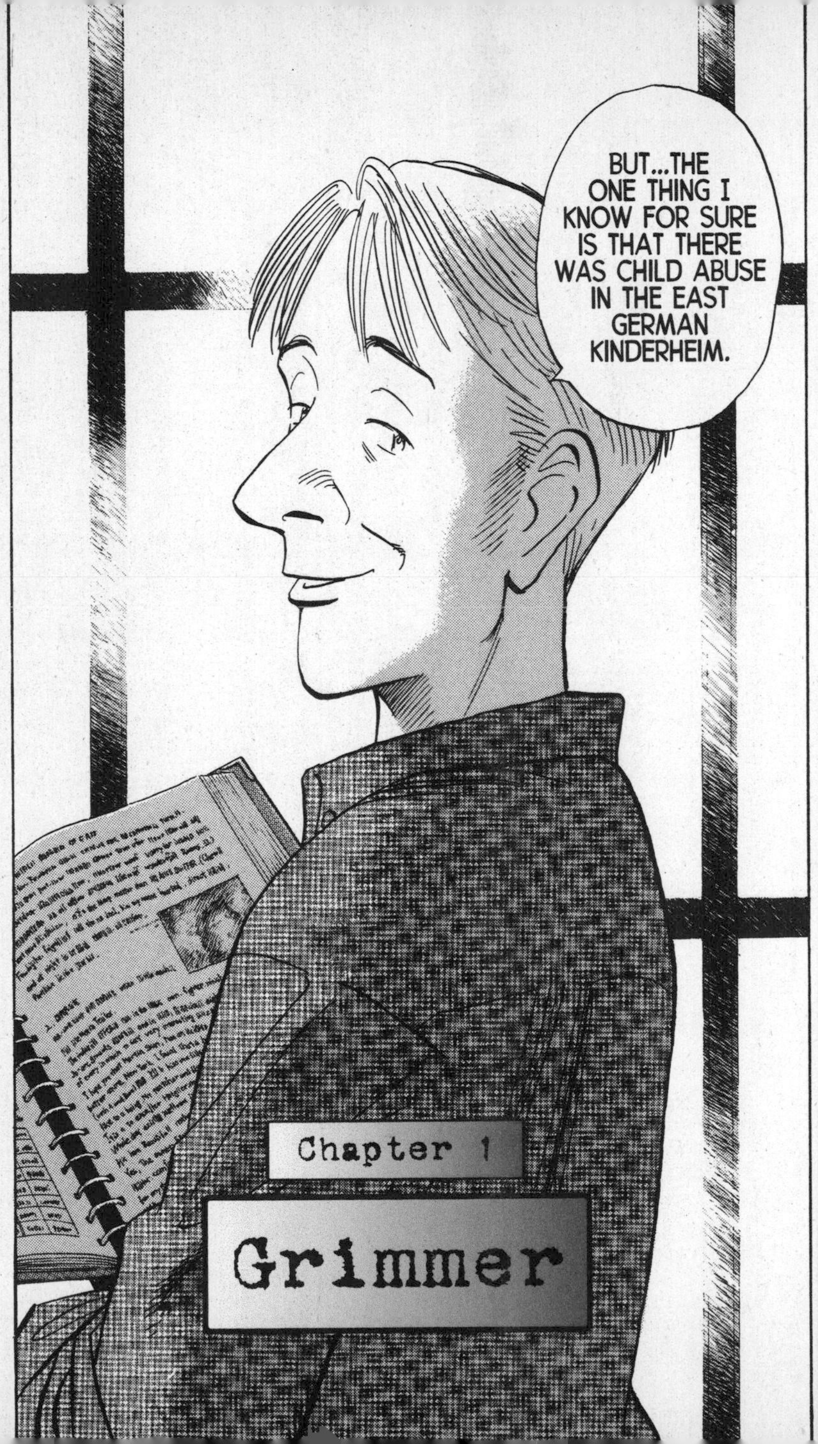
BUT...THE ONE THING I KNOW FOR SURE IS THAT THERE WAS CHILD ABUSE IN THE EAST GERMAN KINDERHEIM.
Chapter 1
Grimmer

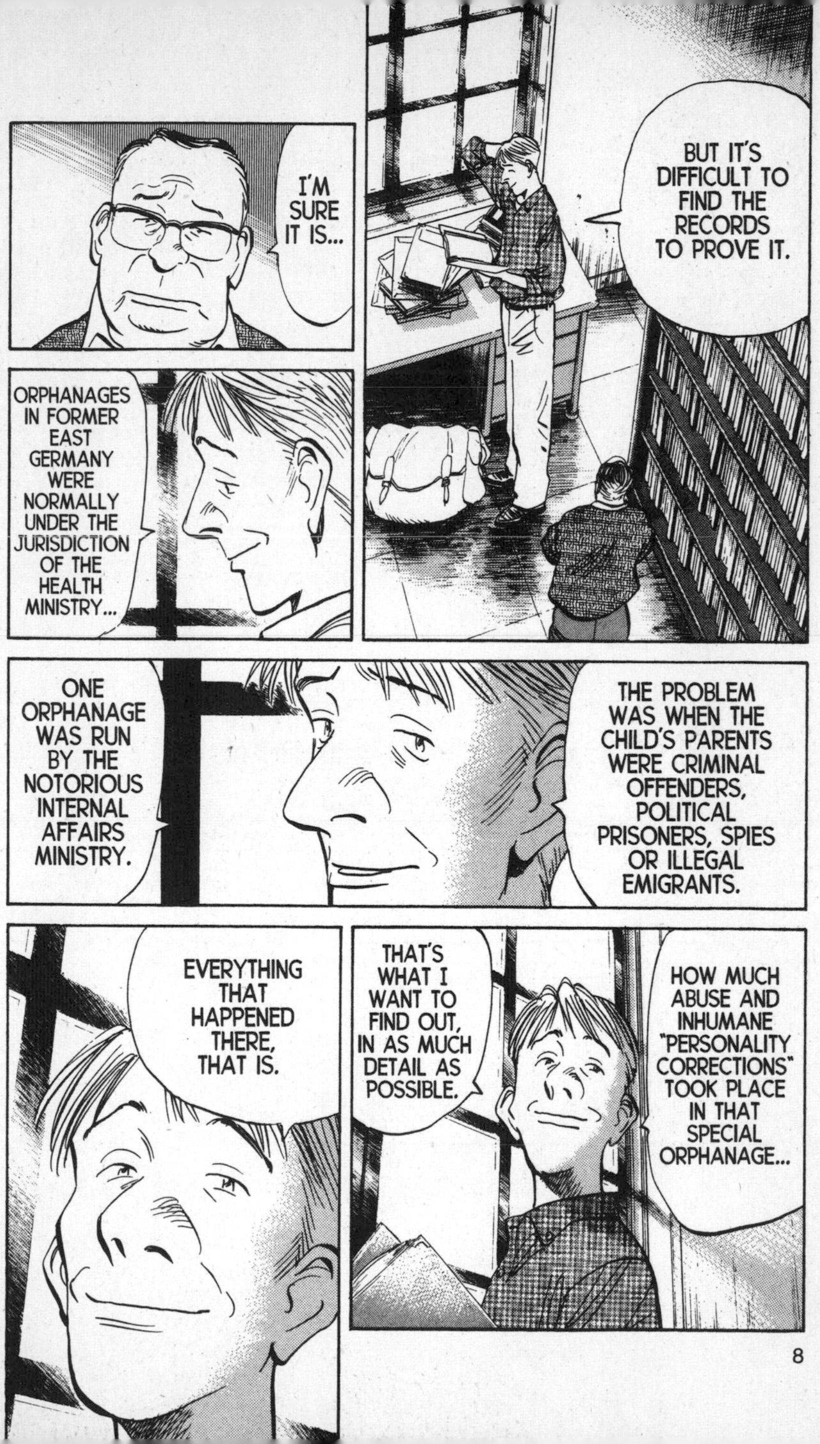
BUT IT'S DIFFICULT TO FIND THE RECORDS TO PROVE IT.
I'M SURE IT IS...
ORPHANAGES IN FORMER EAST GERMANY WERE NORMALLY UNDER THE JURISDICTION OF THE HEALTH MINISTRY...
THE PROBLEM WAS WHEN THE CHILD'S PARENTS WERE CRIMINAL OFFENDERS, POLITICAL PRISONERS, SPIES OR ILLEGAL EMIGRANTS.
ONE ORPHANAGE WAS RUN BY THE NOTORIOUS INTERNAL AFFAIRS MINISTRY.
HOW MUCH ABUSE AND INHUMANE "PERSONALITY CORRECTIONS" TOOK PLACE IN THAT SPECIAL ORPHANAGE...
THAT'S WHAT I WANT TO FIND OUT, IN AS MUCH DETAIL AS POSSIBLE.
EVERYTHING THAT HAPPENED THERE, THAT IS.

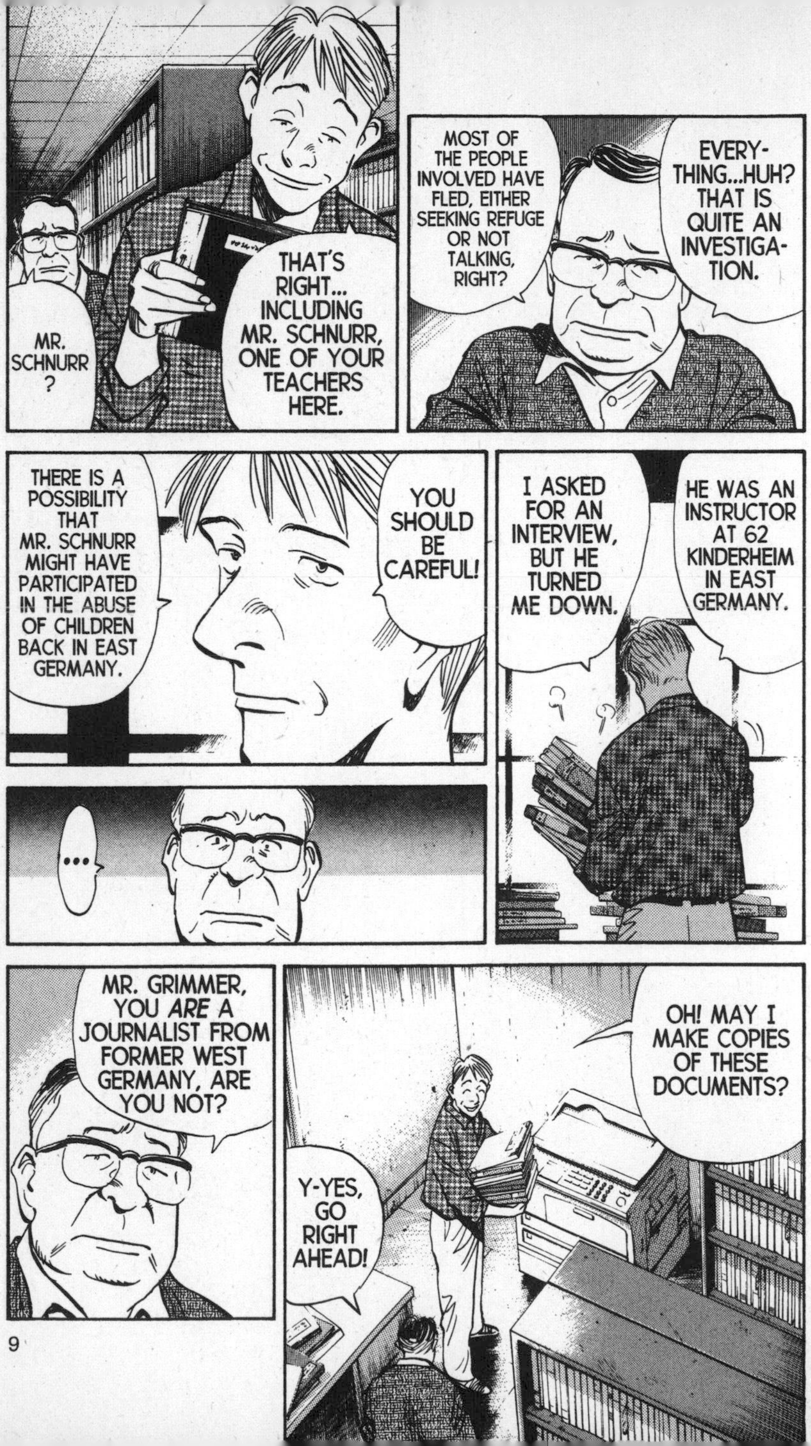
EVERY-THING...HUH? THAT IS QUITE AN INVESTIGA-TION.
MOST OF THE PEOPLE INVOLVED HAVE FLED, EITHER SEEKING REFUGE OR NOT TALKING, RIGHT?
THAT'S RIGHT... INCLUDING MR. SCHNURR, ONE OF YOUR TEACHERS HERE.
MR. SCHNURR ?
HE WAS AN INSTRUCTOR AT 62 KINDERHEIM IN EAST GERMANY.
I ASKED FOR AN INTERVIEW, BUT HE TURNED ME DOWN.
YOU SHOULD BE CAREFUL!
THERE IS A POSSIBILITY THAT MR. SCHNURR MIGHT HAVE PARTICIPATED IN THE ABUSE OF CHILDREN BACK IN EAST GERMANY.
...
OH! MAY I MAKE COPIES OF THESE DOCUMENTS?
Y-YES, GO RIGHT AHEAD!
MR. GRIMMER, YOU *ARE* A JOURNALIST FROM FORMER WEST GERMANY, ARE YOU NOT?

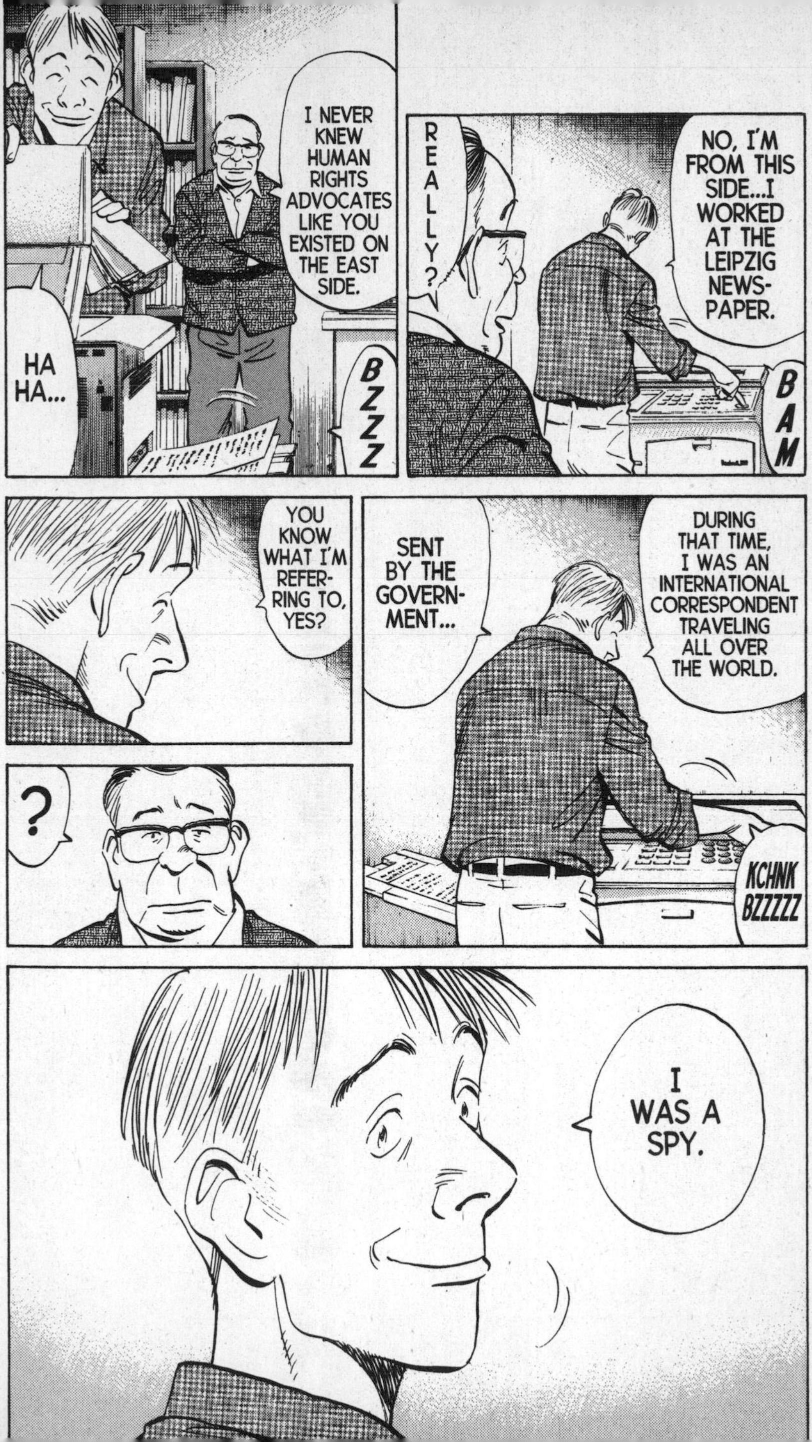
I NEVER KNEW HUMAN RIGHTS ADVOCATES LIKE YOU EXISTED ON THE EAST SIDE.
HA HA...
BZZZ
REALLY?
NO, I'M FROM THIS SIDE...I WORKED AT THE LEIPZIG NEWS-PAPER.
BAM
YOU KNOW WHAT I'M REFER-RING TO, YES?
?
DURING THAT TIME, I WAS AN INTERNATIONAL CORRESPONDENT TRAVELING ALL OVER THE WORLD.
SENT BY THE GOVERN-MENT...
KCHNK BZZZZZ
I WAS A SPY.

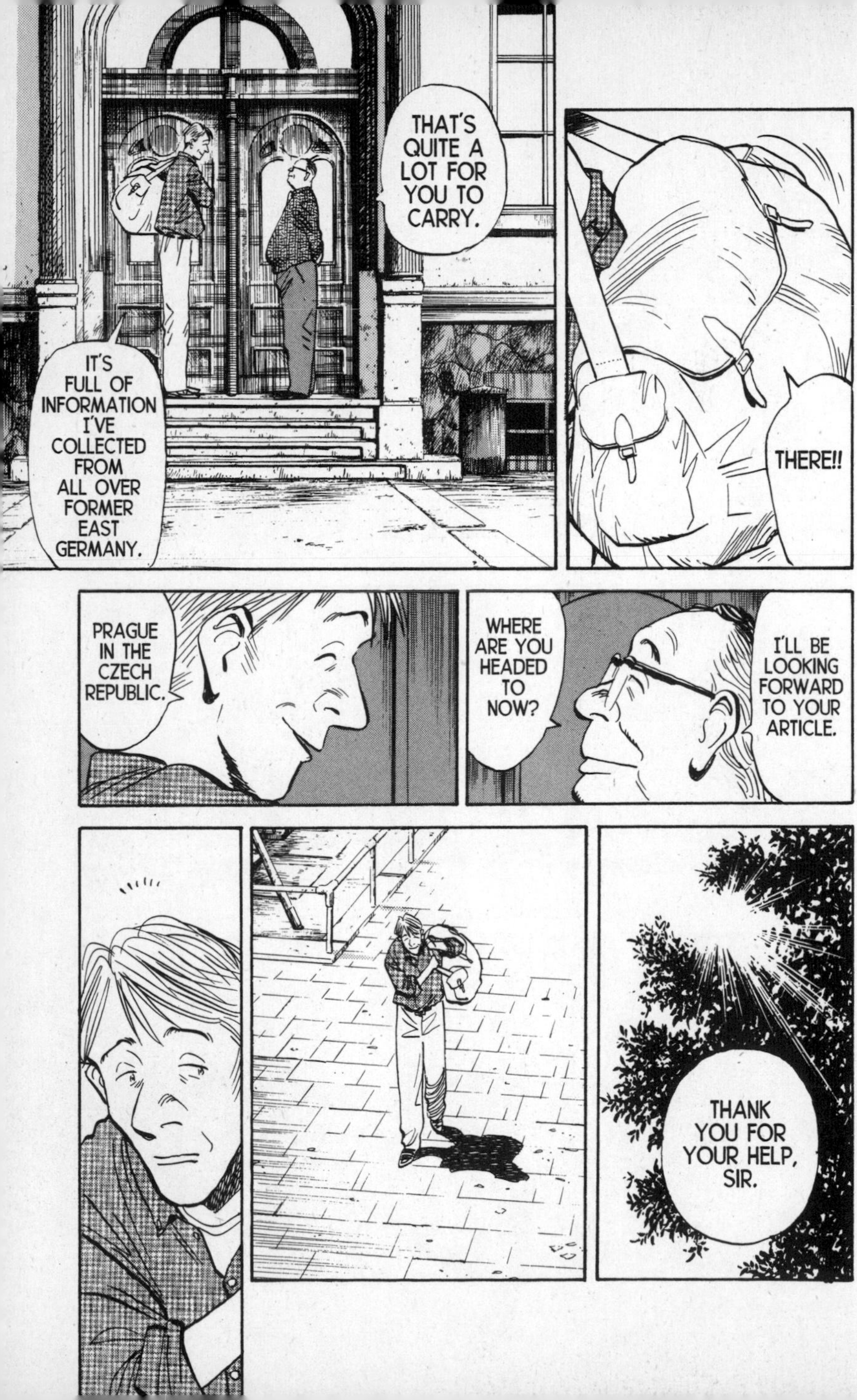
THERE!!
THAT'S QUITE A LOT FOR YOU TO CARRY.
IT'S FULL OF INFORMATION I'VE COLLECTED FROM ALL OVER FORMER EAST GERMANY.
I'LL BE LOOKING FORWARD TO YOUR ARTICLE.
WHERE ARE YOU HEADED TO NOW?
PRAGUE IN THE CZECH REPUBLIC.
THANK YOU FOR YOUR HELP, SIR.

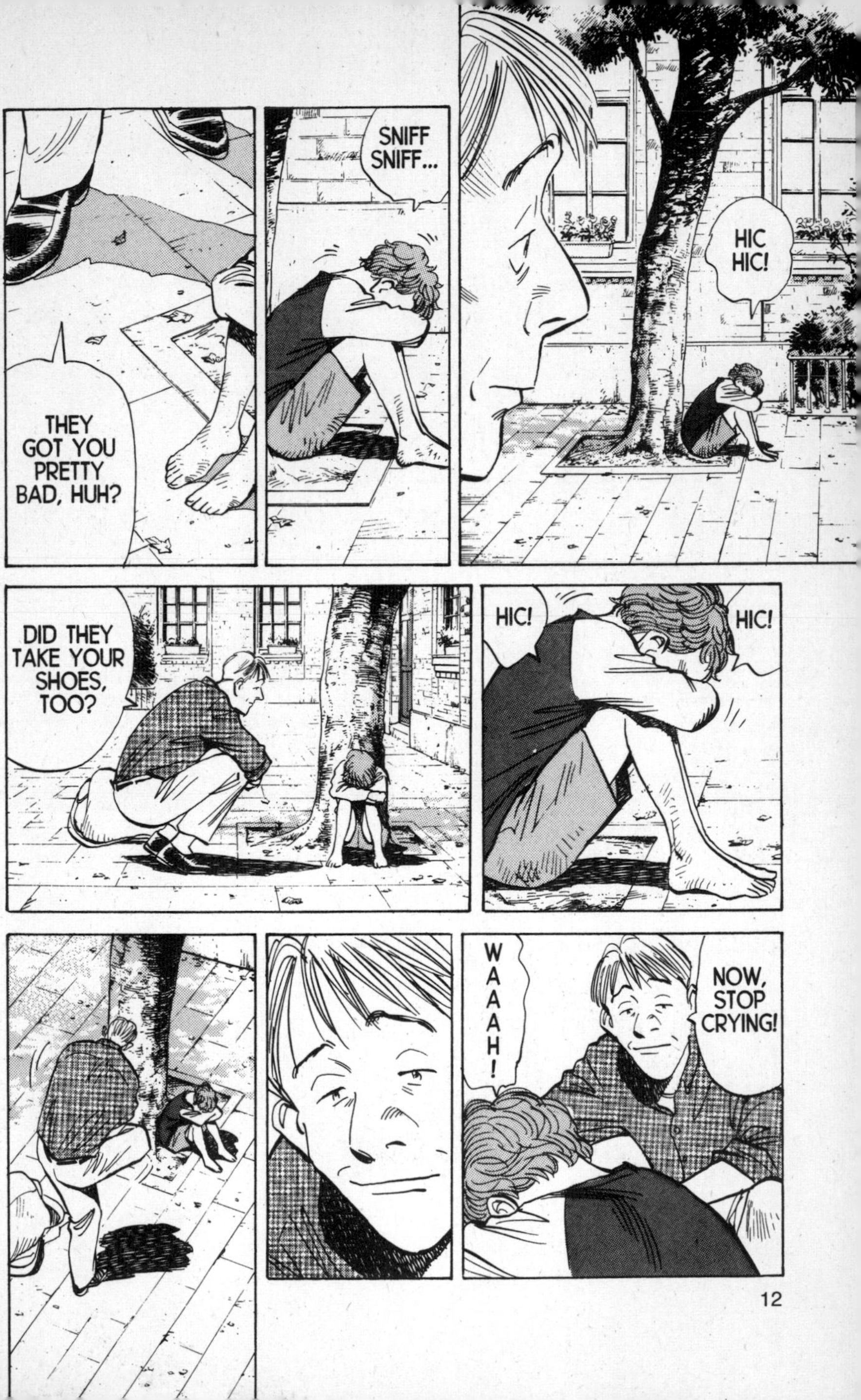
HIC HIC!
SNIFF SNIFF...
THEY GOT YOU PRETTY BAD, HUH?
HIC!
HIC!
DID THEY TAKE YOUR SHOES, TOO?
NOW, STOP CRYING!
WAAAAH!

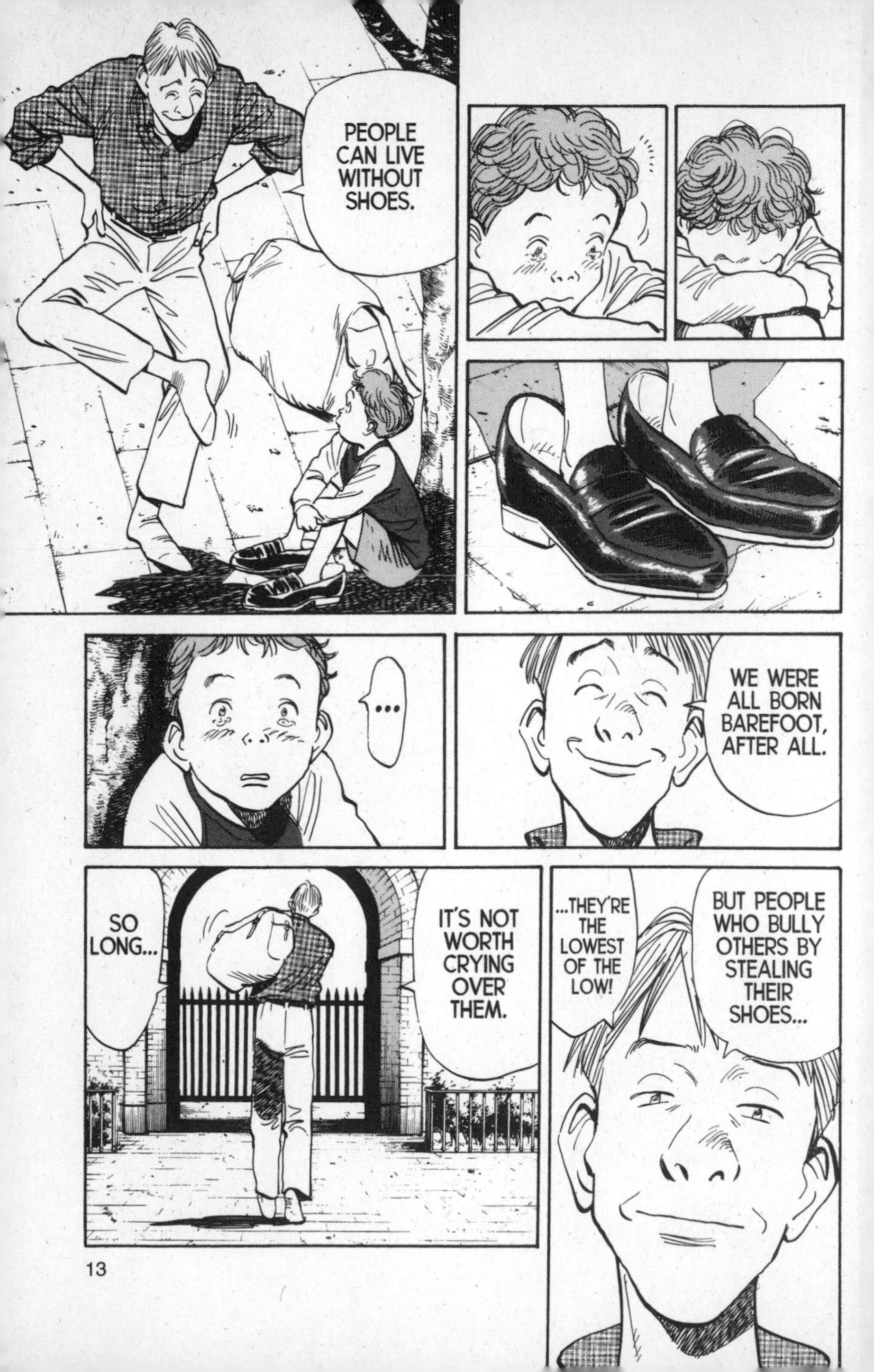
PEOPLE CAN LIVE WITHOUT SHOES.
WE WERE ALL BORN BAREFOOT, AFTER ALL.
...
BUT PEOPLE WHO BULLY OTHERS BY STEALING THEIR SHOES...
...THEY'RE THE LOWEST OF THE LOW!
IT'S NOT WORTH CRYING OVER THEM.
SO LONG...

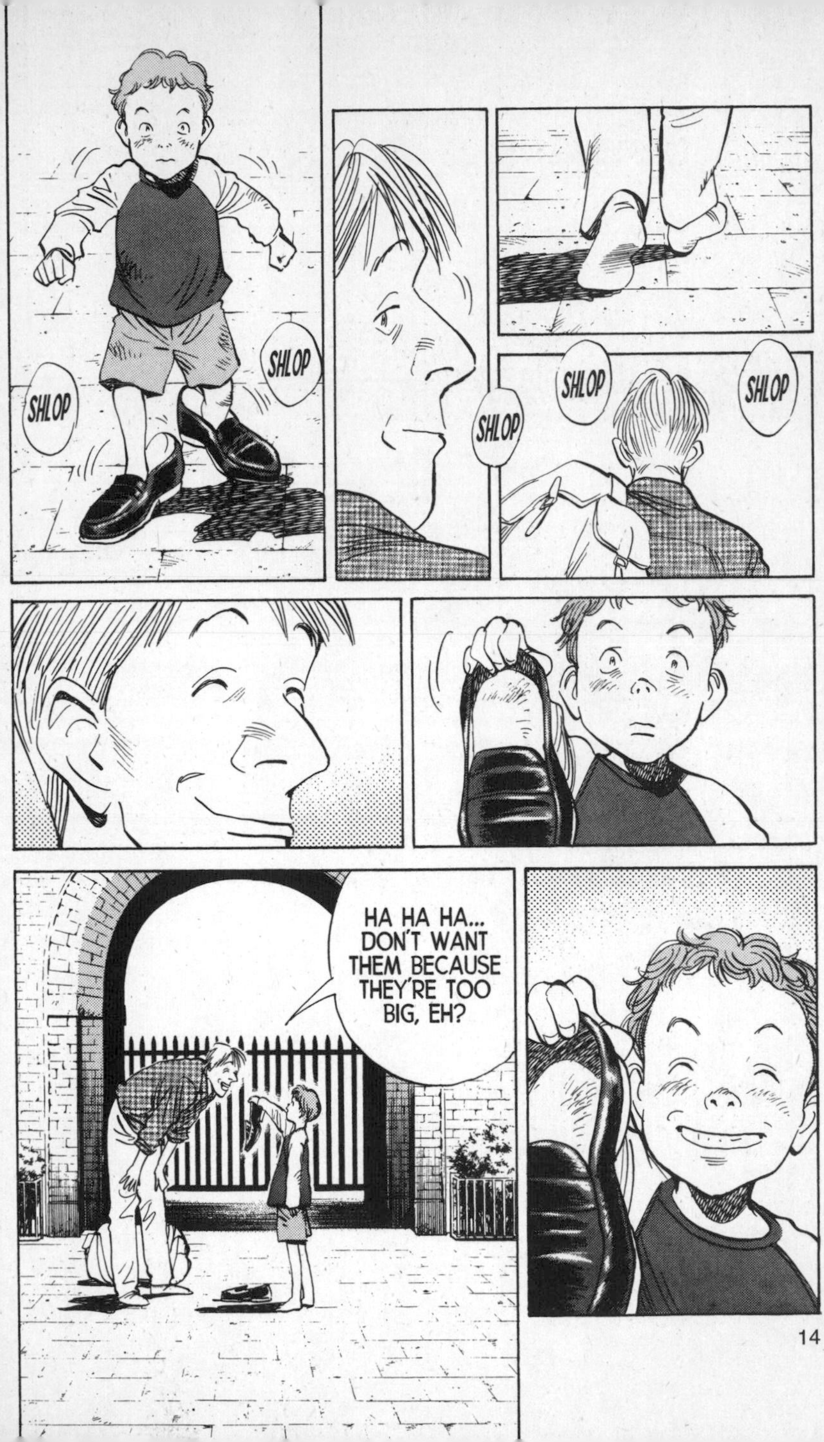
SHLOP
SHLOP
SHLOP
SHLOP
SHLOP
HA HA HA... DON'T WANT THEM BECAUSE THEY'RE TOO BIG, EH?

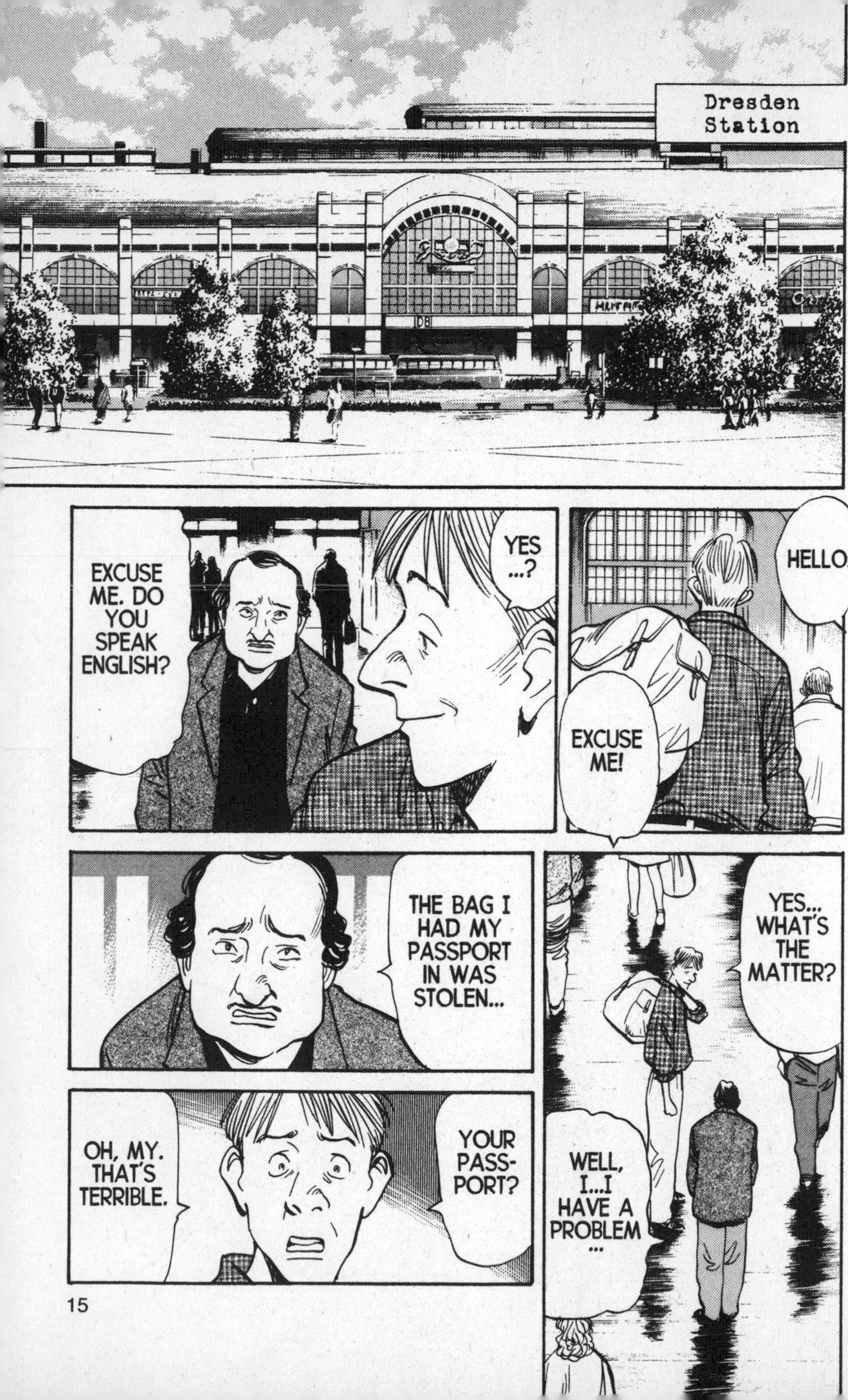
Dresden Station
HELLO!
EXCUSE ME!
YES ...?
EXCUSE ME. DO YOU SPEAK ENGLISH?
YES... WHAT'S THE MATTER?
WELL, I...I HAVE A PROBLEM ...
THE BAG I HAD MY PASSPORT IN WAS STOLEN...
YOUR PASS-PORT?
OH, MY. THAT'S TERRIBLE.

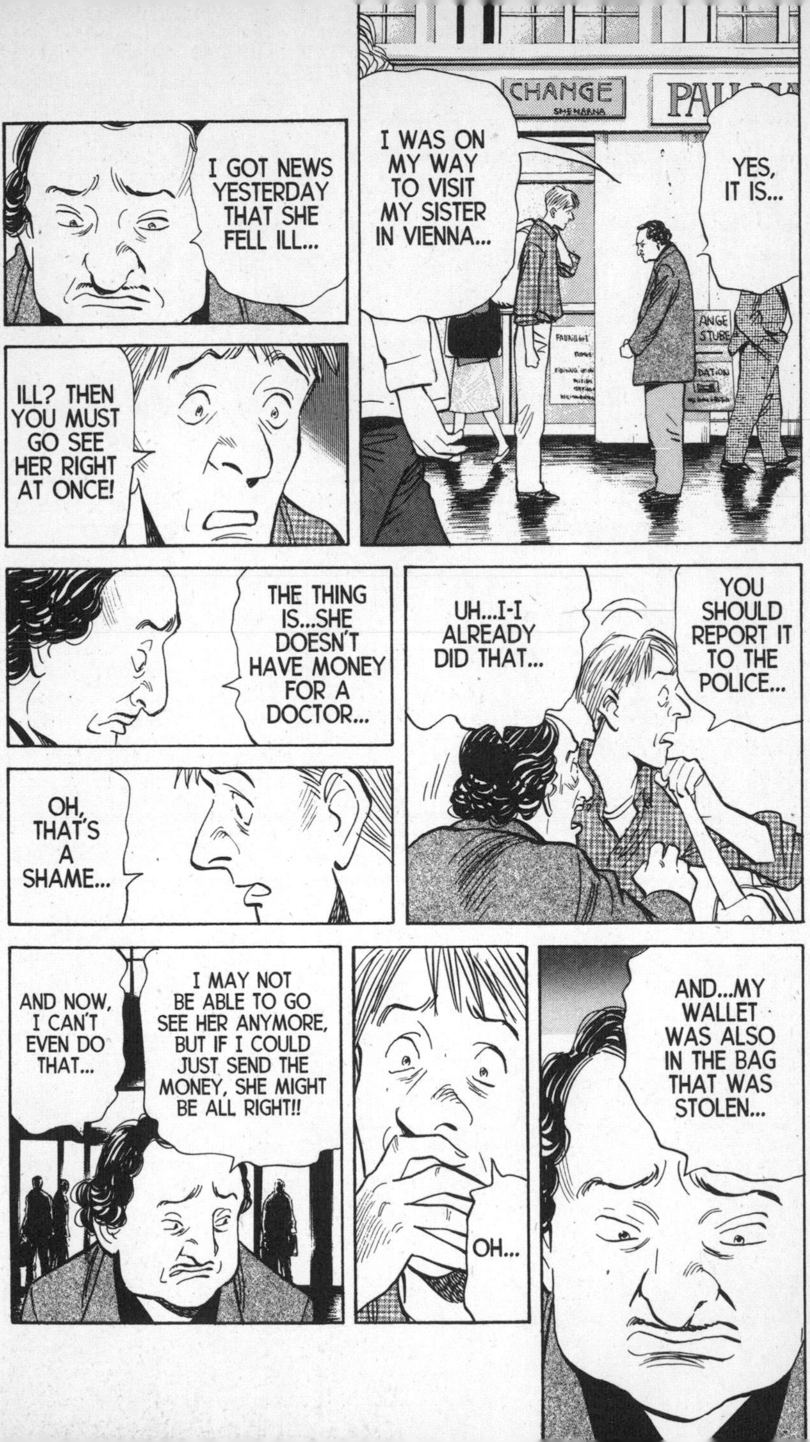
YES, IT IS...
I WAS ON MY WAY TO VISIT MY SISTER IN VIENNA...
CHANGE
I GOT NEWS YESTERDAY THAT SHE FELL ILL...
ILL? THEN YOU MUST GO SEE HER RIGHT AT ONCE!
YOU SHOULD REPORT IT TO THE POLICE...
UH...I-I ALREADY DID THAT...
THE THING IS...SHE DOESN'T HAVE MONEY FOR A DOCTOR...
OH, THAT'S A SHAME...
AND...MY WALLET WAS ALSO IN THE BAG THAT WAS STOLEN...
OH...
I MAY NOT BE ABLE TO GO SEE HER ANYMORE, BUT IF I COULD JUST SEND THE MONEY, SHE MIGHT BE ALL RIGHT!!
AND NOW, I CAN'T EVEN DO THAT...

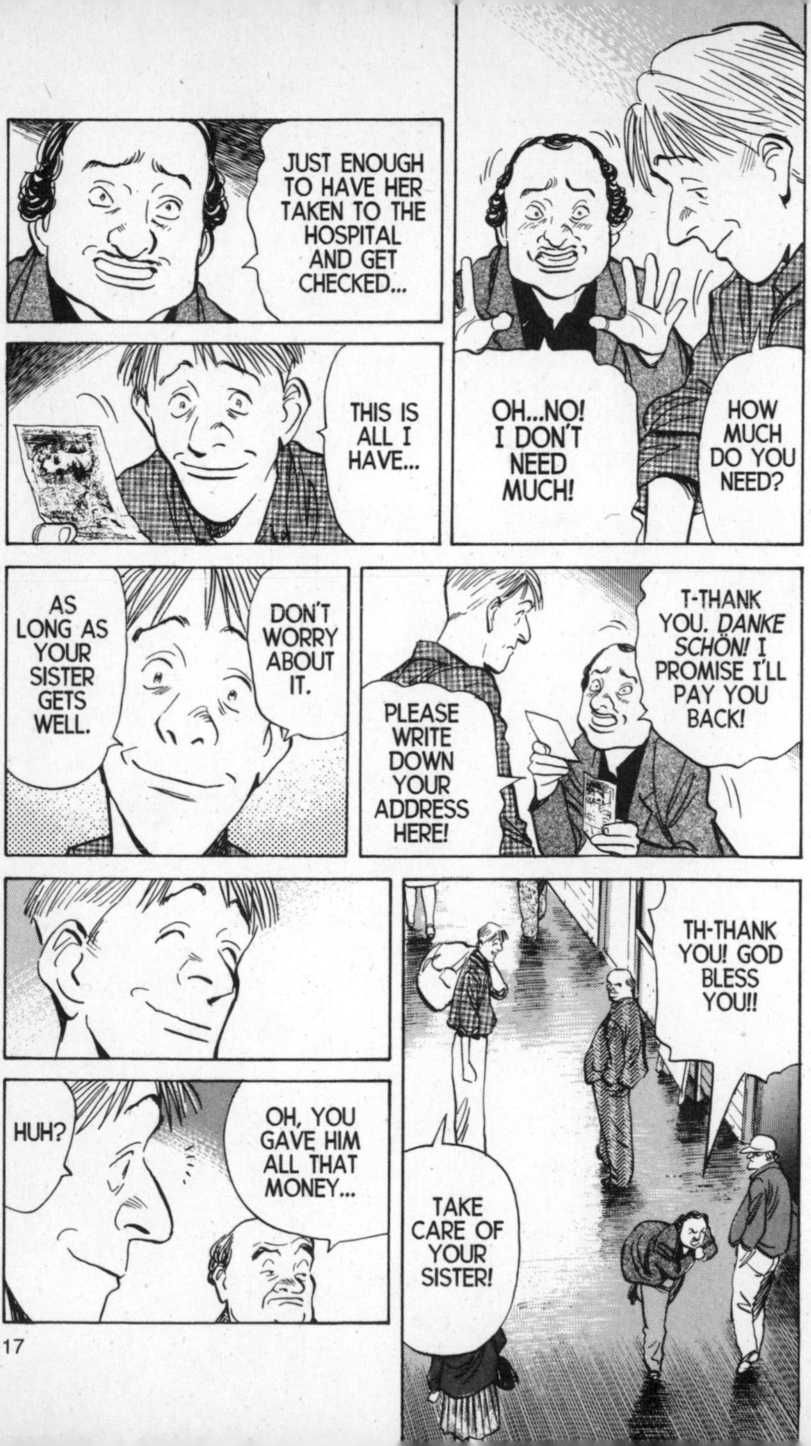
HOW MUCH DO YOU NEED?
OH...NO! I DON'T NEED MUCH!
JUST ENOUGH TO HAVE HER TAKEN TO THE HOSPITAL AND GET CHECKED...
THIS IS ALL I HAVE...
T-THANK YOU. *DANKE SCHÖN!* I PROMISE I'LL PAY YOU BACK!
PLEASE WRITE DOWN YOUR ADDRESS HERE!
DON'T WORRY ABOUT IT.
AS LONG AS YOUR SISTER GETS WELL.
TH-THANK YOU! GOD BLESS YOU!!
TAKE CARE OF YOUR SISTER!
OH, YOU GAVE HIM ALL THAT MONEY...
HUH?

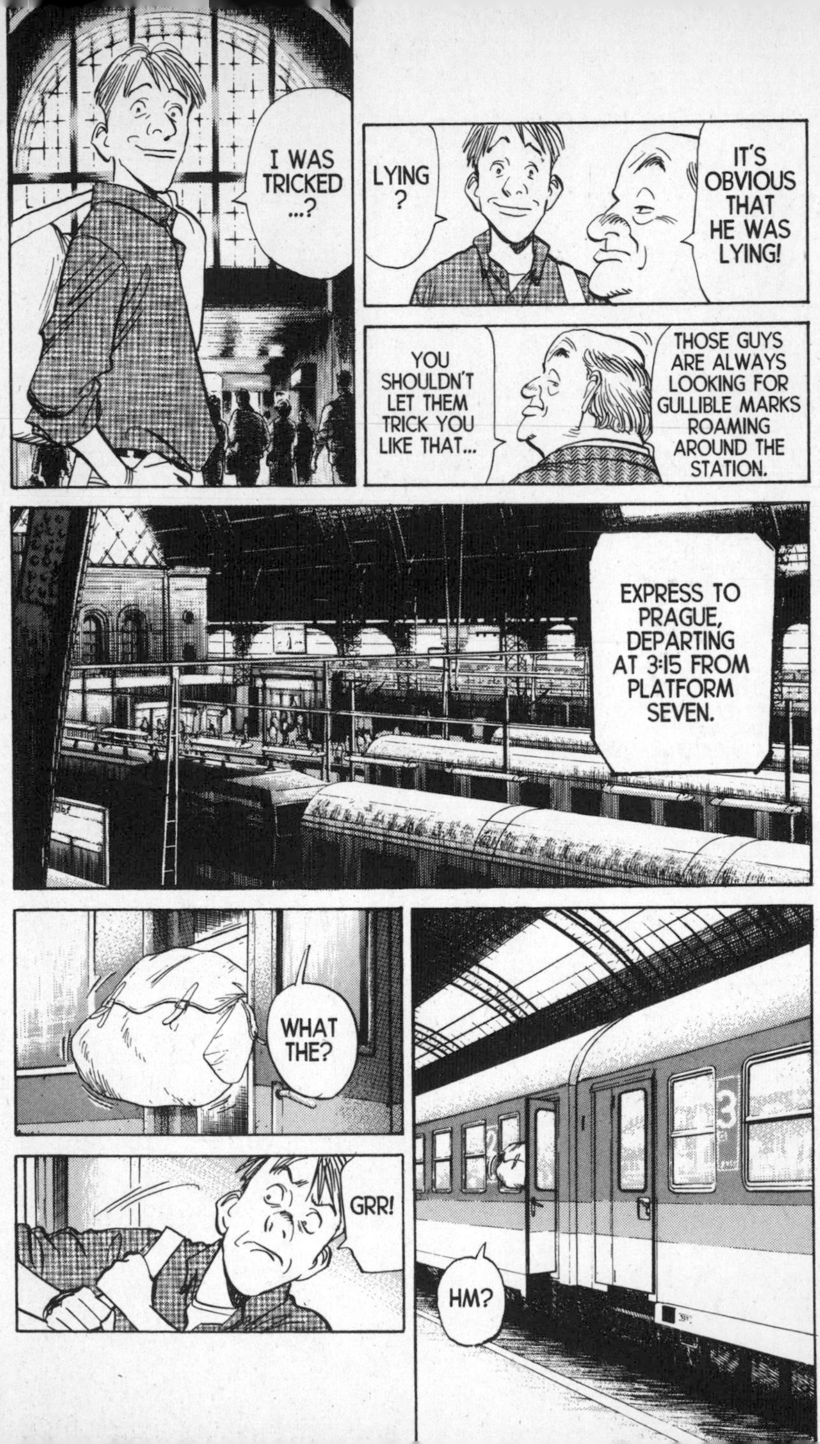
IT'S OBVIOUS THAT HE WAS LYING!
LYING?
THOSE GUYS ARE ALWAYS LOOKING FOR GULLIBLE MARKS ROAMING AROUND THE STATION.
YOU SHOULDN'T LET THEM TRICK YOU LIKE THAT...
I WAS TRICKED ...?
EXPRESS TO PRAGUE, DEPARTING AT 3:15 FROM PLATFORM SEVEN.
HM?
WHAT THE?
GRR!

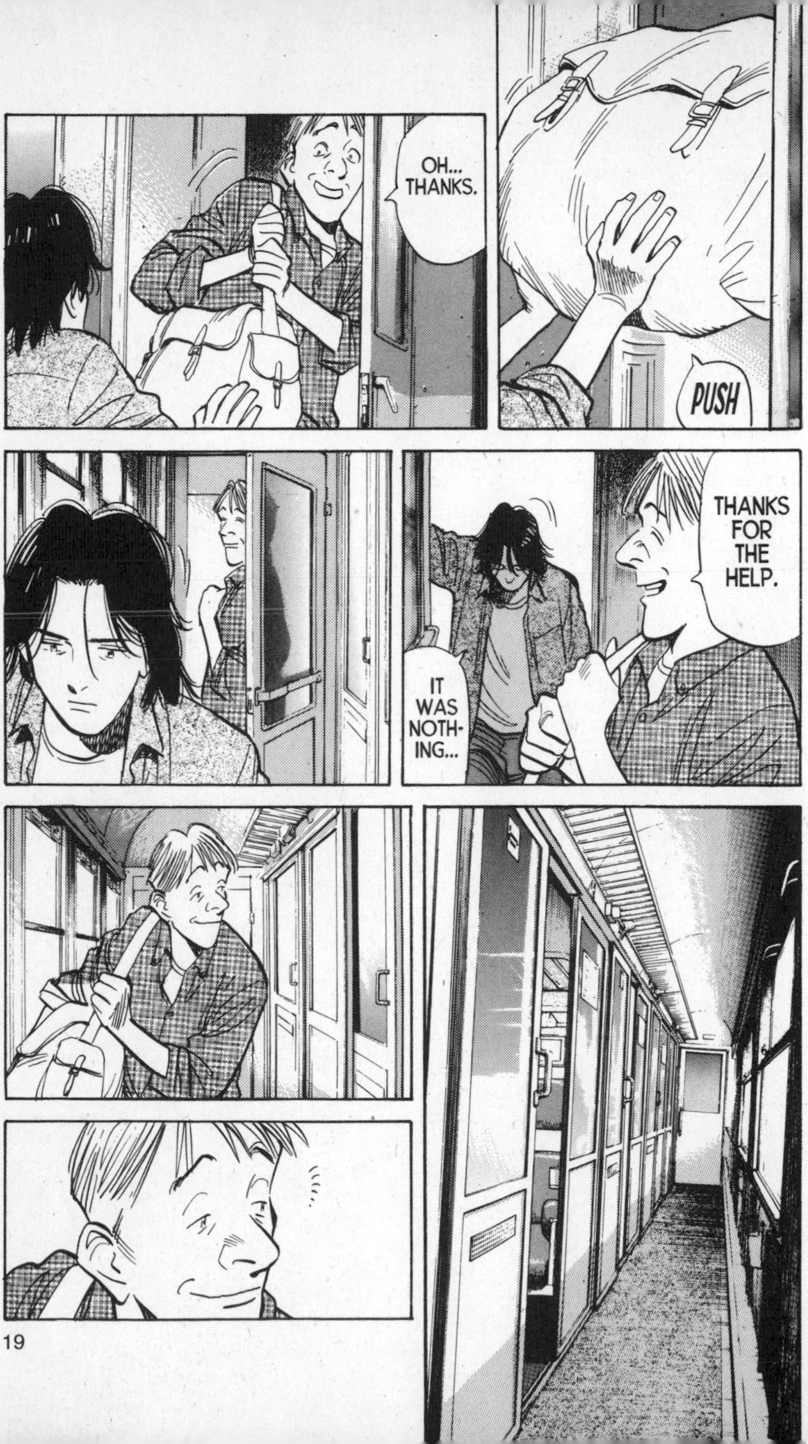
PUSH
OH... THANKS.
THANKS FOR THE HELP.
IT WAS NOTHING...

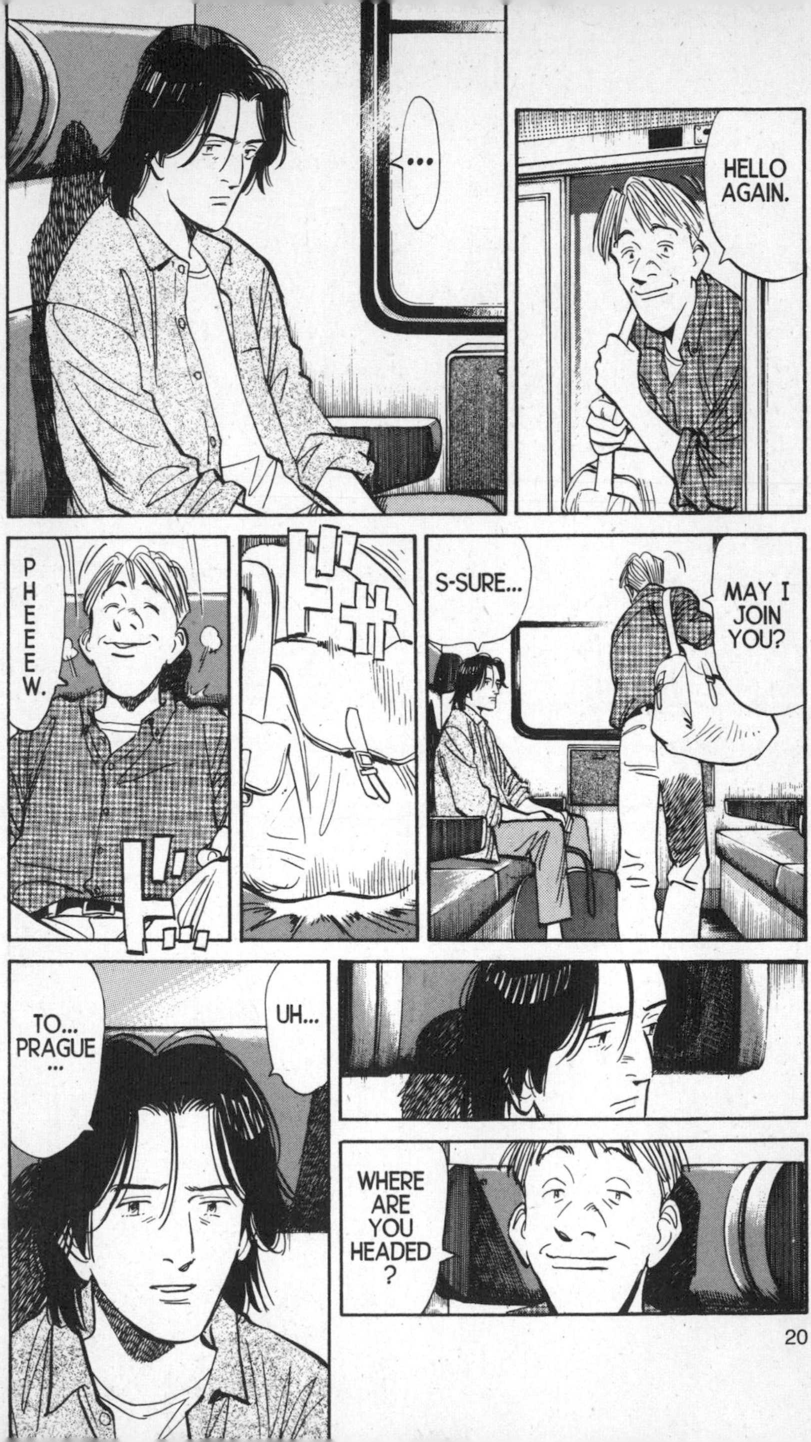
HELLO AGAIN.
...
MAY I JOIN YOU?
S-SURE...
ドサ
PHEEEEW.
WHERE ARE YOU HEADED?
UH...
TO... PRAGUE...

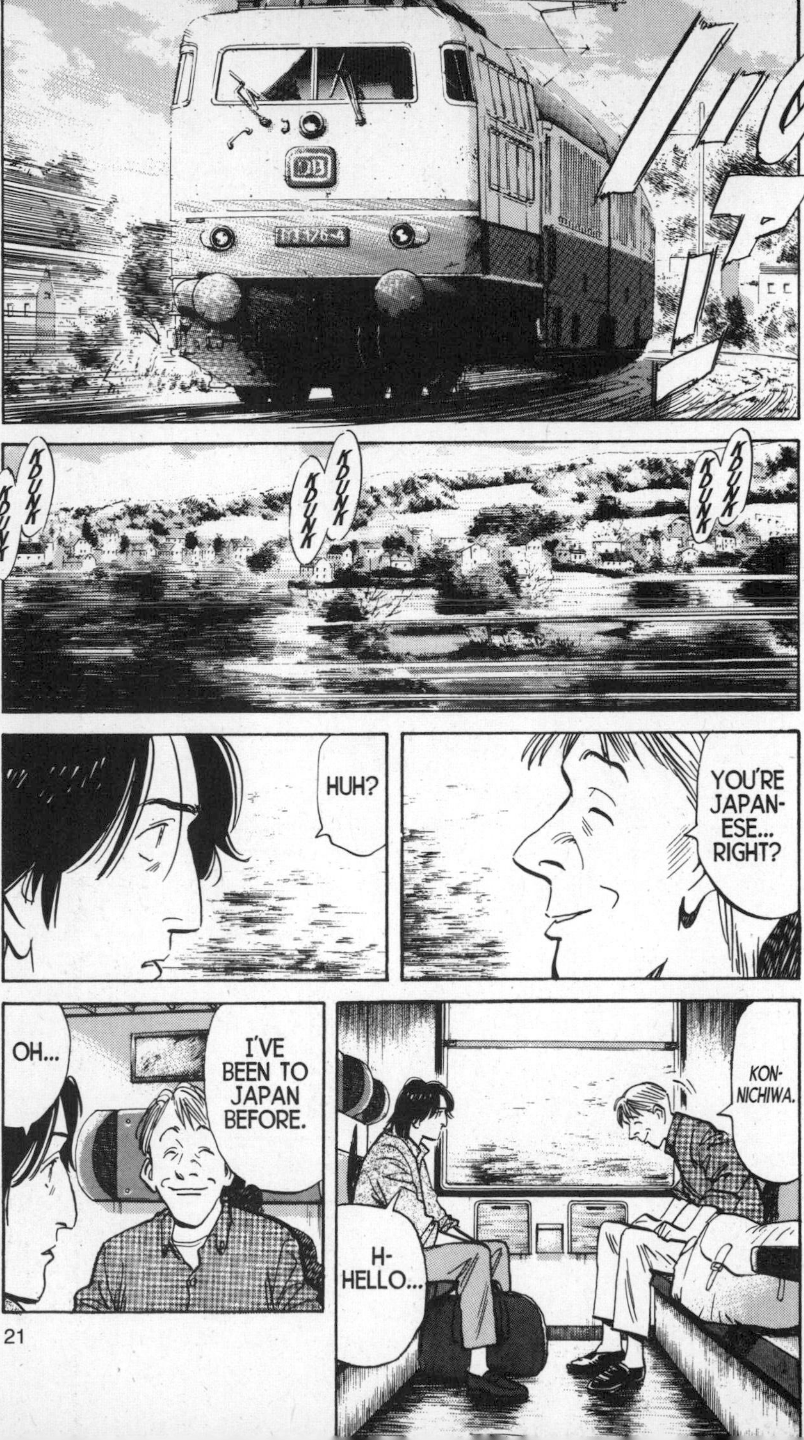

KDUNK KDUNK
KDUNK KDUNK
KDUNK KDUNK
YOU'RE JAPAN-ESE... RIGHT?
HUH?
KON-NICHIWA.
H-HELLO...
I'VE BEEN TO JAPAN BEFORE.
OH...

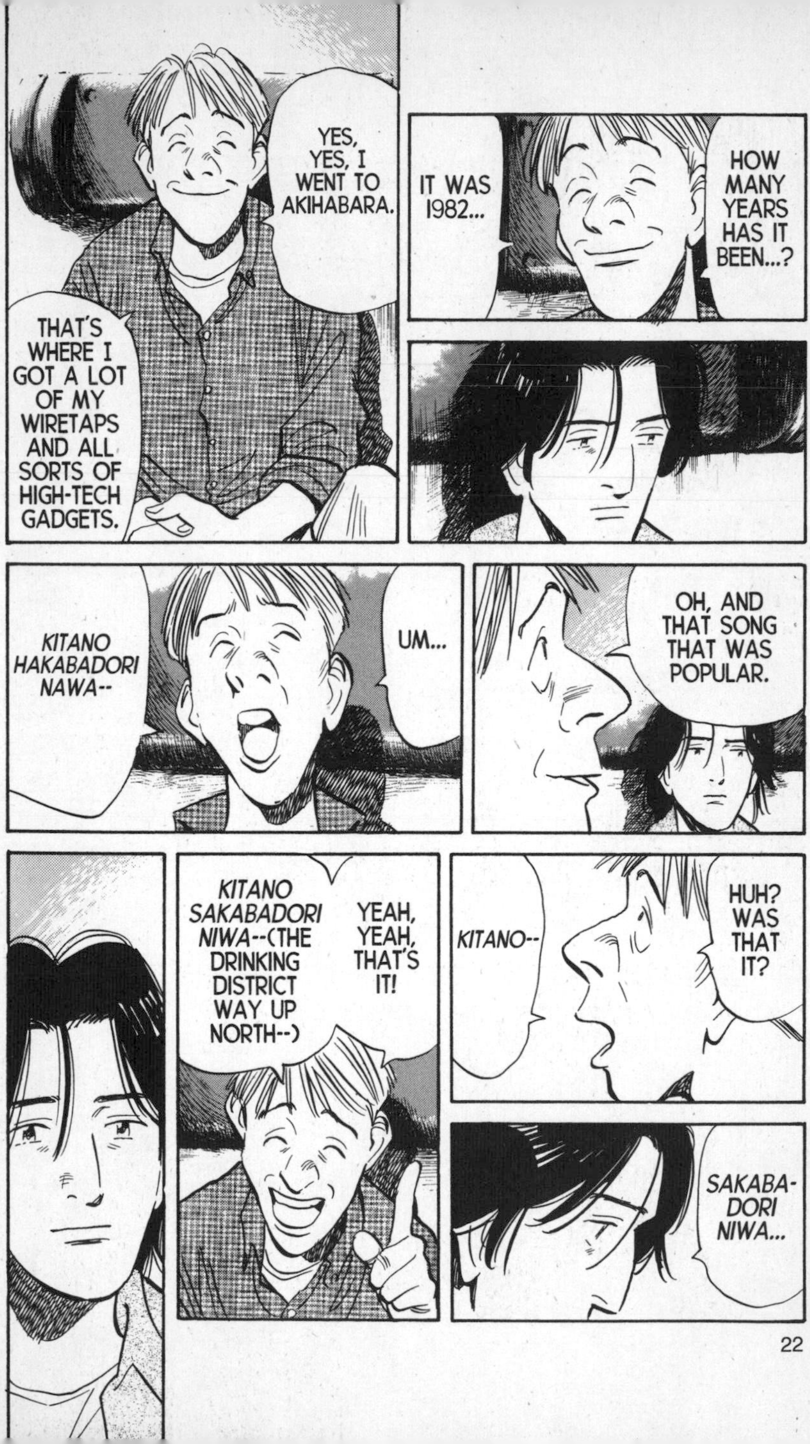
HOW MANY YEARS HAS IT BEEN...?
IT WAS 1982...
YES, YES, I WENT TO AKIHABARA.
THAT'S WHERE I GOT A LOT OF MY WIRETAPS AND ALL SORTS OF HIGH-TECH GADGETS.
OH, AND THAT SONG THAT WAS POPULAR.
UM...
KITANO HAKABADORI NAWA--
HUH? WAS THAT IT?
KITANO--
SAKABA-DORI NIWA...
YEAH, YEAH, THAT'S IT!
KITANO SAKABADORI NIWA--(THE DRINKING DISTRICT WAY UP NORTH--)

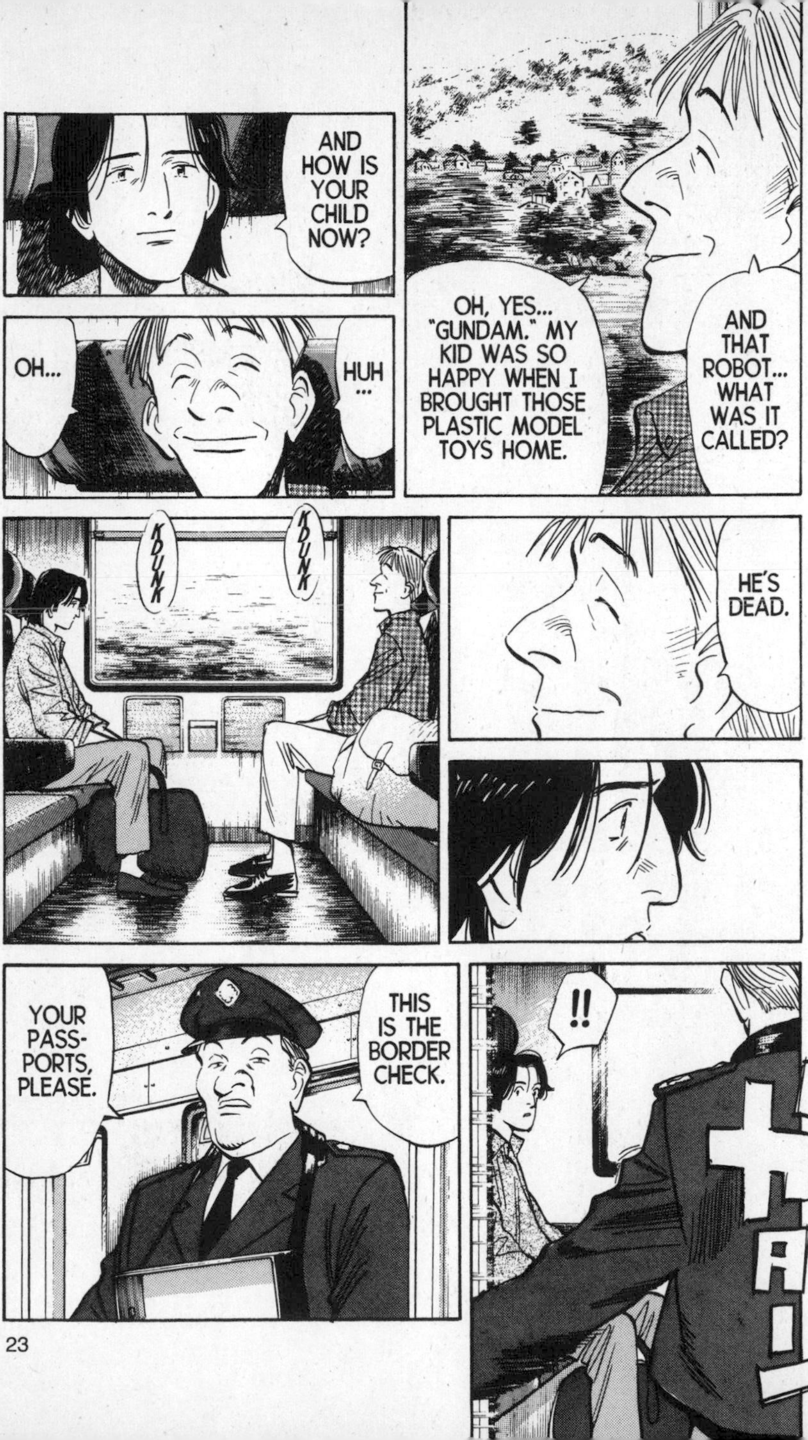
AND THAT ROBOT... WHAT WAS IT CALLED?
OH, YES... "GUNDAM." MY KID WAS SO HAPPY WHEN I BROUGHT THOSE PLASTIC MODEL TOYS HOME.
AND HOW IS YOUR CHILD NOW?
HUH ...
OH...
HE'S DEAD.
KDUNK
KDUNK
!!
THIS IS THE BORDER CHECK.
YOUR PASSPORTS, PLEASE.

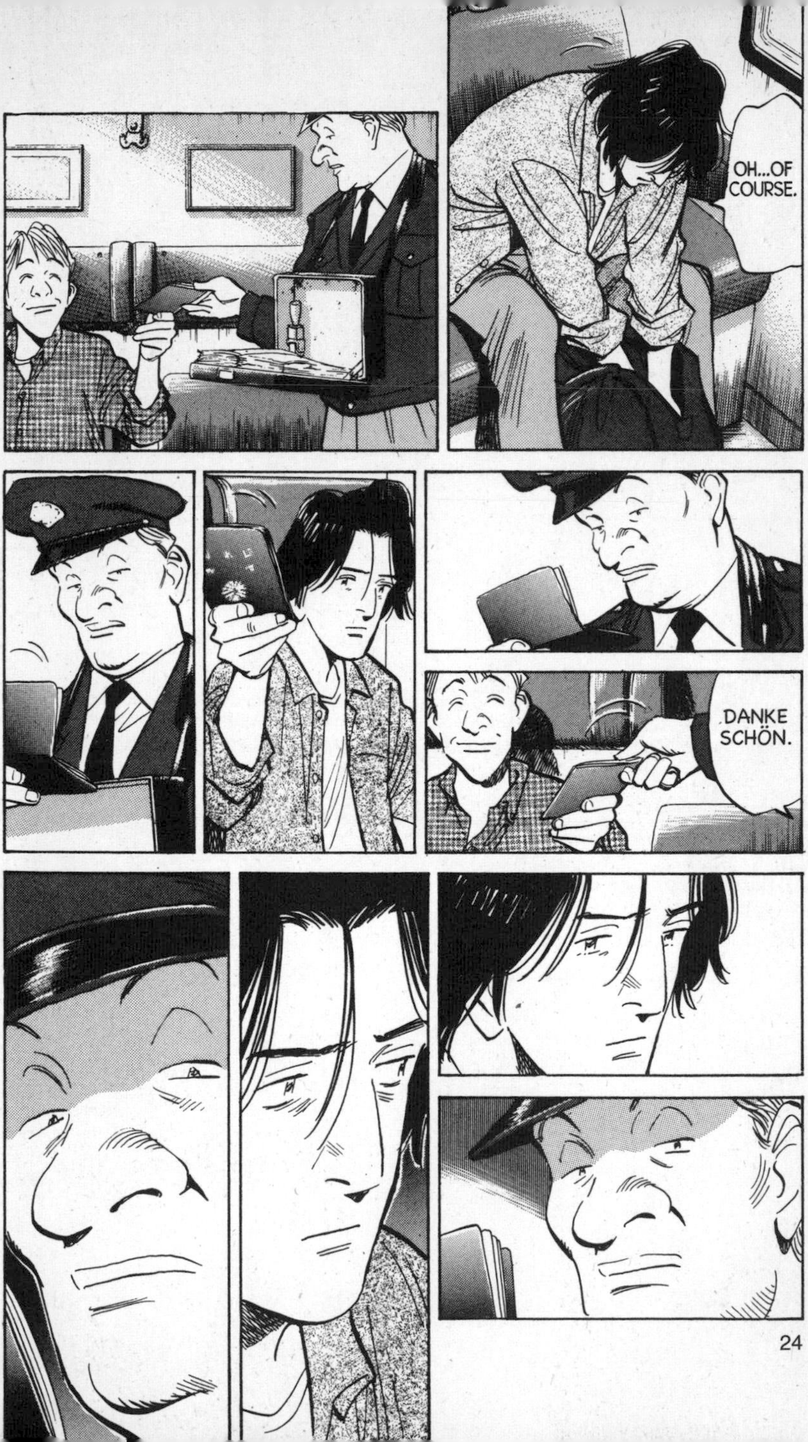
OH...OF COURSE.
DANKE SCHÖN.

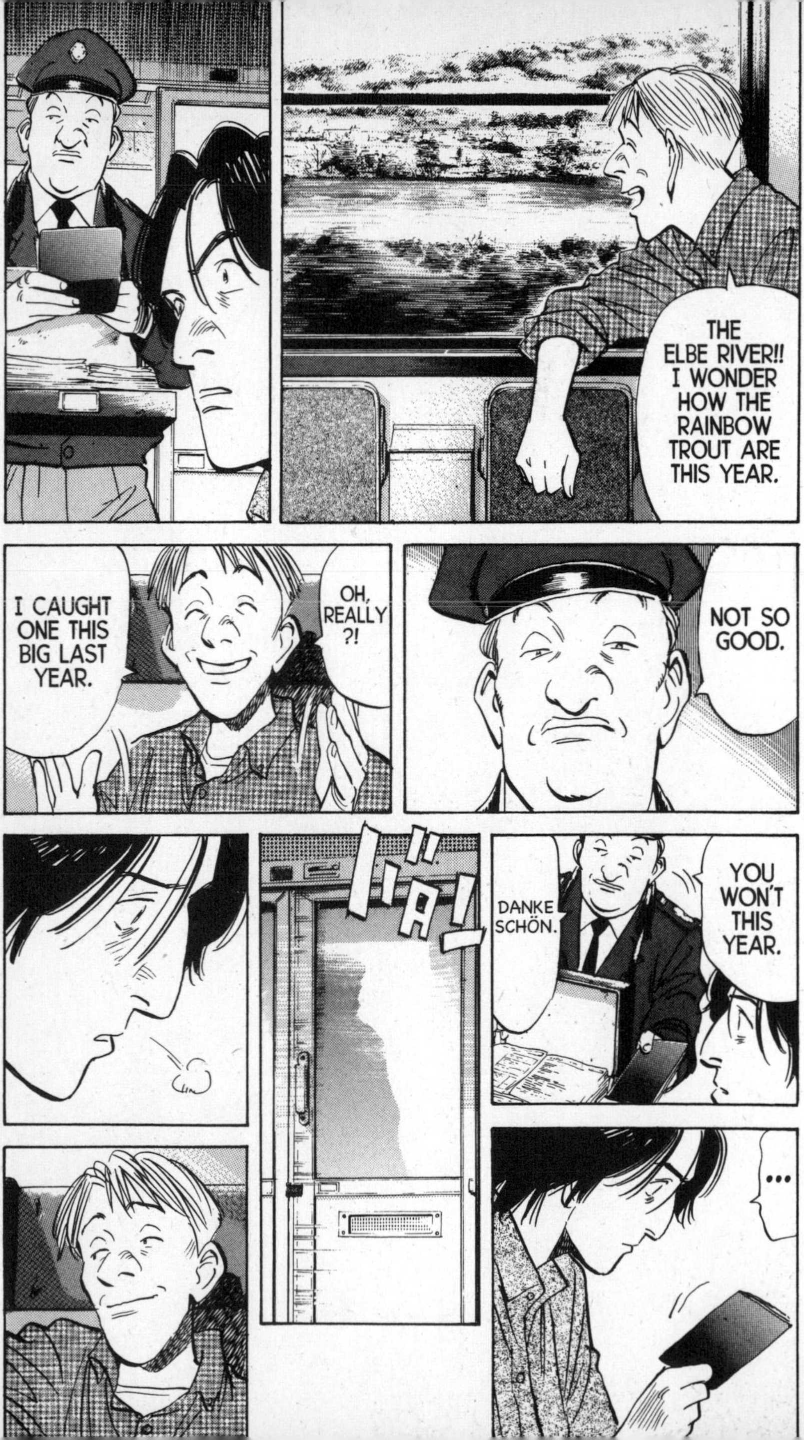
THE ELBE RIVER!! I WONDER HOW THE RAINBOW TROUT ARE THIS YEAR.
NOT SO GOOD.
OH, REALLY?!
I CAUGHT ONE THIS BIG LAST YEAR.
YOU WON'T THIS YEAR.
DANKE SCHÖN.
...

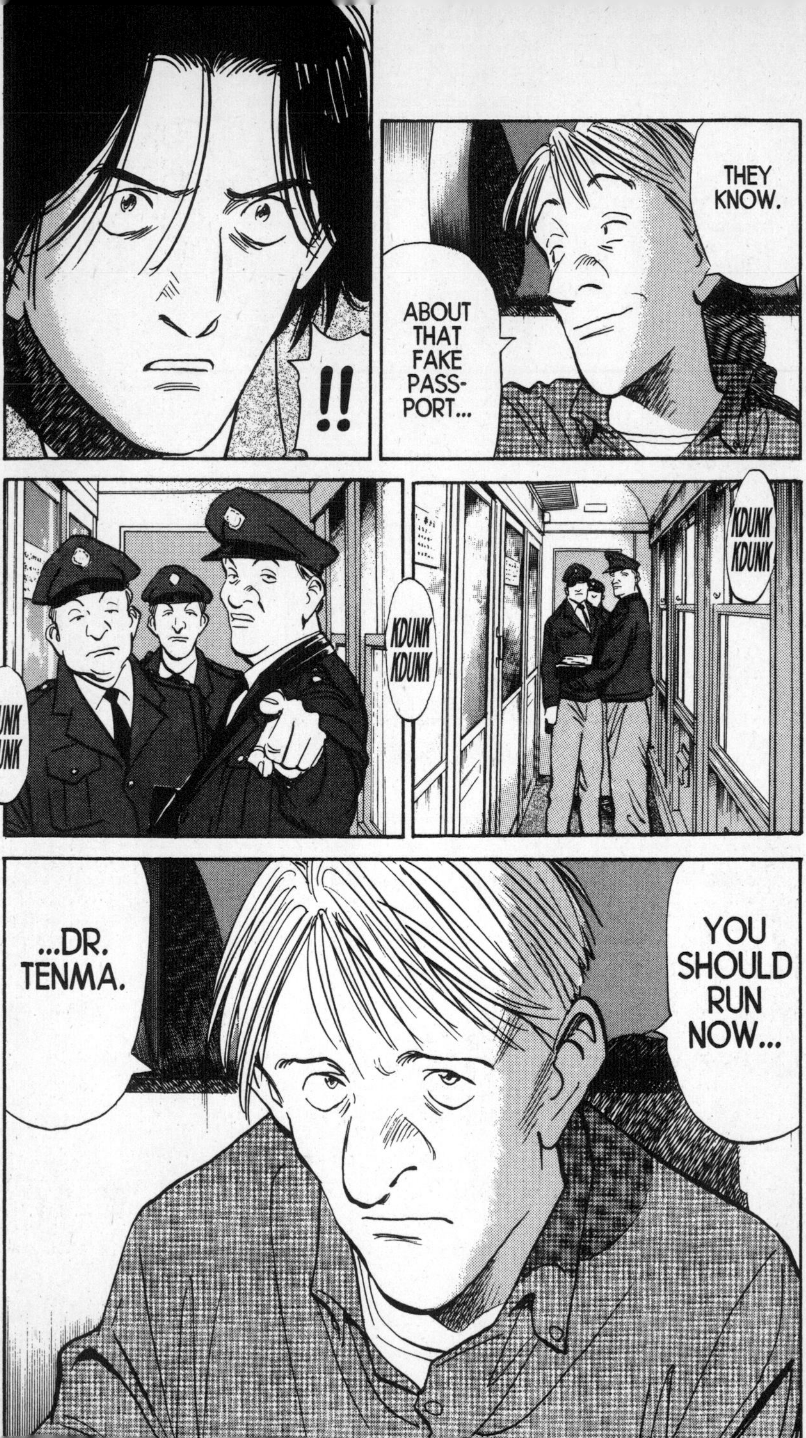
THEY KNOW.
ABOUT THAT FAKE PASSPORT...
!!
KDUNK KDUNK
KDUNK KDUNK
KDUNK KDUNK
YOU SHOULD RUN NOW...
...DR. TENMA.

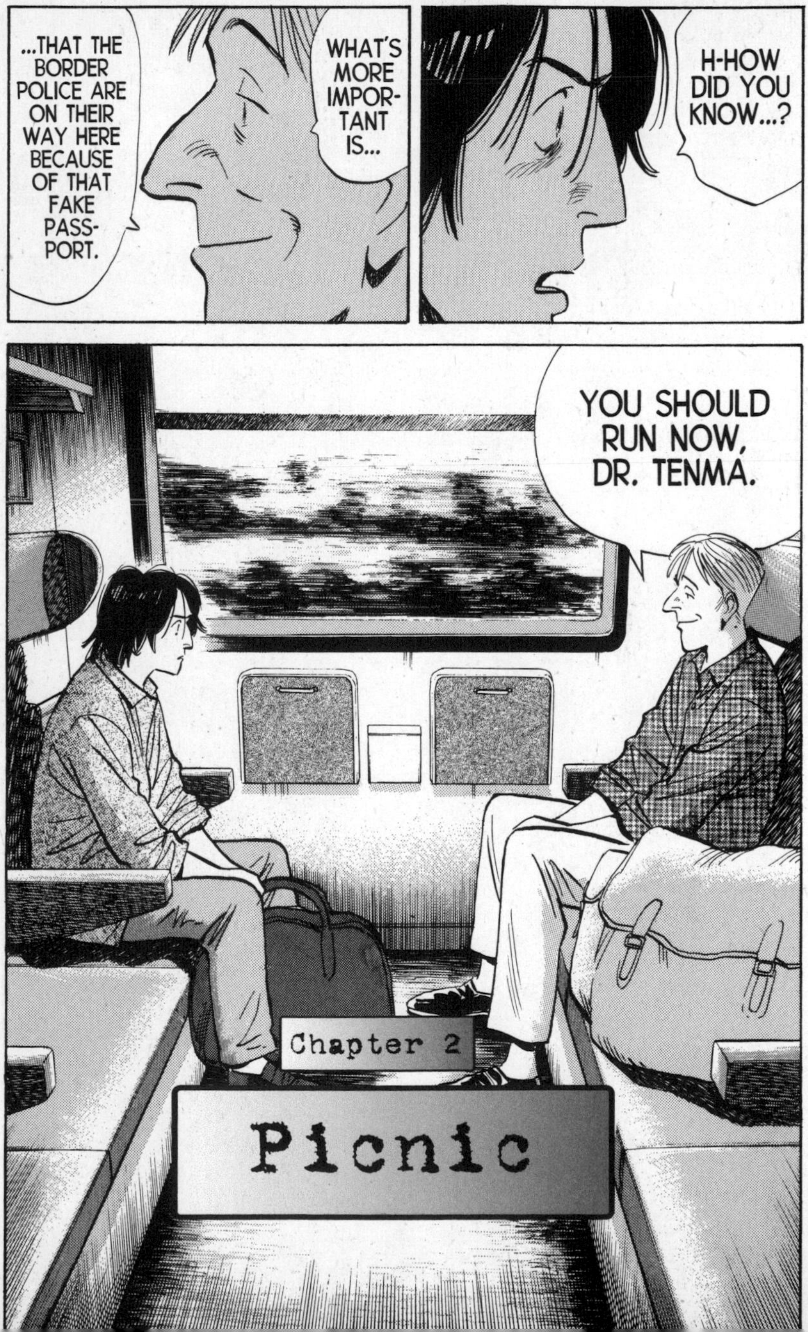
H-HOW DID YOU KNOW...?
WHAT'S MORE IMPOR-TANT IS...
...THAT THE BORDER POLICE ARE ON THEIR WAY HERE BECAUSE OF THAT FAKE PASS-PORT.
YOU SHOULD RUN NOW, DR. TENMA.
Chapter 2
Picnic

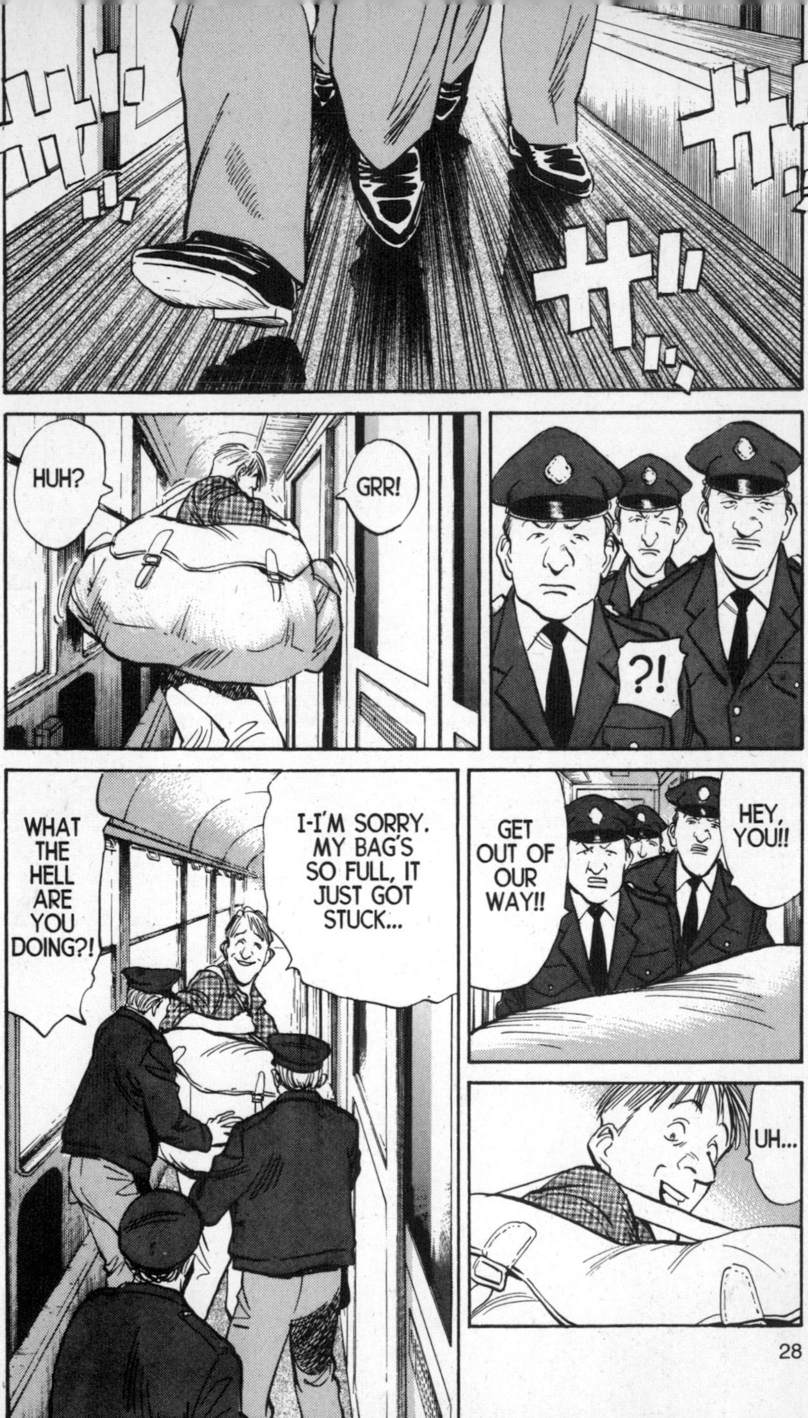
?!
GRR!
HUH?
HEY, YOU!!
GET OUT OF OUR WAY!!
UH...
I-I'M SORRY. MY BAG'S SO FULL, IT JUST GOT STUCK...
WHAT THE HELL ARE YOU DOING?!

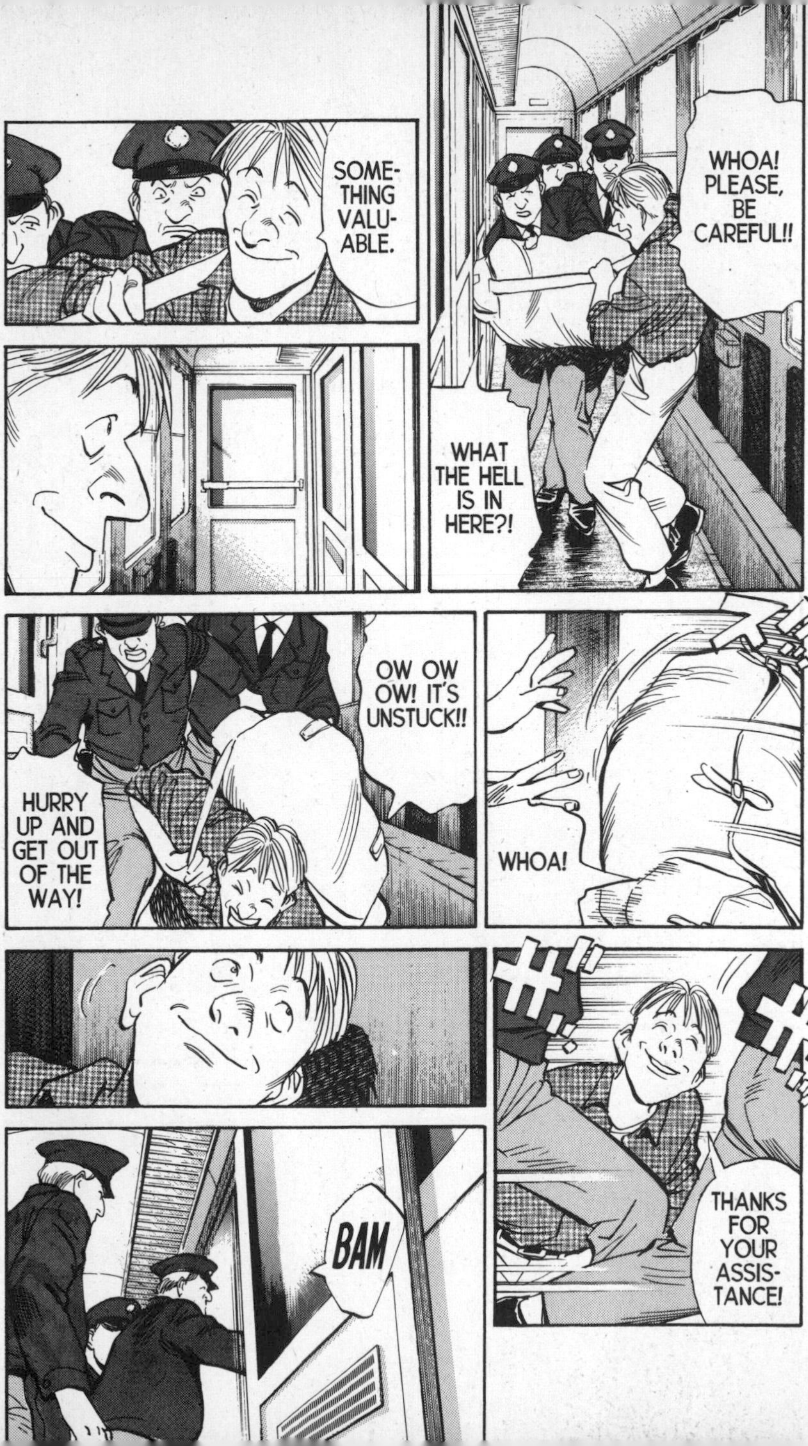
WHOA! PLEASE, BE CAREFUL!!
WHAT THE HELL IS IN HERE?!
SOMETHING VALUABLE.
WHOA!
OW OW OW! IT'S UNSTUCK!!
HURRY UP AND GET OUT OF THE WAY!
THANKS FOR YOUR ASSISTANCE!
BAM

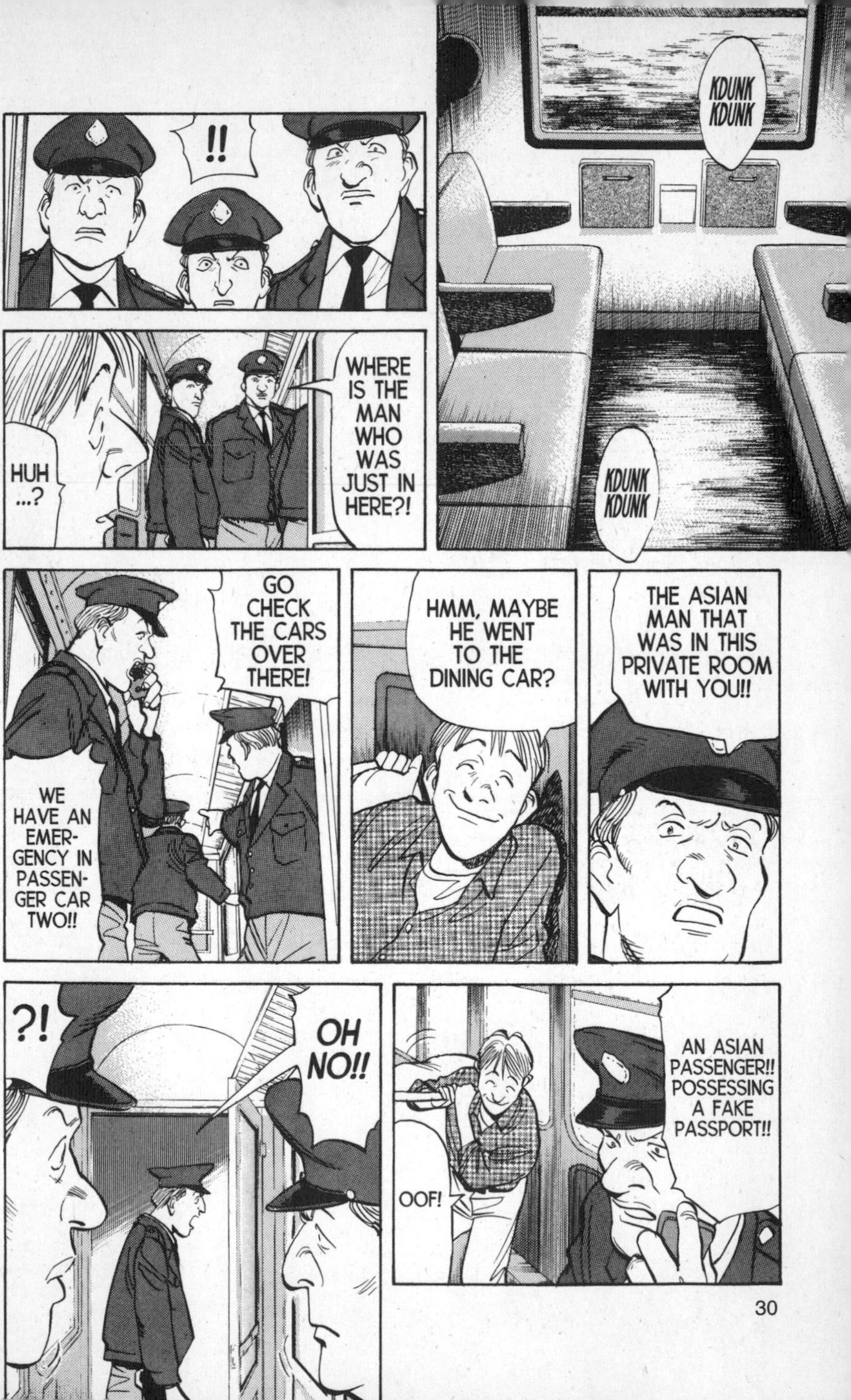
KDUNK KDUNK
KDUNK KDUNK
!!
WHERE IS THE MAN WHO WAS JUST IN HERE?!
HUH ...?
THE ASIAN MAN THAT WAS IN THIS PRIVATE ROOM WITH YOU!!
HMM, MAYBE HE WENT TO THE DINING CAR?
GO CHECK THE CARS OVER THERE!
WE HAVE AN EMERGENCY IN PASSENGER CAR TWO!!
AN ASIAN PASSENGER!! POSSESSING A FAKE PASSPORT!!
OOF!
OH NO!!
?!

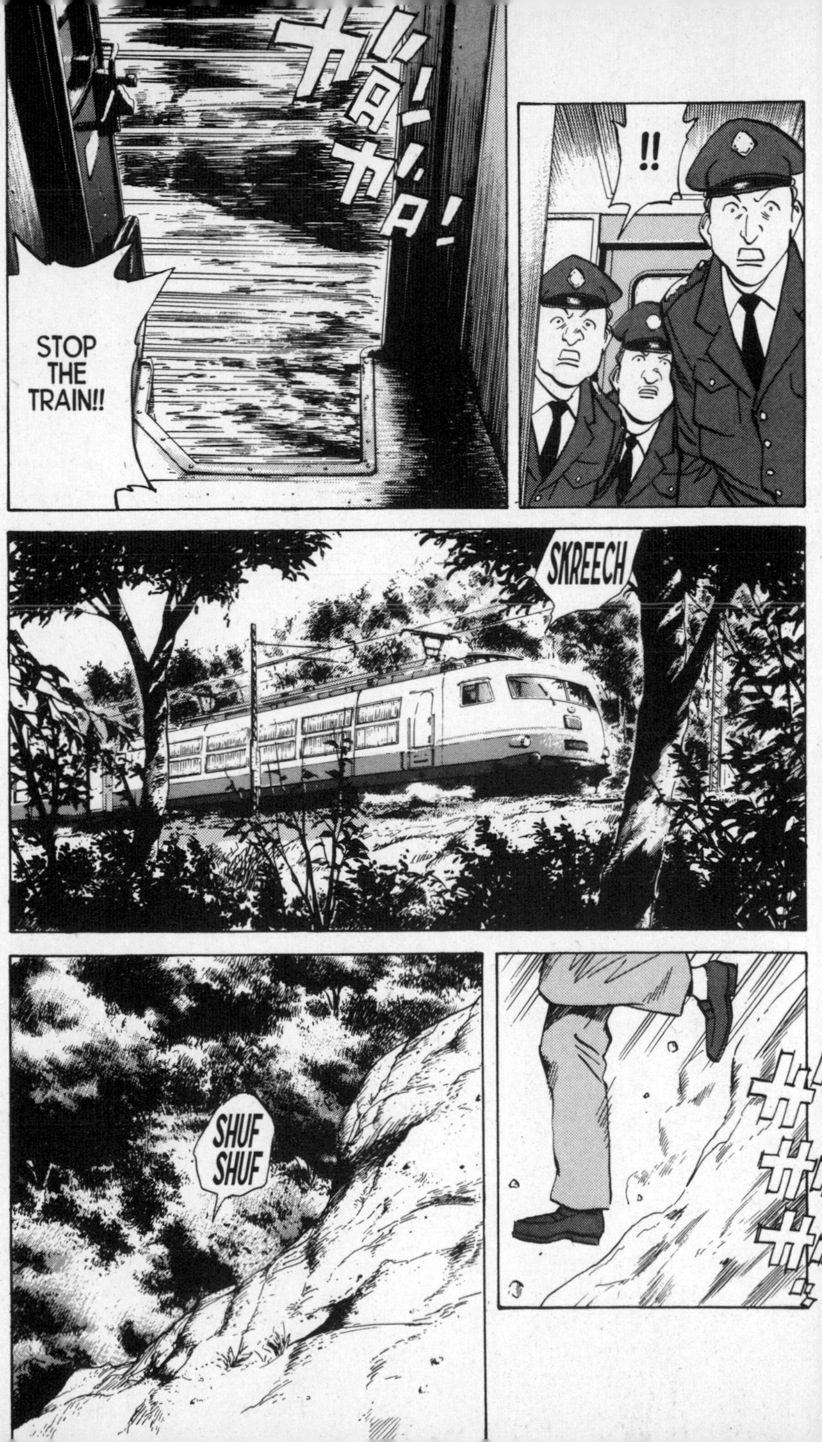
!!
STOP THE TRAIN!!
SKREECH
SHUF SHUF

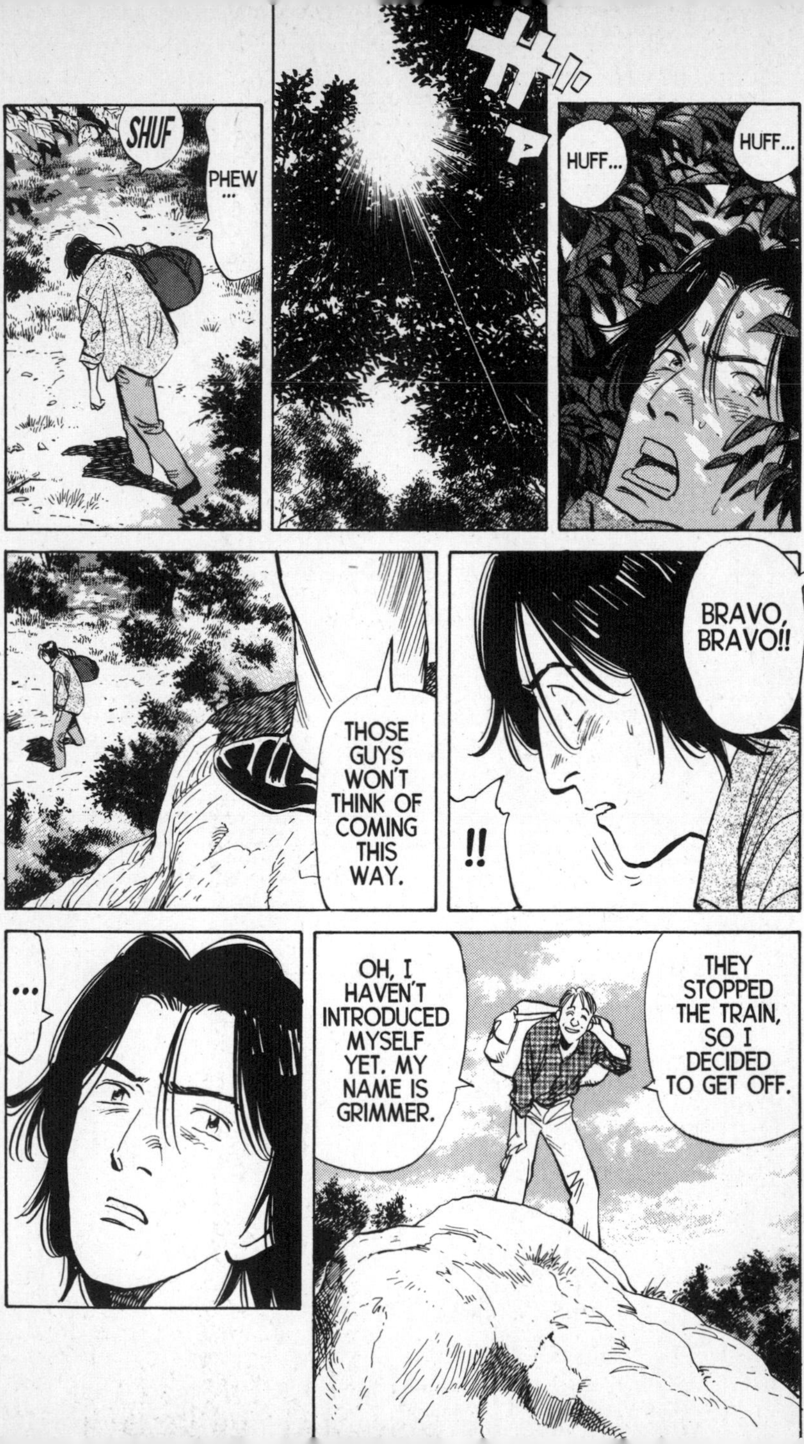
HUFF...
HUFF...
SHUF
PHEW...
BRAVO, BRAVO!!
!!
THOSE GUYS WON'T THINK OF COMING THIS WAY.
THEY STOPPED THE TRAIN, SO I DECIDED TO GET OFF.
OH, I HAVEN'T INTRODUCED MYSELF YET. MY NAME IS GRIMMER.
...

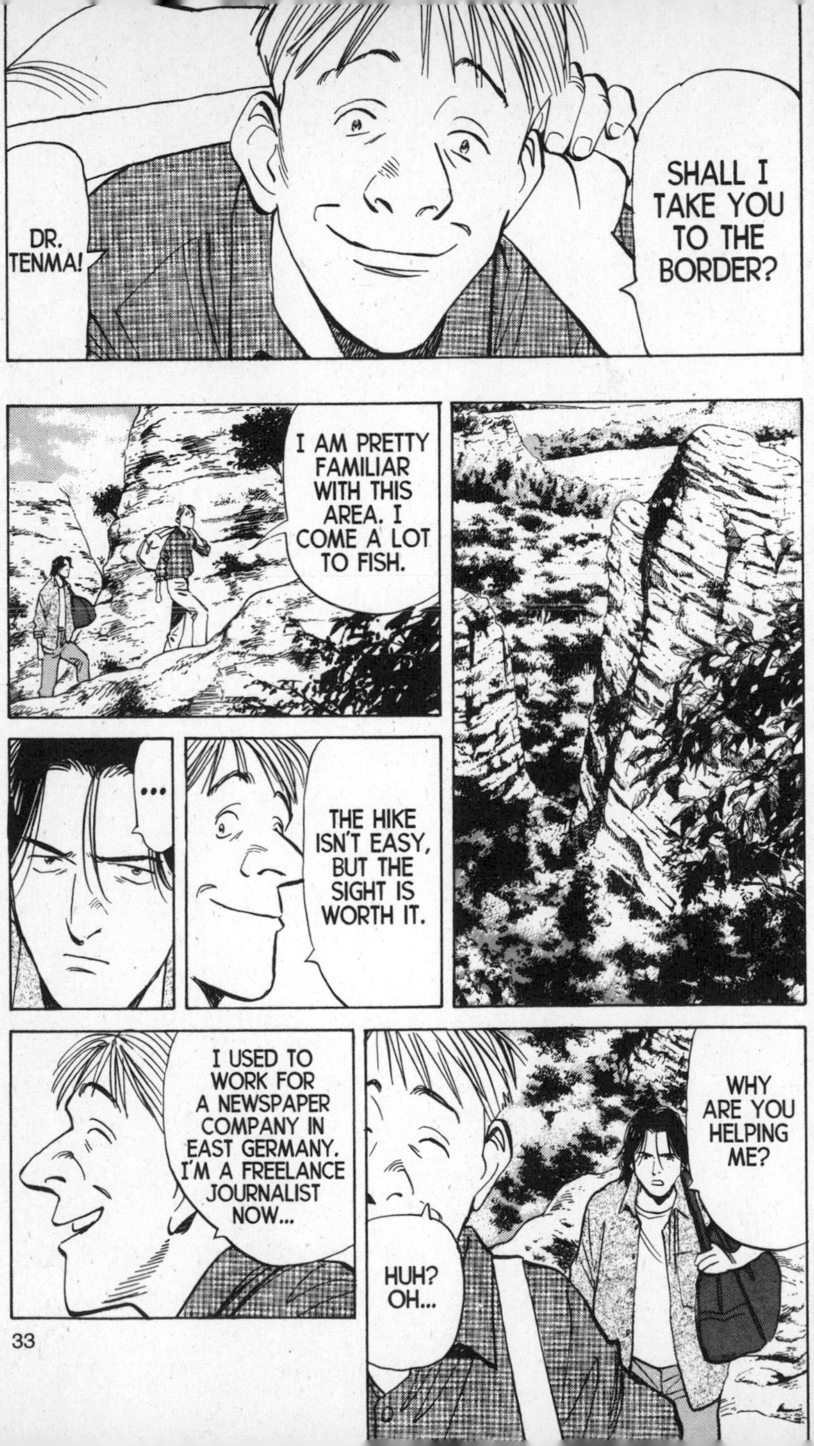
SHALL I TAKE YOU TO THE BORDER?
DR. TENMA!
I AM PRETTY FAMILIAR WITH THIS AREA. I COME A LOT TO FISH.
THE HIKE ISN'T EASY, BUT THE SIGHT IS WORTH IT.
...
WHY ARE YOU HELPING ME?
HUH? OH...
I USED TO WORK FOR A NEWSPAPER COMPANY IN EAST GERMANY. I'M A FREELANCE JOURNALIST NOW...

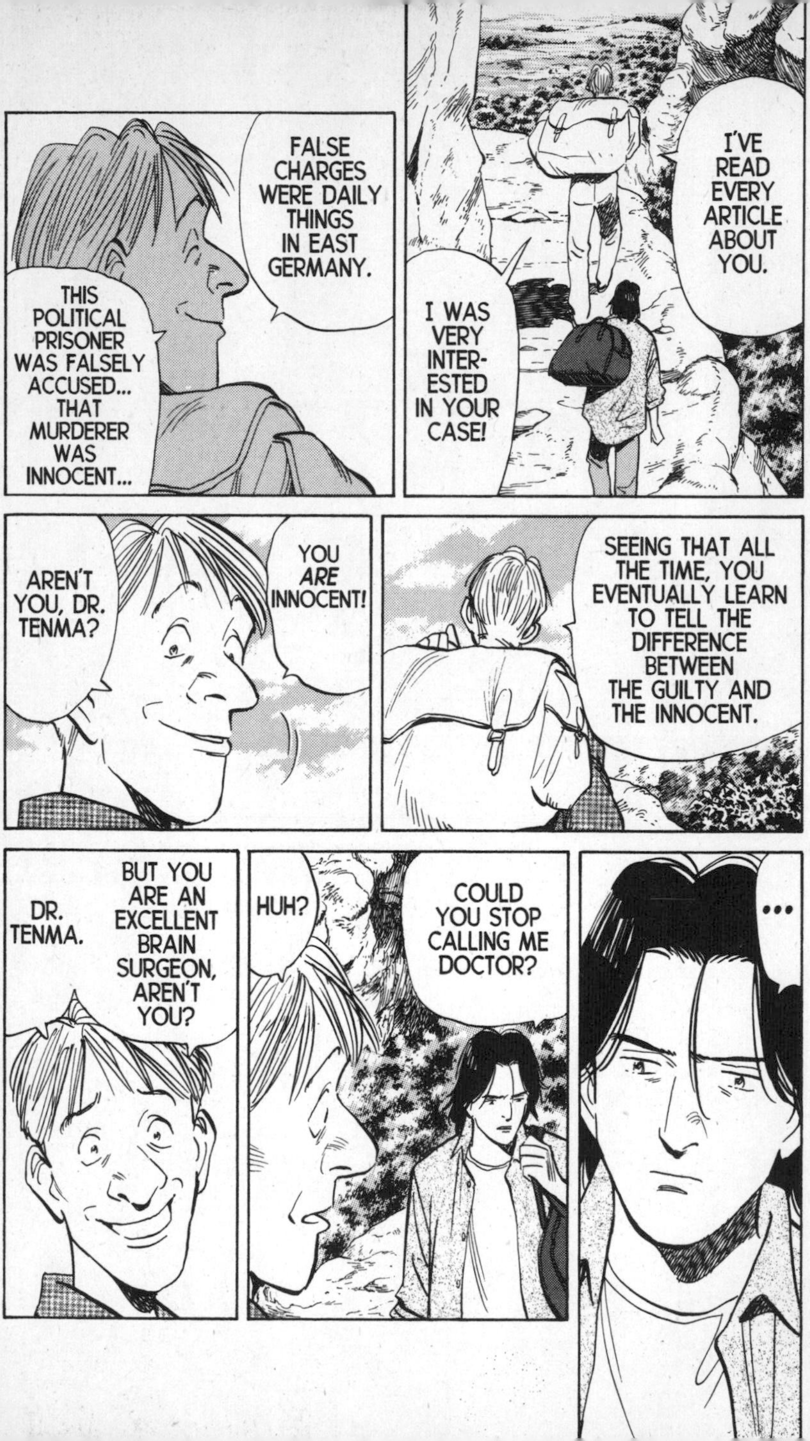
I'VE READ EVERY ARTICLE ABOUT YOU.
I WAS VERY INTERESTED IN YOUR CASE!
FALSE CHARGES WERE DAILY THINGS IN EAST GERMANY.
THIS POLITICAL PRISONER WAS FALSELY ACCUSED... THAT MURDERER WAS INNOCENT...
SEEING THAT ALL THE TIME, YOU EVENTUALLY LEARN TO TELL THE DIFFERENCE BETWEEN THE GUILTY AND THE INNOCENT.
YOU *ARE* INNOCENT!
AREN'T YOU, DR. TENMA?
...
COULD YOU STOP CALLING ME DOCTOR?
HUH?
BUT YOU ARE AN EXCELLENT BRAIN SURGEON, AREN'T YOU?
DR. TENMA.

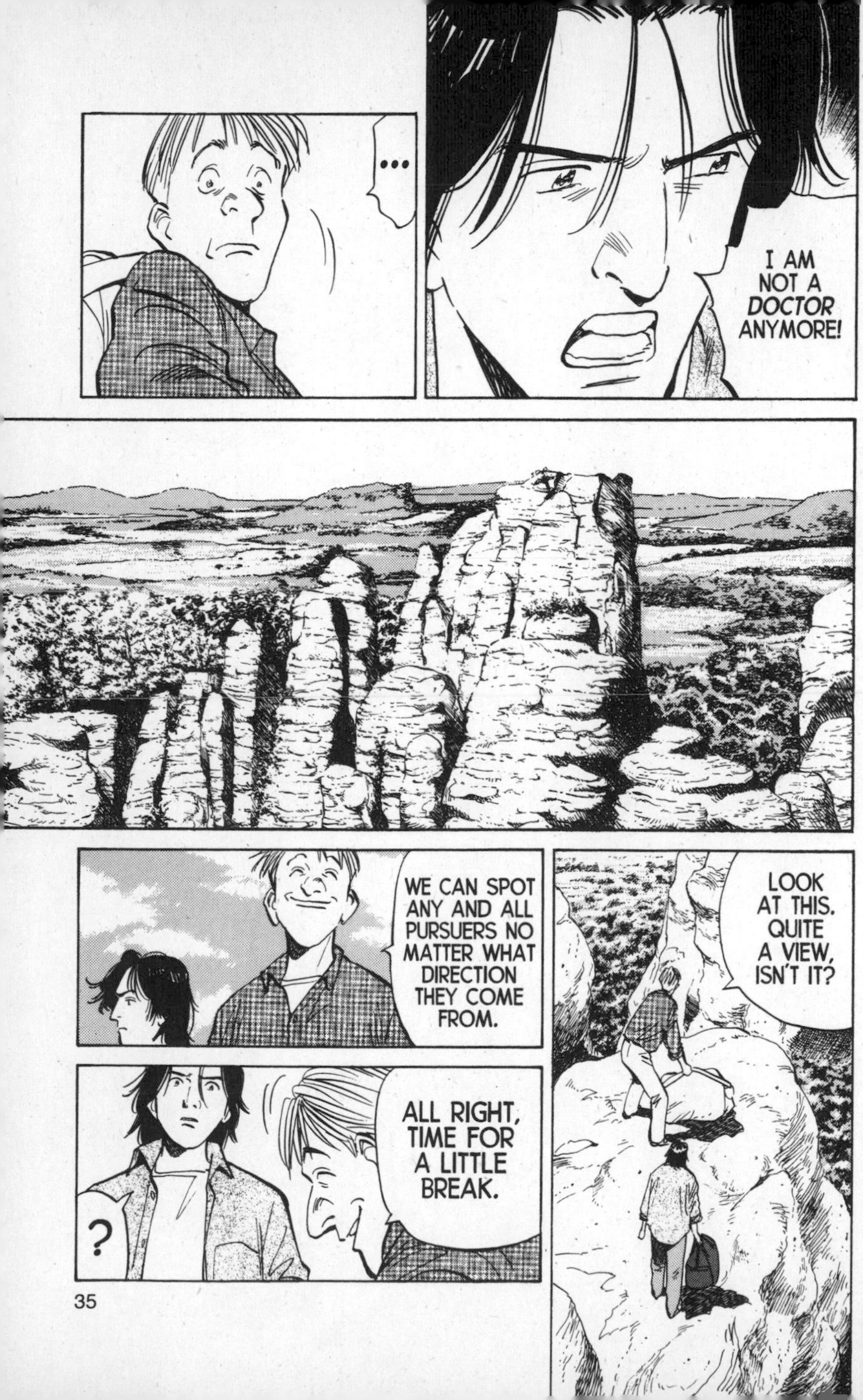
I AM NOT A *DOCTOR* ANYMORE!
...
LOOK AT THIS. QUITE A VIEW, ISN'T IT?
WE CAN SPOT ANY AND ALL PURSUERS NO MATTER WHAT DIRECTION THEY COME FROM.
ALL RIGHT, TIME FOR A LITTLE BREAK.
?

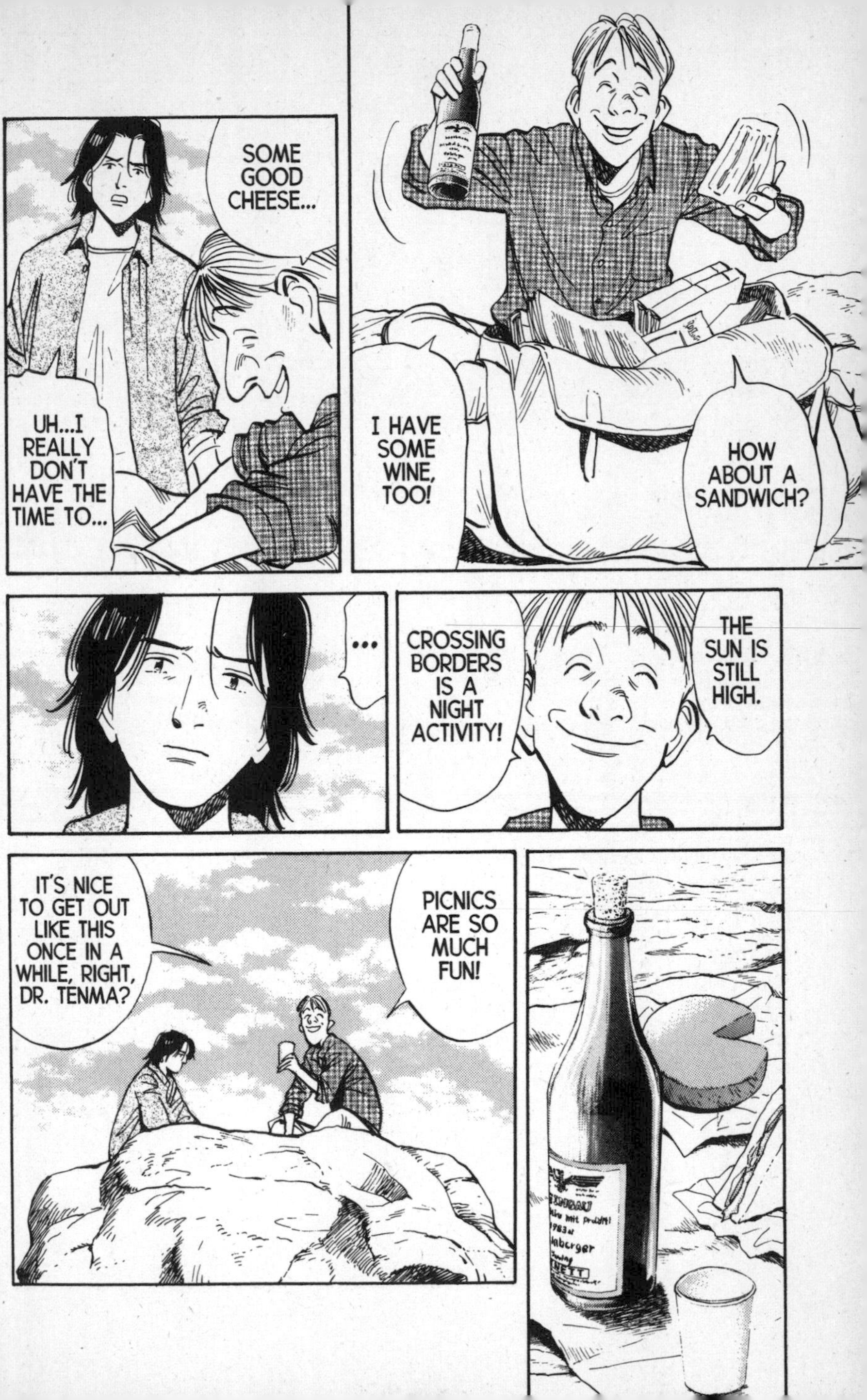
HOW ABOUT A SANDWICH?
I HAVE SOME WINE, TOO!
SOME GOOD CHEESE...
UH...I REALLY DON'T HAVE THE TIME TO...
THE SUN IS STILL HIGH.
CROSSING BORDERS IS A NIGHT ACTIVITY!
...
PICNICS ARE SO MUCH FUN!
IT'S NICE TO GET OUT LIKE THIS ONCE IN A WHILE, RIGHT, DR. TENMA?

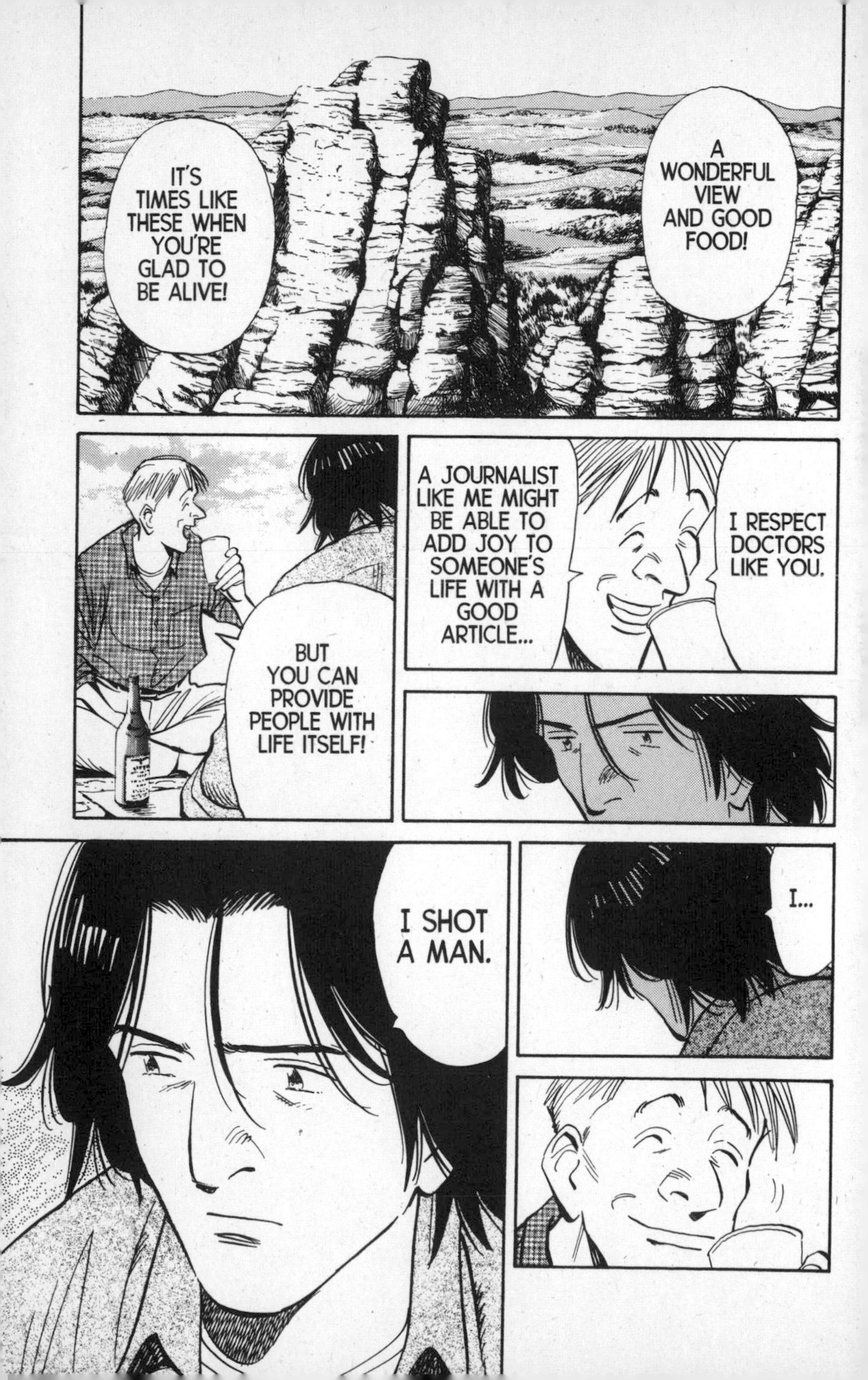
A WONDERFUL VIEW AND GOOD FOOD!
IT'S TIMES LIKE THESE WHEN YOU'RE GLAD TO BE ALIVE!
I RESPECT DOCTORS LIKE YOU.
A JOURNALIST LIKE ME MIGHT BE ABLE TO ADD JOY TO SOMEONE'S LIFE WITH A GOOD ARTICLE...
BUT YOU CAN PROVIDE PEOPLE WITH LIFE ITSELF!
I...
I SHOT A MAN.

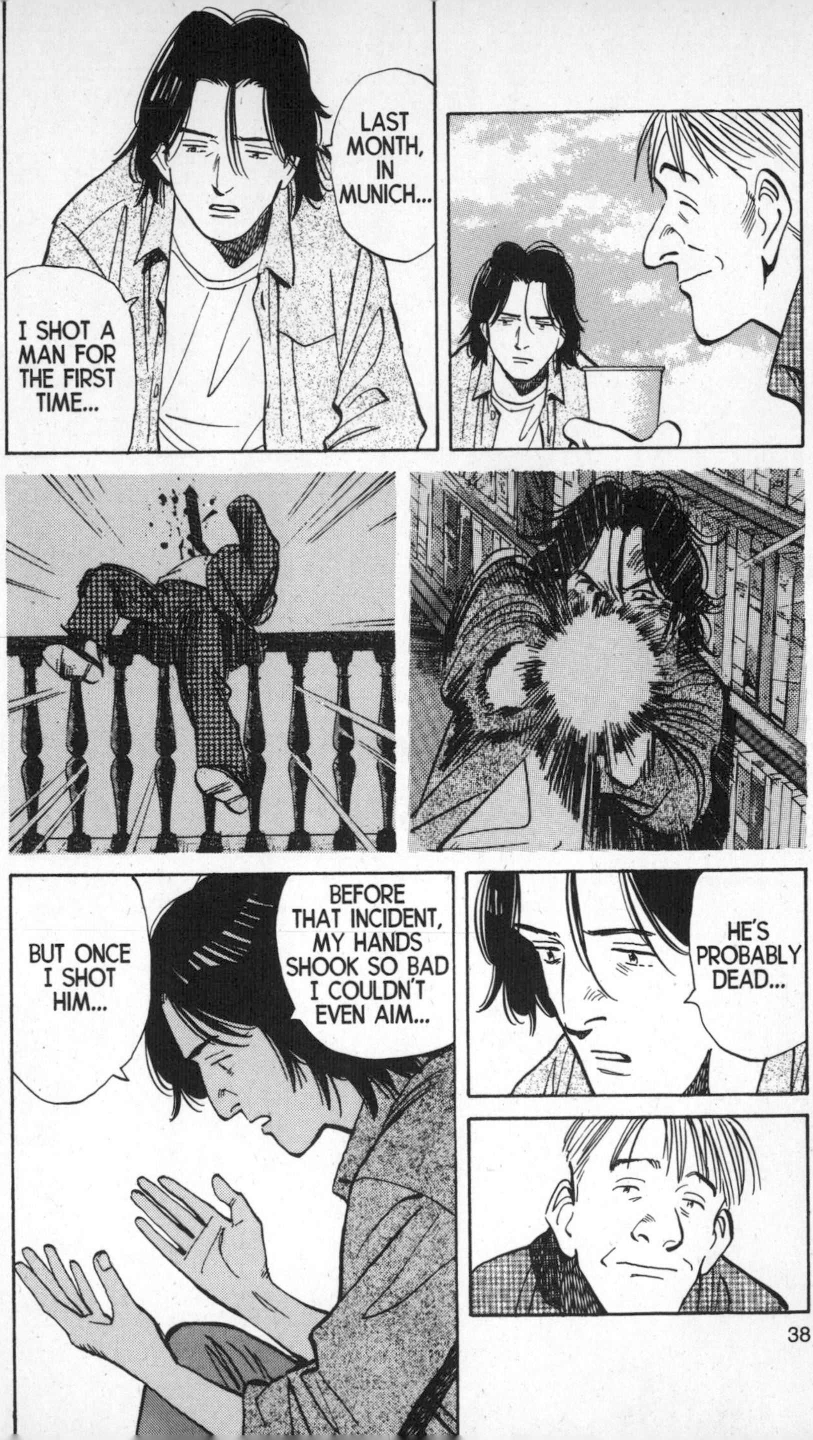
LAST MONTH, IN MUNICH...
I SHOT A MAN FOR THE FIRST TIME...
HE'S PROBABLY DEAD...
BEFORE THAT INCIDENT, MY HANDS SHOOK SO BAD I COULDN'T EVEN AIM...
BUT ONCE I SHOT HIM...

AND STILL...

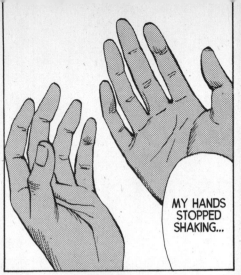

MY HANDS STOPPED SHAKING...

THERE IS ONE MORE PERSON I HAVE TO SHOOT...

...A DOCTOR ANYMORE...

I AM NOT...

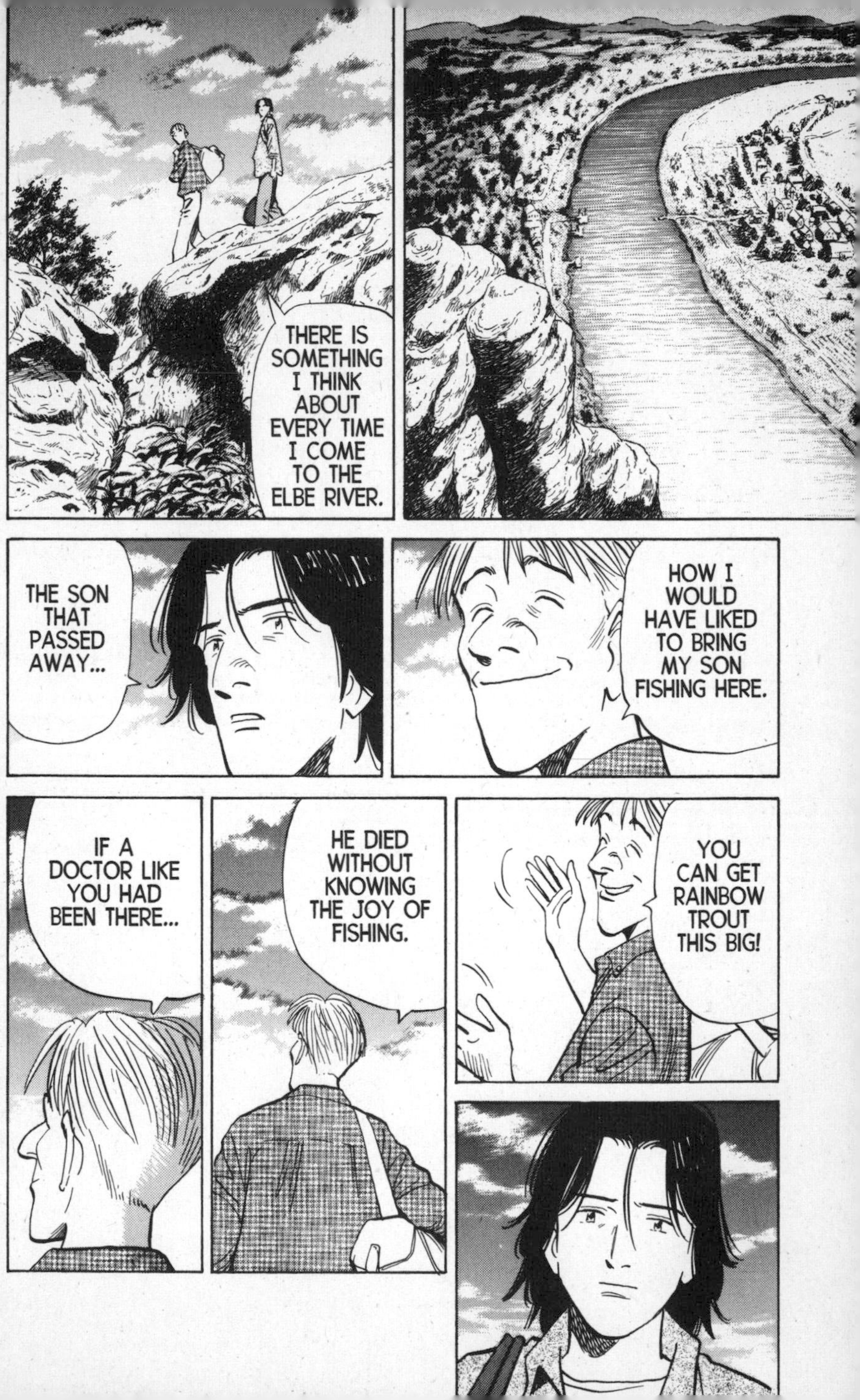
THERE IS SOMETHING I THINK ABOUT EVERY TIME I COME TO THE ELBE RIVER.
HOW I WOULD HAVE LIKED TO BRING MY SON FISHING HERE.
THE SON THAT PASSED AWAY...
YOU CAN GET RAINBOW TROUT THIS BIG!
HE DIED WITHOUT KNOWING THE JOY OF FISHING.
IF A DOCTOR LIKE YOU HAD BEEN THERE...

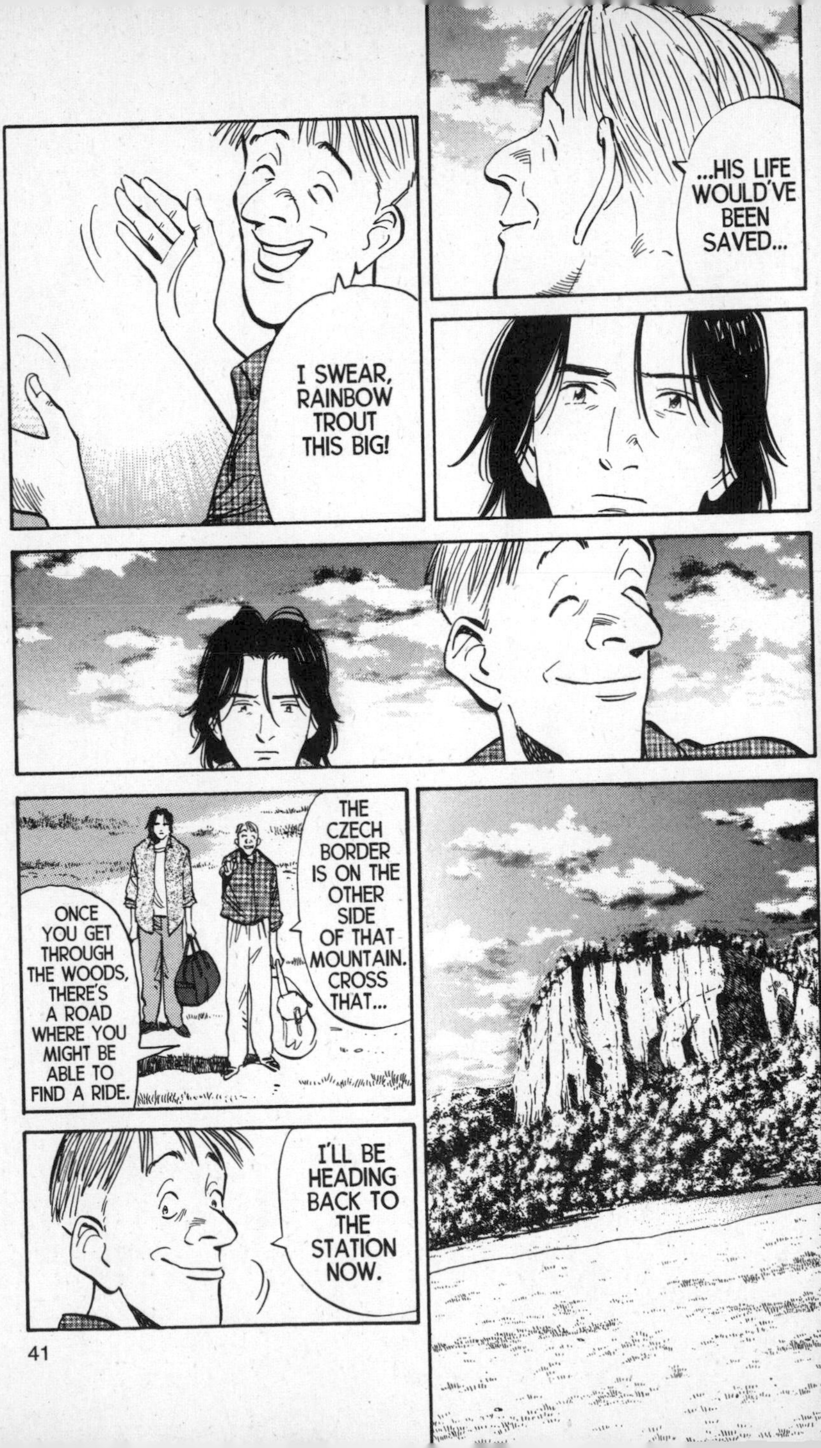

...HIS LIFE WOULD'VE BEEN SAVED...
I SWEAR, RAINBOW TROUT THIS BIG!
THE CZECH BORDER IS ON THE OTHER SIDE OF THAT MOUNTAIN. CROSS THAT...
ONCE YOU GET THROUGH THE WOODS, THERE'S A ROAD WHERE YOU MIGHT BE ABLE TO FIND A RIDE.
I'LL BE HEADING BACK TO THE STATION NOW.

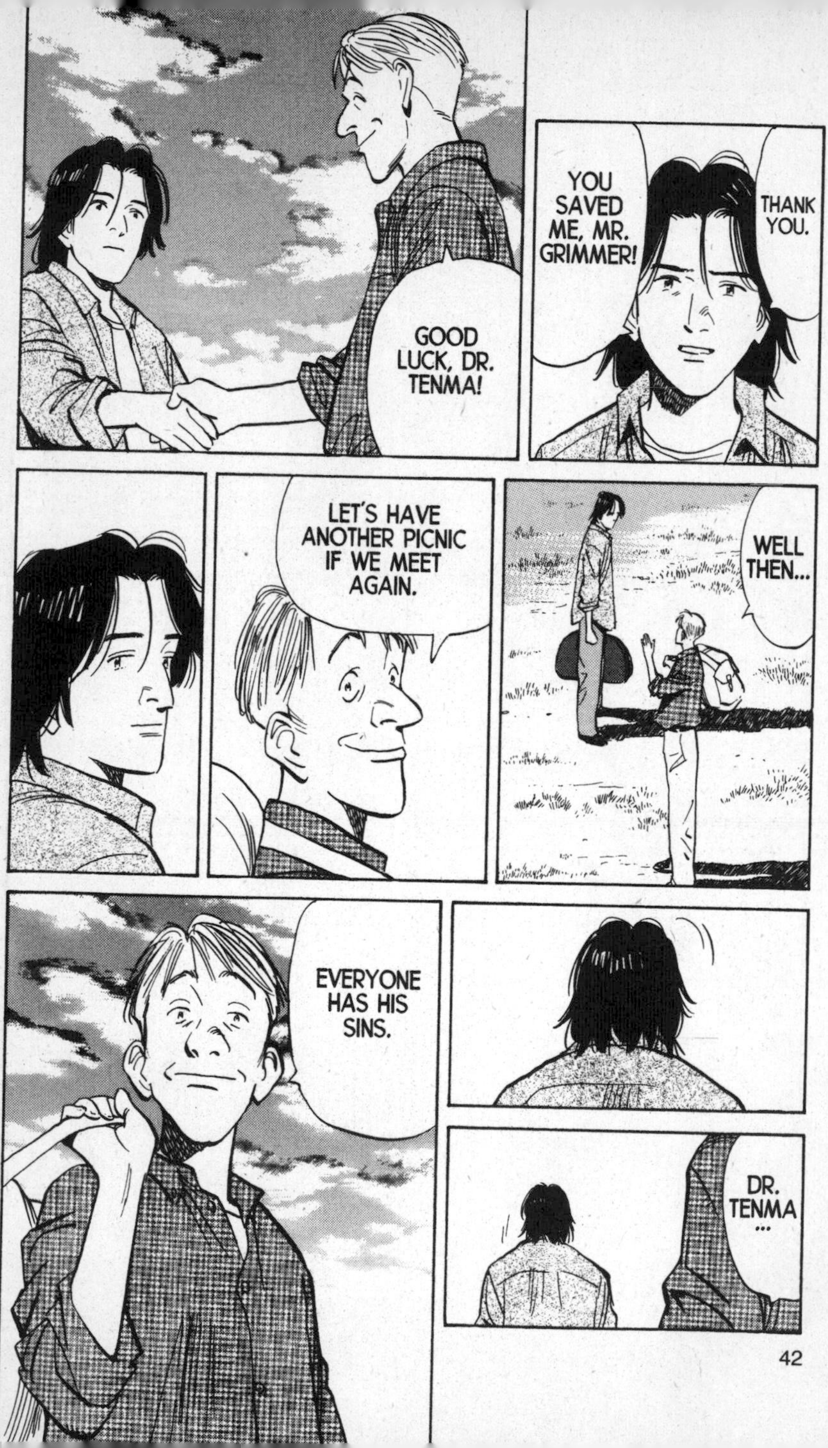
YOU SAVED ME, MR. GRIMMER!
THANK YOU.
GOOD LUCK, DR. TENMA!
WELL THEN...
LET'S HAVE ANOTHER PICNIC IF WE MEET AGAIN.
DR. TENMA...
EVERYONE HAS HIS SINS.

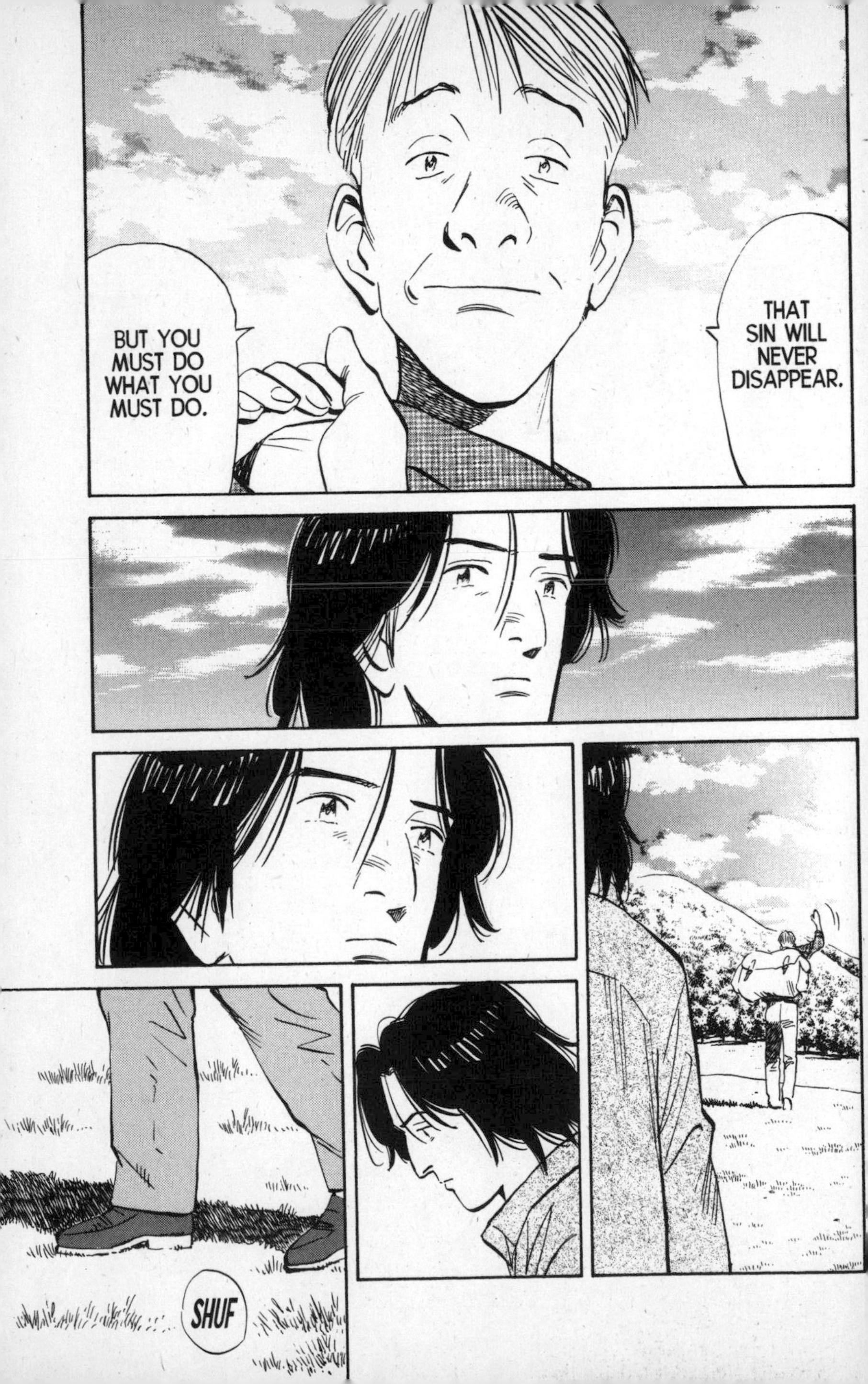
THAT SIN WILL NEVER DISAPPEAR.
BUT YOU MUST DO WHAT YOU MUST DO.
SHUF

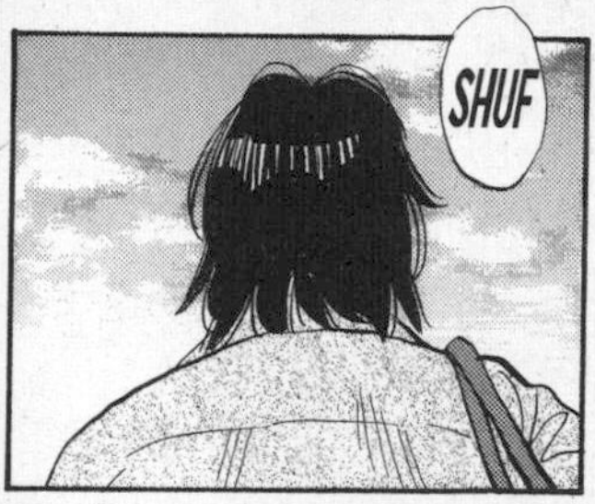
SHUF
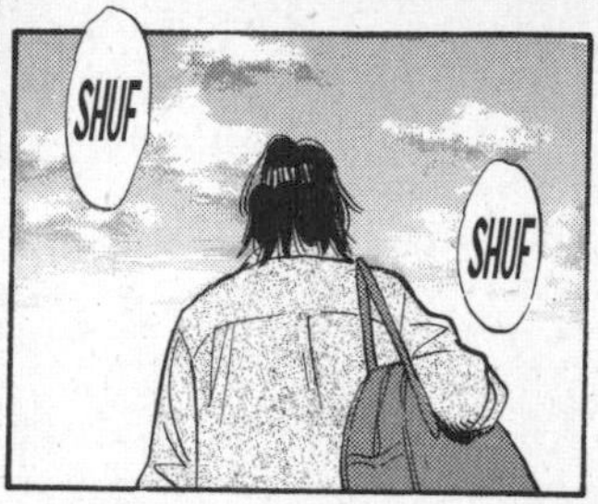
SHUF
SHUF
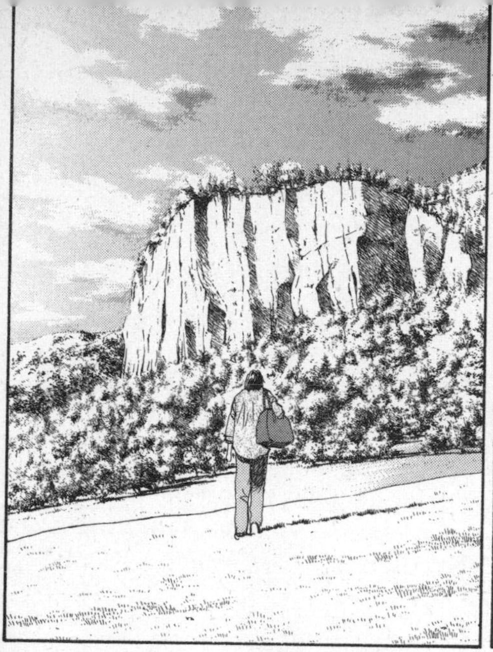
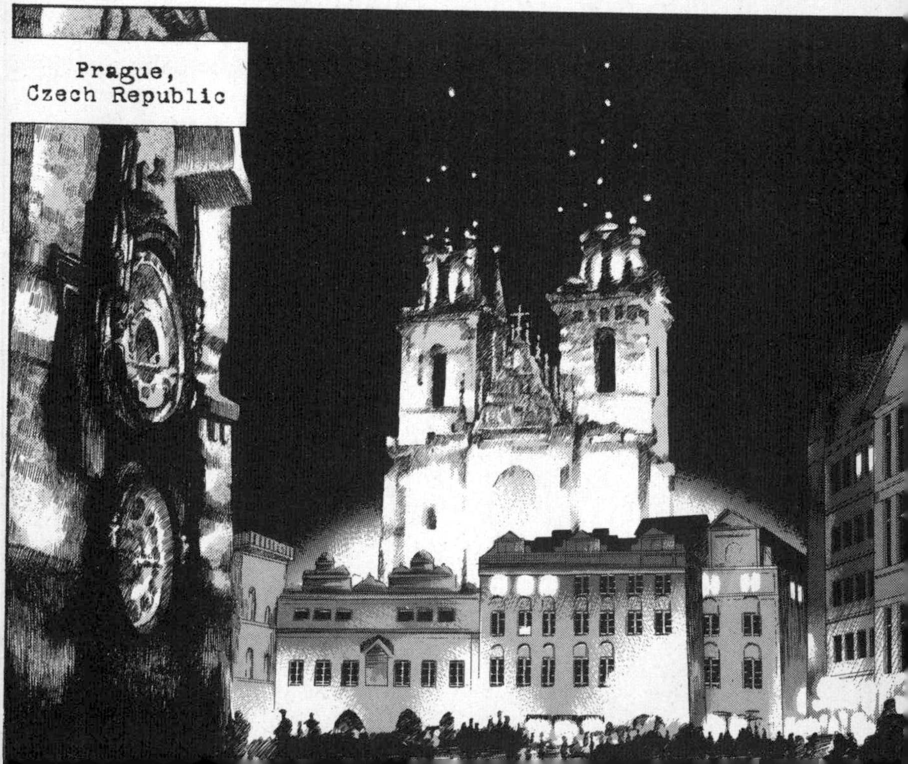
Prague,
Czech Republic

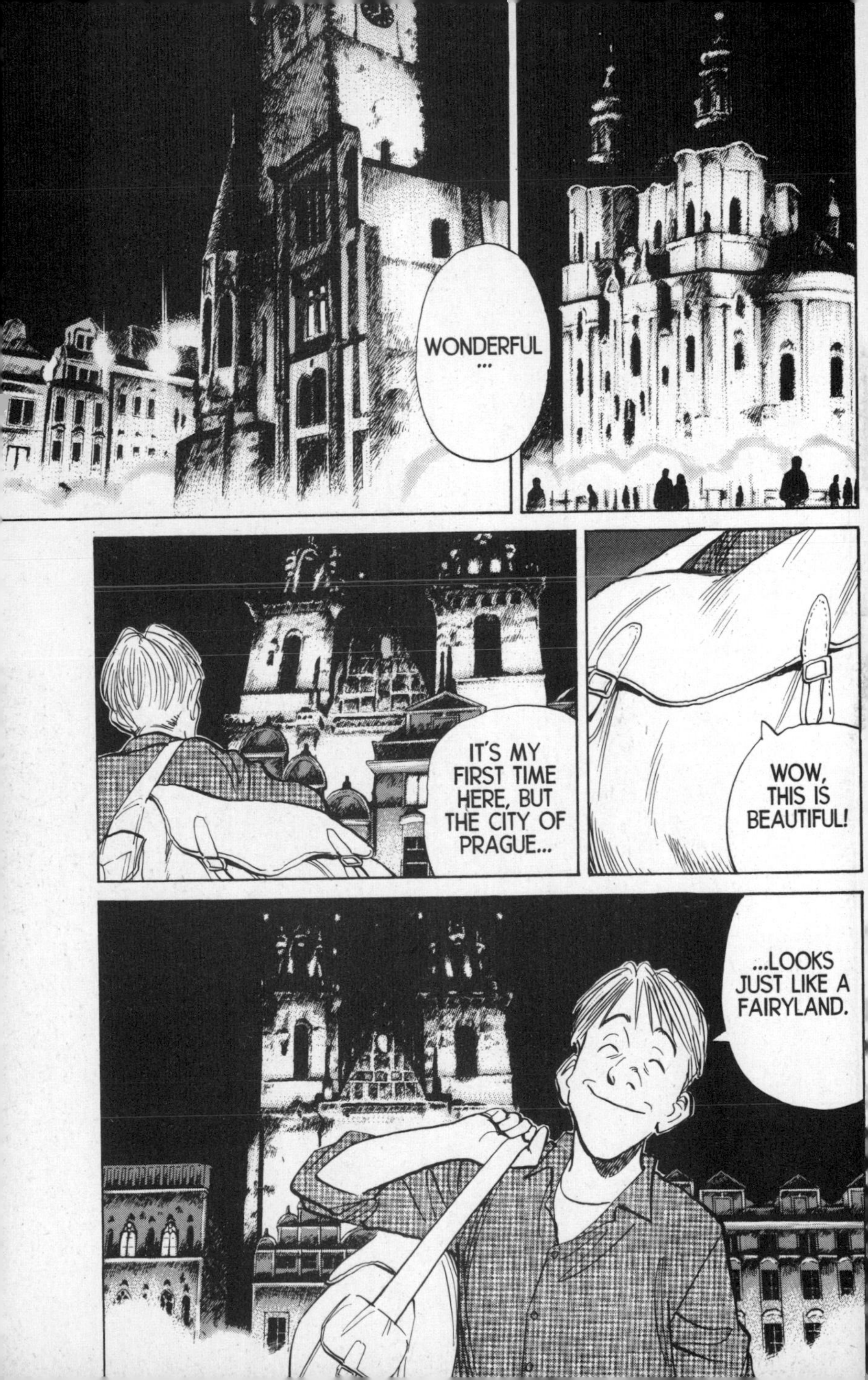
WONDERFUL ...
WOW, THIS IS BEAUTIFUL!
IT'S MY FIRST TIME HERE, BUT THE CITY OF PRAGUE...
...LOOKS JUST LIKE A FAIRYLAND.

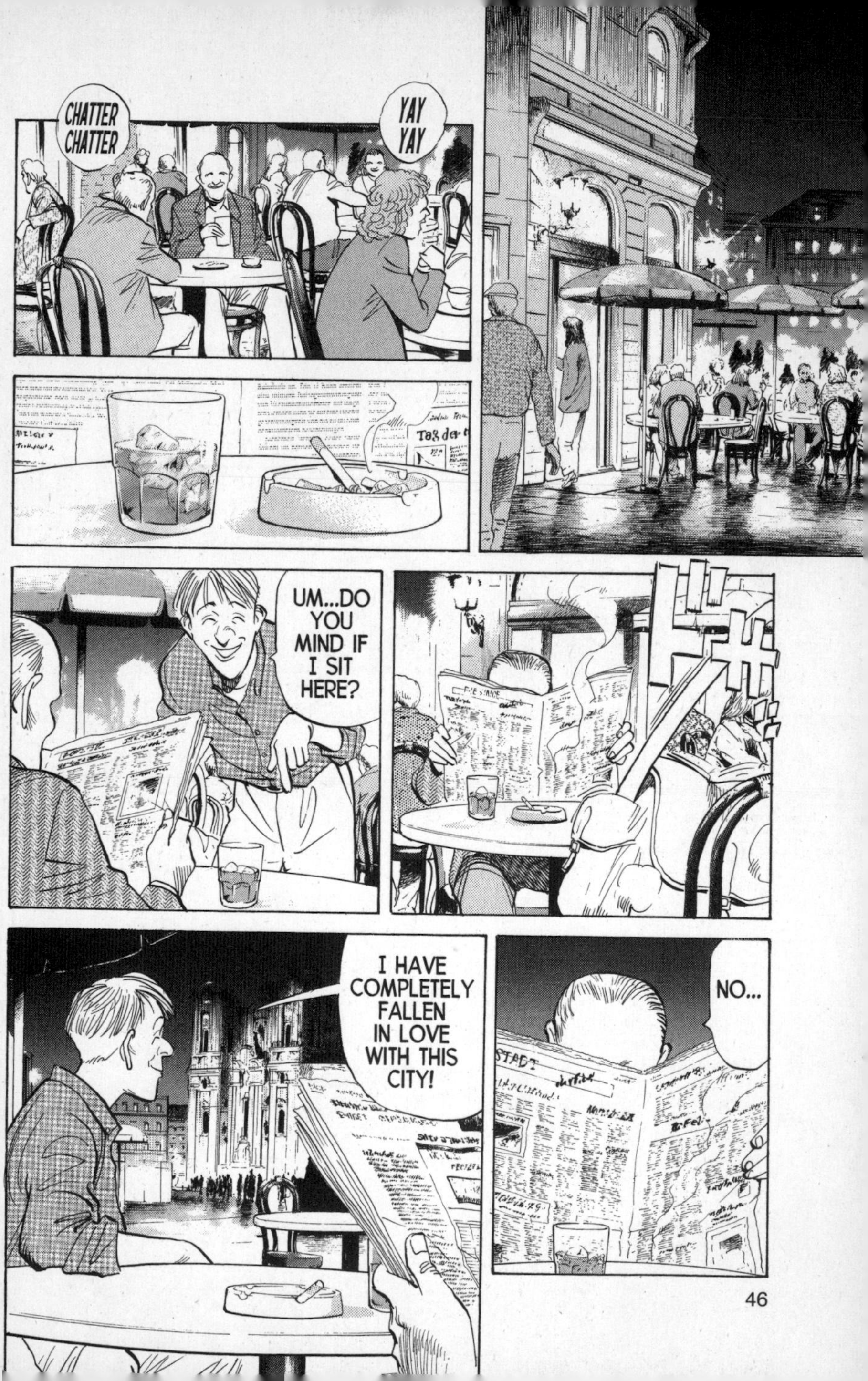
YAY YAY
CHATTER CHATTER
UM...DO YOU MIND IF I SIT HERE?
NO...
I HAVE COMPLETELY FALLEN IN LOVE WITH THIS CITY!

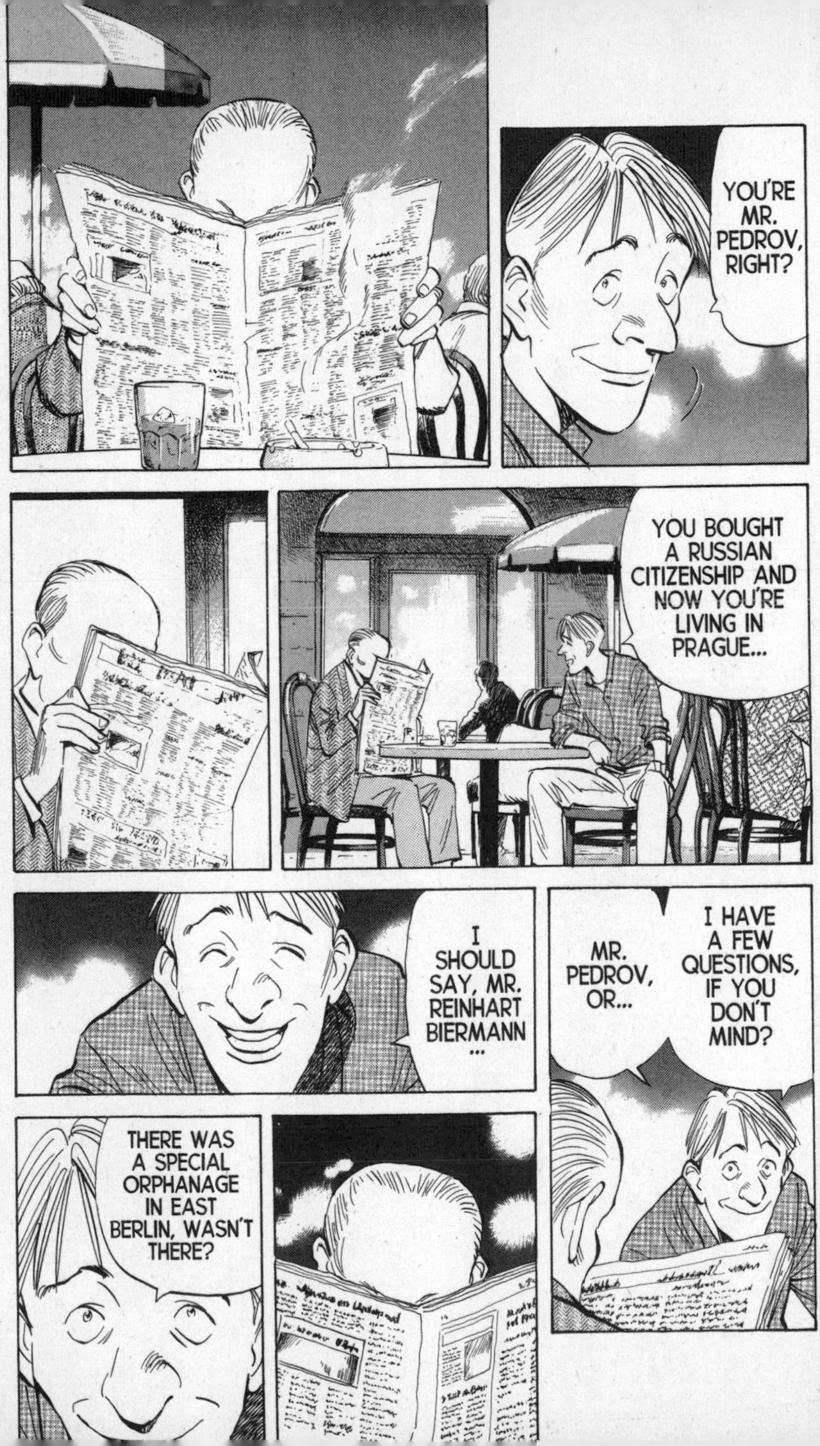
YOU'RE MR. PEDROV, RIGHT?
YOU BOUGHT A RUSSIAN CITIZENSHIP AND NOW YOU'RE LIVING IN PRAGUE...
MR. PEDROV, OR...
I SHOULD SAY, MR. REINHART BIERMANN...
I HAVE A FEW QUESTIONS, IF YOU DON'T MIND?
THERE WAS A SPECIAL ORPHANAGE IN EAST BERLIN, WASN'T THERE?

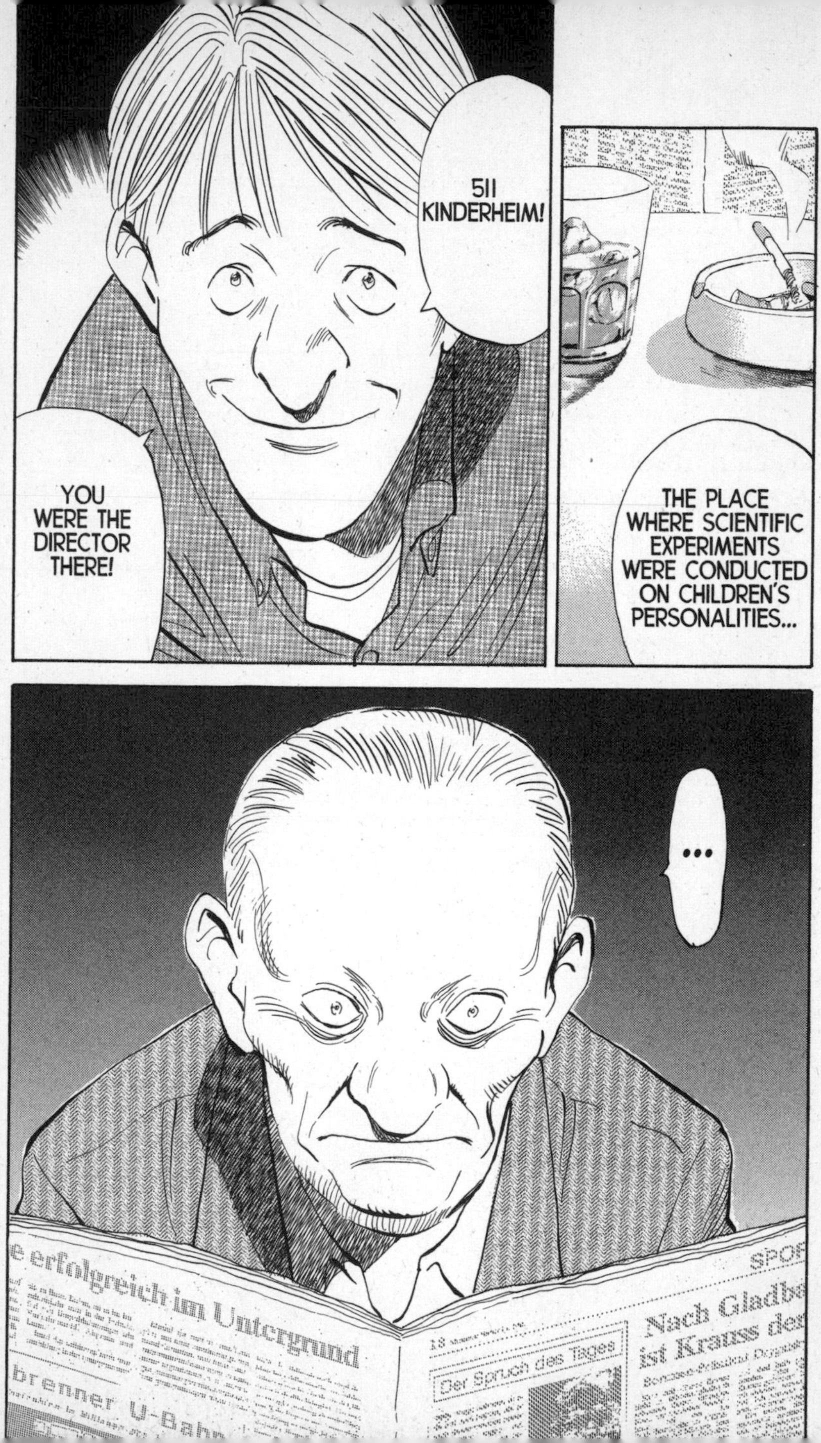
THE PLACE WHERE SCIENTIFIC EXPERIMENTS WERE CONDUCTED ON CHILDREN'S PERSONALITIES...
511 KINDERHEIM!
YOU WERE THE DIRECTOR THERE!
...
erfolgreich im Untergrund
Der Spruch des Tages
Nach
ist

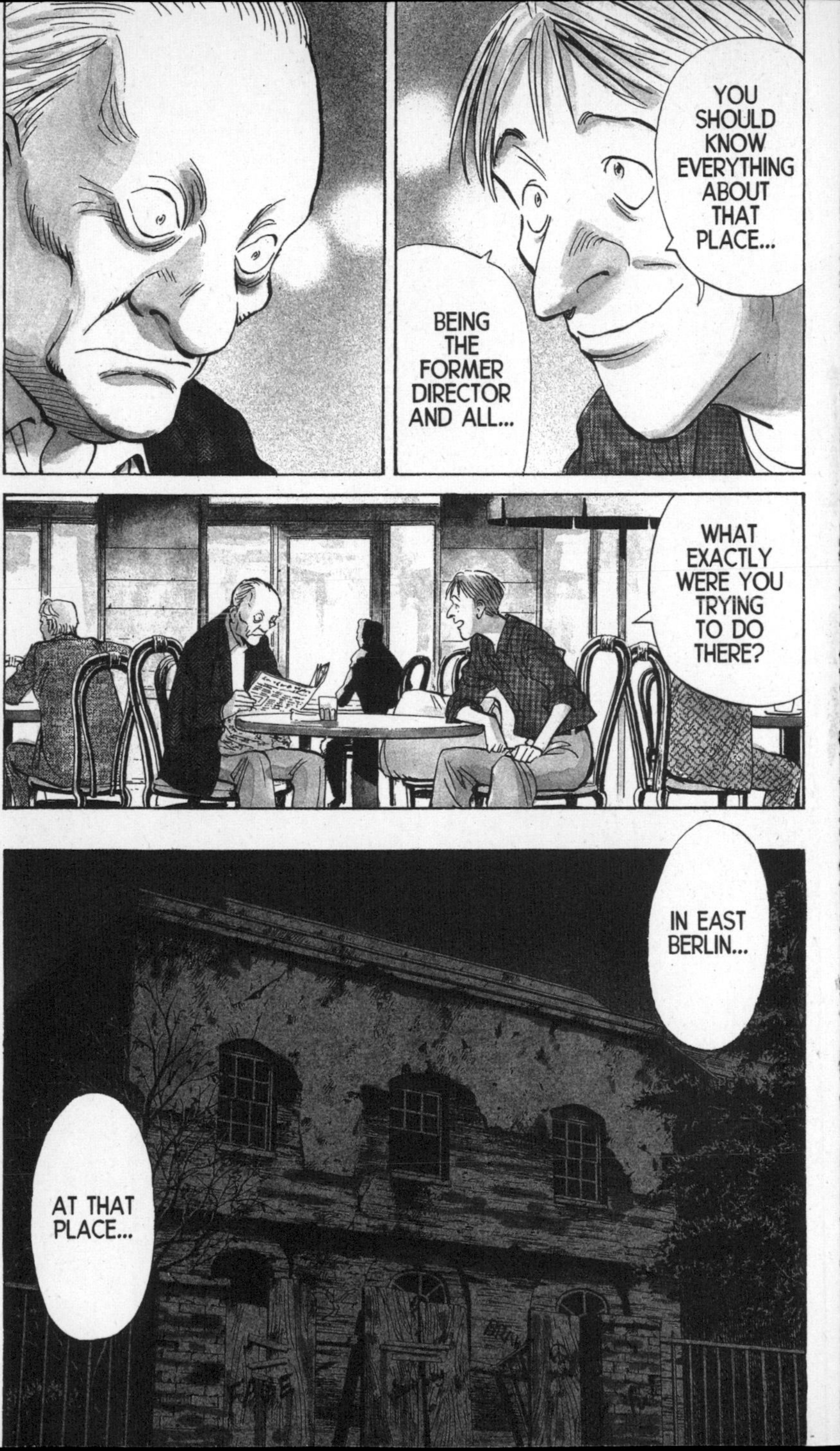
YOU SHOULD KNOW EVERYTHING ABOUT THAT PLACE...
BEING THE FORMER DIRECTOR AND ALL...
WHAT EXACTLY WERE YOU TRYING TO DO THERE?
IN EAST BERLIN...
AT THAT PLACE...

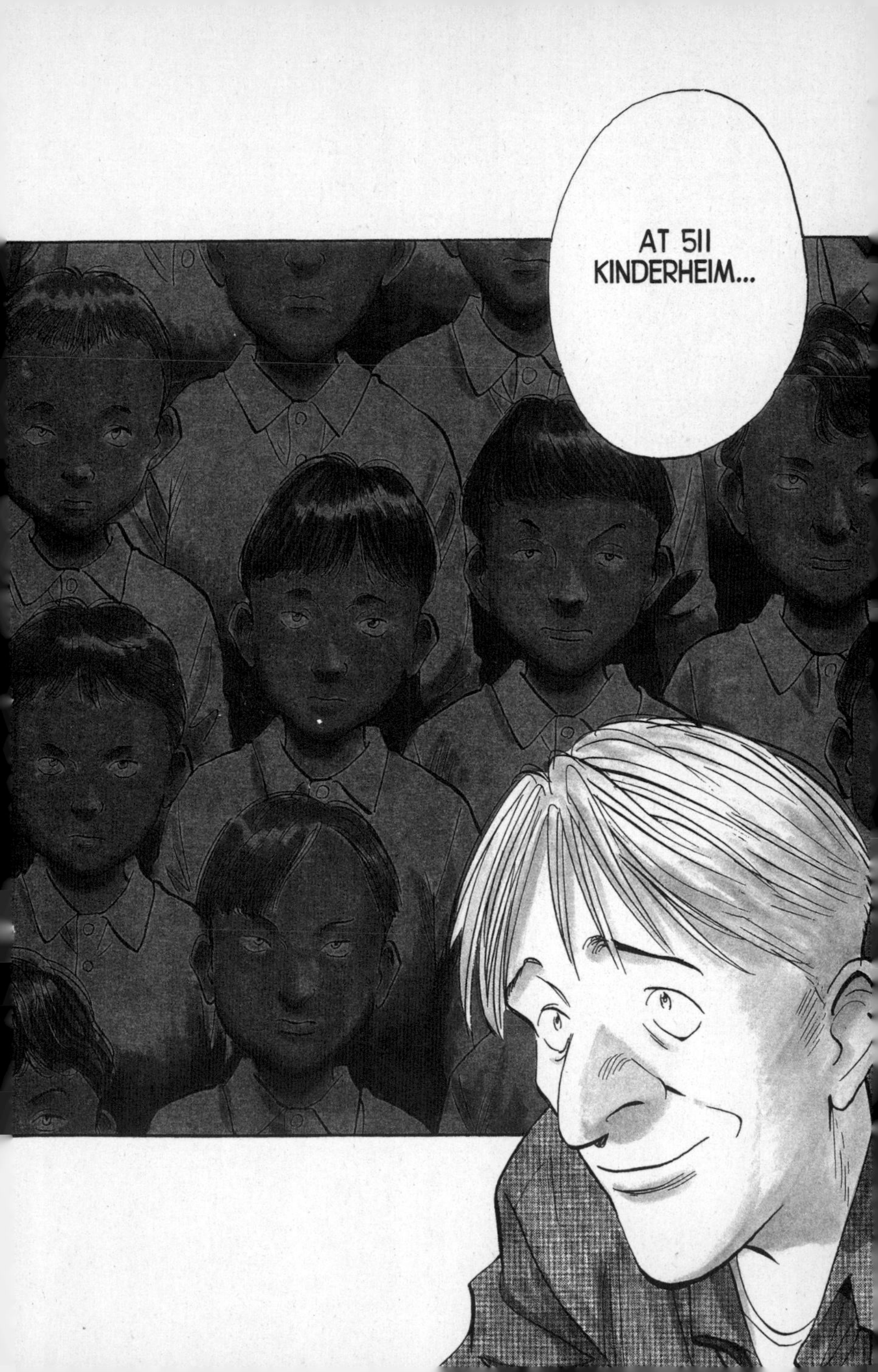
AT 511
KINDERHEIM...

Chapter 3
The Ghost of 511

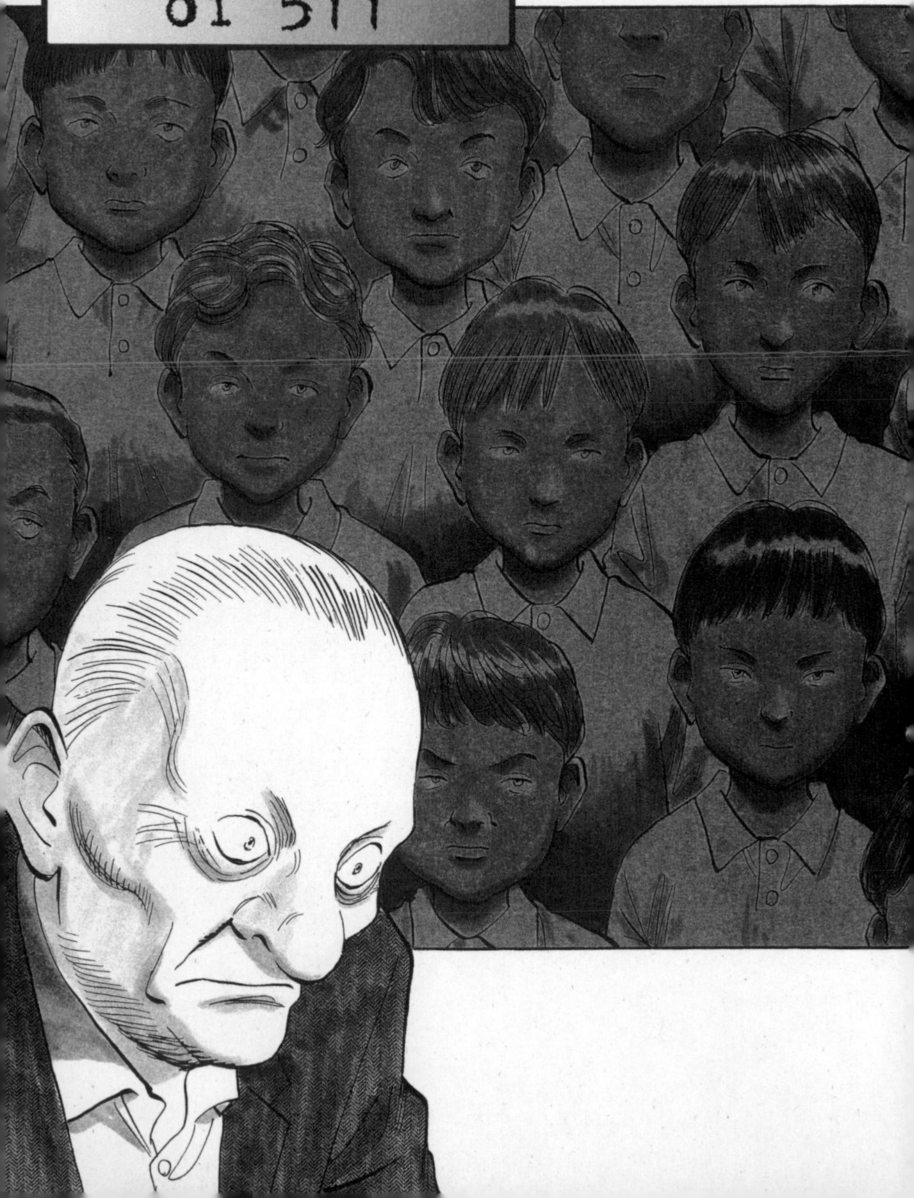

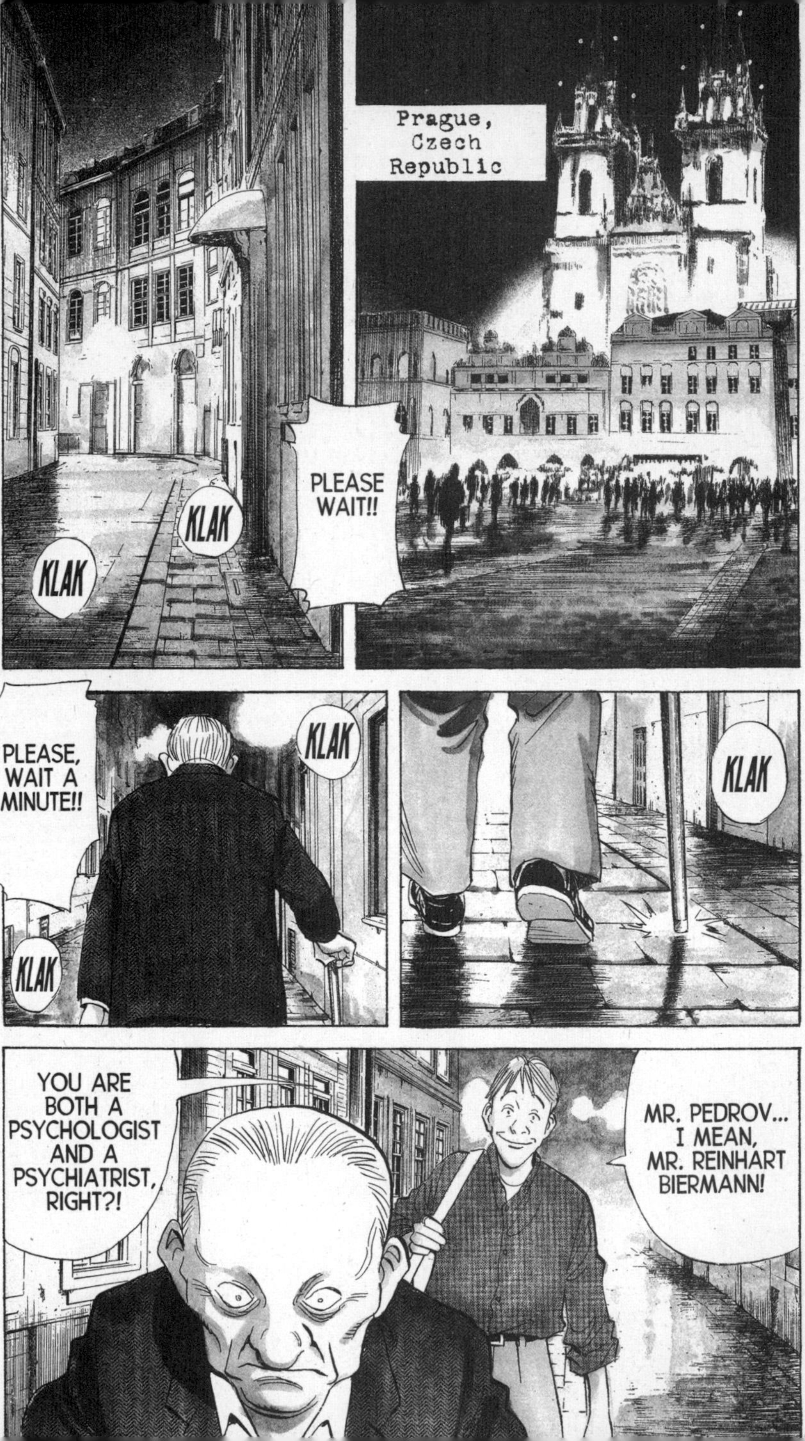
Prague, Czech Republic
PLEASE WAIT!!
KLAK
KLAK
KLAK
PLEASE, WAIT A MINUTE!!
KLAK
KLAK
MR. PEDROV... I MEAN, MR. REINHART BIERMANN!
YOU ARE BOTH A PSYCHOLOGIST AND A PSYCHIATRIST, RIGHT?!

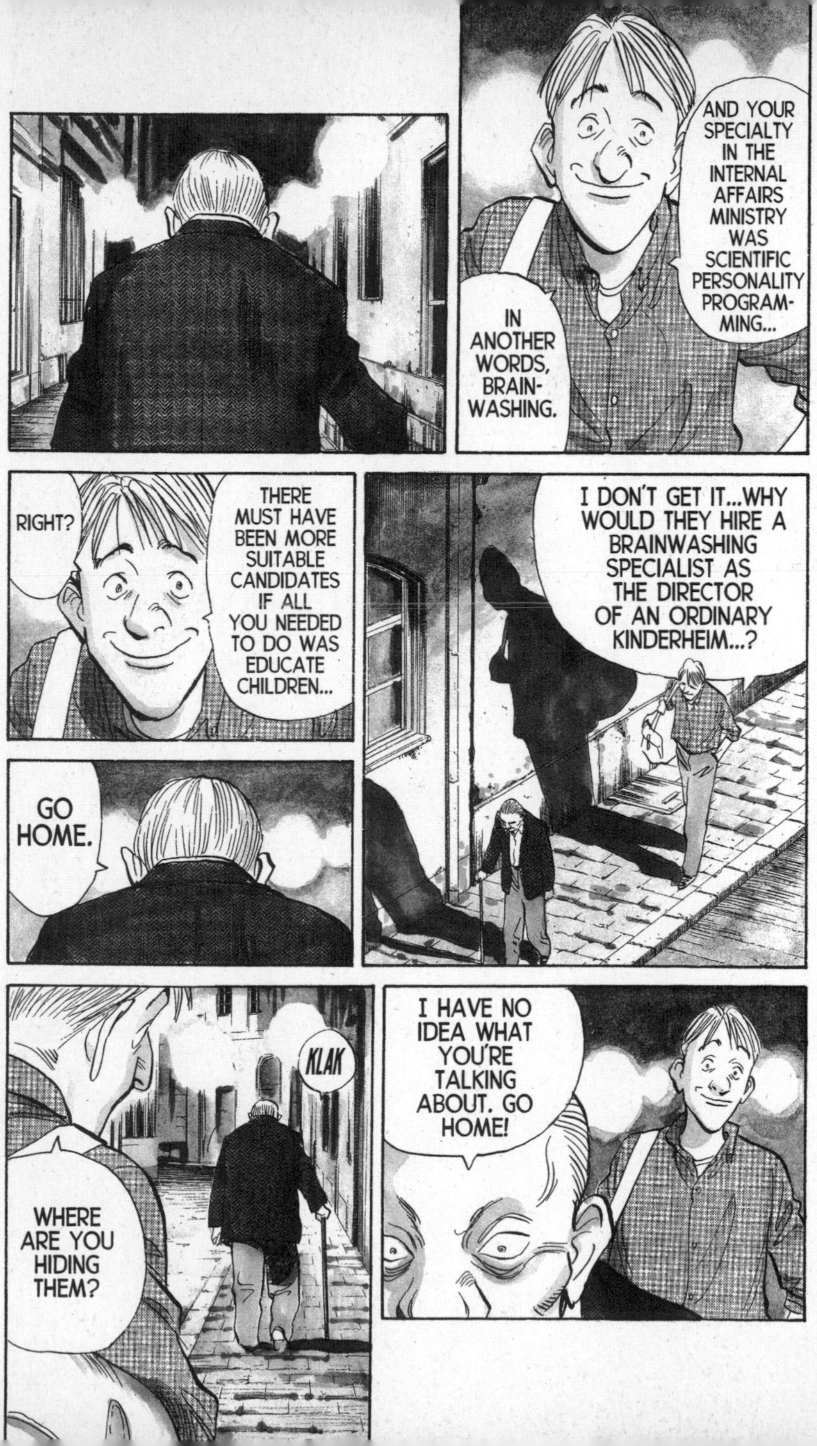
AND YOUR SPECIALTY IN THE INTERNAL AFFAIRS MINISTRY WAS SCIENTIFIC PERSONALITY PROGRAM-MING...
IN ANOTHER WORDS, BRAIN-WASHING.
I DON'T GET IT...WHY WOULD THEY HIRE A BRAINWASHING SPECIALIST AS THE DIRECTOR OF AN ORDINARY KINDERHEIM...?
THERE MUST HAVE BEEN MORE SUITABLE CANDIDATES IF ALL YOU NEEDED TO DO WAS EDUCATE CHILDREN...
RIGHT?
GO HOME.
I HAVE NO IDEA WHAT YOU'RE TALKING ABOUT. GO HOME!
KLAK
WHERE ARE YOU HIDING THEM?

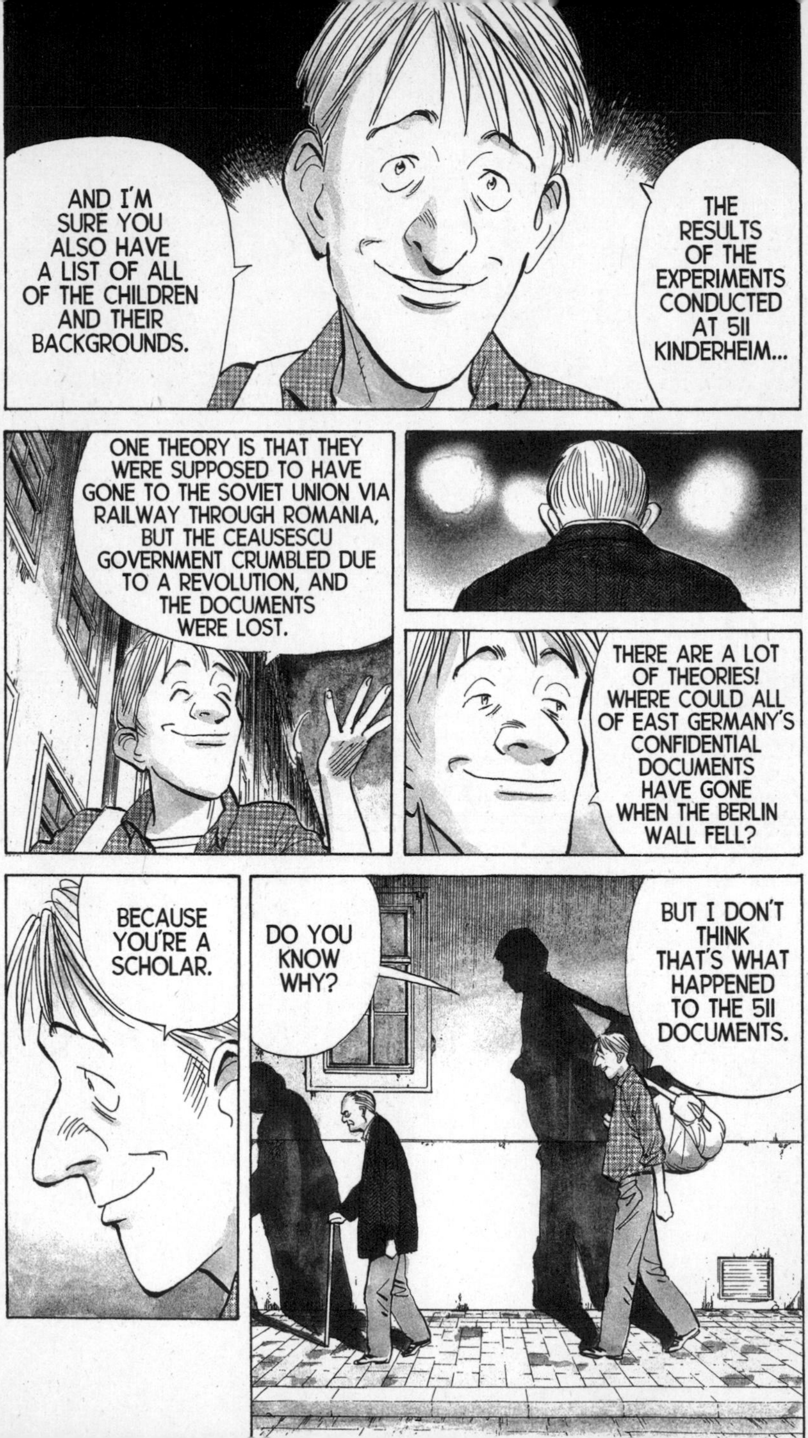
THE RESULTS OF THE EXPERIMENTS CONDUCTED AT 511 KINDERHEIM...
AND I'M SURE YOU ALSO HAVE A LIST OF ALL OF THE CHILDREN AND THEIR BACKGROUNDS.
THERE ARE A LOT OF THEORIES! WHERE COULD ALL OF EAST GERMANY'S CONFIDENTIAL DOCUMENTS HAVE GONE WHEN THE BERLIN WALL FELL?
ONE THEORY IS THAT THEY WERE SUPPOSED TO HAVE GONE TO THE SOVIET UNION VIA RAILWAY THROUGH ROMANIA, BUT THE CEAUSESCU GOVERNMENT CRUMBLED DUE TO A REVOLUTION, AND THE DOCUMENTS WERE LOST.
BUT I DON'T THINK THAT'S WHAT HAPPENED TO THE 511 DOCUMENTS.
DO YOU KNOW WHY?
BECAUSE YOU'RE A SCHOLAR.

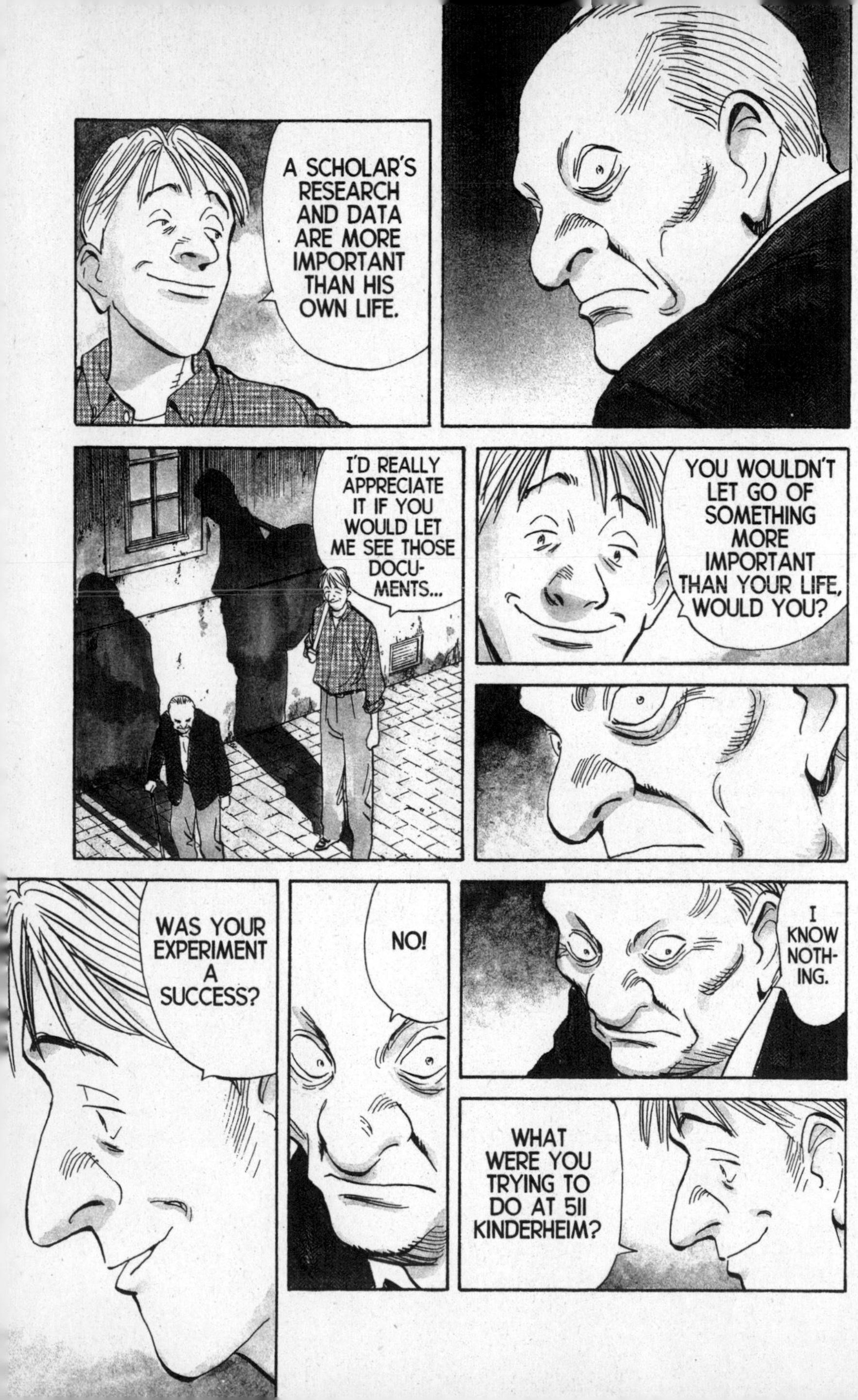
A SCHOLAR'S RESEARCH AND DATA ARE MORE IMPORTANT THAN HIS OWN LIFE.
I'D REALLY APPRECIATE IT IF YOU WOULD LET ME SEE THOSE DOCU-MENTS...
YOU WOULDN'T LET GO OF SOMETHING MORE IMPORTANT THAN YOUR LIFE, WOULD YOU?
WAS YOUR EXPERIMENT A SUCCESS?
NO!
I KNOW NOTH-ING.
WHAT WERE YOU TRYING TO DO AT 511 KINDERHEIM?

DO YOU ENJOY TREATING HUMAN BEINGS LIKE GUINEA PIGS?

THE EXPERIMENT...

...WAS A FAILURE, RIGHT?

...

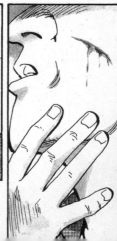

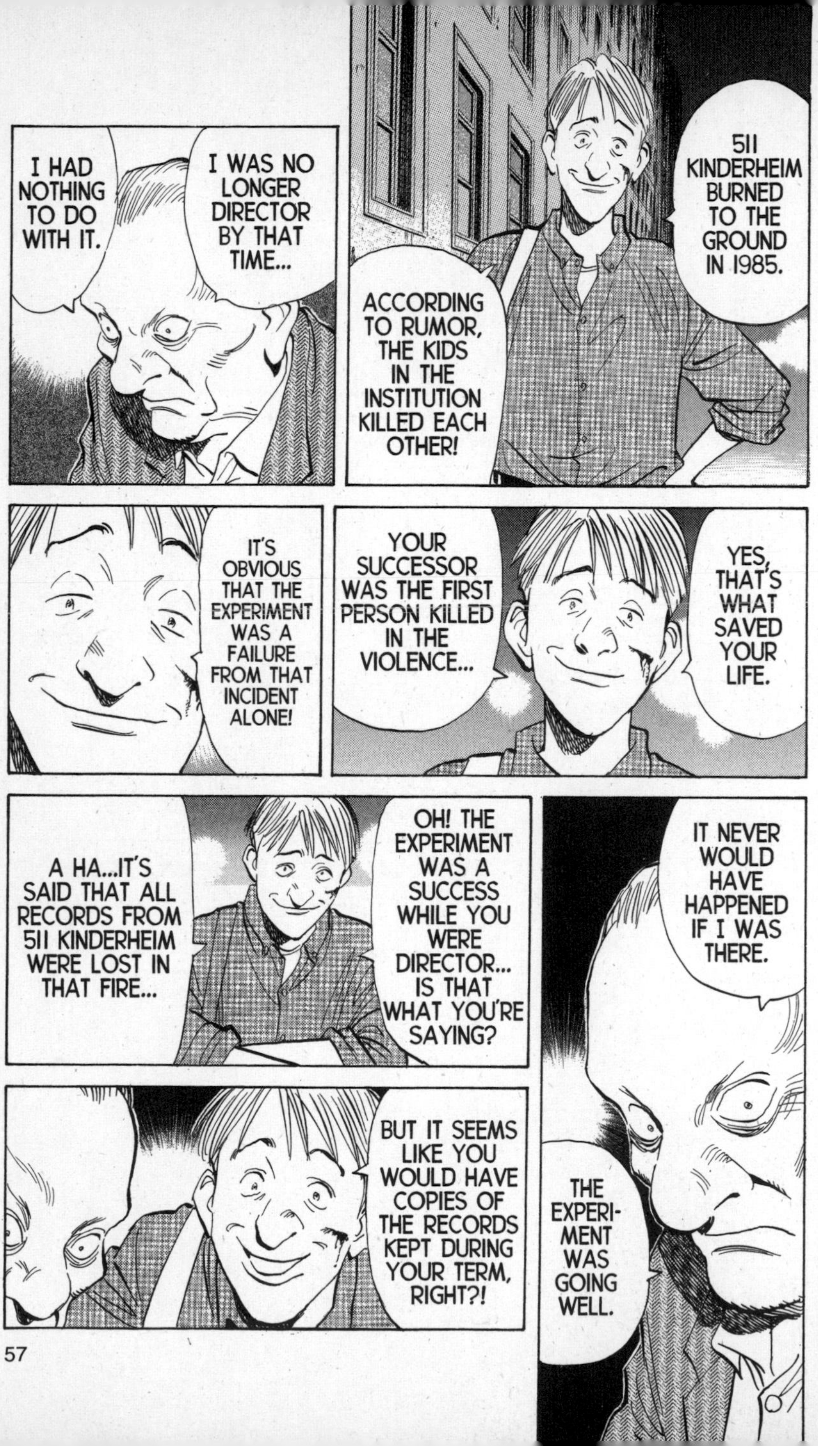
511 KINDERHEIM BURNED TO THE GROUND IN 1985.
ACCORDING TO RUMOR, THE KIDS IN THE INSTITUTION KILLED EACH OTHER!
I WAS NO LONGER DIRECTOR BY THAT TIME...
I HAD NOTHING TO DO WITH IT.
YES, THAT'S WHAT SAVED YOUR LIFE.
YOUR SUCCESSOR WAS THE FIRST PERSON KILLED IN THE VIOLENCE...
IT'S OBVIOUS THAT THE EXPERIMENT WAS A FAILURE FROM THAT INCIDENT ALONE!
IT NEVER WOULD HAVE HAPPENED IF I WAS THERE.
THE EXPERIMENT WAS GOING WELL.
OH! THE EXPERIMENT WAS A SUCCESS WHILE YOU WERE DIRECTOR... IS THAT WHAT YOU'RE SAYING?
A HA...IT'S SAID THAT ALL RECORDS FROM 511 KINDERHEIM WERE LOST IN THAT FIRE...
BUT IT SEEMS LIKE YOU WOULD HAVE COPIES OF THE RECORDS KEPT DURING YOUR TERM, RIGHT?!

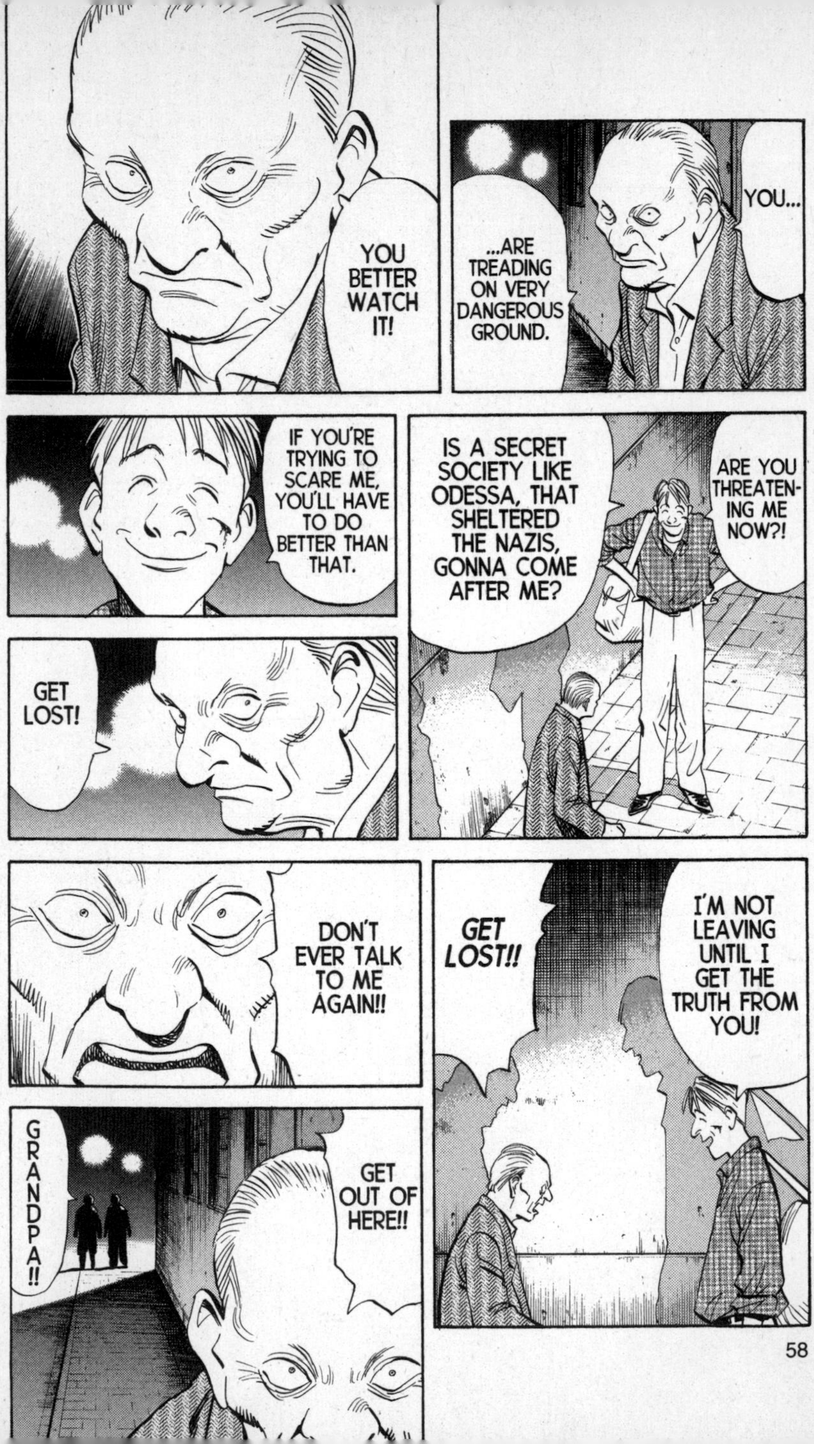
YOU...
...ARE TREADING ON VERY DANGEROUS GROUND.
YOU BETTER WATCH IT!
ARE YOU THREATENING ME NOW?!
IS A SECRET SOCIETY LIKE ODESSA, THAT SHELTERED THE NAZIS, GONNA COME AFTER ME?
IF YOU'RE TRYING TO SCARE ME, YOU'LL HAVE TO DO BETTER THAN THAT.
GET LOST!
I'M NOT LEAVING UNTIL I GET THE TRUTH FROM YOU!
GET LOST!!
DON'T EVER TALK TO ME AGAIN!!
GET OUT OF HERE!!
GRANDPA!!

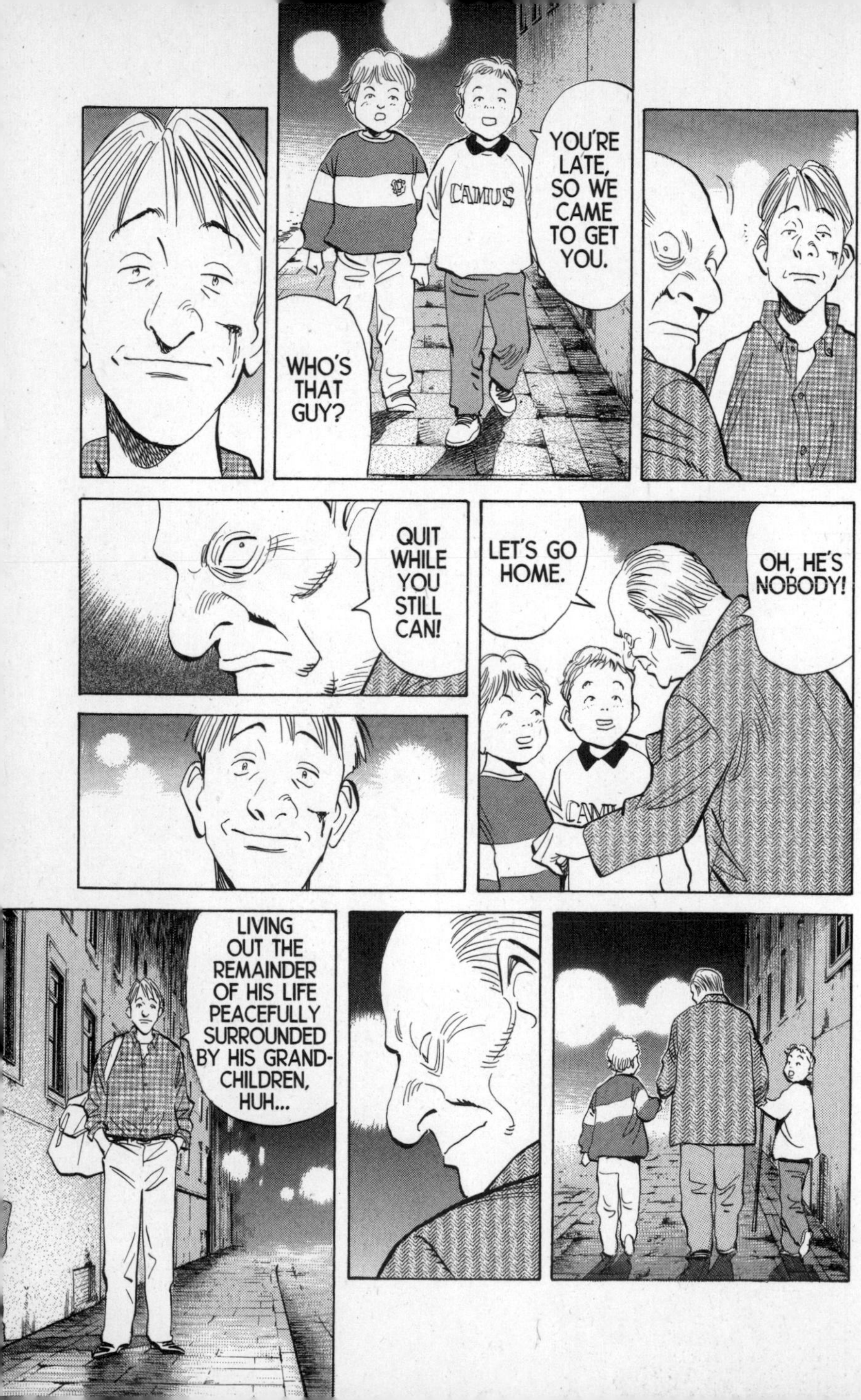
YOU'RE LATE, SO WE CAME TO GET YOU.
WHO'S THAT GUY?
OH, HE'S NOBODY!
LET'S GO HOME.
QUIT WHILE YOU STILL CAN!
LIVING OUT THE REMAINDER OF HIS LIFE PEACEFULLY SURROUNDED BY HIS GRAND-CHILDREN, HUH...

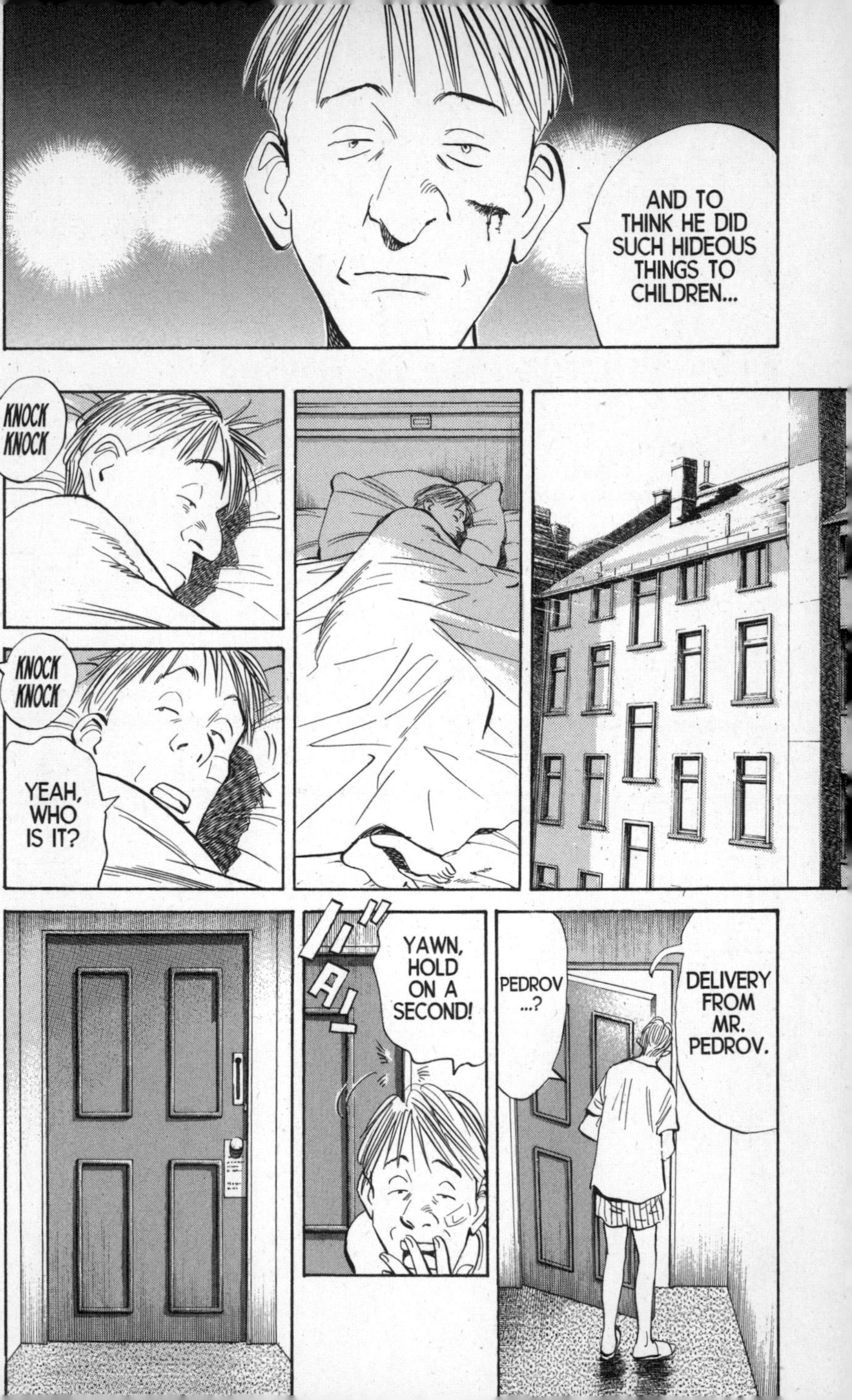
AND TO THINK HE DID SUCH HIDEOUS THINGS TO CHILDREN...
KNOCK KNOCK
KNOCK KNOCK
YEAH, WHO IS IT?
DELIVERY FROM MR. PEDROV.
PEDROV ...?
YAWN, HOLD ON A SECOND!

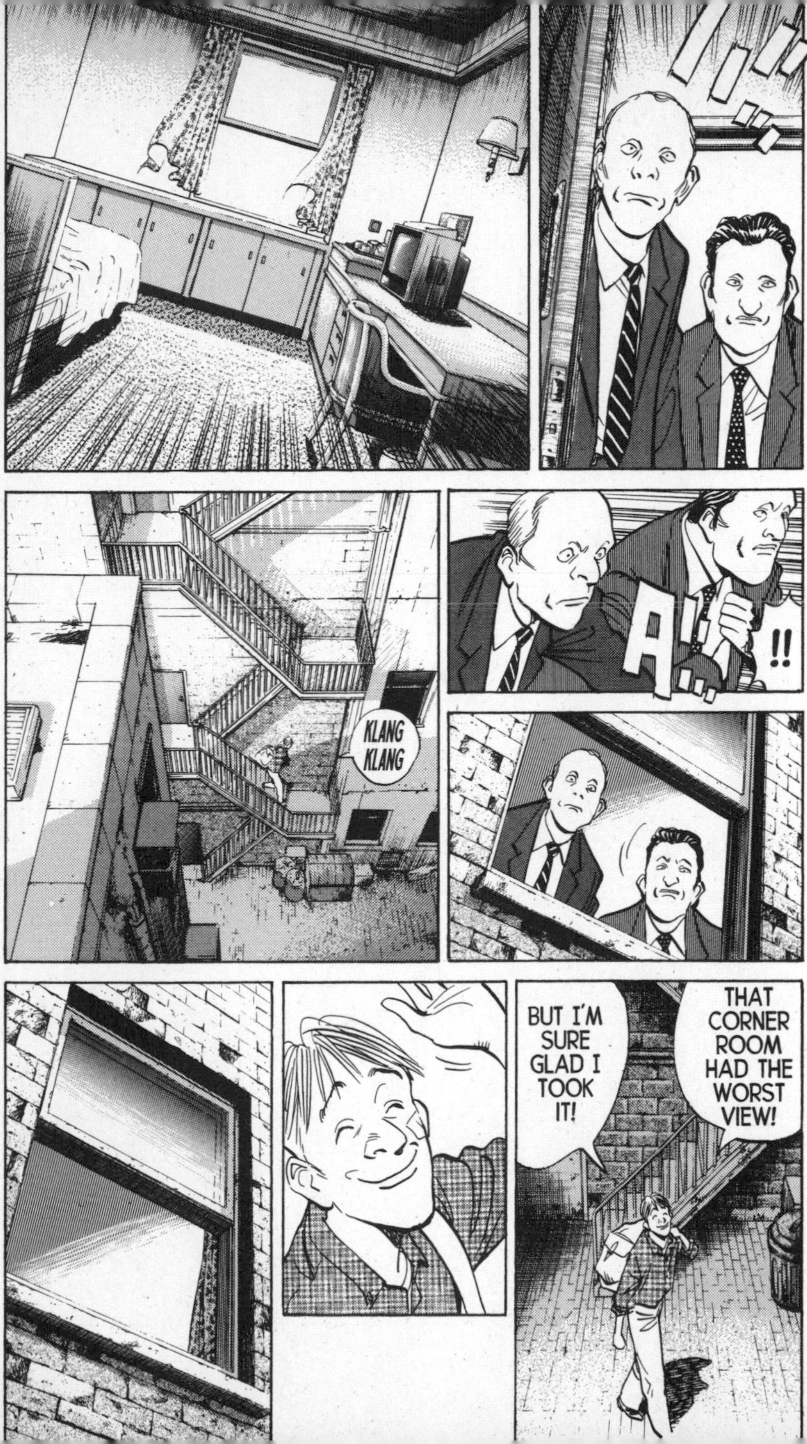
A...!!
KLANG KLANG
THAT CORNER ROOM HAD THE WORST VIEW!
BUT I'M SURE GLAD I TOOK IT!

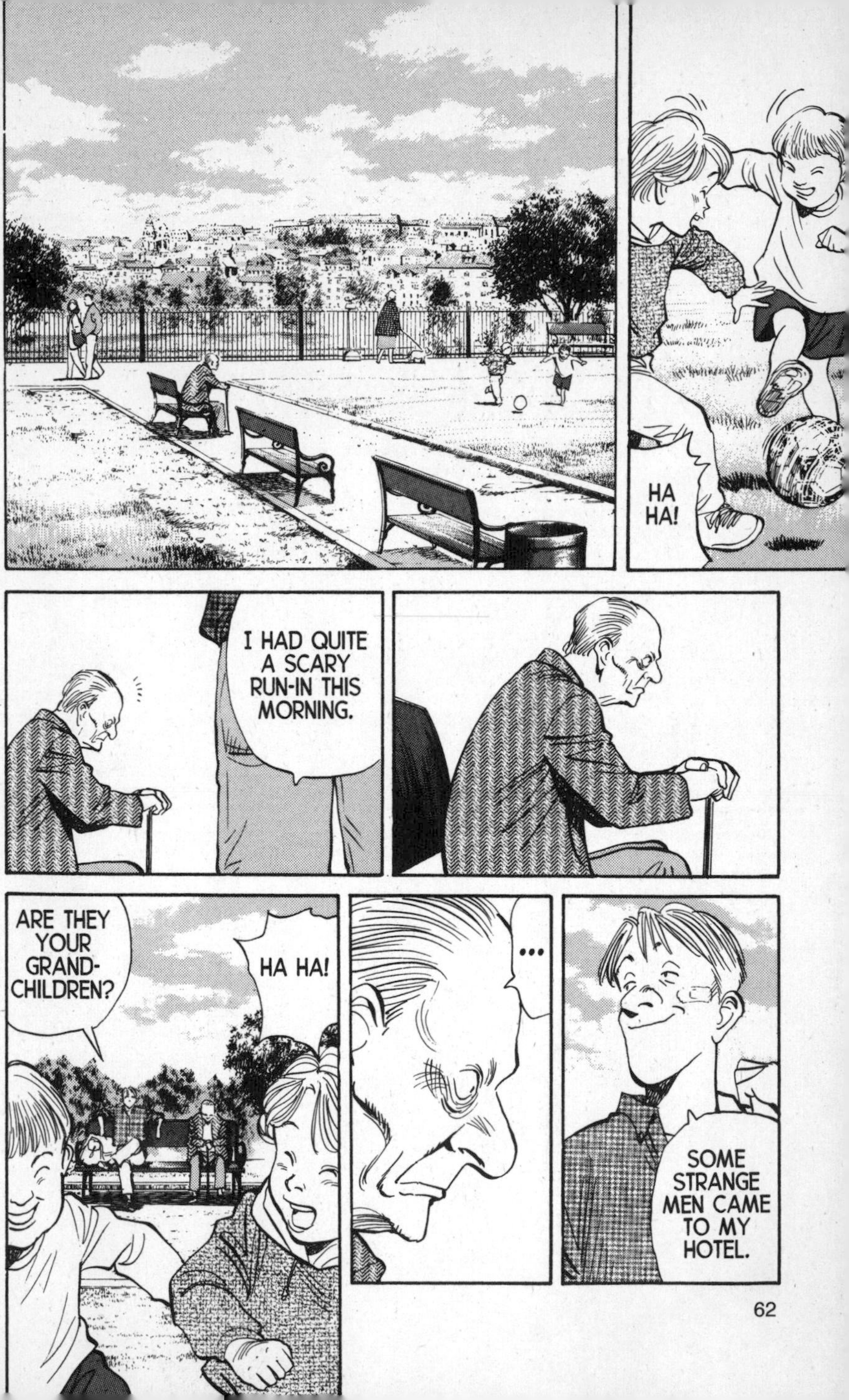
HA HA!
I HAD QUITE A SCARY RUN-IN THIS MORNING.
SOME STRANGE MEN CAME TO MY HOTEL.
...
ARE THEY YOUR GRAND-CHILDREN?
HA HA!

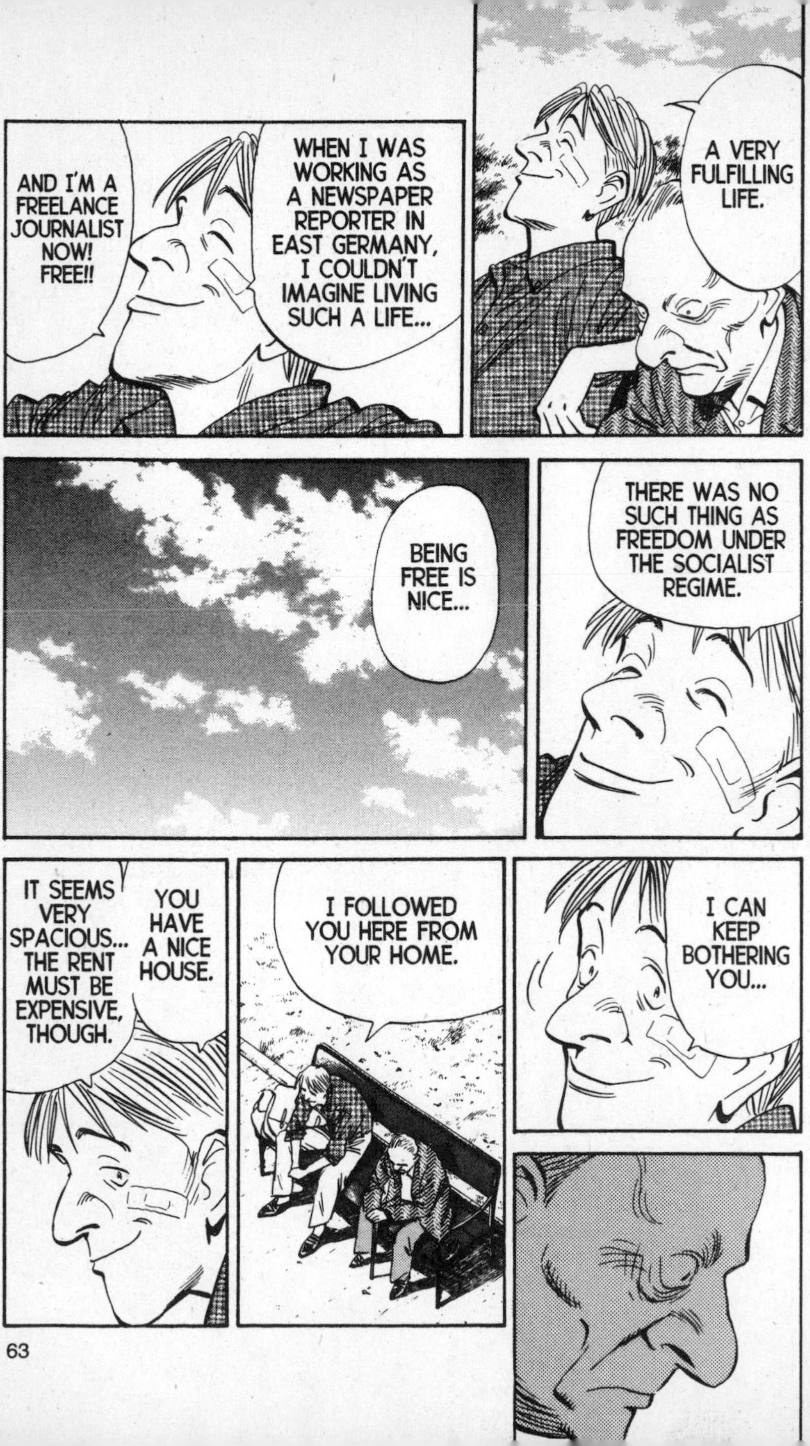
AND I'M A FREELANCE JOURNALIST NOW! FREE!!
WHEN I WAS WORKING AS A NEWSPAPER REPORTER IN EAST GERMANY, I COULDN'T IMAGINE LIVING SUCH A LIFE...
A VERY FULFILLING LIFE.
BEING FREE IS NICE...
THERE WAS NO SUCH THING AS FREEDOM UNDER THE SOCIALIST REGIME.
IT SEEMS VERY SPACIOUS... THE RENT MUST BE EXPENSIVE, THOUGH.
YOU HAVE A NICE HOUSE.
I FOLLOWED YOU HERE FROM YOUR HOME.
I CAN KEEP BOTHERING YOU...

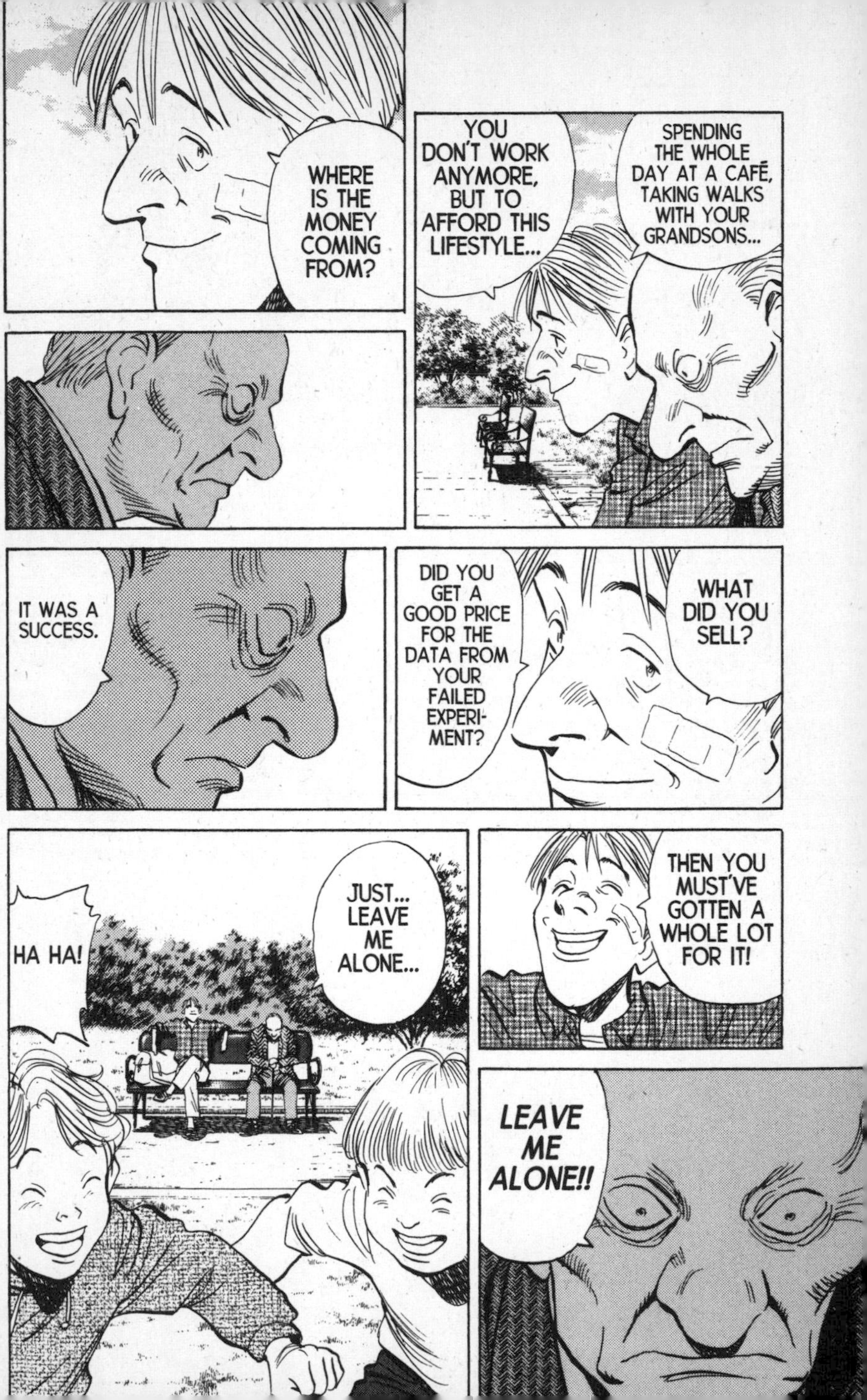
SPENDING THE WHOLE DAY AT A CAFÉ, TAKING WALKS WITH YOUR GRANDSONS...
YOU DON'T WORK ANYMORE, BUT TO AFFORD THIS LIFESTYLE...
WHERE IS THE MONEY COMING FROM?
WHAT DID YOU SELL?
DID YOU GET A GOOD PRICE FOR THE DATA FROM YOUR FAILED EXPERI-MENT?
IT WAS A SUCCESS.
THEN YOU MUST'VE GOTTEN A WHOLE LOT FOR IT!
LEAVE ME ALONE!!
JUST... LEAVE ME ALONE...
HA HA!

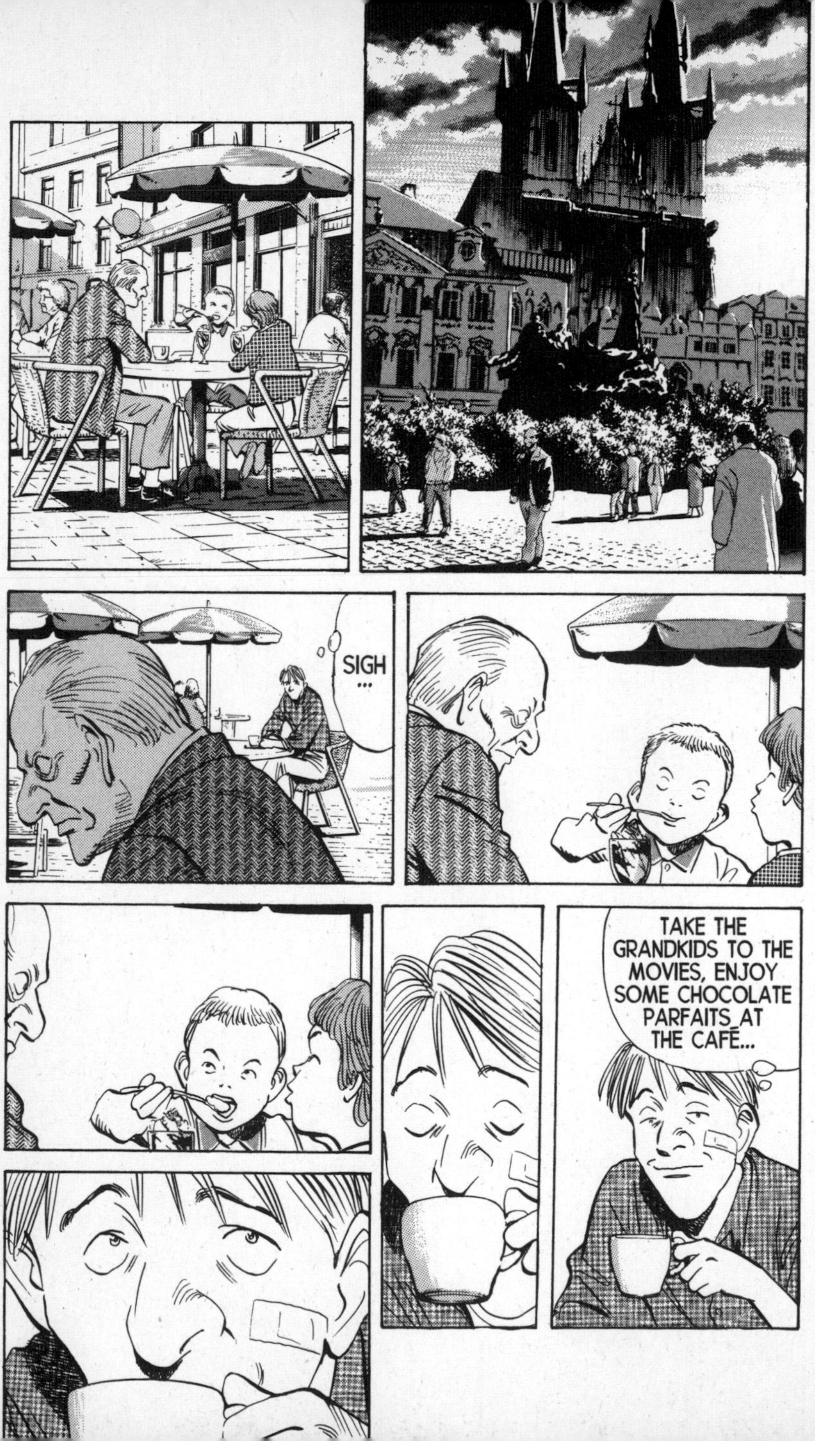
SIGH...
TAKE THE GRANDKIDS TO THE MOVIES, ENJOY SOME CHOCOLATE PARFAITS AT THE CAFÉ...

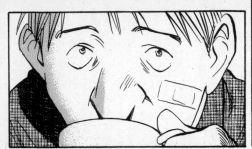

TWO...

ONE...

DIFFERENT KIDS AGAIN...

FOUR...

THREE...

FIVE...

SIX...

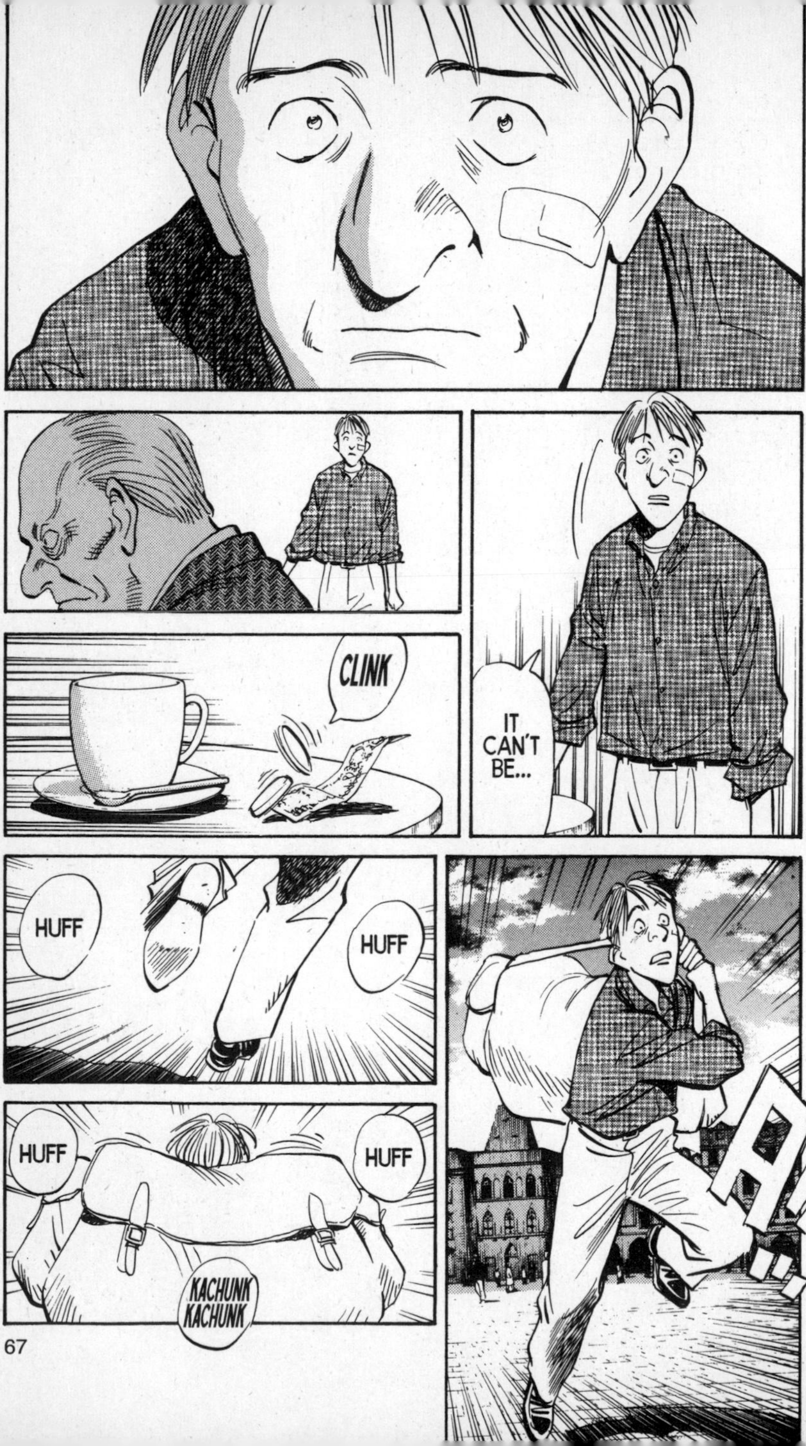
IT CAN'T BE...
CLINK
A!!
HUFF
HUFF
HUFF
HUFF
KACHUNK KACHUNK

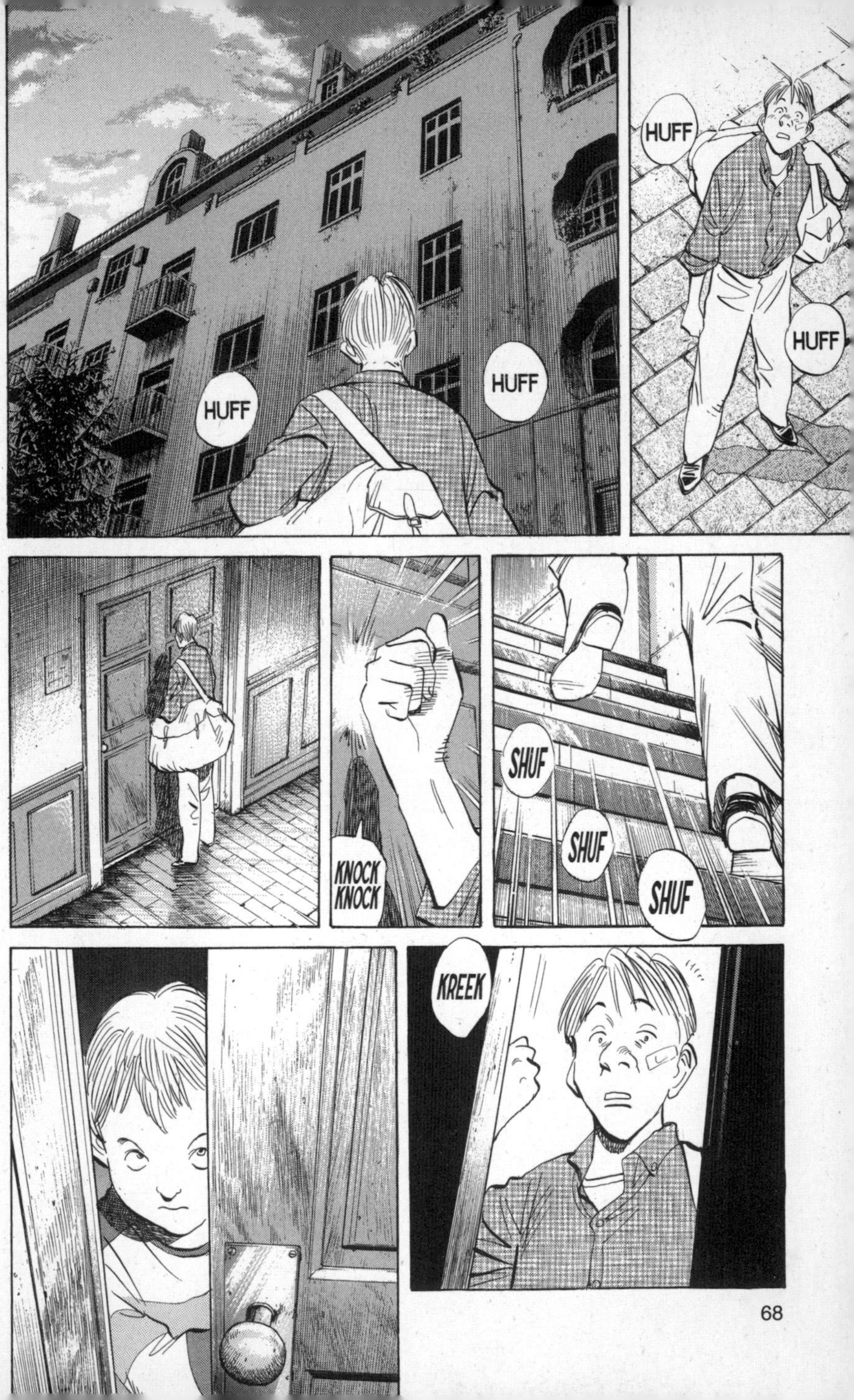
HUFF
HUFF
HUFF
HUFF
SHUF
SHUF
SHUF
KNOCK KNOCK
KREEK

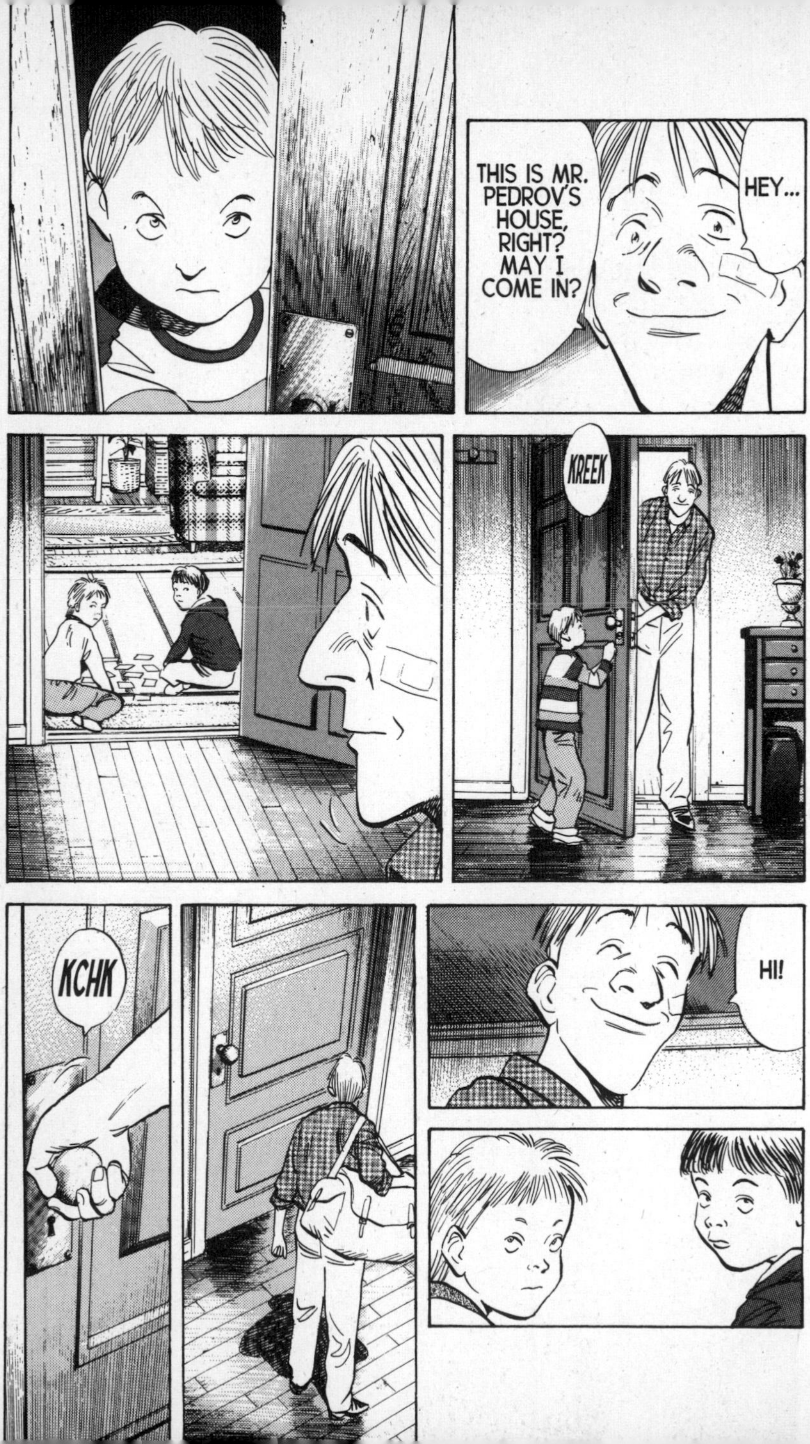
HEY...
THIS IS MR. PEDROV'S HOUSE, RIGHT? MAY I COME IN?
KREEK
HI!
KCHK

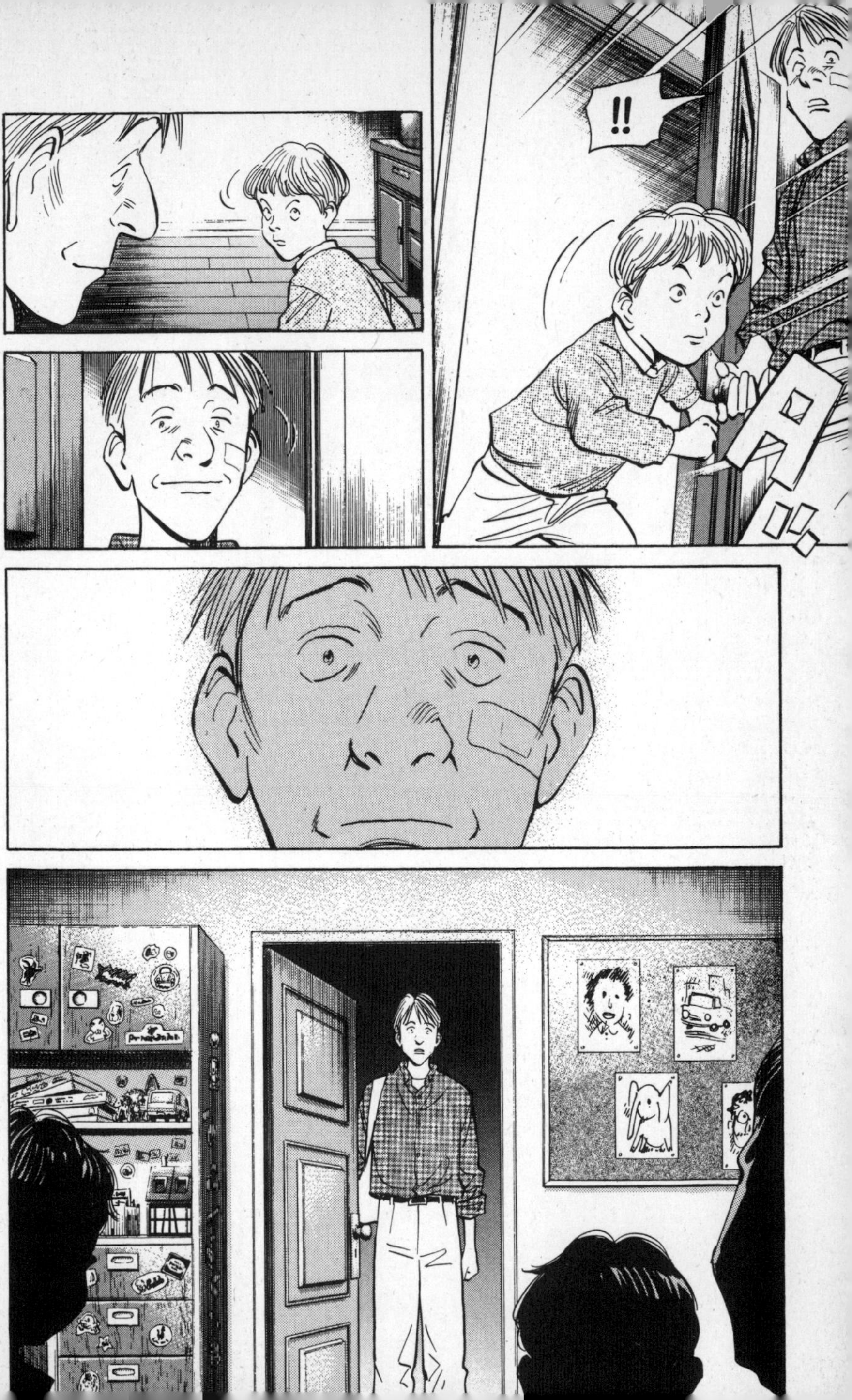
!!

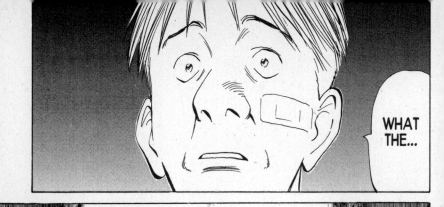

WHAT
THE...

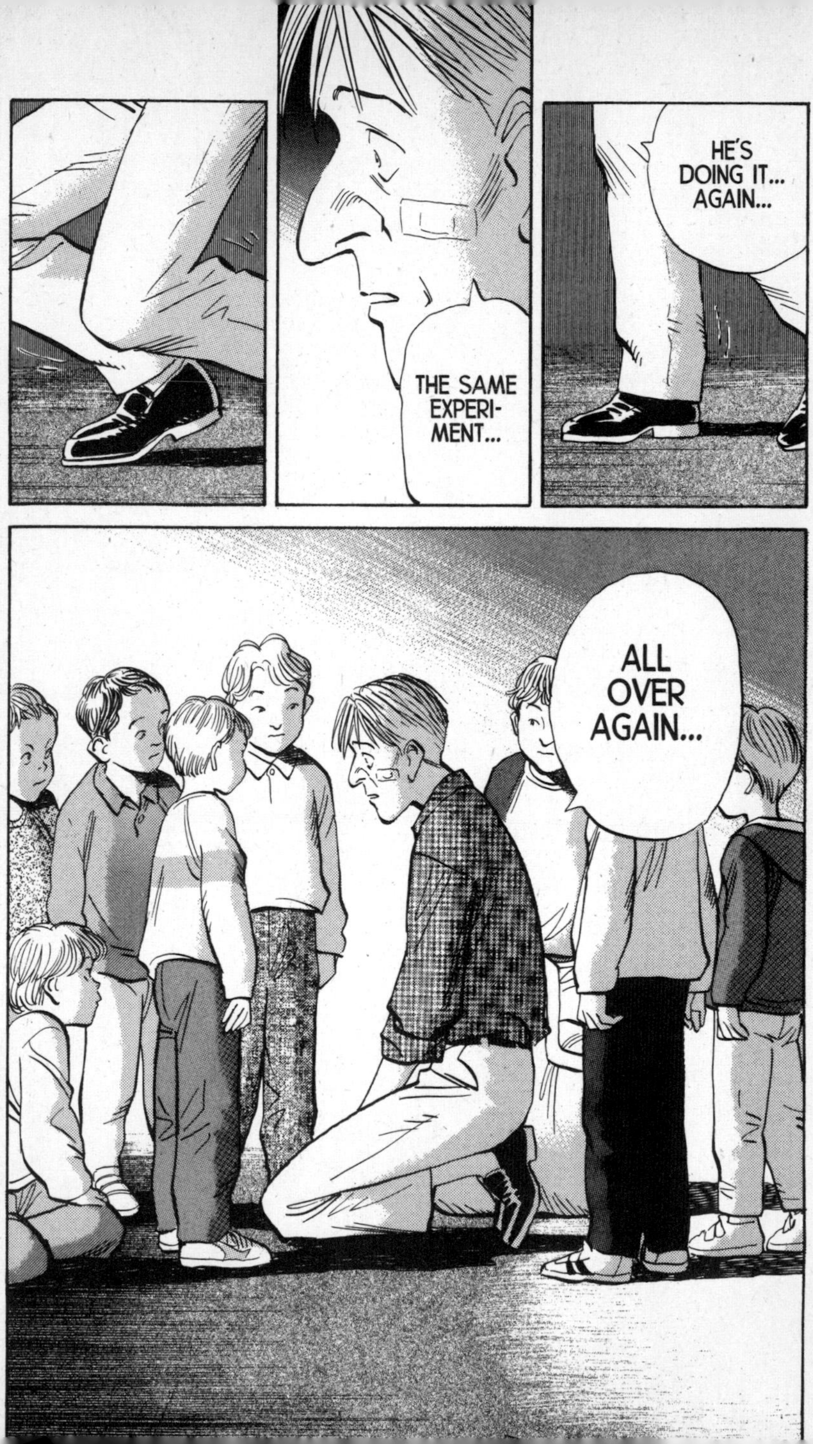
HE'S DOING IT... AGAIN...
THE SAME EXPERIMENT...
ALL OVER AGAIN...

Chapter 4 The New Experiment

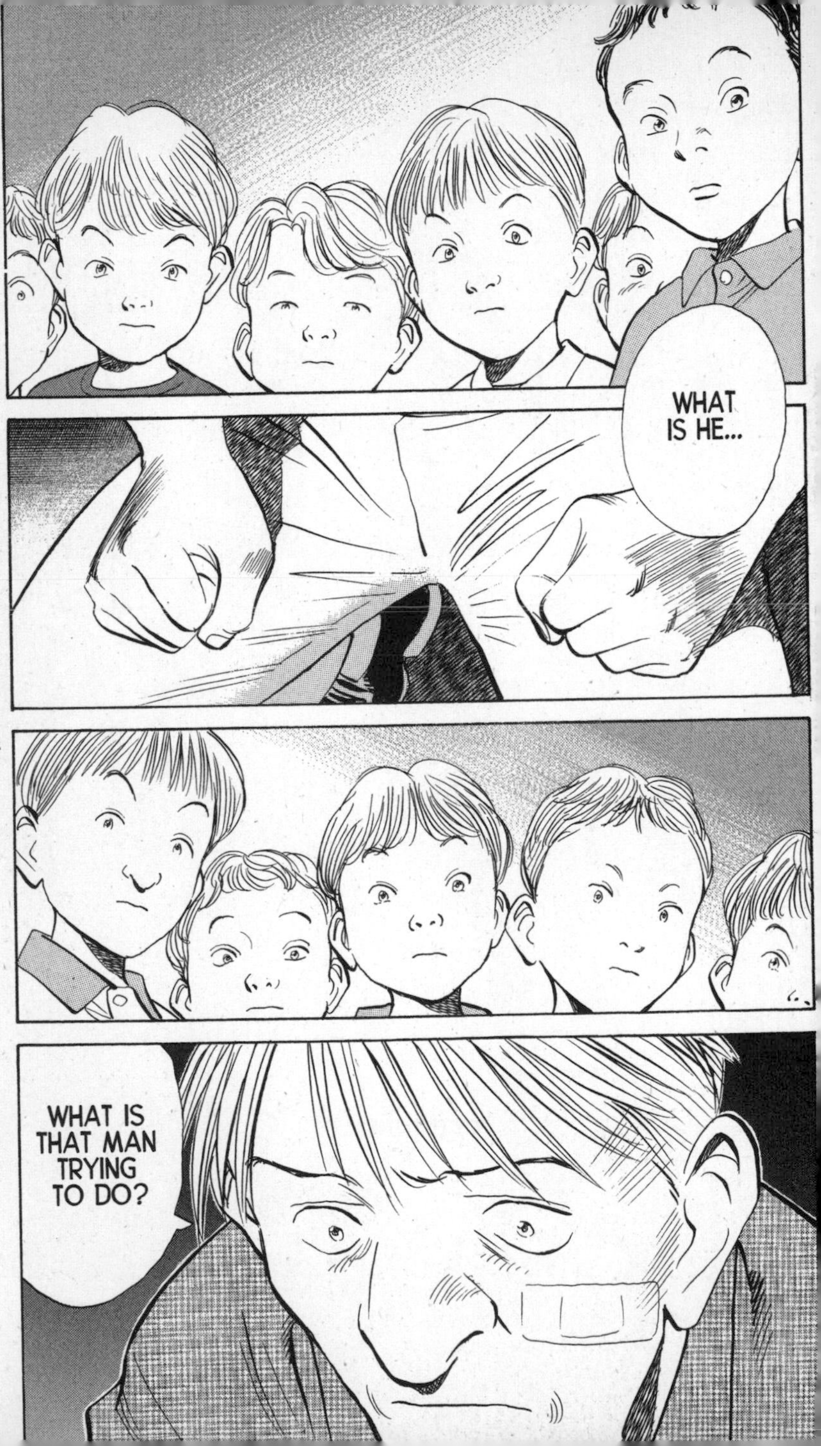
WHAT IS HE...
WHAT IS THAT MAN TRYING TO DO?

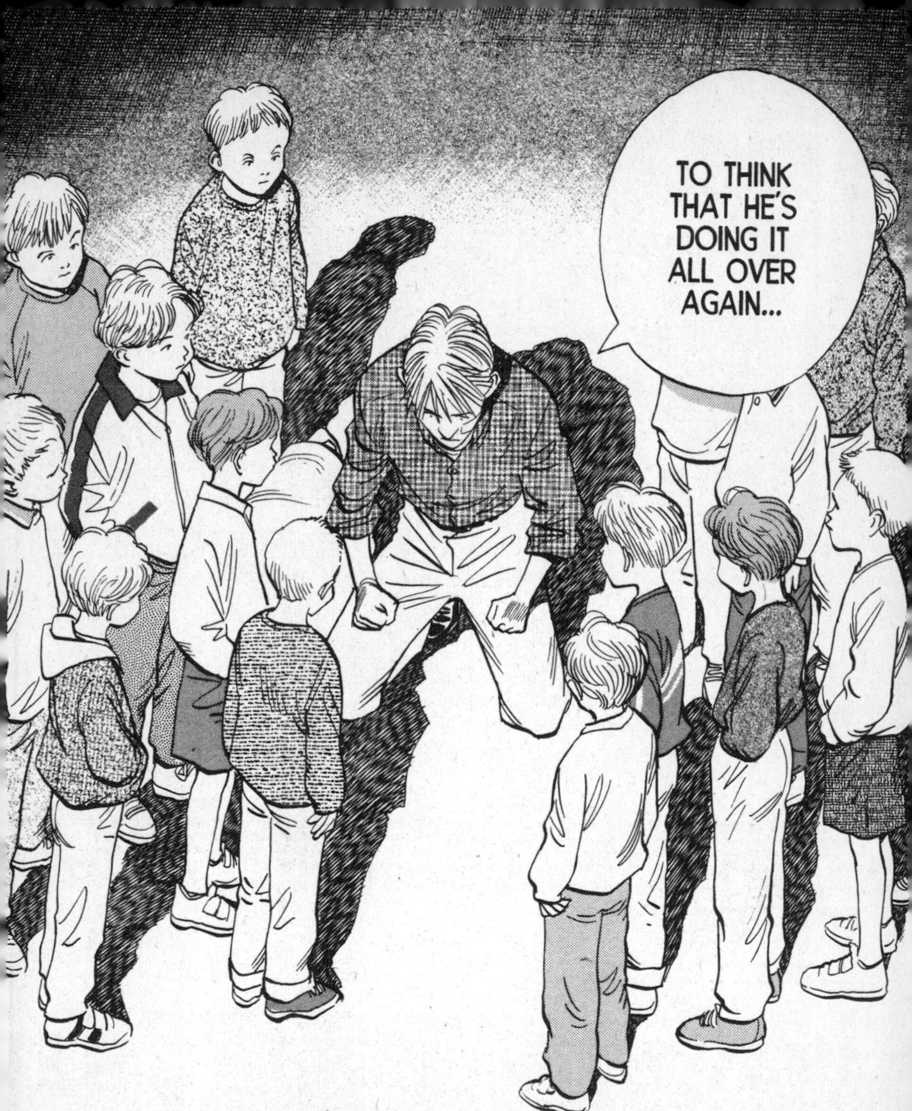
TO THINK THAT HE'S DOING IT ALL OVER AGAIN...

Chapter 4

The New Experiment

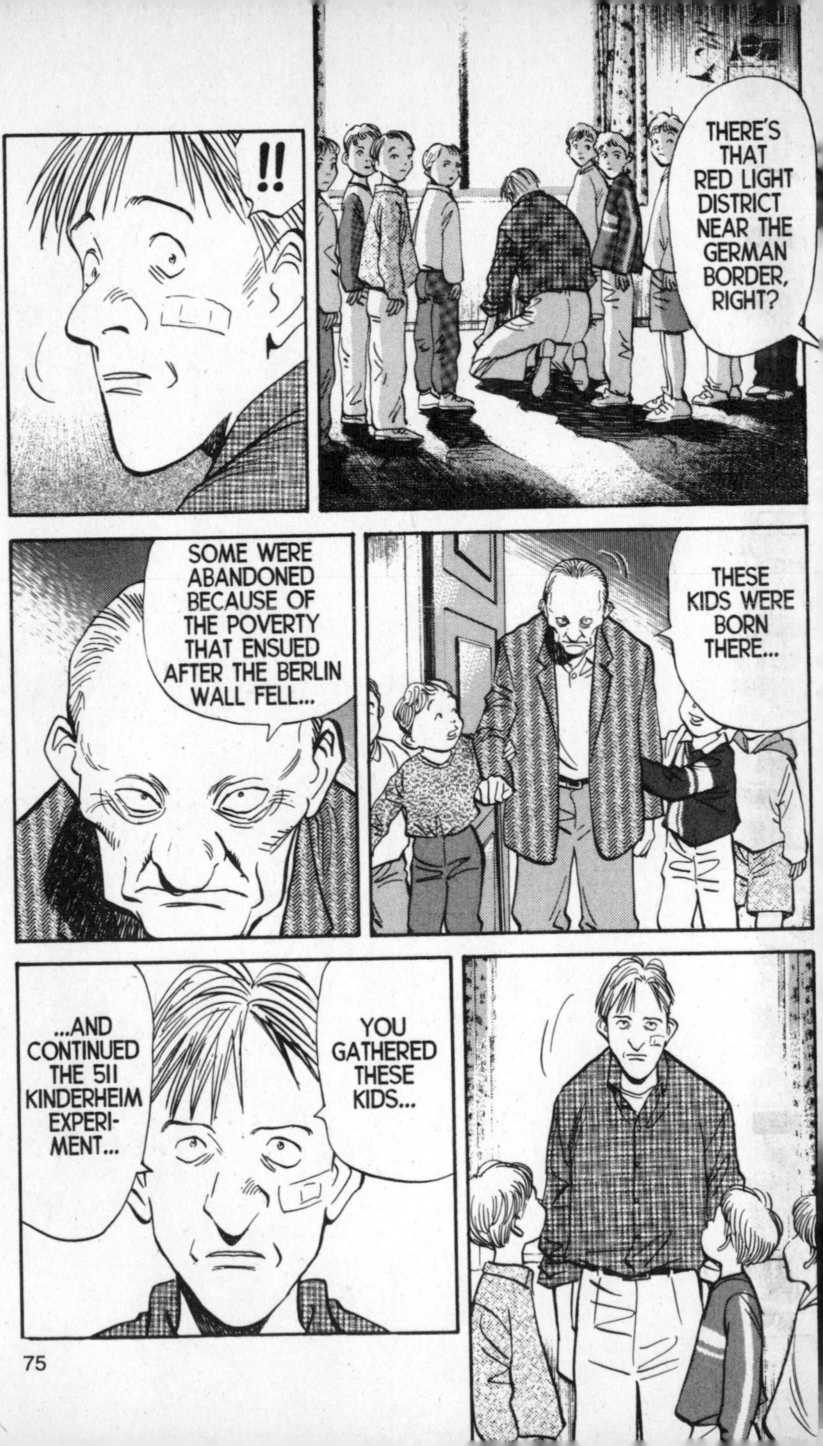
THERE'S THAT RED LIGHT DISTRICT NEAR THE GERMAN BORDER, RIGHT?
!!
THESE KIDS WERE BORN THERE...
SOME WERE ABANDONED BECAUSE OF THE POVERTY THAT ENSUED AFTER THE BERLIN WALL FELL...
YOU GATHERED THESE KIDS...
...AND CONTINUED THE 511 KINDERHEIM EXPERI-MENT...

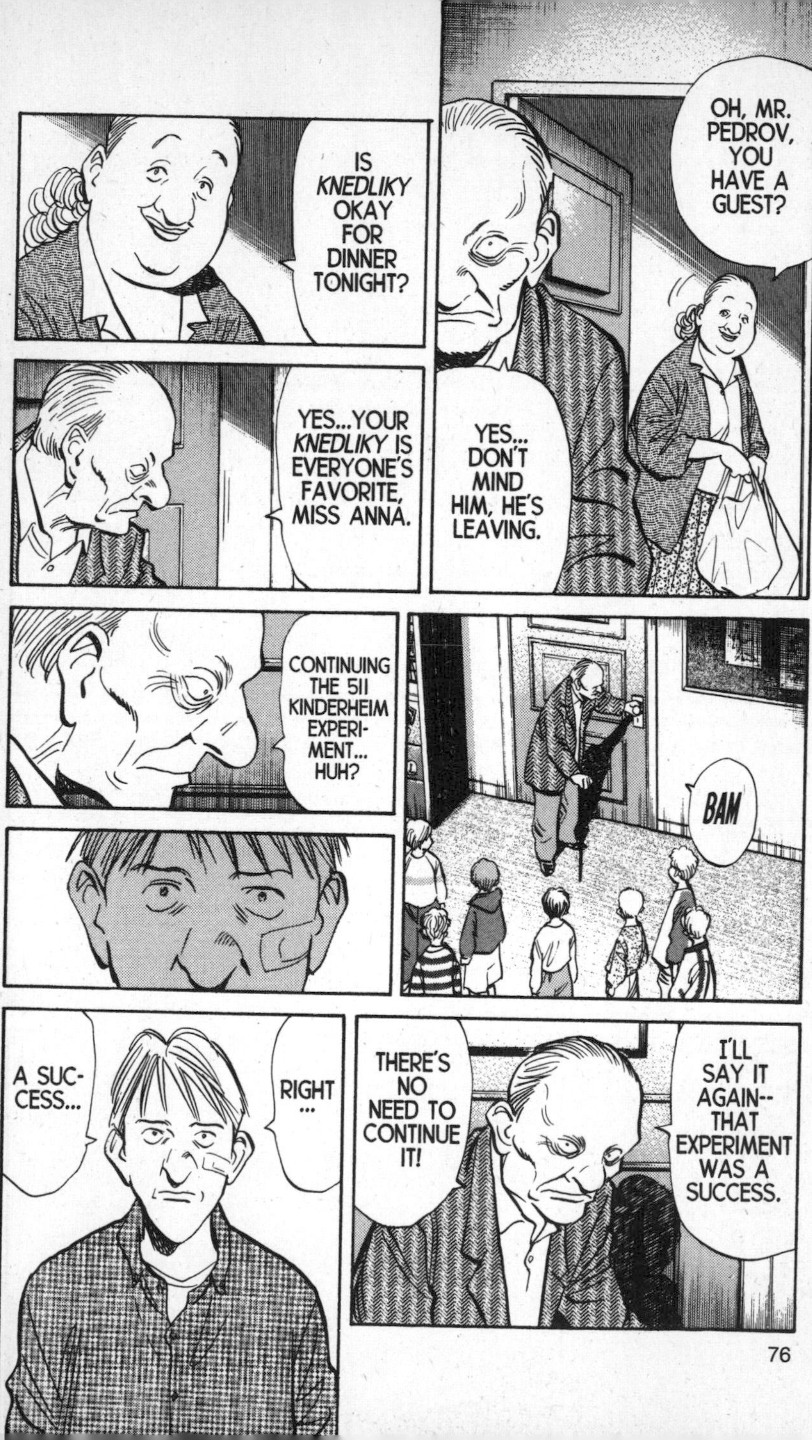
OH, MR. PEDROV, YOU HAVE A GUEST?
YES... DON'T MIND HIM, HE'S LEAVING.
IS *KNEDLIKY* OKAY FOR DINNER TONIGHT?
YES...YOUR *KNEDLIKY* IS EVERYONE'S FAVORITE, MISS ANNA.
BAM
CONTINUING THE 511 KINDERHEIM EXPERIMENT... HUH?
I'LL SAY IT AGAIN-- THAT EXPERIMENT WAS A SUCCESS.
THERE'S NO NEED TO CONTINUE IT!
RIGHT ...
A SUC-CESS...

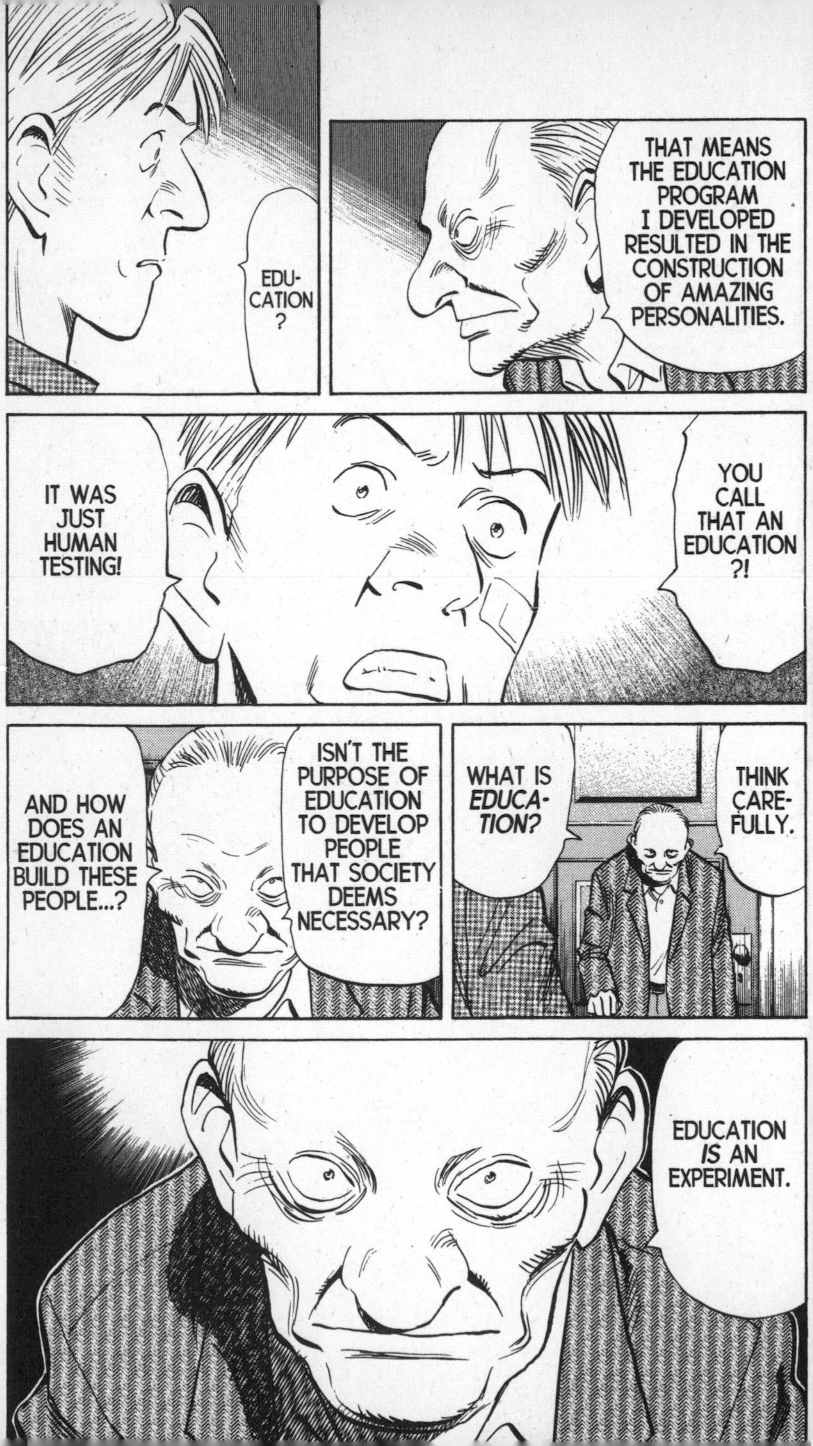
THAT MEANS THE EDUCATION PROGRAM I DEVELOPED RESULTED IN THE CONSTRUCTION OF AMAZING PERSONALITIES.
EDU-CATION?
YOU CALL THAT AN EDUCATION?!
IT WAS JUST HUMAN TESTING!
THINK CARE-FULLY.
WHAT IS *EDUCA-TION?*
ISN'T THE PURPOSE OF EDUCATION TO DEVELOP PEOPLE THAT SOCIETY DEEMS NECESSARY?
AND HOW DOES AN EDUCATION BUILD THESE PEOPLE...?
EDUCATION *IS* AN EXPERIMENT.

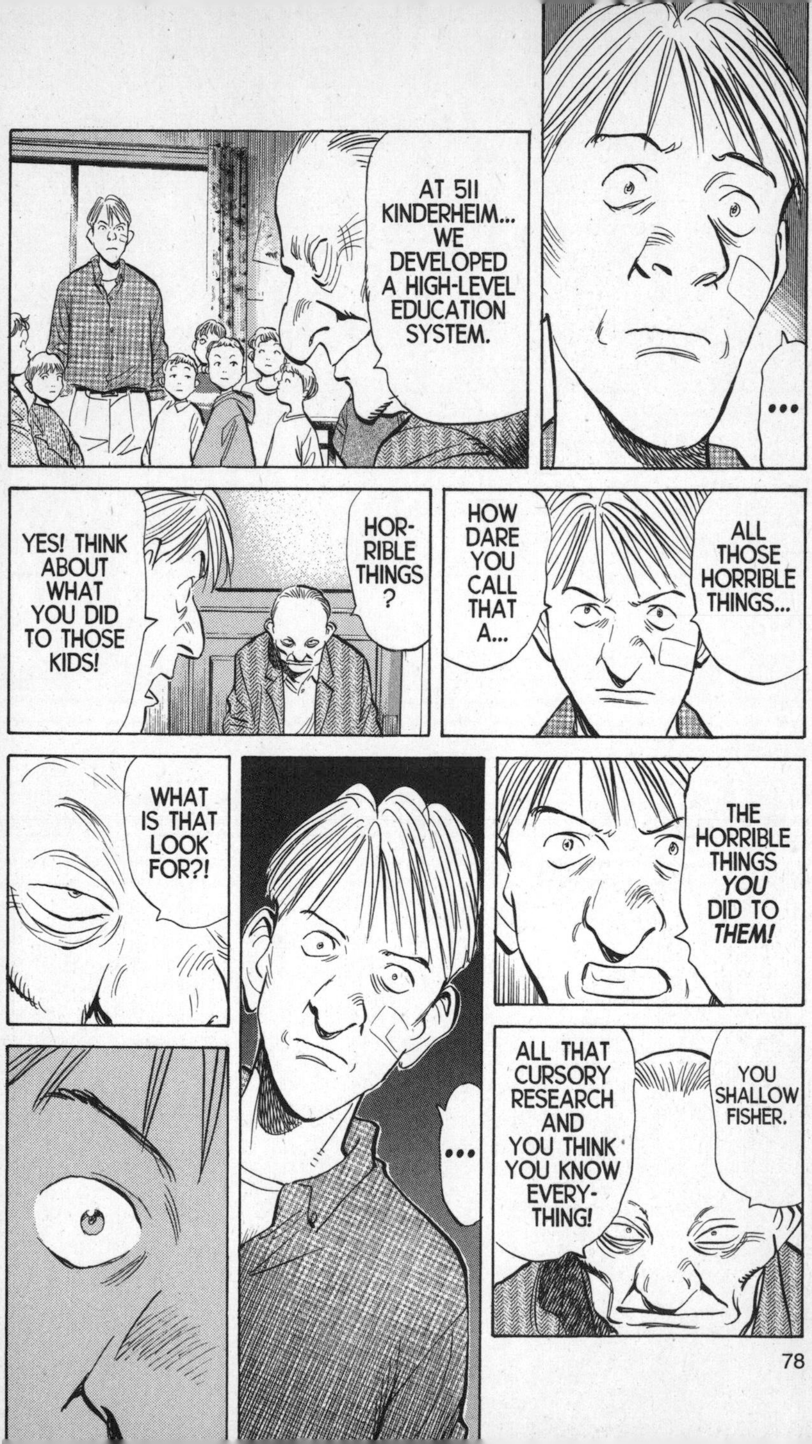
...
AT 511 KINDERHEIM... WE DEVELOPED A HIGH-LEVEL EDUCATION SYSTEM.
ALL THOSE HORRIBLE THINGS...
HOW DARE YOU CALL THAT A...
HOR-RIBLE THINGS?
YES! THINK ABOUT WHAT YOU DID TO THOSE KIDS!
THE HORRIBLE THINGS *YOU* DID TO *THEM!*
YOU SHALLOW FISHER.
ALL THAT CURSORY RESEARCH AND YOU THINK YOU KNOW EVERY-THING!
...
WHAT IS THAT LOOK FOR?!

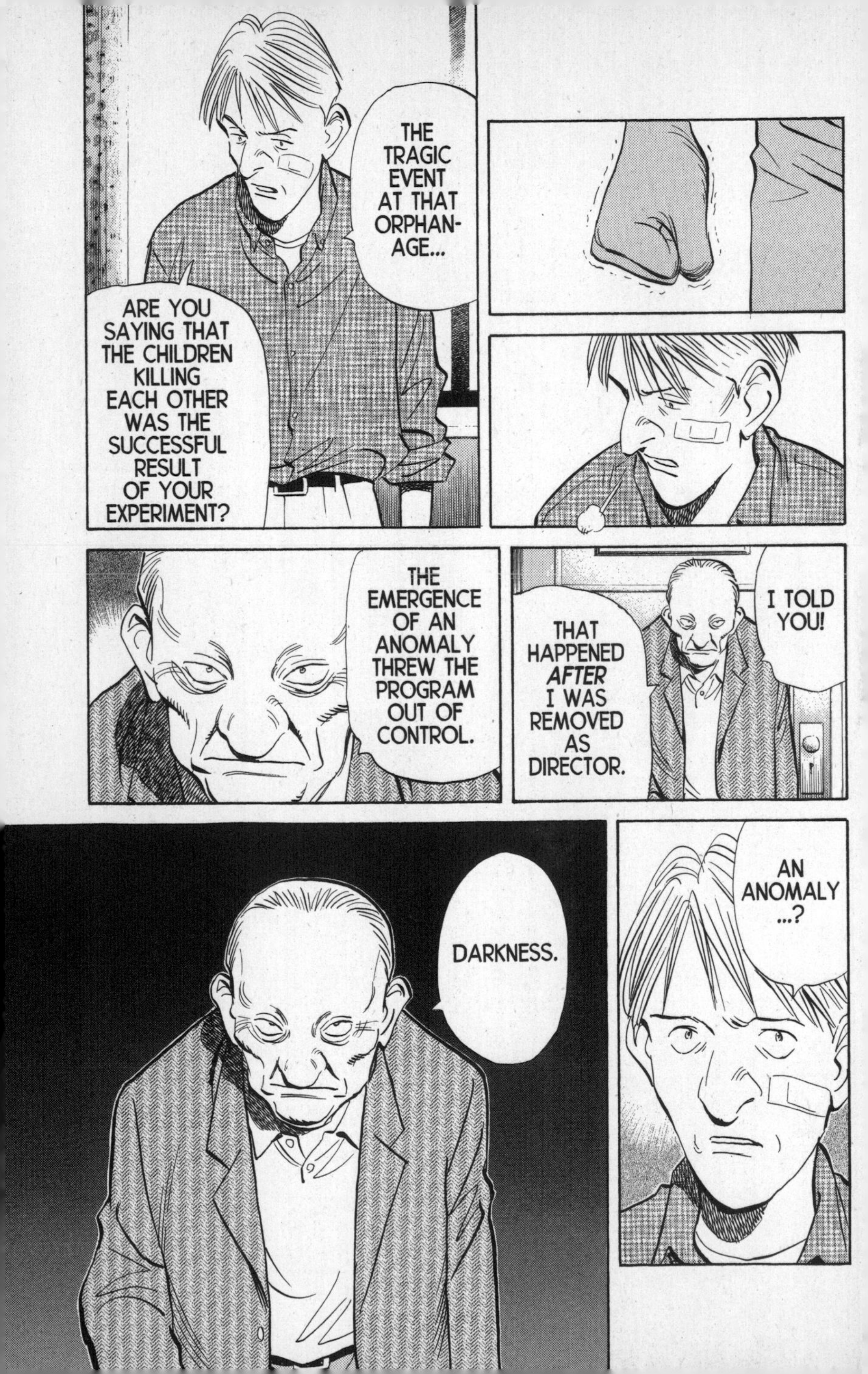
THE TRAGIC EVENT AT THAT ORPHAN-AGE...
ARE YOU SAYING THAT THE CHILDREN KILLING EACH OTHER WAS THE SUCCESSFUL RESULT OF YOUR EXPERIMENT?
I TOLD YOU!
THAT HAPPENED *AFTER* I WAS REMOVED AS DIRECTOR.
THE EMERGENCE OF AN ANOMALY THREW THE PROGRAM OUT OF CONTROL.
AN ANOMALY ...?
DARKNESS.

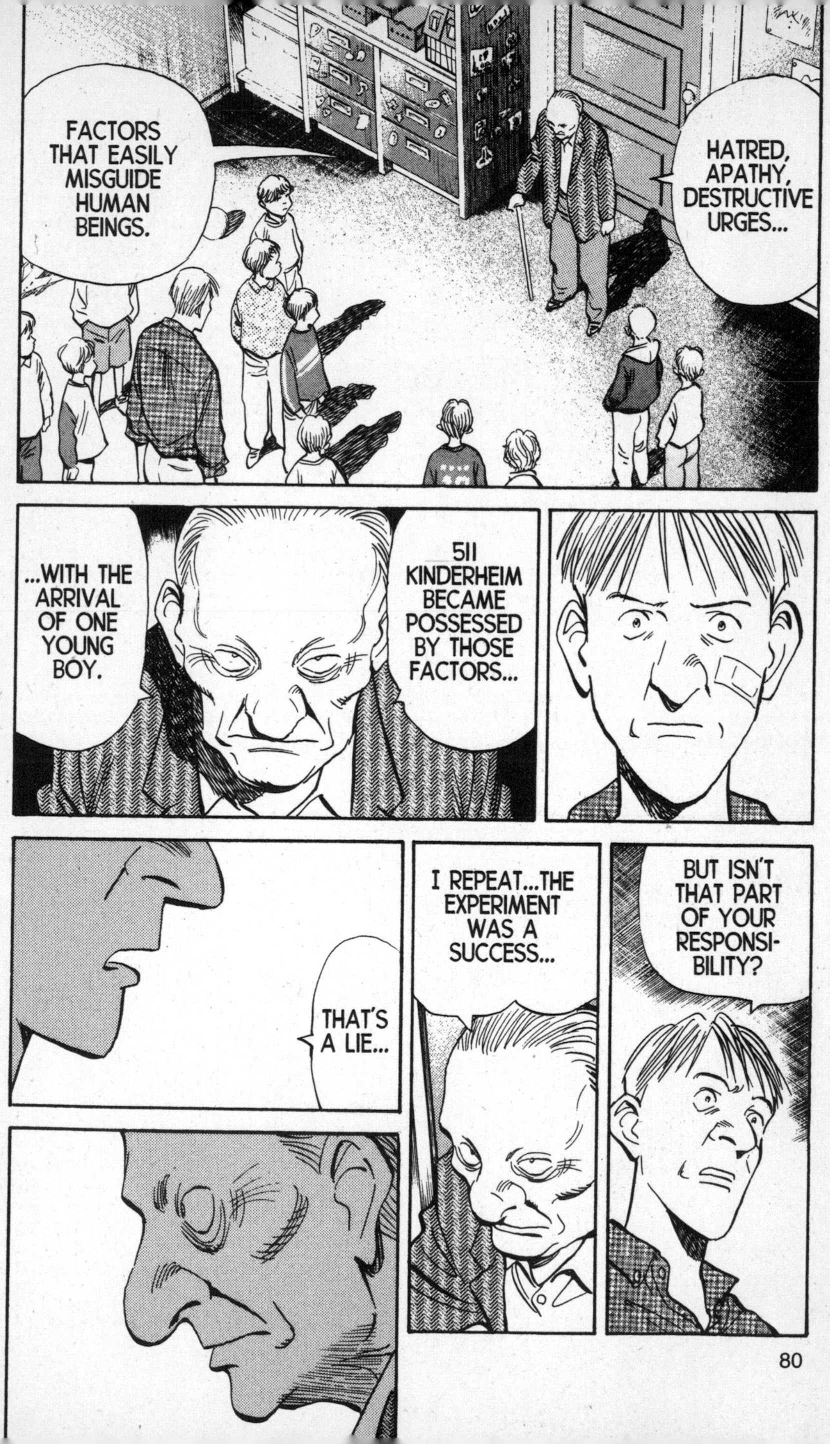
HATRED, APATHY, DESTRUCTIVE URGES...
FACTORS THAT EASILY MISGUIDE HUMAN BEINGS.
511 KINDERHEIM BECAME POSSESSED BY THOSE FACTORS...
...WITH THE ARRIVAL OF ONE YOUNG BOY.
BUT ISN'T THAT PART OF YOUR RESPONSI-BILITY?
I REPEAT...THE EXPERIMENT WAS A SUCCESS...
THAT'S A LIE...

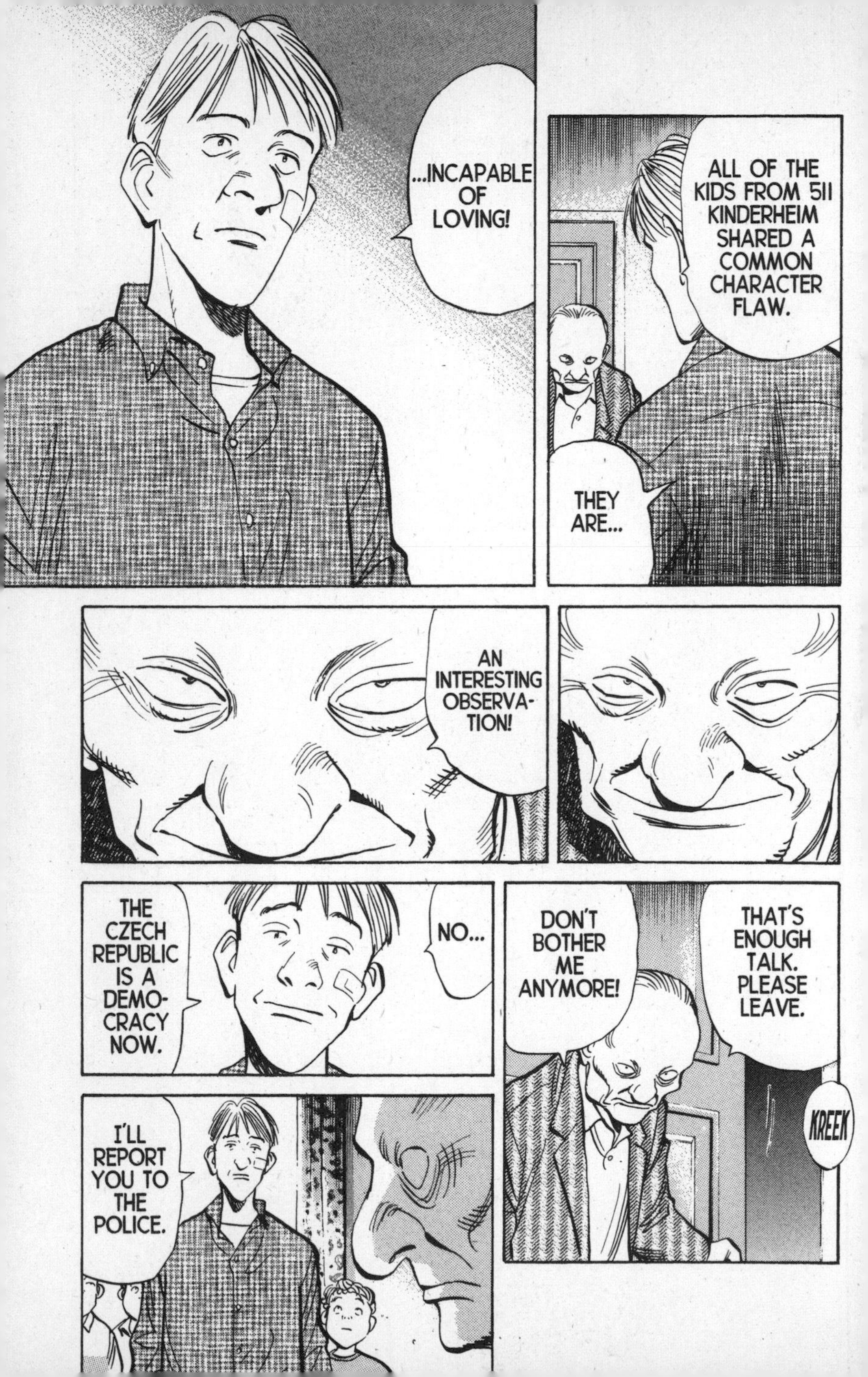
ALL OF THE KIDS FROM 511 KINDERHEIM SHARED A COMMON CHARACTER FLAW.
THEY ARE...
...INCAPABLE OF LOVING!
AN INTERESTING OBSERVATION!
THAT'S ENOUGH TALK. PLEASE LEAVE.
DON'T BOTHER ME ANYMORE!
KREEK
NO...
THE CZECH REPUBLIC IS A DEMOCRACY NOW.
I'LL REPORT YOU TO THE POLICE.

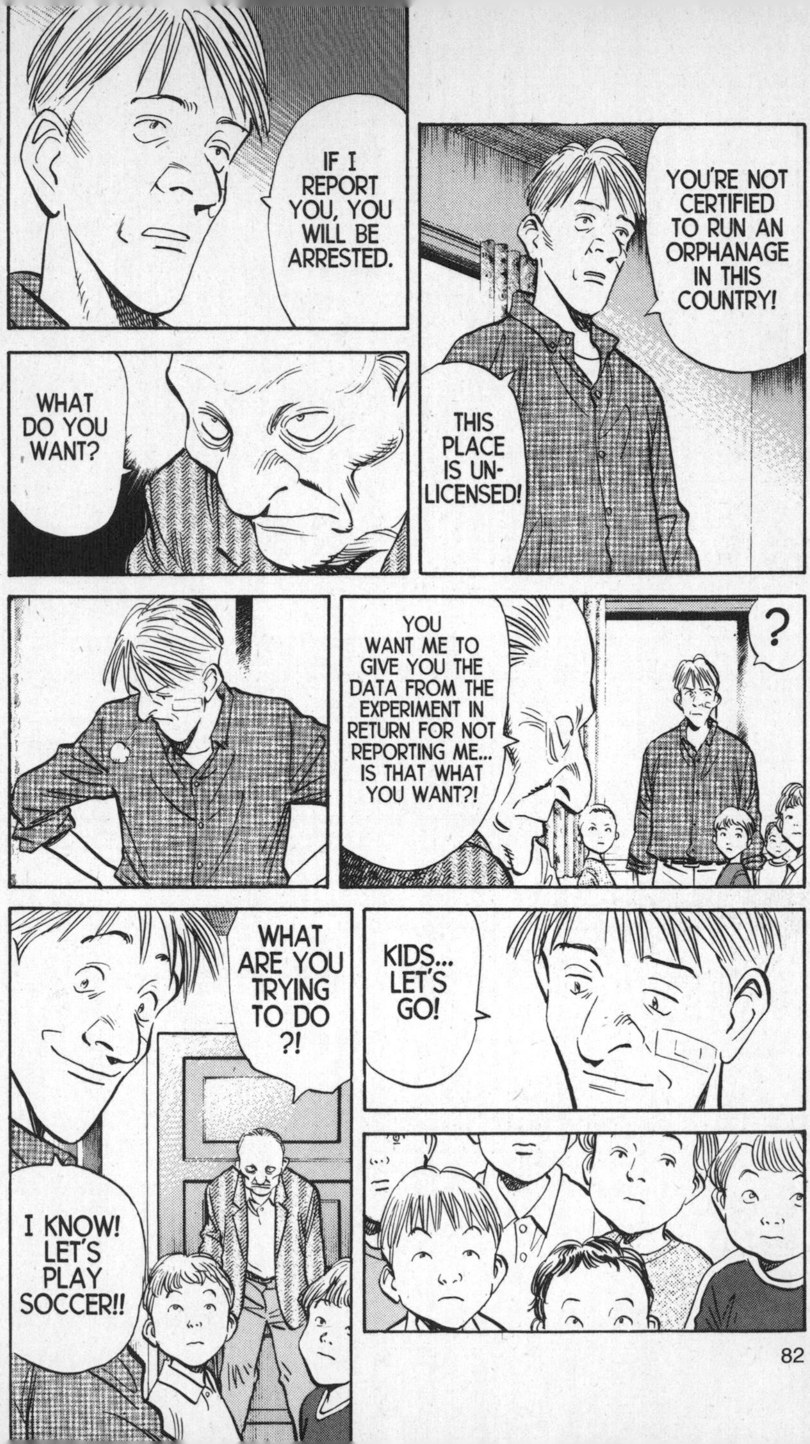
YOU'RE NOT CERTIFIED TO RUN AN ORPHANAGE IN THIS COUNTRY!
THIS PLACE IS UN-LICENSED!
IF I REPORT YOU, YOU WILL BE ARRESTED.
WHAT DO YOU WANT?
YOU WANT ME TO GIVE YOU THE DATA FROM THE EXPERIMENT IN RETURN FOR NOT REPORTING ME... IS THAT WHAT YOU WANT?!
?
KIDS... LET'S GO!
WHAT ARE YOU TRYING TO DO ?!
I KNOW! LET'S PLAY SOCCER!!

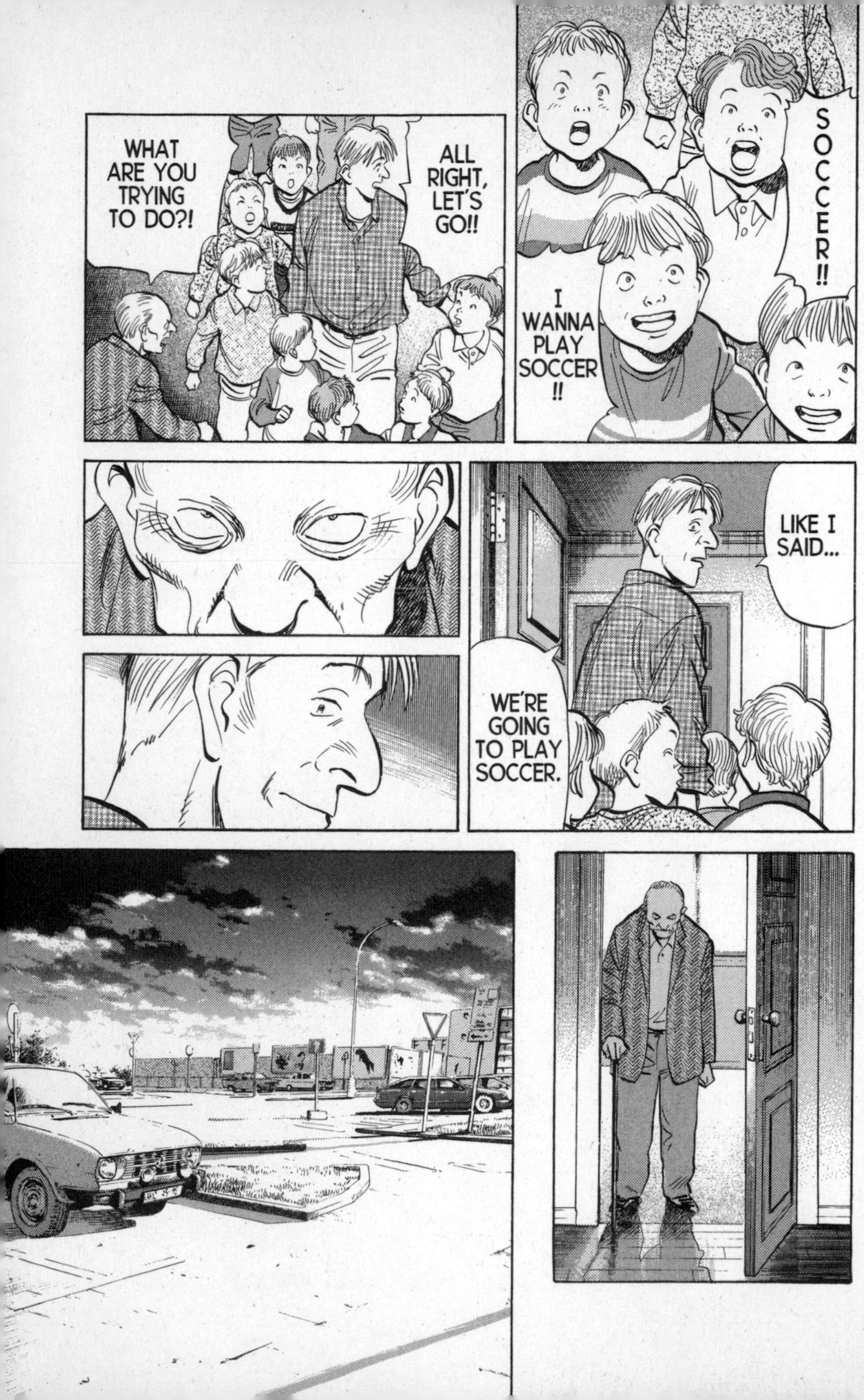
SOCCER!!
I WANNA PLAY SOCCER !!
ALL RIGHT, LET'S GO!!
WHAT ARE YOU TRYING TO DO?!
LIKE I SAID...
WE'RE GOING TO PLAY SOCCER.

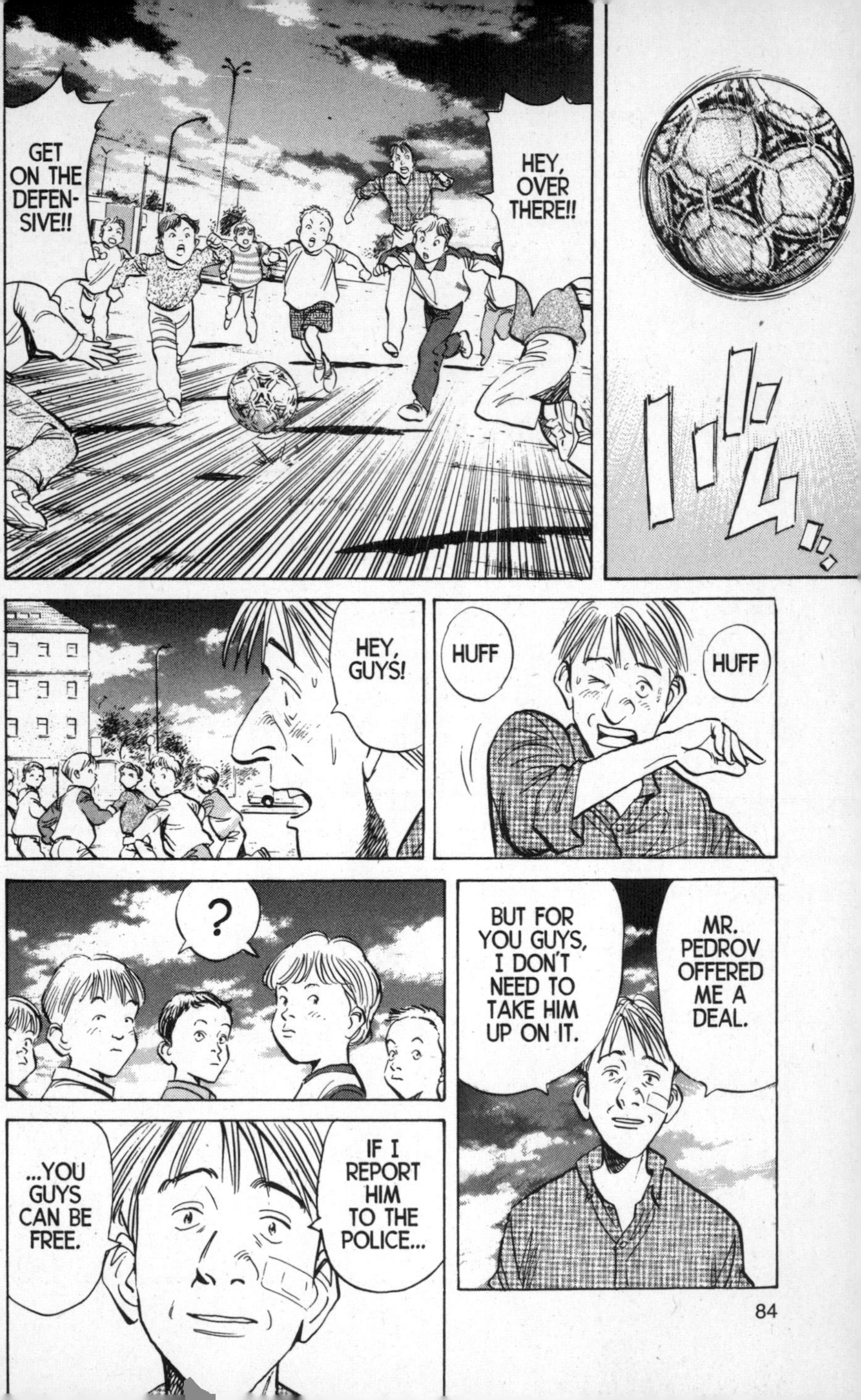
HEY, OVER THERE!!
GET ON THE DEFEN-SIVE!!
HUFF
HUFF
HEY, GUYS!
MR. PEDROV OFFERED ME A DEAL.
BUT FOR YOU GUYS, I DON'T NEED TO TAKE HIM UP ON IT.
?
IF I REPORT HIM TO THE POLICE...
...YOU GUYS CAN BE FREE.

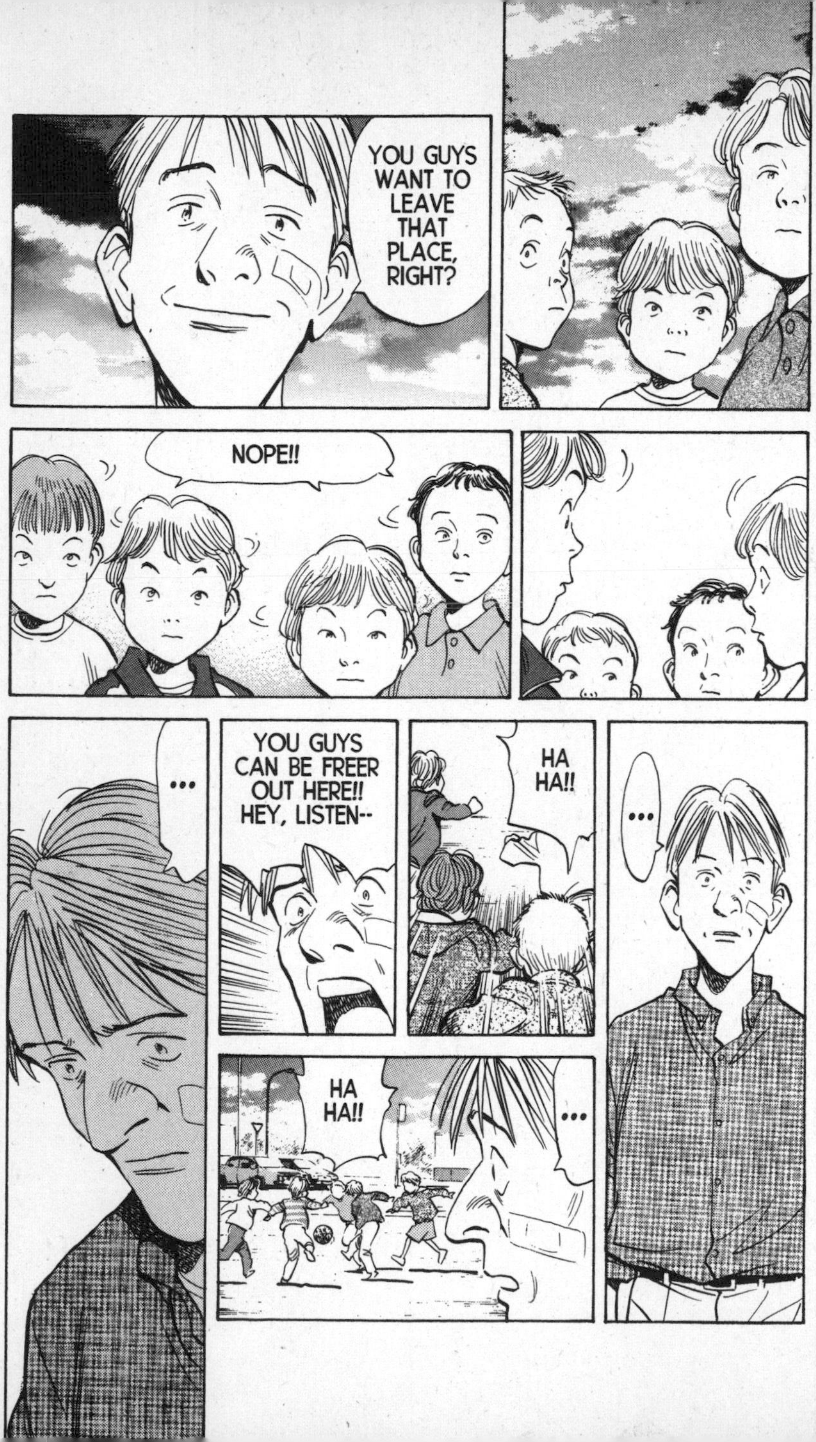
YOU GUYS WANT TO LEAVE THAT PLACE, RIGHT?
NOPE!!
...
HA HA!!
YOU GUYS CAN BE FREER OUT HERE!! HEY, LISTEN--
...
HA HA!!
...

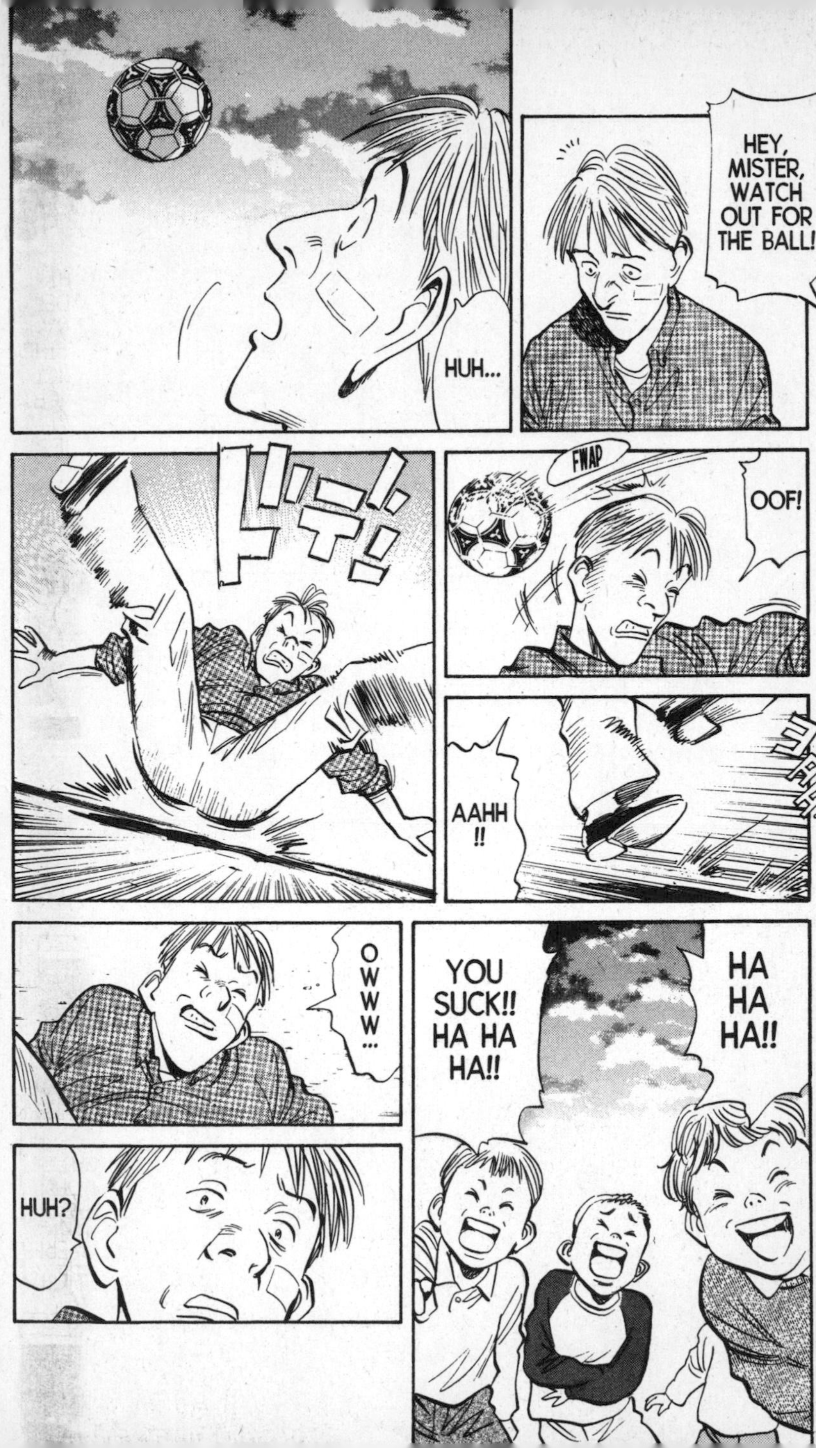
HEY, MISTER, WATCH OUT FOR THE BALL!
HUH...
FWAP
OOF!
AAHH !!
HA HA HA!!
YOU SUCK!! HA HA HA!!
OWWW...
HUH?

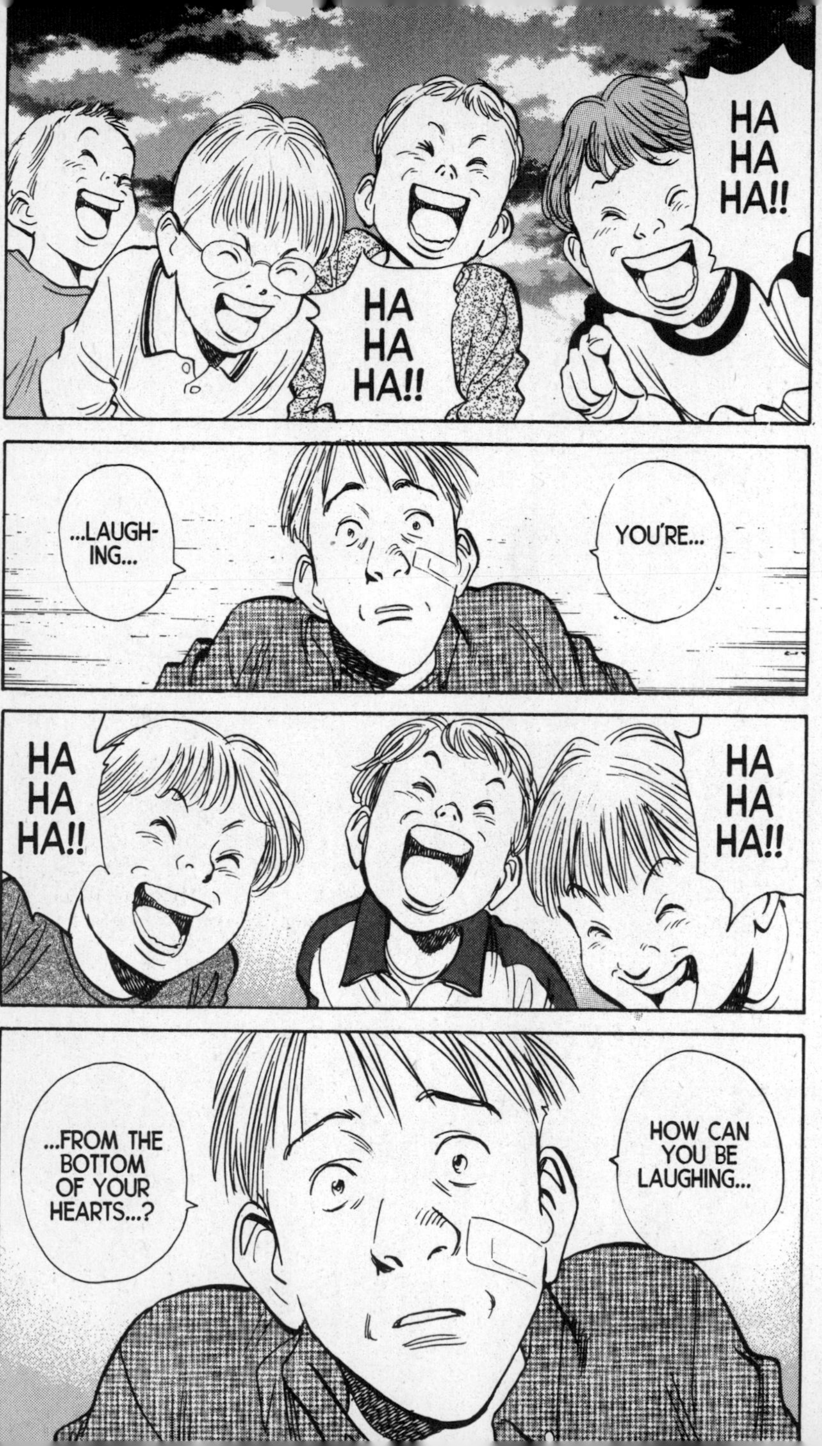
HA HA HA!!
HA HA HA!!
YOU'RE...
...LAUGHING...
HA HA HA!!
HA HA HA!!
HOW CAN YOU BE LAUGHING...
...FROM THE BOTTOM OF YOUR HEARTS...?

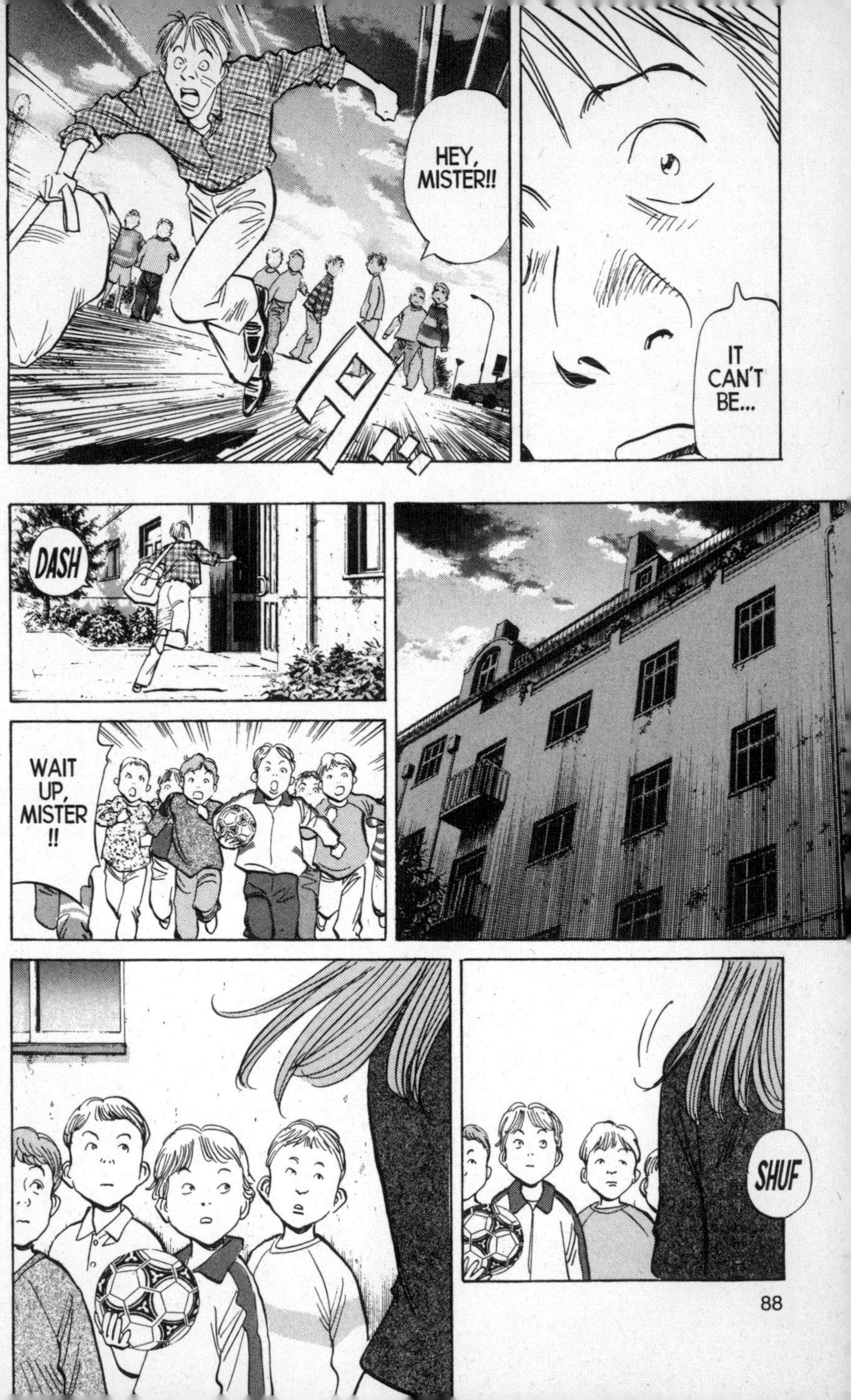
IT CAN'T BE...
HEY, MISTER!!
DASH
WAIT UP, MISTER !!
SHUF

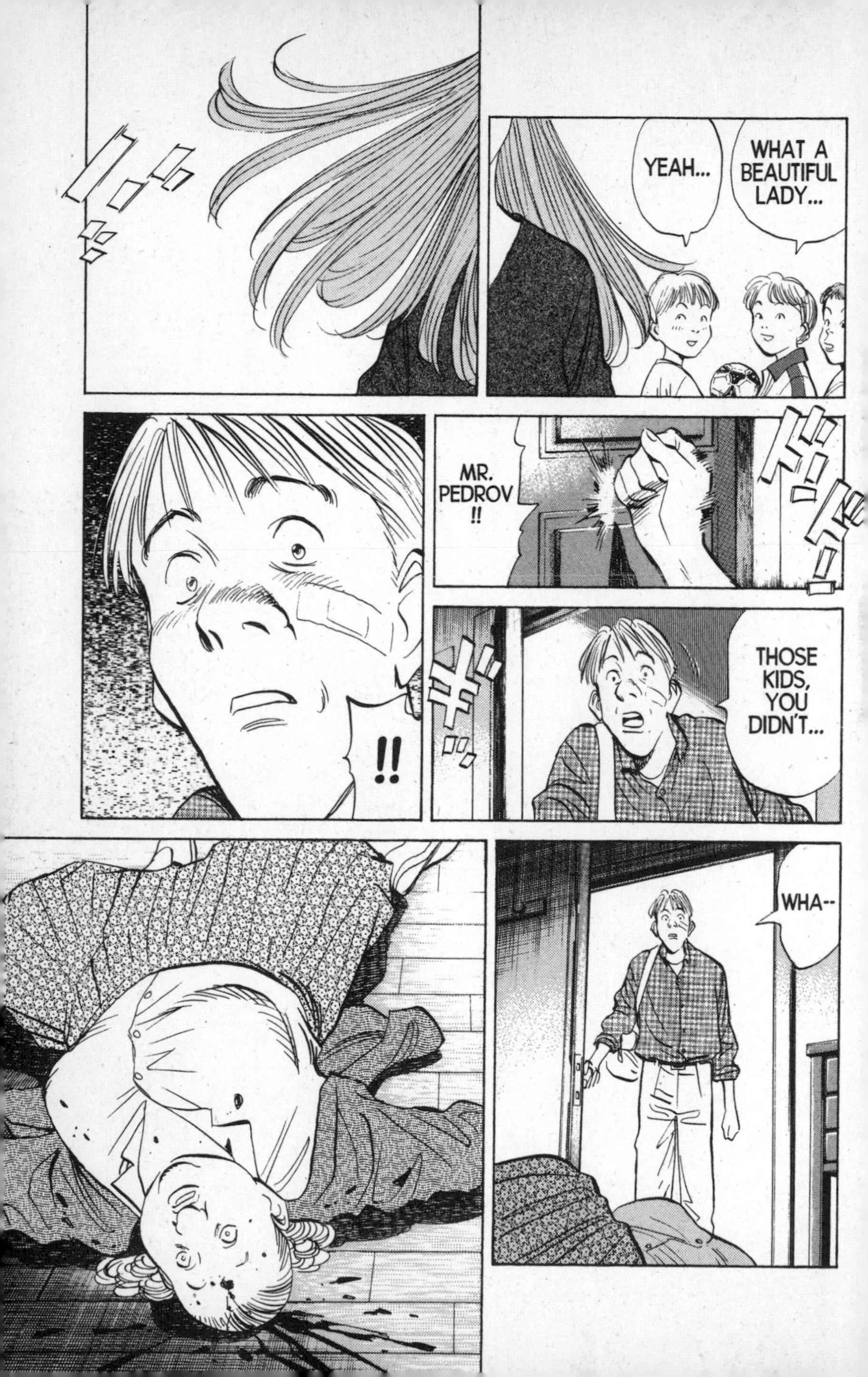
WHAT A BEAUTIFUL LADY...
YEAH...
MR. PEDROV !!
THOSE KIDS, YOU DIDN'T...
!!
WHA--

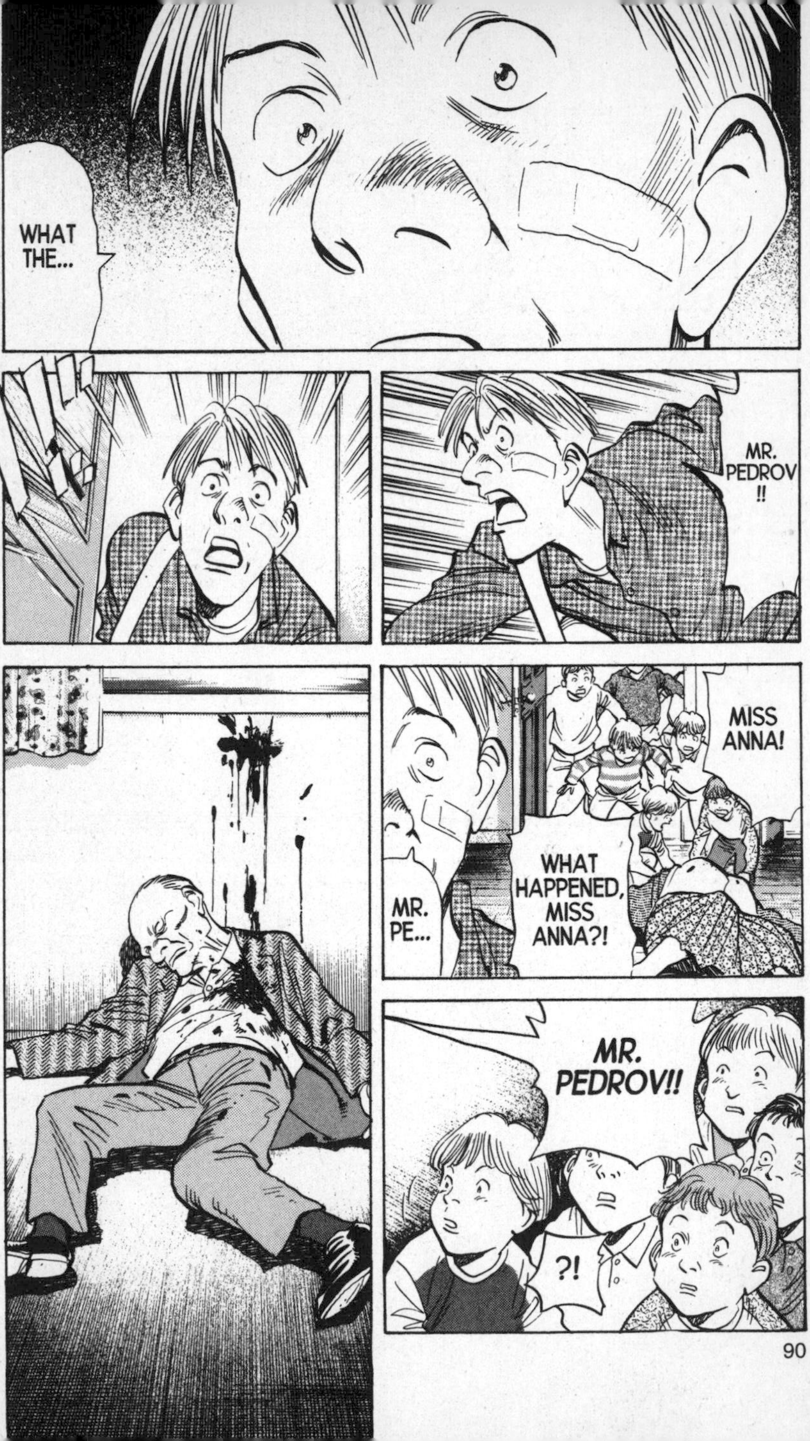
WHAT THE...
MR. PEDROV !!
MISS ANNA!
WHAT HAPPENED, MISS ANNA?!
MR. PE...
MR. PEDROV!!
?!

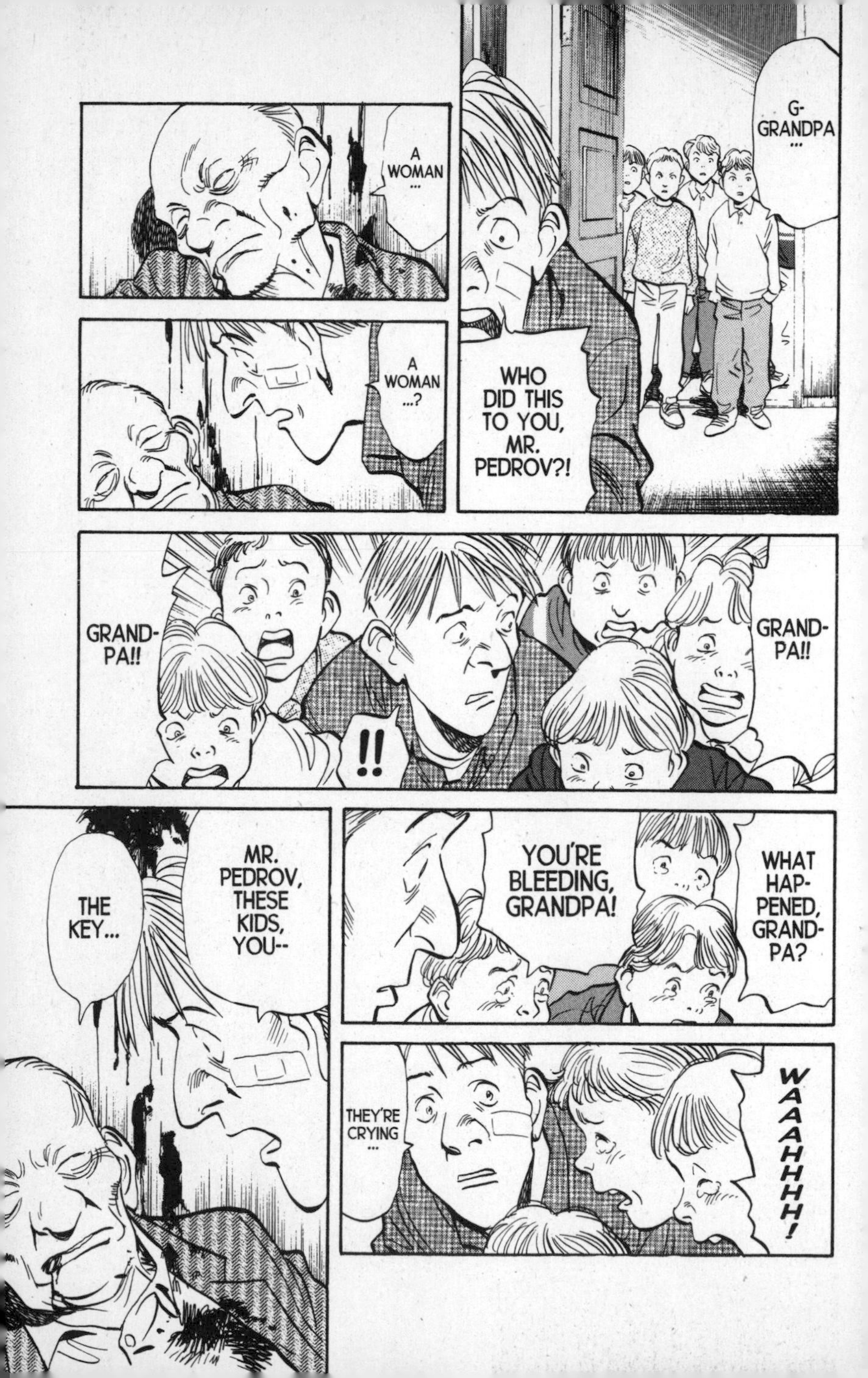
G-GRANDPA...
WHO DID THIS TO YOU, MR. PEDROV?!
A WOMAN...
A WOMAN...?
GRAND-PA!!
GRAND-PA!!
!!
WHAT HAP-PENED, GRAND-PA?
YOU'RE BLEEDING, GRANDPA!
WAAAHHHH!
THEY'RE CRYING...
MR. PEDROV, THESE KIDS, YOU--
THE KEY...

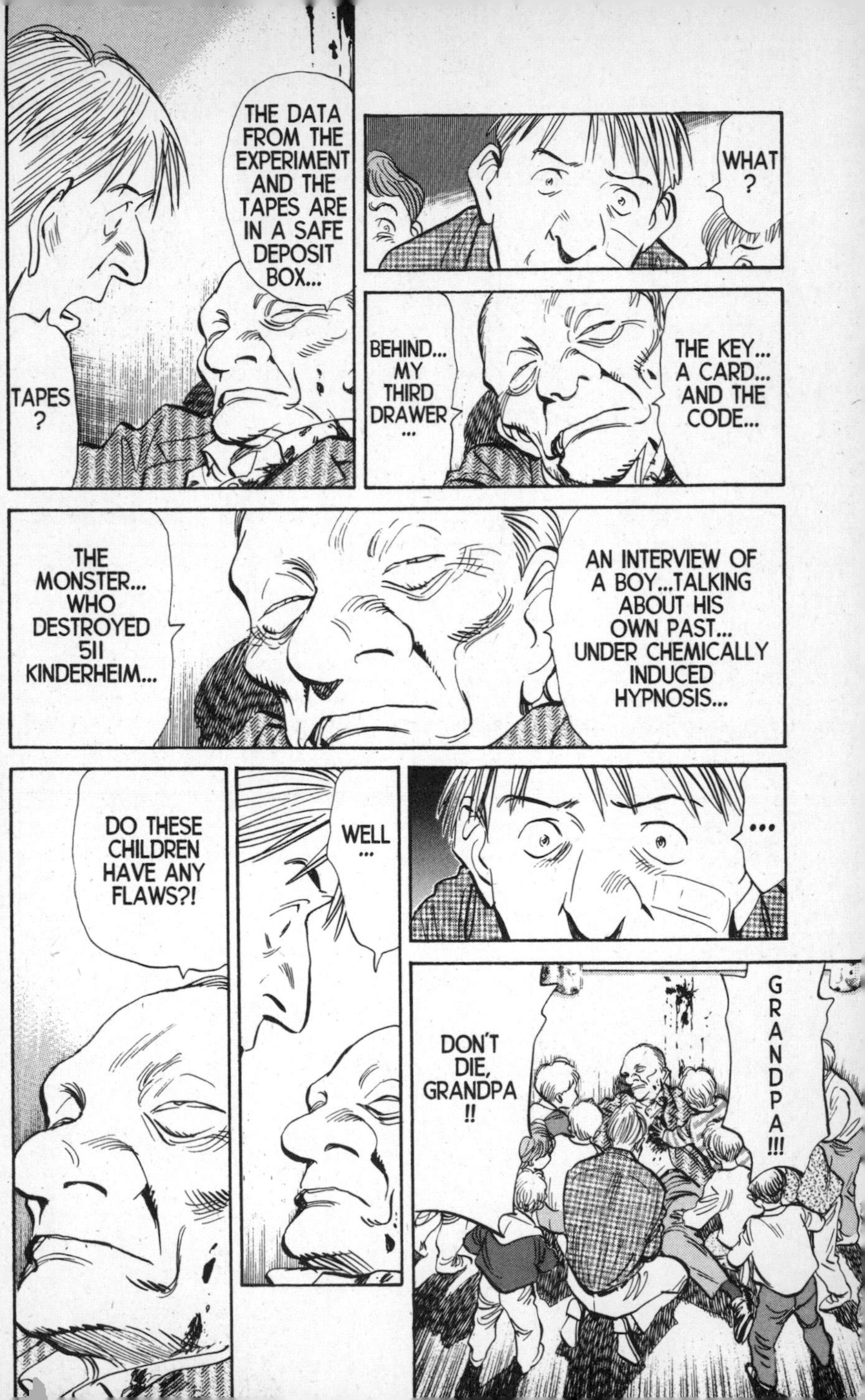
THE DATA FROM THE EXPERIMENT AND THE TAPES ARE IN A SAFE DEPOSIT BOX...
TAPES ?
WHAT ?
THE KEY... A CARD... AND THE CODE...
BEHIND... MY THIRD DRAWER ...
AN INTERVIEW OF A BOY...TALKING ABOUT HIS OWN PAST... UNDER CHEMICALLY INDUCED HYPNOSIS...
THE MONSTER... WHO DESTROYED 511 KINDERHEIM...
DO THESE CHILDREN HAVE ANY FLAWS?!
WELL ...
...
GRANDPA!!!
DON'T DIE, GRANDPA !!

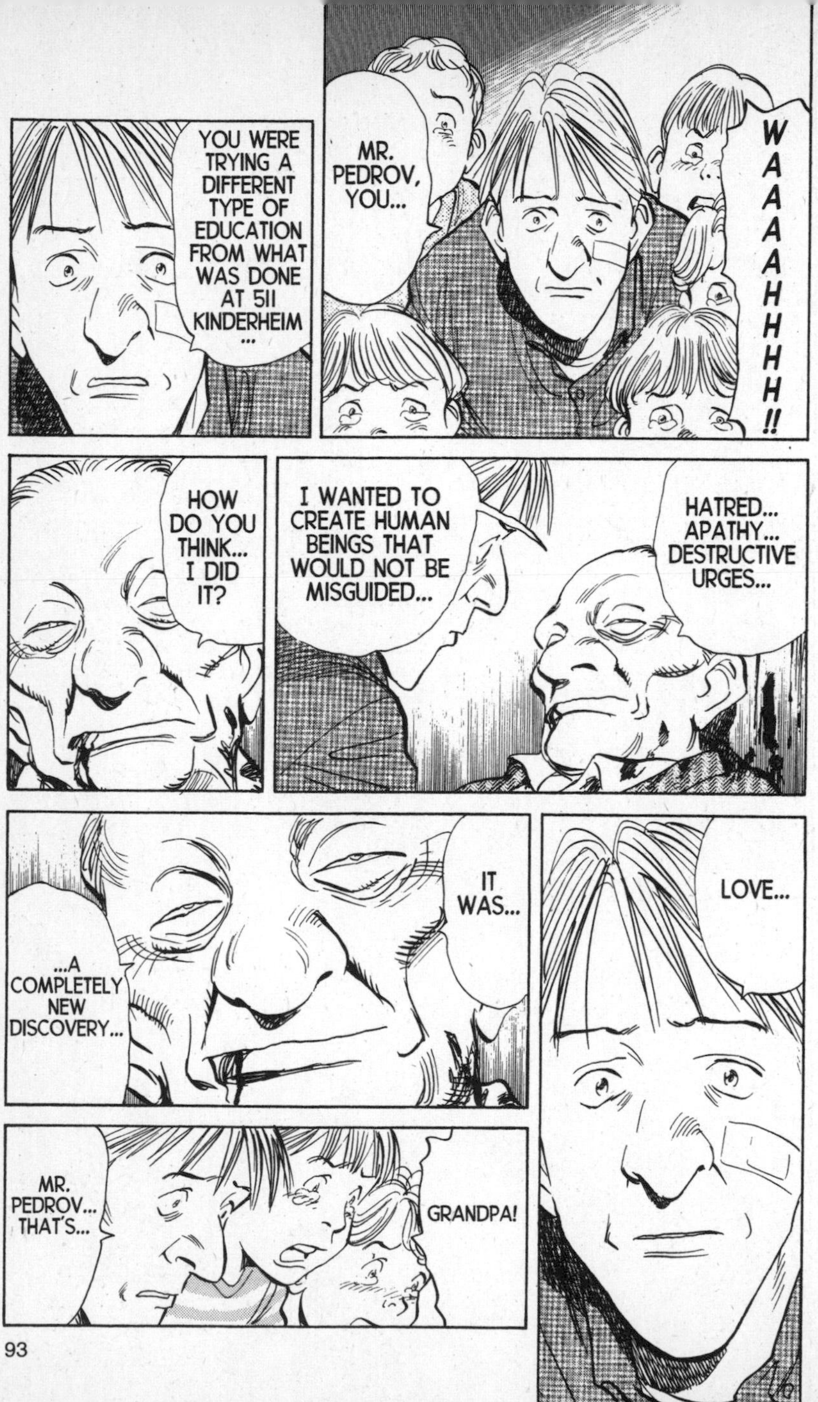
WAAAAHHHH!!
MR. PEDROV, YOU...
YOU WERE TRYING A DIFFERENT TYPE OF EDUCATION FROM WHAT WAS DONE AT 511 KINDERHEIM ...
HATRED... APATHY... DESTRUCTIVE URGES...
I WANTED TO CREATE HUMAN BEINGS THAT WOULD NOT BE MISGUIDED...
HOW DO YOU THINK... I DID IT?
IT WAS...
...A COMPLETELY NEW DISCOVERY...
LOVE...
GRANDPA!
MR. PEDROV... THAT'S...

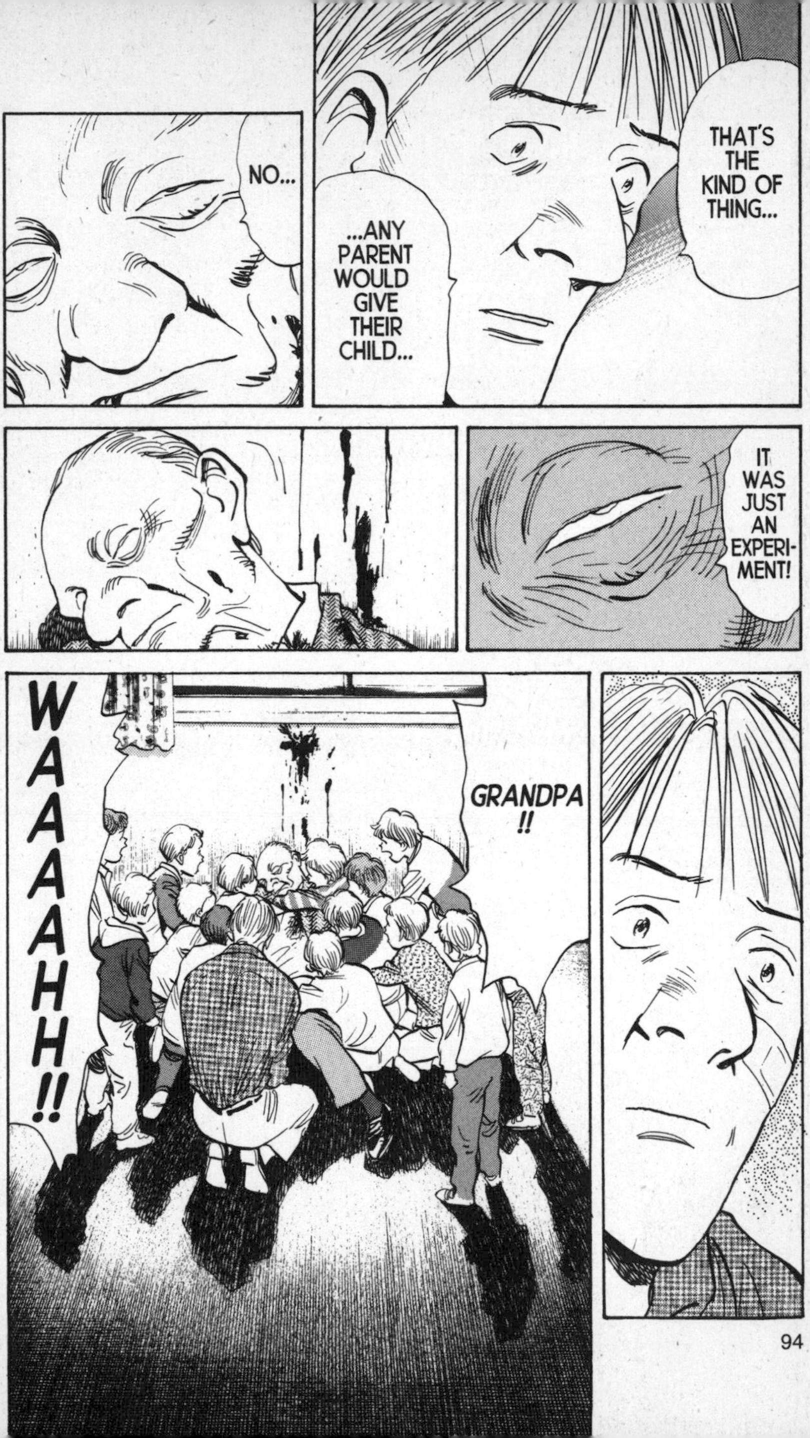
THAT'S THE KIND OF THING...
...ANY PARENT WOULD GIVE THEIR CHILD...
NO...
IT WAS JUST AN EXPERIMENT!
GRANDPA!!
WAAAAAHH!!

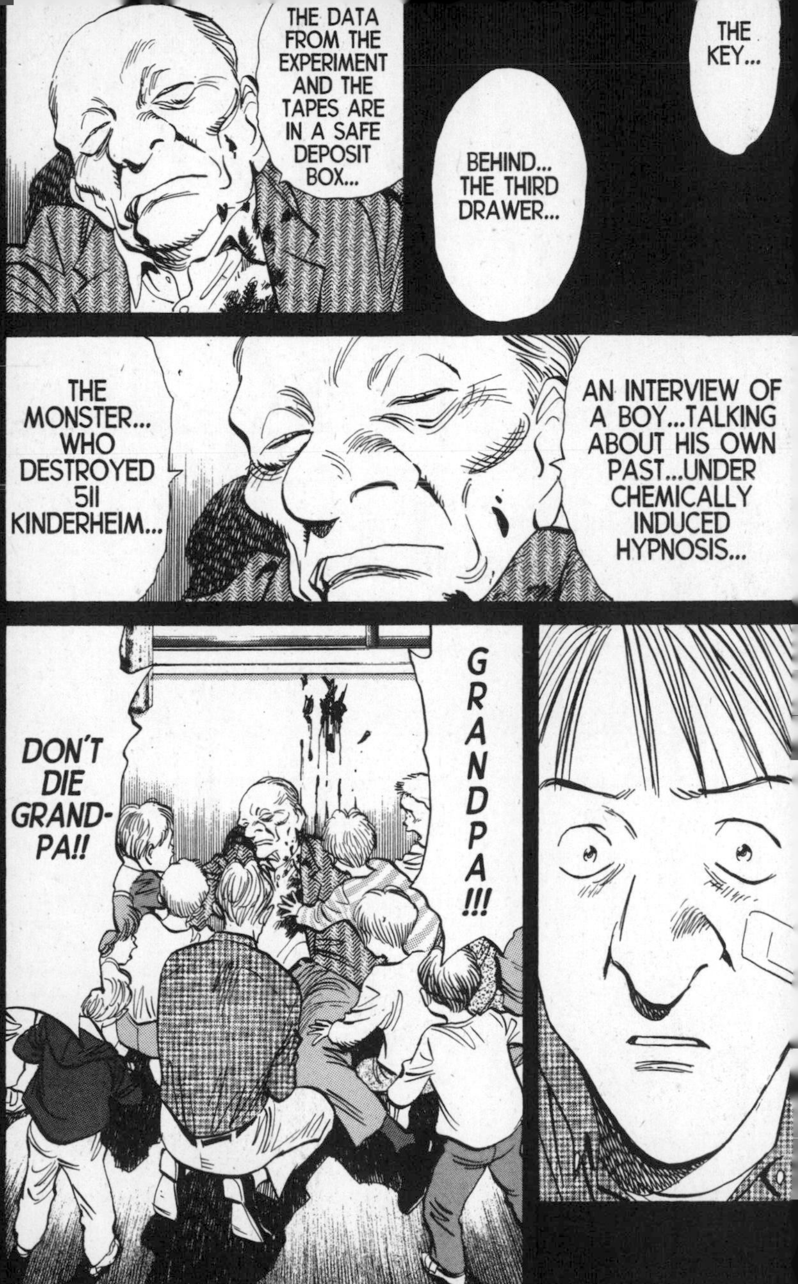
THE KEY...
BEHIND... THE THIRD DRAWER...
THE DATA FROM THE EXPERIMENT AND THE TAPES ARE IN A SAFE DEPOSIT BOX...
AN INTERVIEW OF A BOY...TALKING ABOUT HIS OWN PAST...UNDER CHEMICALLY INDUCED HYPNOSIS...
THE MONSTER... WHO DESTROYED 511 KINDERHEIM...
GRANDPA!!!
DON'T DIE GRAND-PA!!

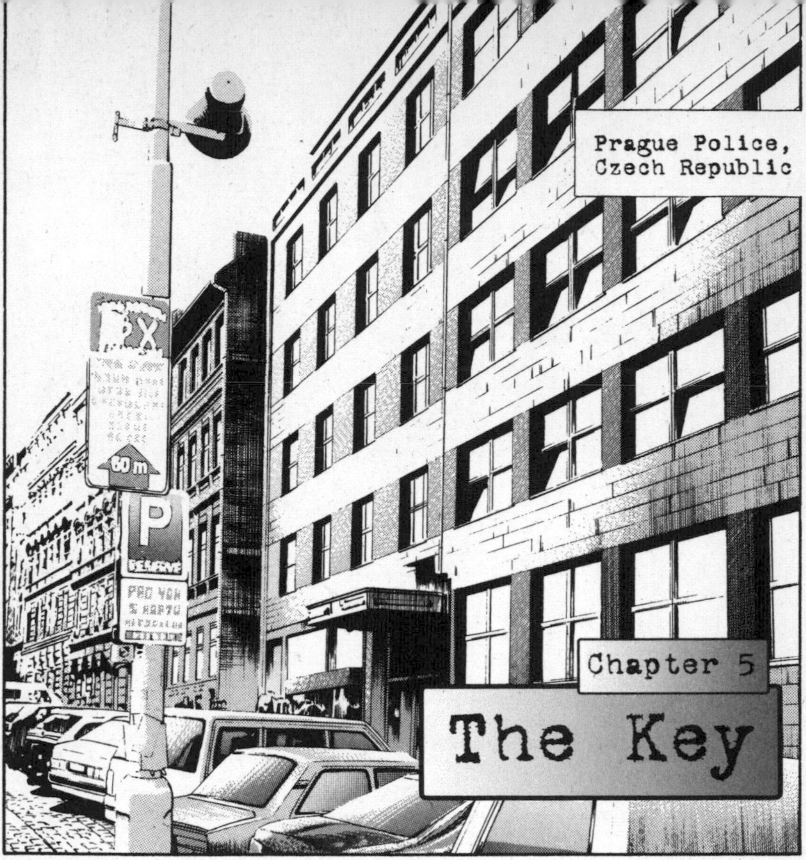
Prague Police,
Czech Republic
60 m
P
Chapter 5
The Key

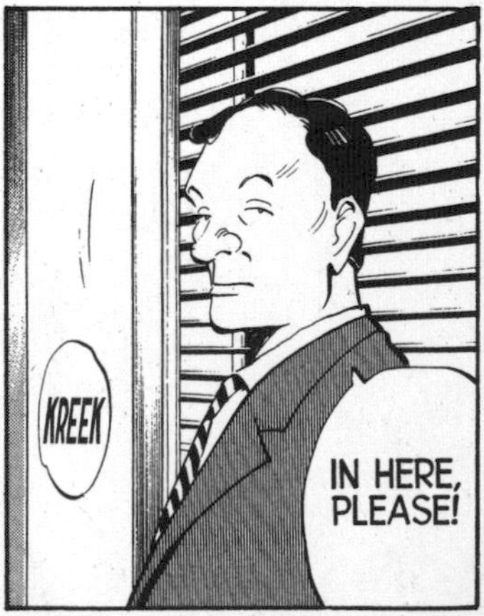
KREEK
IN HERE, PLEASE!

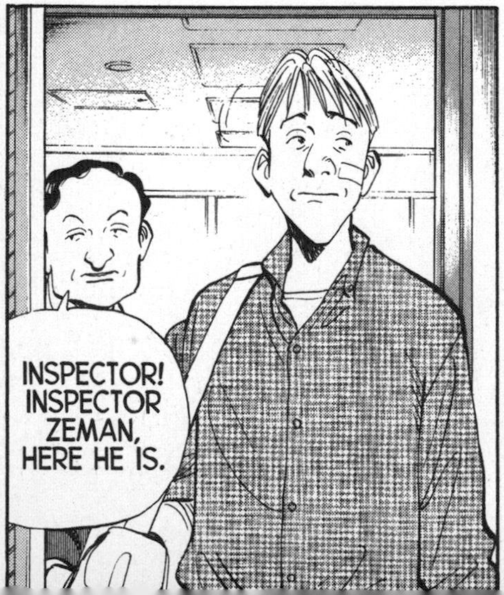
INSPECTOR! INSPECTOR ZEMAN, HERE HE IS.

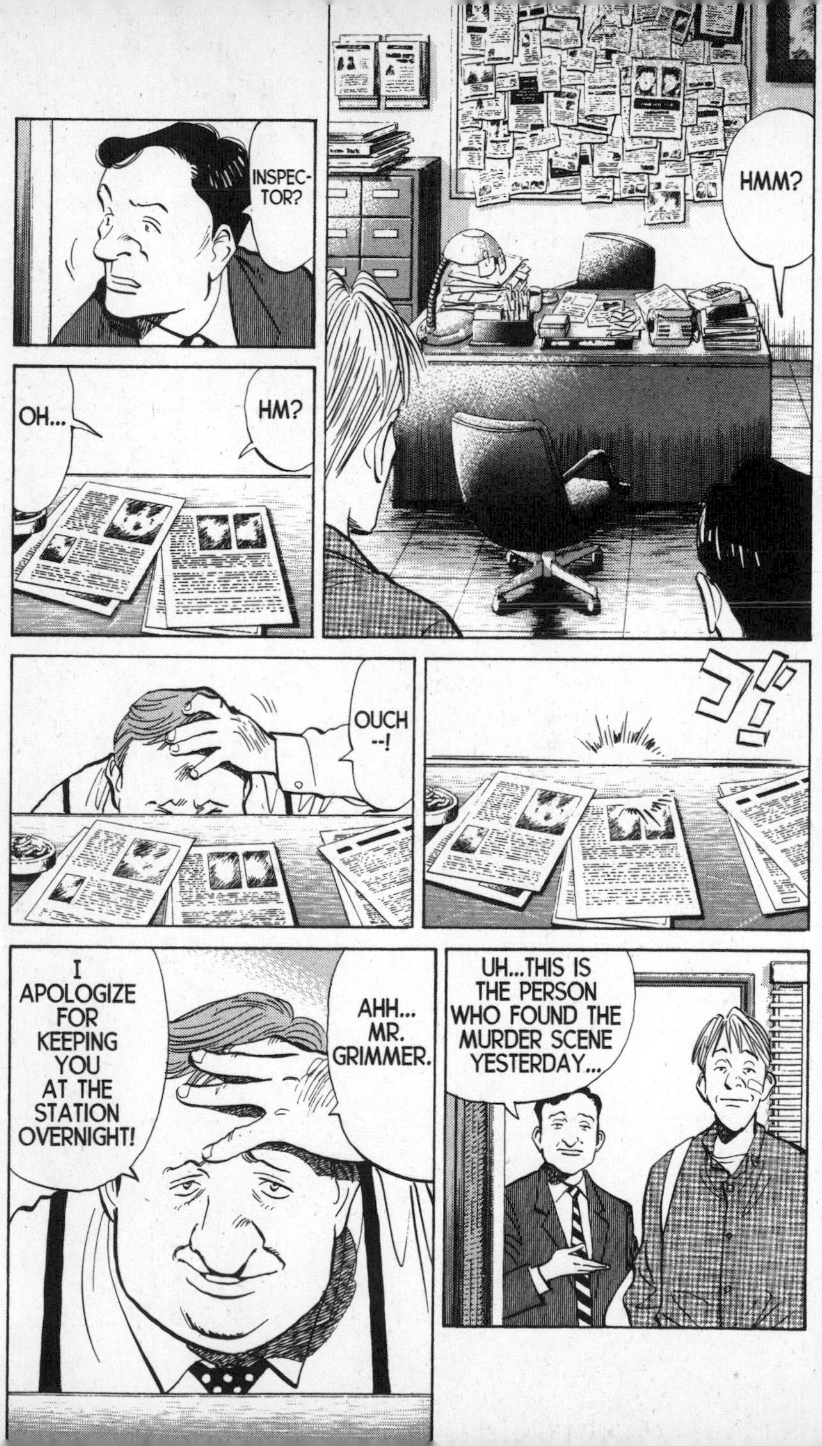
HMM?
INSPECTOR?
HM?
OH...
OUCH --!
UH...THIS IS THE PERSON WHO FOUND THE MURDER SCENE YESTERDAY...
AHH... MR. GRIMMER.
I APOLOGIZE FOR KEEPING YOU AT THE STATION OVERNIGHT!

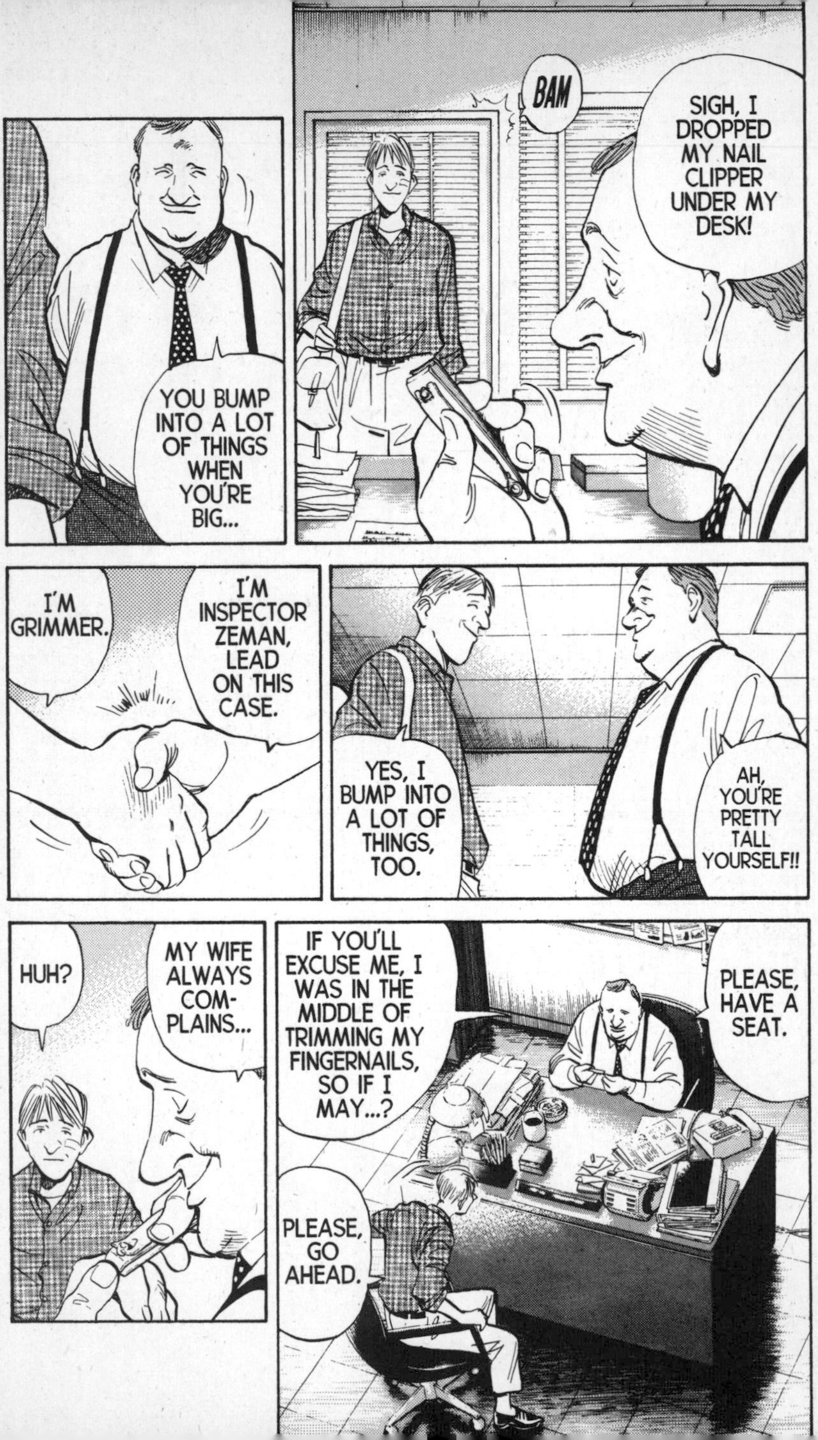
BAM
SIGH, I DROPPED MY NAIL CLIPPER UNDER MY DESK!
YOU BUMP INTO A LOT OF THINGS WHEN YOU'RE BIG...
AH, YOU'RE PRETTY TALL YOURSELF!!
YES, I BUMP INTO A LOT OF THINGS, TOO.
I'M INSPECTOR ZEMAN, LEAD ON THIS CASE.
I'M GRIMMER.
PLEASE, HAVE A SEAT.
IF YOU'LL EXCUSE ME, I WAS IN THE MIDDLE OF TRIMMING MY FINGERNAILS, SO IF I MAY...?
PLEASE, GO AHEAD.
MY WIFE ALWAYS COM-PLAINS...
HUH?

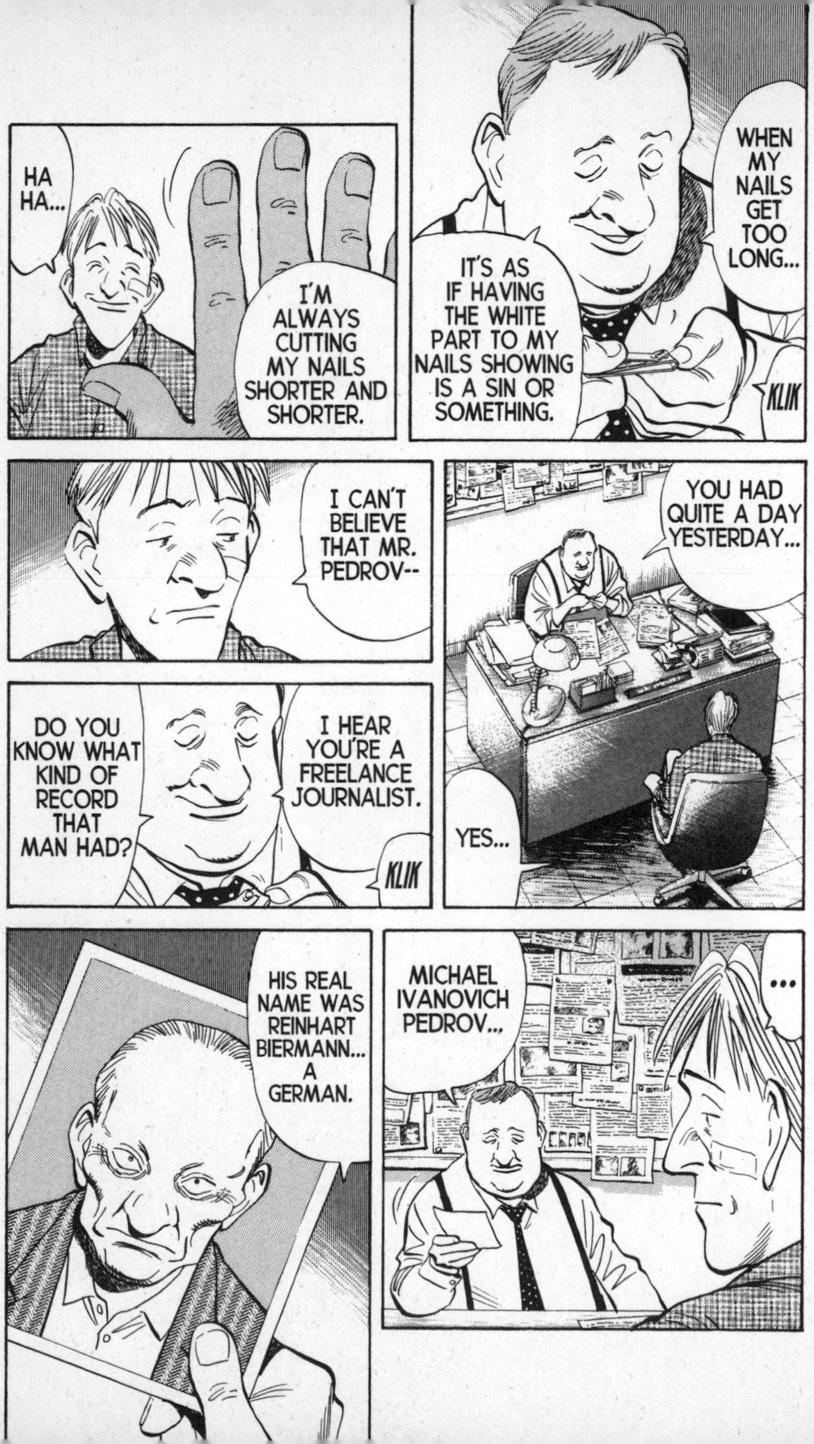
WHEN MY NAILS GET TOO LONG...
IT'S AS IF HAVING THE WHITE PART TO MY NAILS SHOWING IS A SIN OR SOMETHING.
KLIK
I'M ALWAYS CUTTING MY NAILS SHORTER AND SHORTER.
HA HA...
YOU HAD QUITE A DAY YESTERDAY...
YES...
I CAN'T BELIEVE THAT MR. PEDROV--
I HEAR YOU'RE A FREELANCE JOURNALIST.
KLIK
DO YOU KNOW WHAT KIND OF RECORD THAT MAN HAD?
...
MICHAEL IVANOVICH PEDROV...
HIS REAL NAME WAS REINHART BIERMANN... A GERMAN.

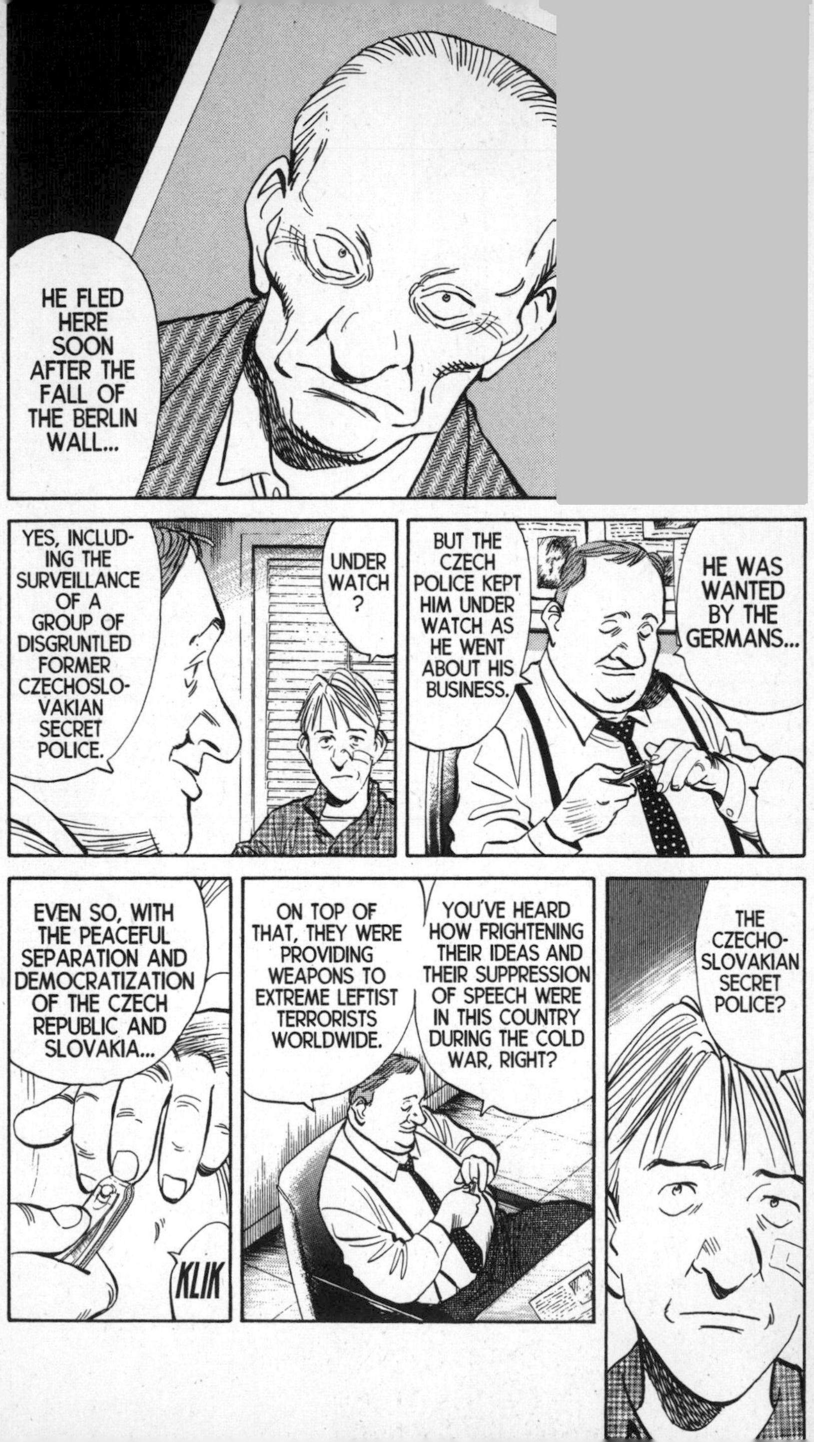
HE FLED HERE SOON AFTER THE FALL OF THE BERLIN WALL...
HE WAS WANTED BY THE GERMANS...
BUT THE CZECH POLICE KEPT HIM UNDER WATCH AS HE WENT ABOUT HIS BUSINESS.
UNDER WATCH?
YES, INCLUDING THE SURVEILLANCE OF A GROUP OF DISGRUNTLED FORMER CZECHOSLOVAKIAN SECRET POLICE.
THE CZECHOSLOVAKIAN SECRET POLICE?
YOU'VE HEARD HOW FRIGHTENING THEIR IDEAS AND THEIR SUPPRESSION OF SPEECH WERE IN THIS COUNTRY DURING THE COLD WAR, RIGHT?
ON TOP OF THAT, THEY WERE PROVIDING WEAPONS TO EXTREME LEFTIST TERRORISTS WORLDWIDE.
EVEN SO, WITH THE PEACEFUL SEPARATION AND DEMOCRATIZATION OF THE CZECH REPUBLIC AND SLOVAKIA...
KLIK

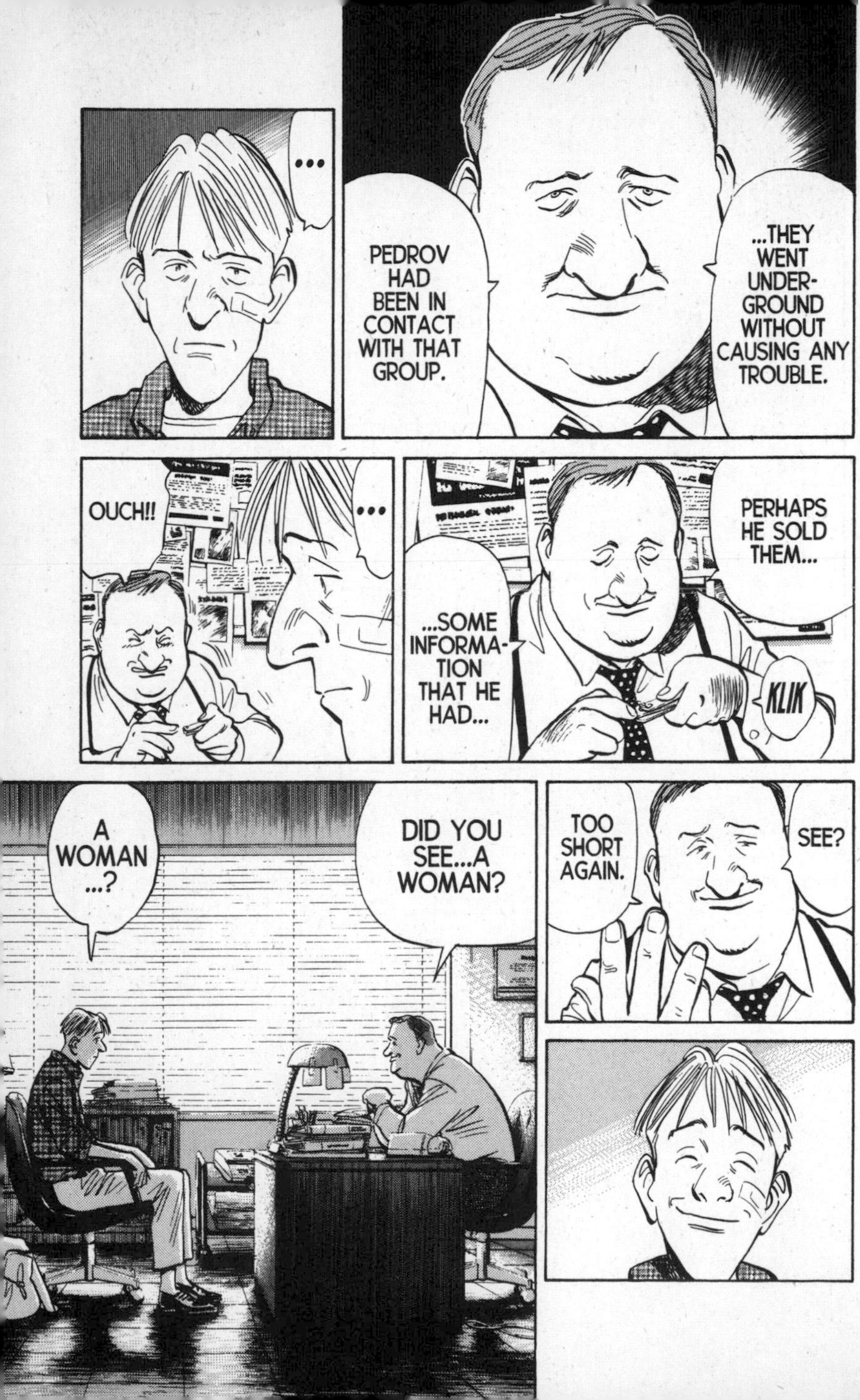
...THEY WENT UNDER-GROUND WITHOUT CAUSING ANY TROUBLE.
PEDROV HAD BEEN IN CONTACT WITH THAT GROUP.
...
PERHAPS HE SOLD THEM...
...SOME INFORMATION THAT HE HAD...
KLIK
...
OUCH!!
SEE?
TOO SHORT AGAIN.
DID YOU SEE...A WOMAN?
A WOMAN ...?

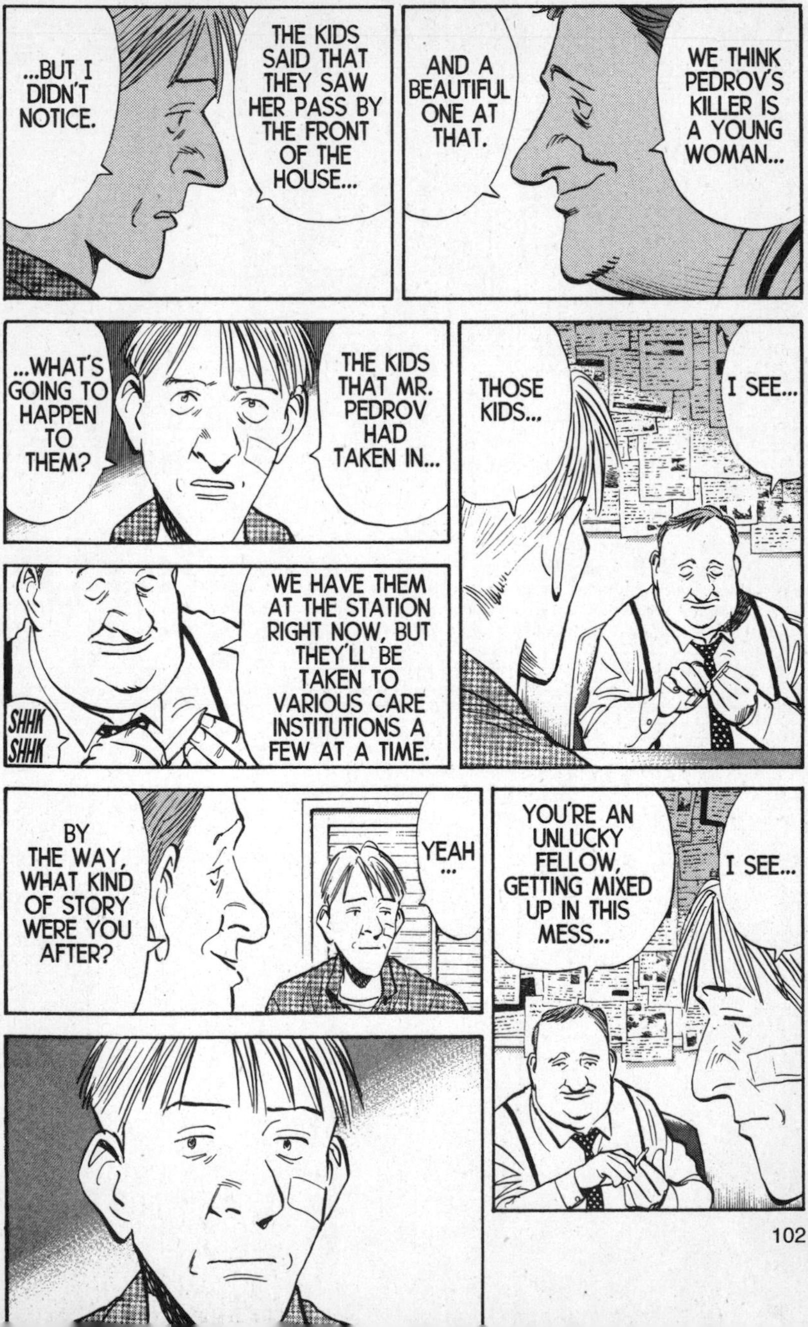
WE THINK PEDROV'S KILLER IS A YOUNG WOMAN...
AND A BEAUTIFUL ONE AT THAT.
THE KIDS SAID THAT THEY SAW HER PASS BY THE FRONT OF THE HOUSE...
...BUT I DIDN'T NOTICE.
I SEE...
THOSE KIDS...
THE KIDS THAT MR. PEDROV HAD TAKEN IN...
...WHAT'S GOING TO HAPPEN TO THEM?
WE HAVE THEM AT THE STATION RIGHT NOW, BUT THEY'LL BE TAKEN TO VARIOUS CARE INSTITUTIONS A FEW AT A TIME.
SHHK SHHK
I SEE...
YOU'RE AN UNLUCKY FELLOW, GETTING MIXED UP IN THIS MESS...
YEAH ...
BY THE WAY, WHAT KIND OF STORY WERE YOU AFTER?

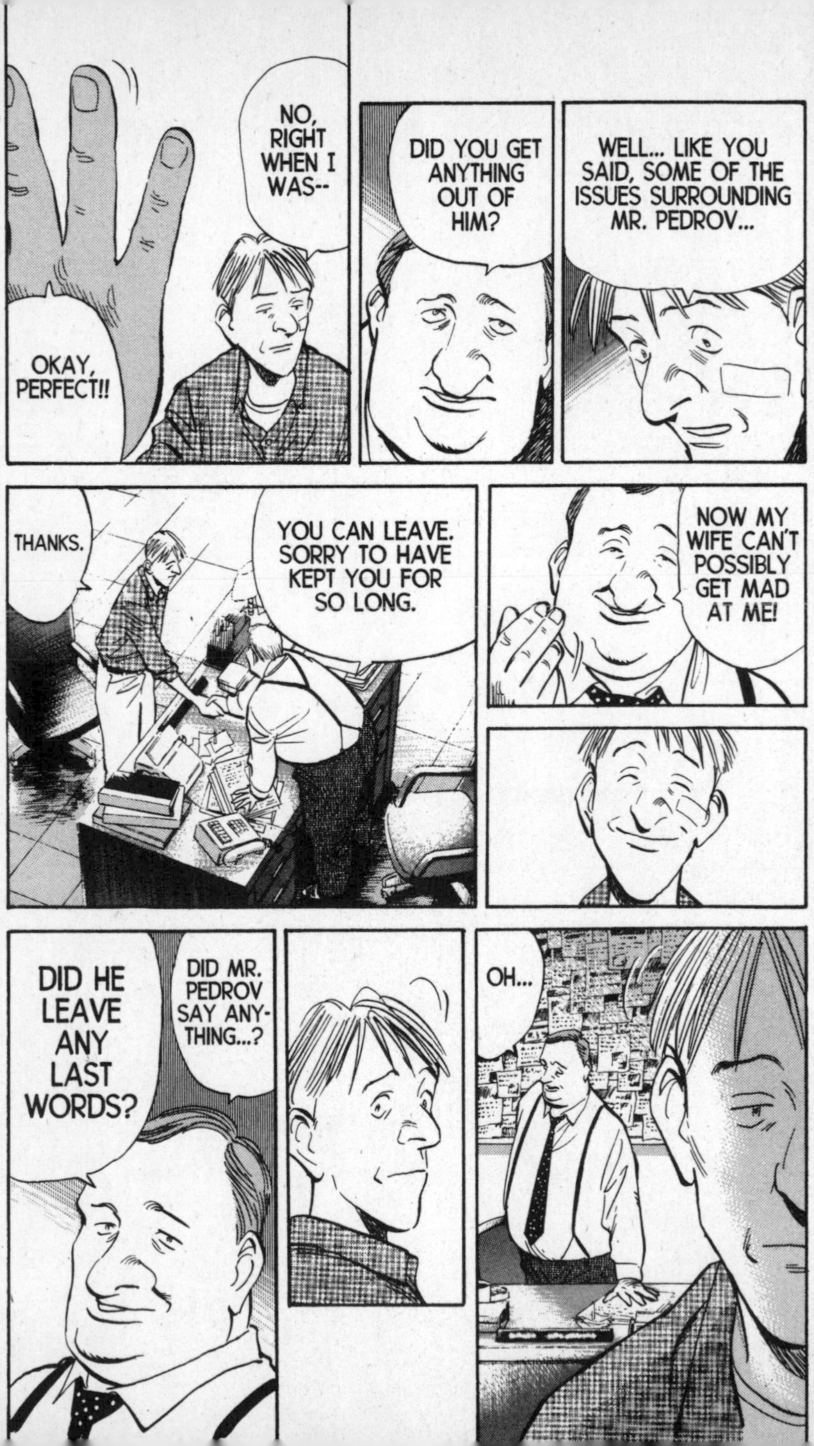
NO, RIGHT WHEN I WAS--
OKAY, PERFECT!!
DID YOU GET ANYTHING OUT OF HIM?
WELL... LIKE YOU SAID, SOME OF THE ISSUES SURROUNDING MR. PEDROV...
YOU CAN LEAVE. SORRY TO HAVE KEPT YOU FOR SO LONG.
THANKS.
NOW MY WIFE CAN'T POSSIBLY GET MAD AT ME!
DID HE LEAVE ANY LAST WORDS?
DID MR. PEDROV SAY ANY-THING...?
OH...

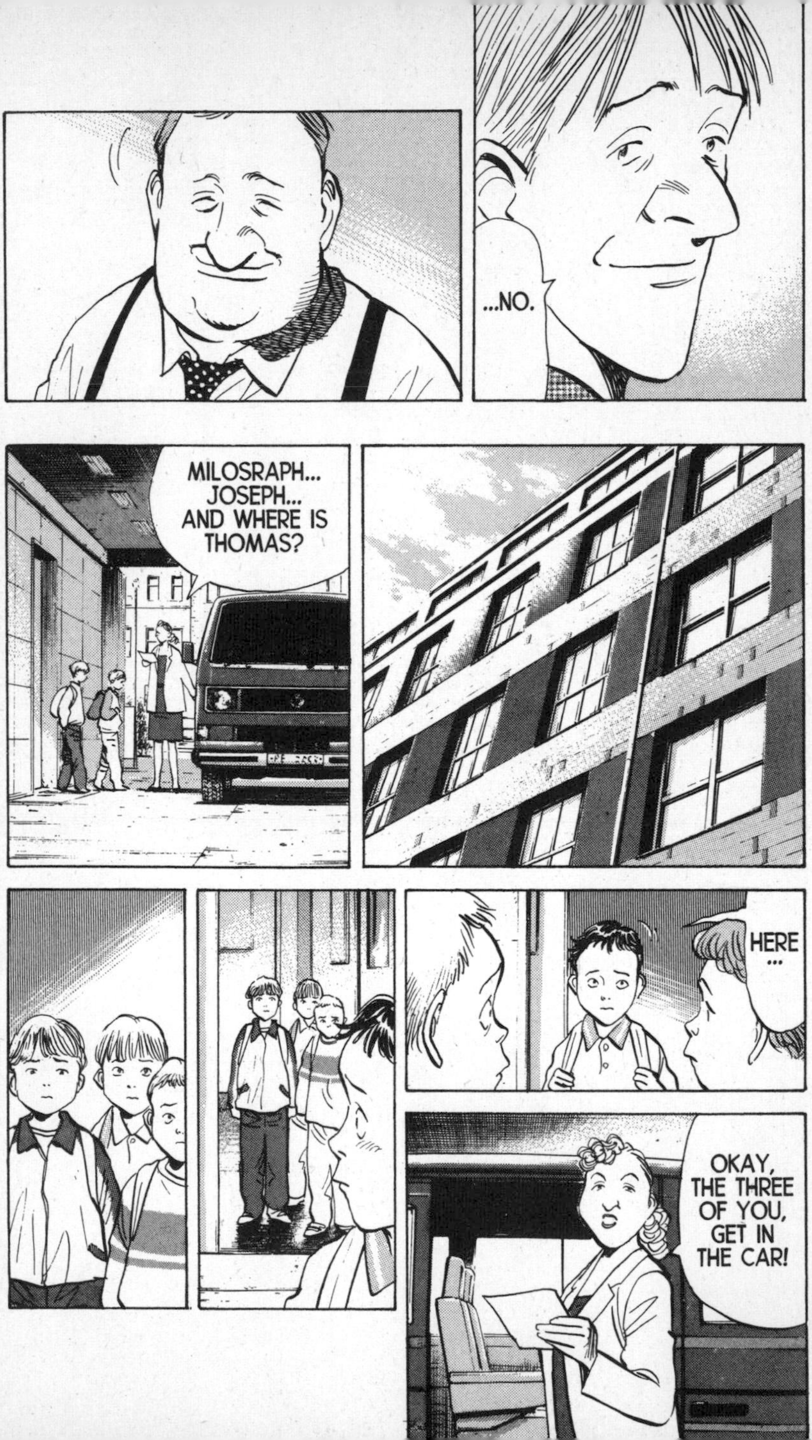
...NO.
MILOSRAPH... JOSEPH... AND WHERE IS THOMAS?
HERE ...
OKAY, THE THREE OF YOU, GET IN THE CAR!

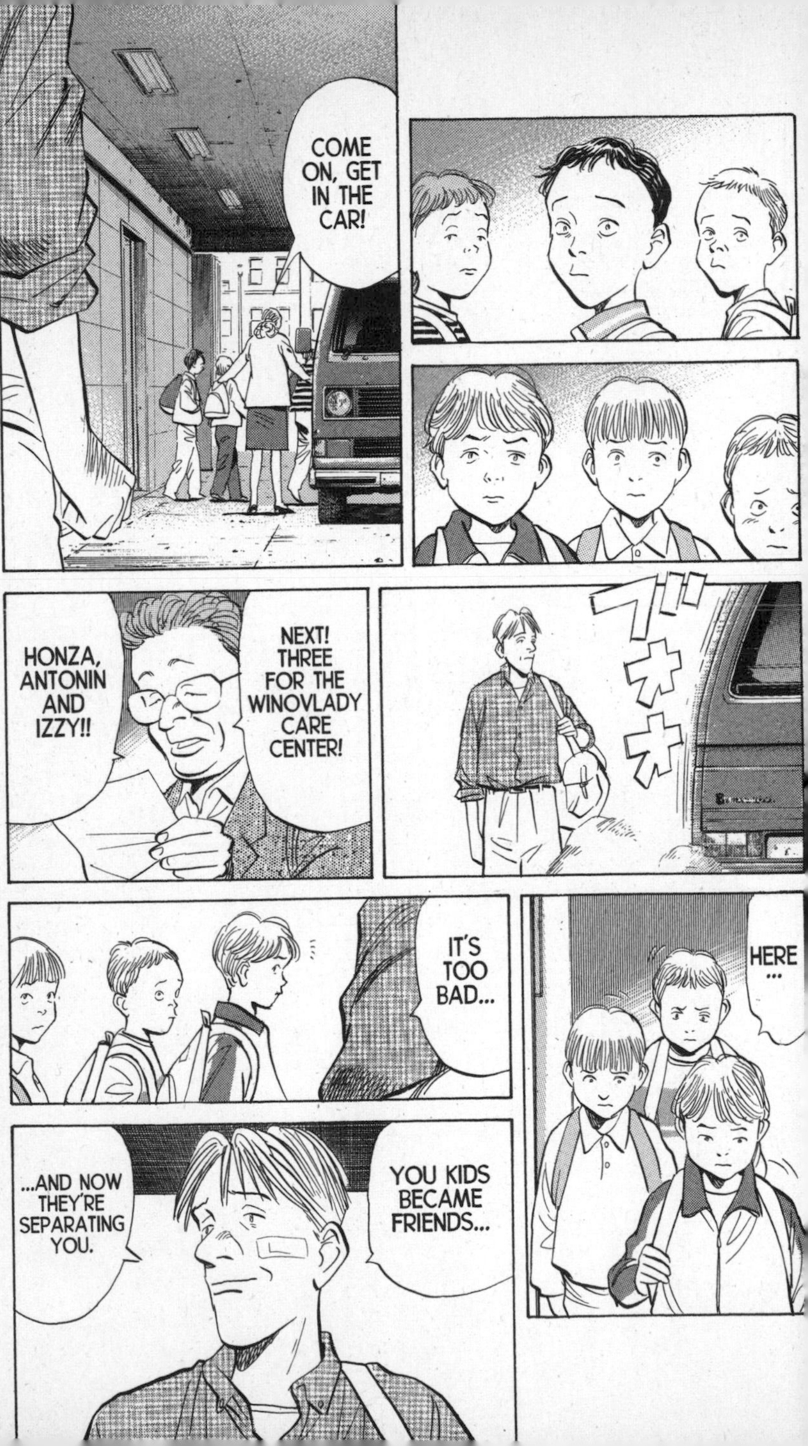
COME ON, GET IN THE CAR!
ブォォ
NEXT! THREE FOR THE WINOVLADY CARE CENTER!
HONZA, ANTONIN AND IZZY!!
HERE...
IT'S TOO BAD...
YOU KIDS BECAME FRIENDS...
...AND NOW THEY'RE SEPARATING YOU.

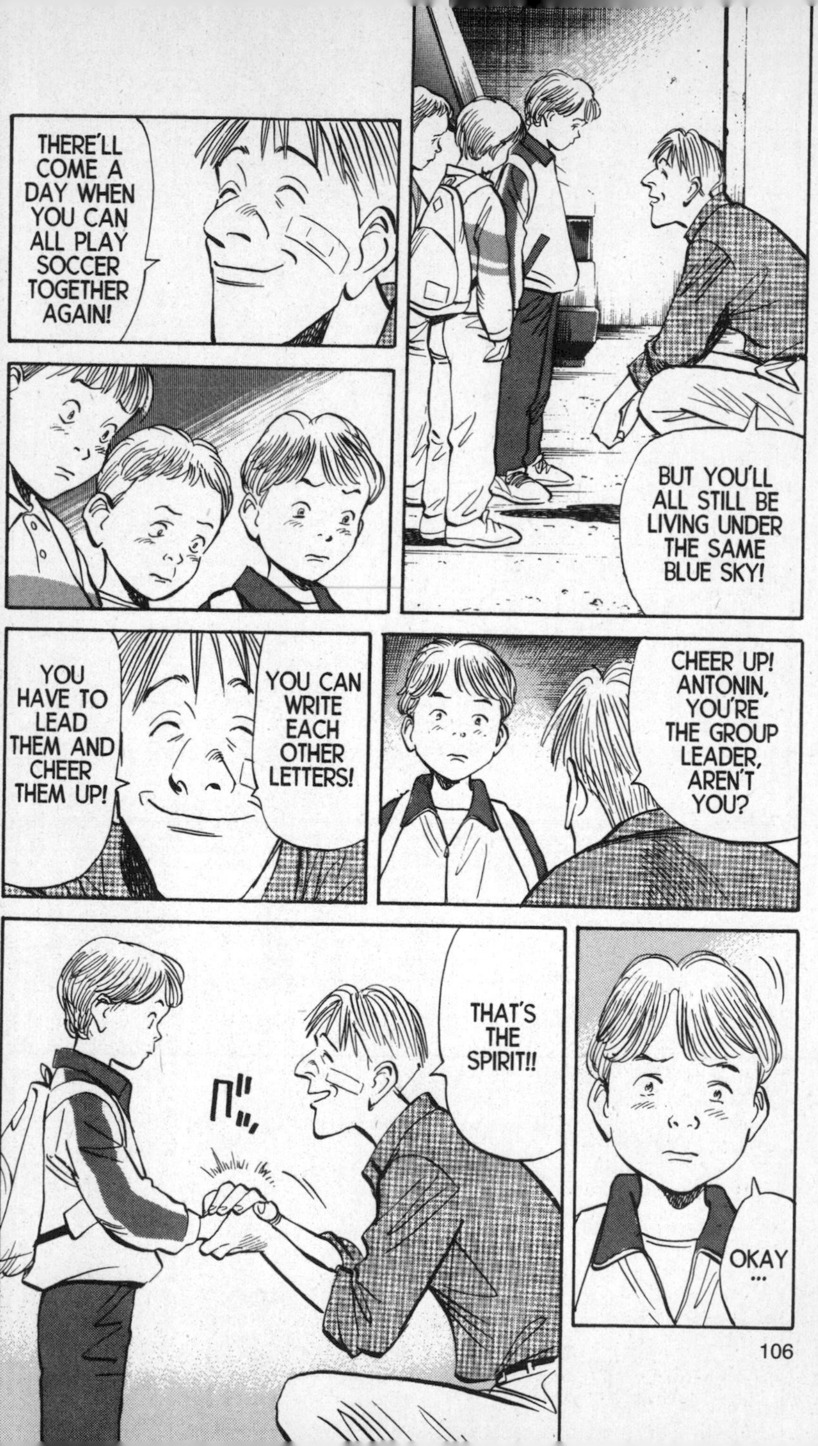
BUT YOU'LL ALL STILL BE LIVING UNDER THE SAME BLUE SKY!
THERE'LL COME A DAY WHEN YOU CAN ALL PLAY SOCCER TOGETHER AGAIN!
CHEER UP! ANTONIN, YOU'RE THE GROUP LEADER, AREN'T YOU?
YOU CAN WRITE EACH OTHER LETTERS!
YOU HAVE TO LEAD THEM AND CHEER THEM UP!
OKAY ...
THAT'S THE SPIRIT!!

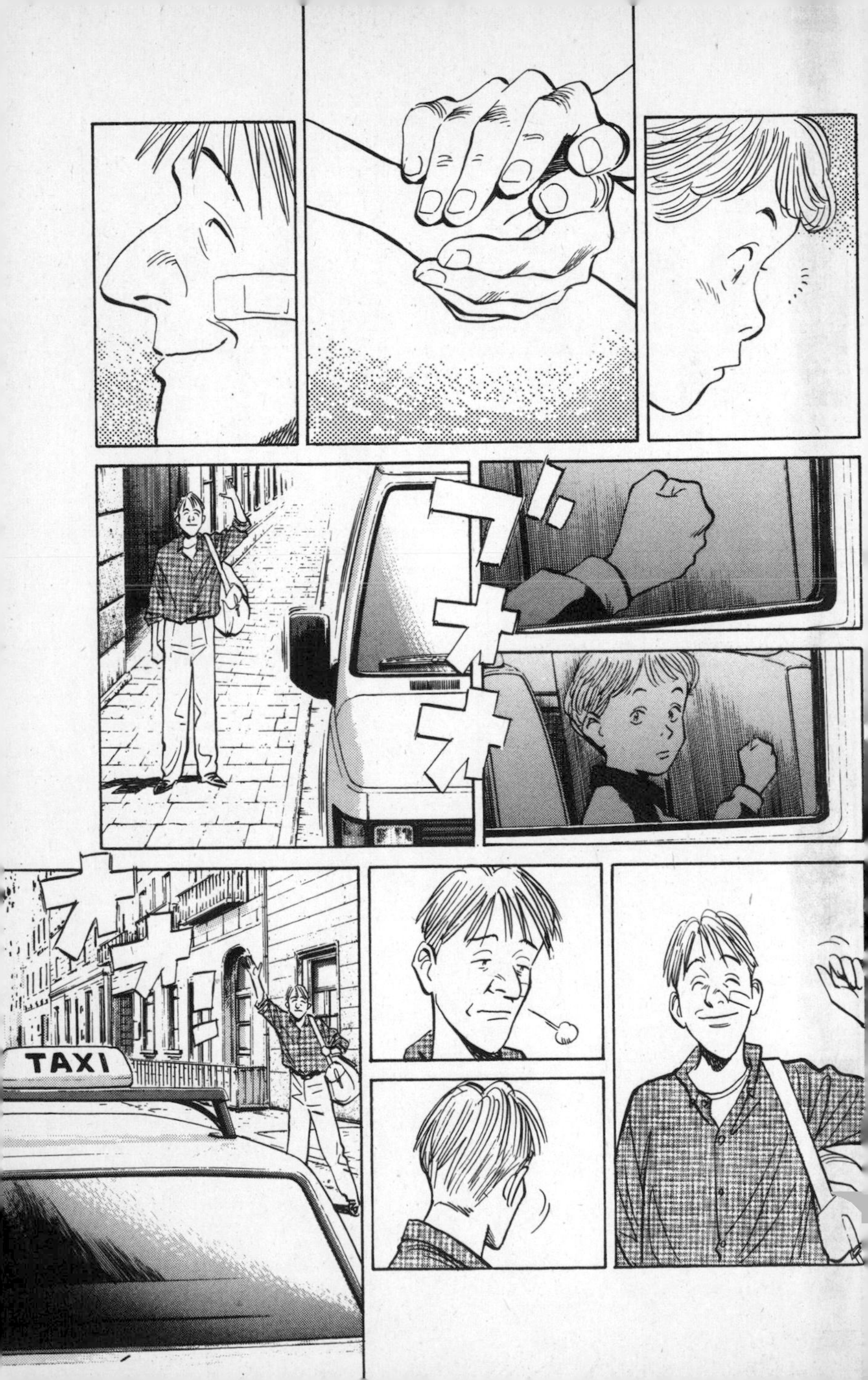
ブオオ
オオ
TAXI

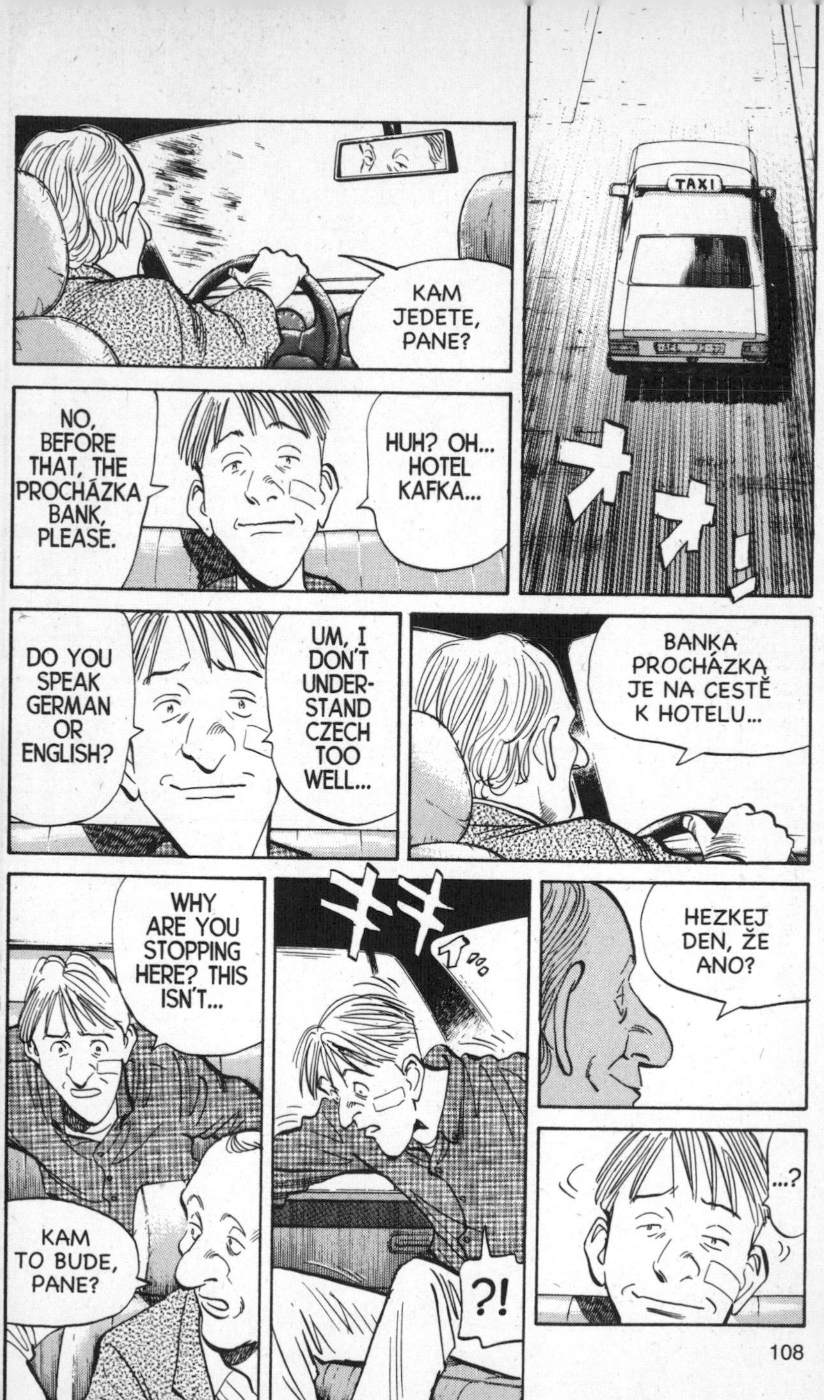
KAM JEDETE, PANE?
HUH? OH... HOTEL KAFKA...
NO, BEFORE THAT, THE PROCHÁZKA BANK, PLEASE.
BANKA PROCHÁZKA JE NA CESTĚ K HOTELU...
UM, I DON'T UNDERSTAND CZECH TOO WELL...
DO YOU SPEAK GERMAN OR ENGLISH?
HEZKEJ DEN, ŽE ANO?
...?
?!
WHY ARE YOU STOPPING HERE? THIS ISN'T...
KAM TO BUDE, PANE?

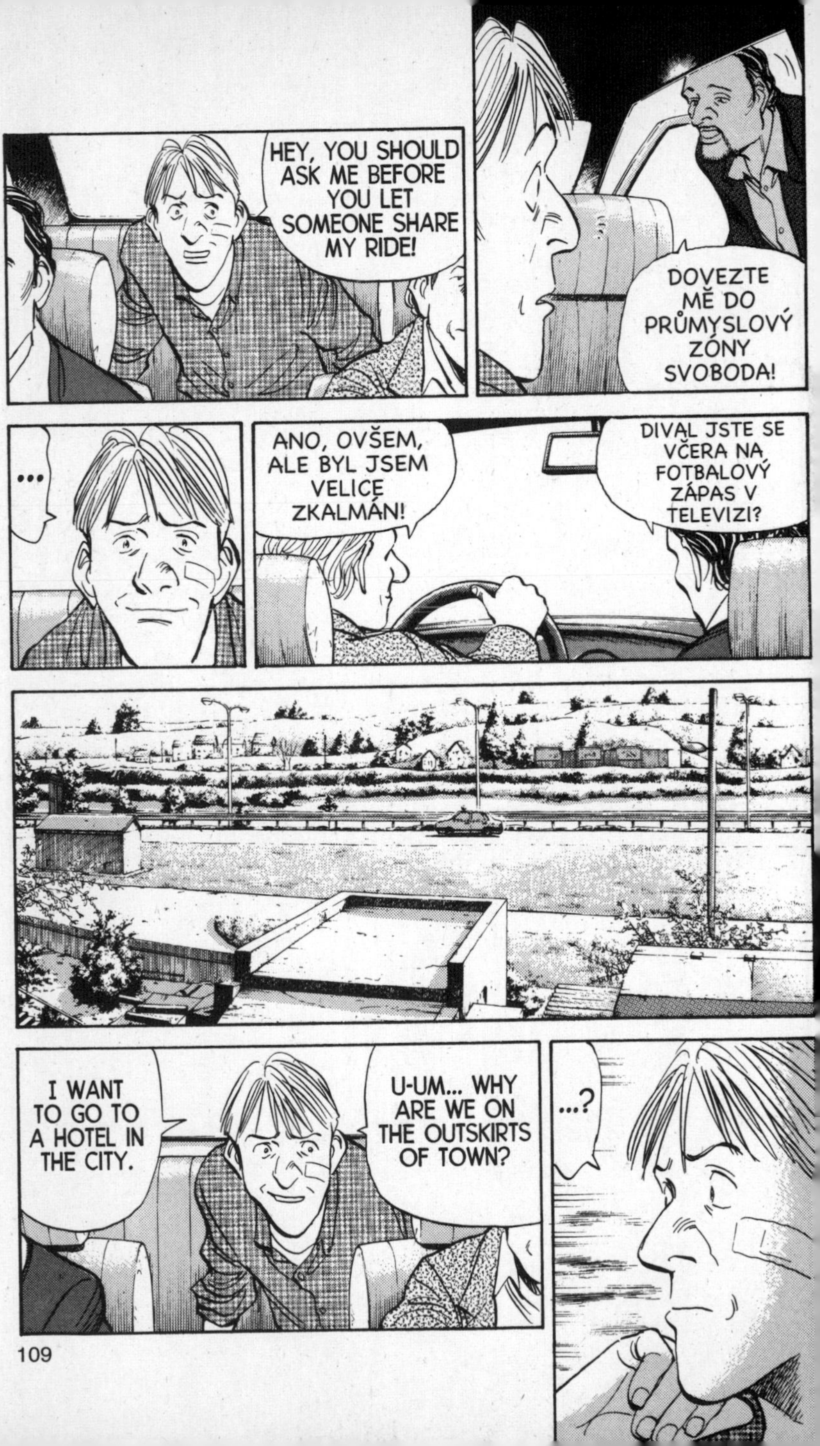
DOVEZTE MĚ DO PRŮMYSLOVÝ ZÓNY SVOBODA!
HEY, YOU SHOULD ASK ME BEFORE YOU LET SOMEONE SHARE MY RIDE!
DIVAL JSTE SE VČERA NA FOTBALOVÝ ZÁPAS V TELEVIZI?
ANO, OVŠEM, ALE BYL JSEM VELICE ZKALMÁN!
...
...?
U-UM... WHY ARE WE ON THE OUTSKIRTS OF TOWN?
I WANT TO GO TO A HOTEL IN THE CITY.

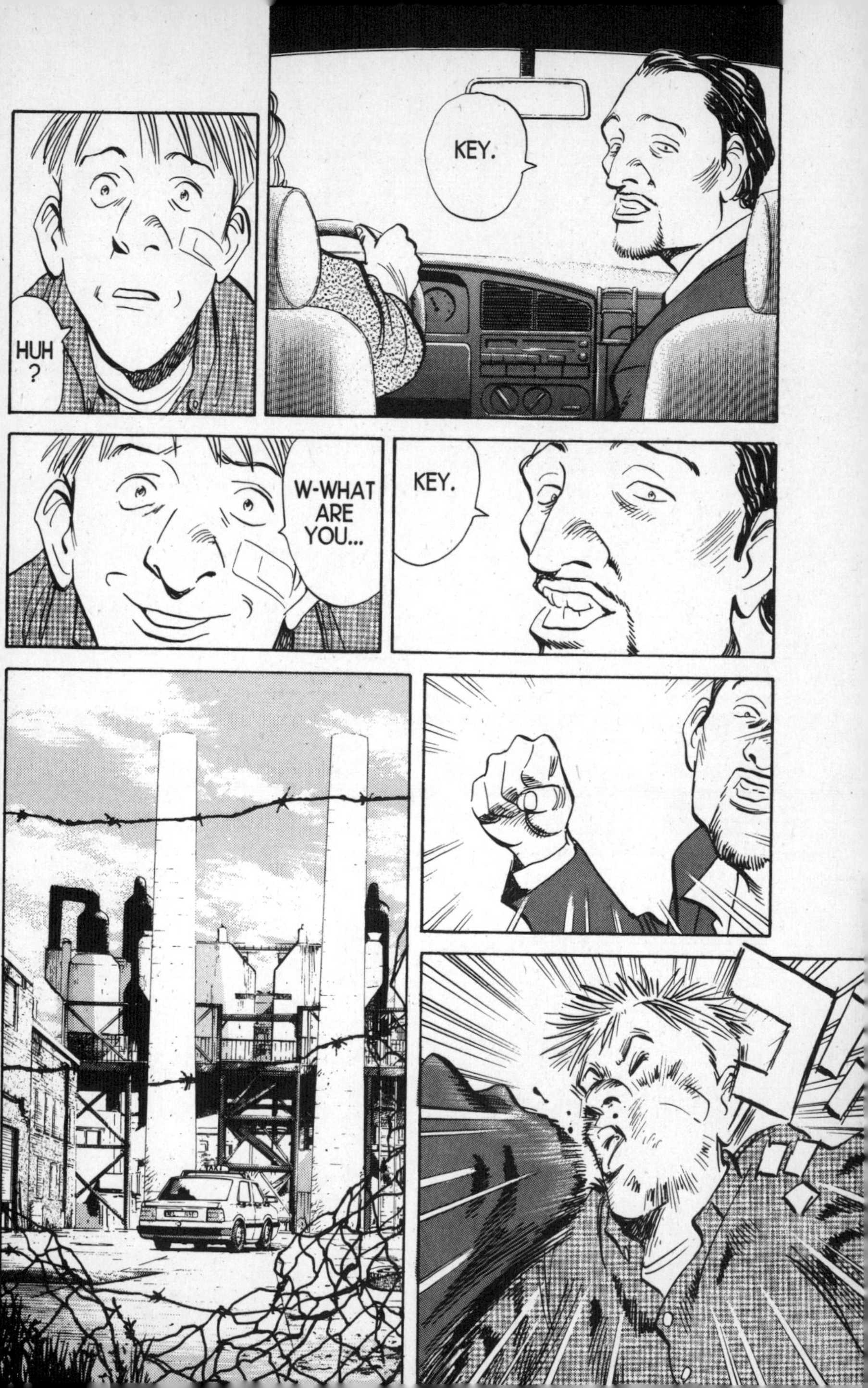
KEY.
HUH ?
KEY.
W-WHAT ARE YOU...

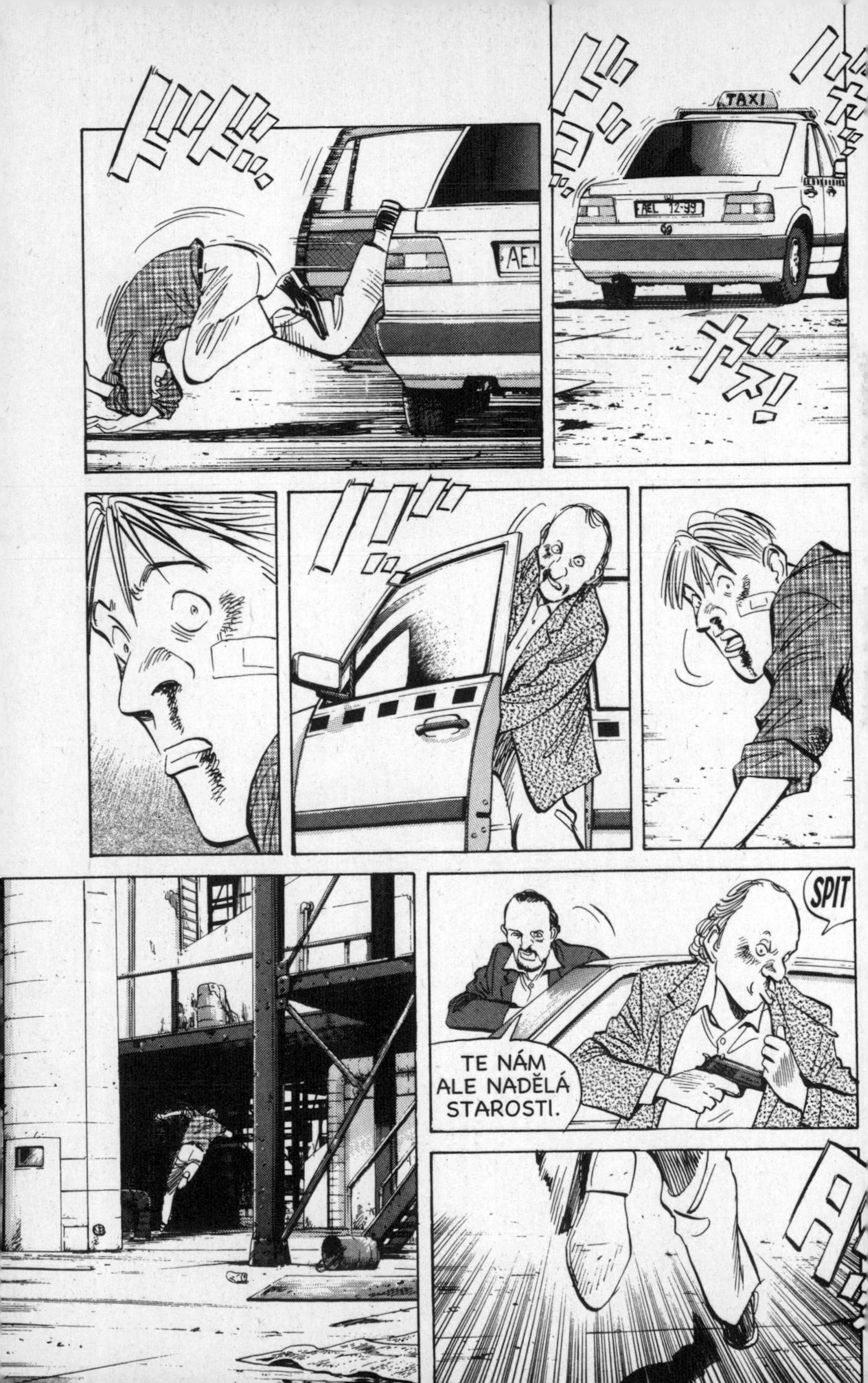
TAXI
AEL 12-99
SPIT
TE NÁM ALE NADĚLÁ STAROSTI.

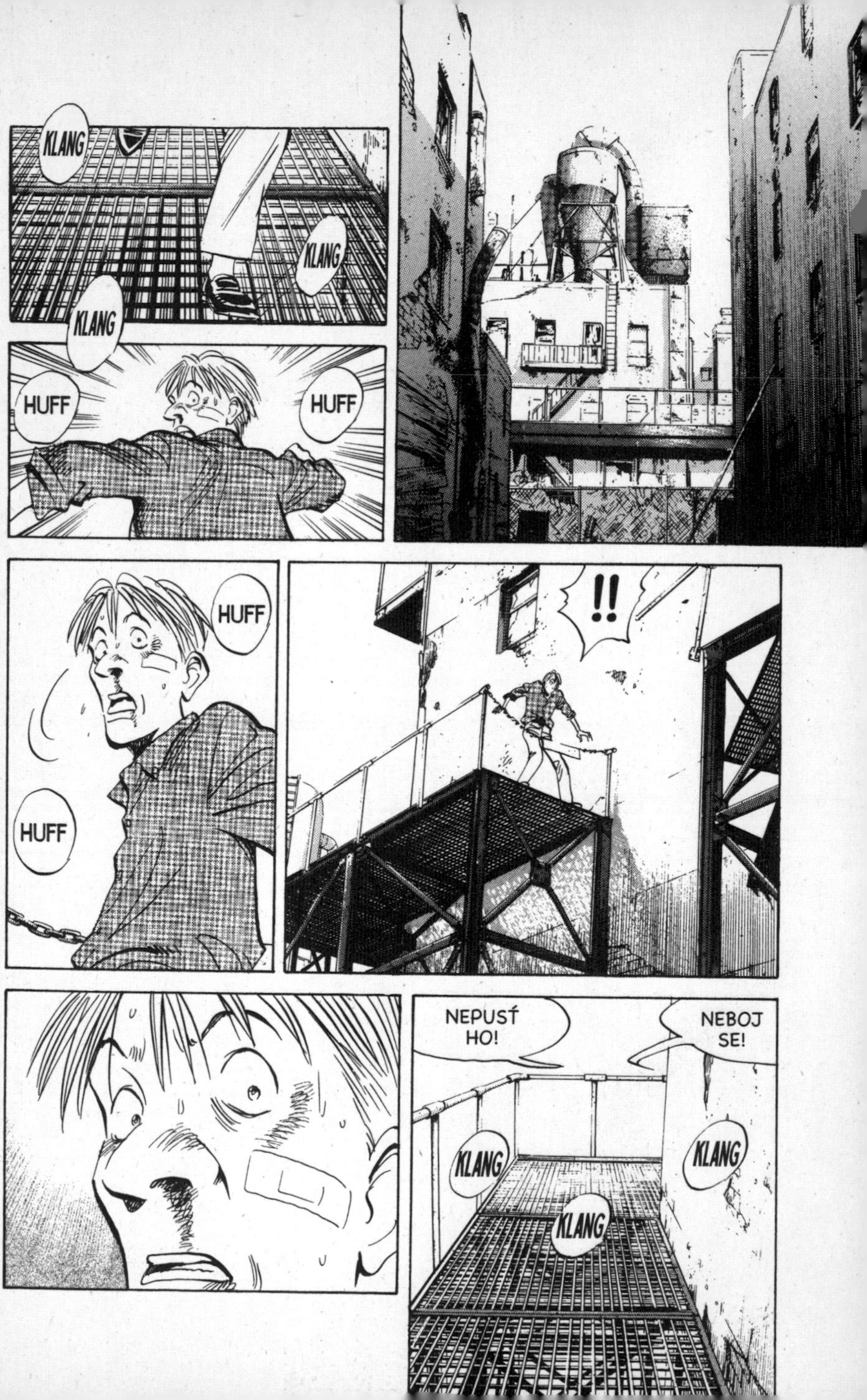
KLANG
KLANG
KLANG
HUFF
HUFF
!!
HUFF
HUFF
NEBOJ SE!
NEPUSŤ HO!
KLANG
KLANG
KLANG

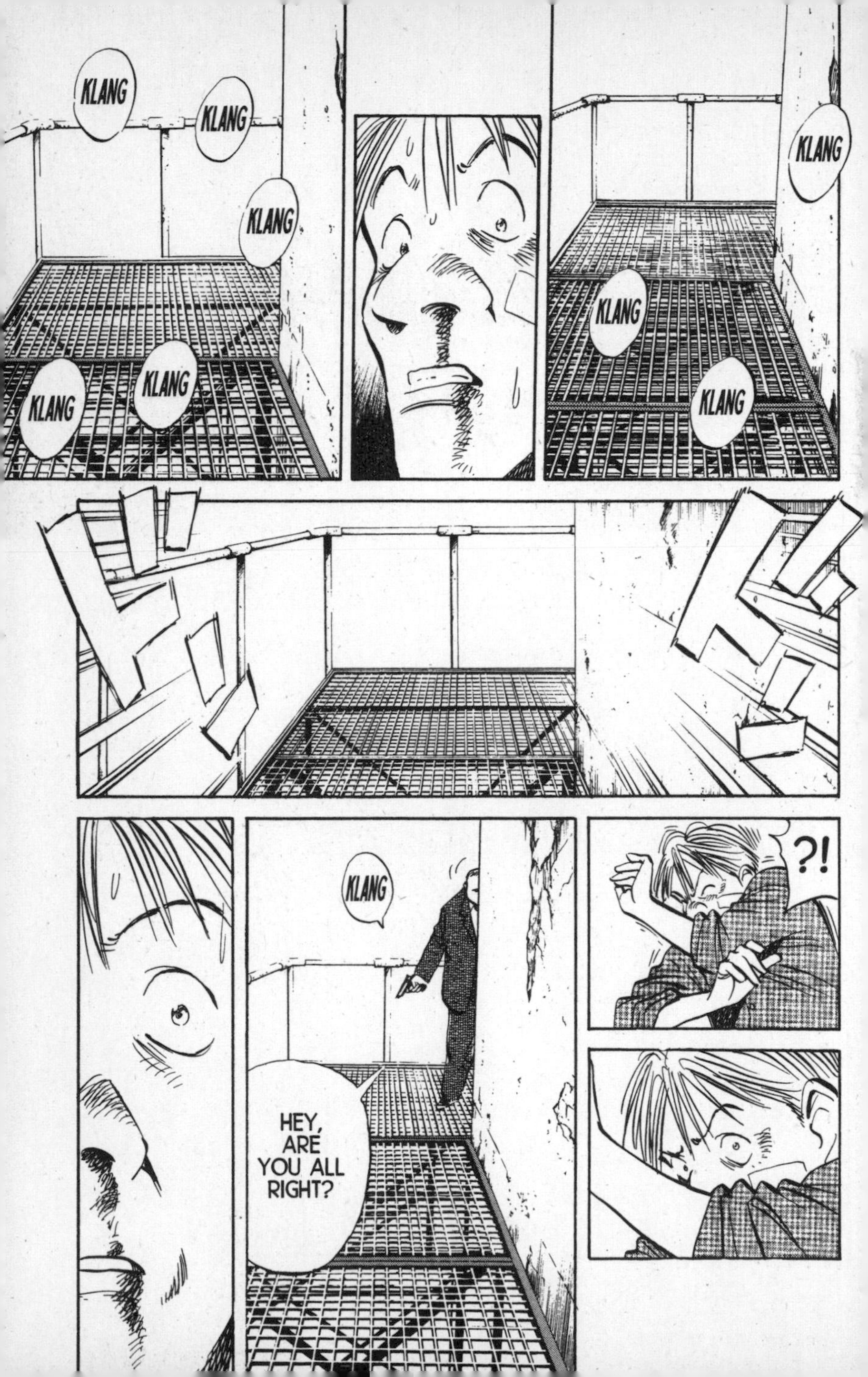
KLANG
KLANG
KLANG
KLANG
KLANG
KLANG
KLANG
KLANG
?!
KLANG
HEY, ARE YOU ALL RIGHT?

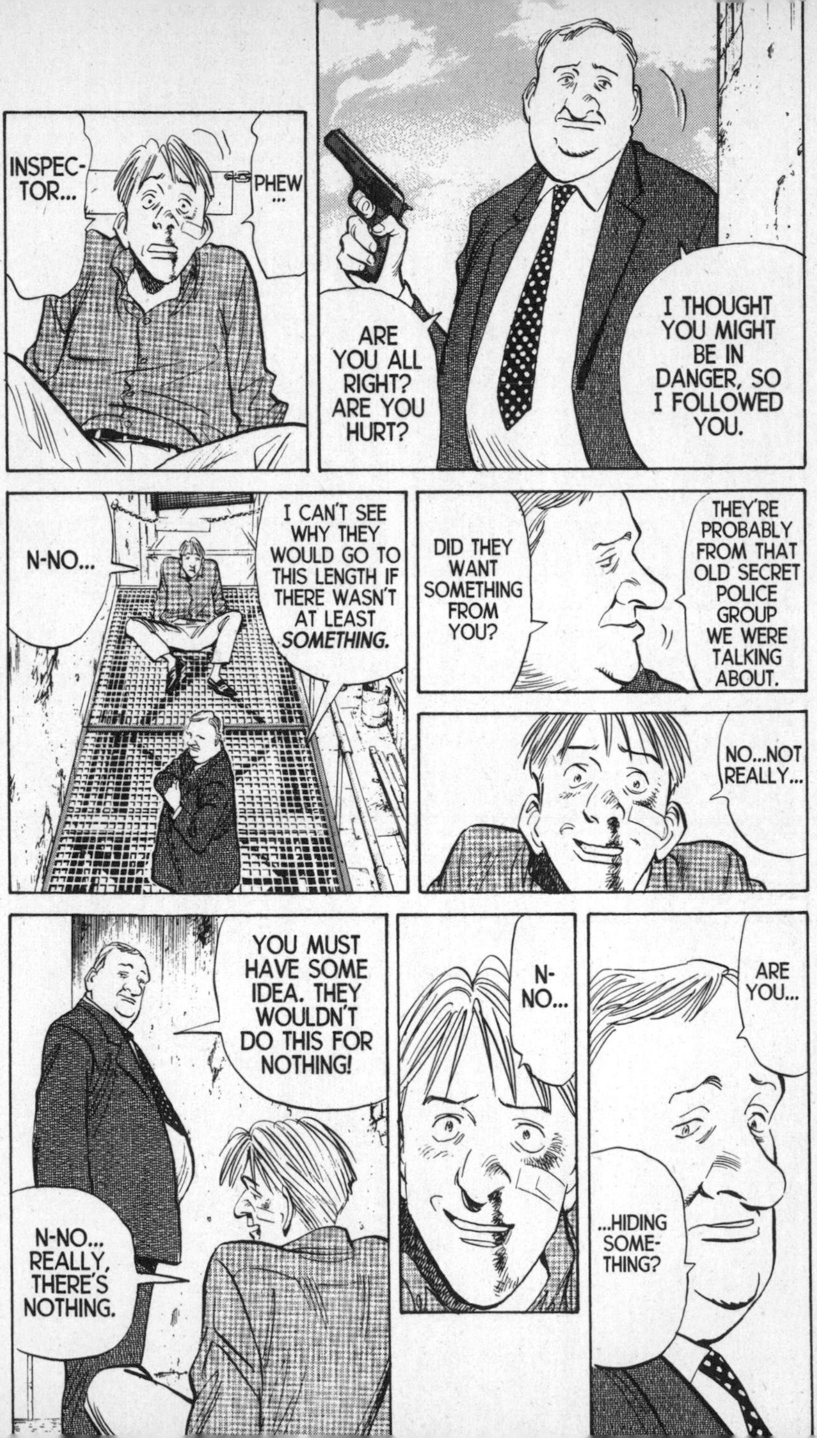
I THOUGHT YOU MIGHT BE IN DANGER, SO I FOLLOWED YOU.
ARE YOU ALL RIGHT? ARE YOU HURT?
PHEW...
INSPEC-TOR...
THEY'RE PROBABLY FROM THAT OLD SECRET POLICE GROUP WE WERE TALKING ABOUT.
DID THEY WANT SOMETHING FROM YOU?
NO...NOT REALLY...
I CAN'T SEE WHY THEY WOULD GO TO THIS LENGTH IF THERE WASN'T AT LEAST *SOMETHING.*
N-NO...
ARE YOU...
...HIDING SOME-THING?
N-NO...
YOU MUST HAVE SOME IDEA. THEY WOULDN'T DO THIS FOR NOTHING!
N-NO... REALLY, THERE'S NOTHING.

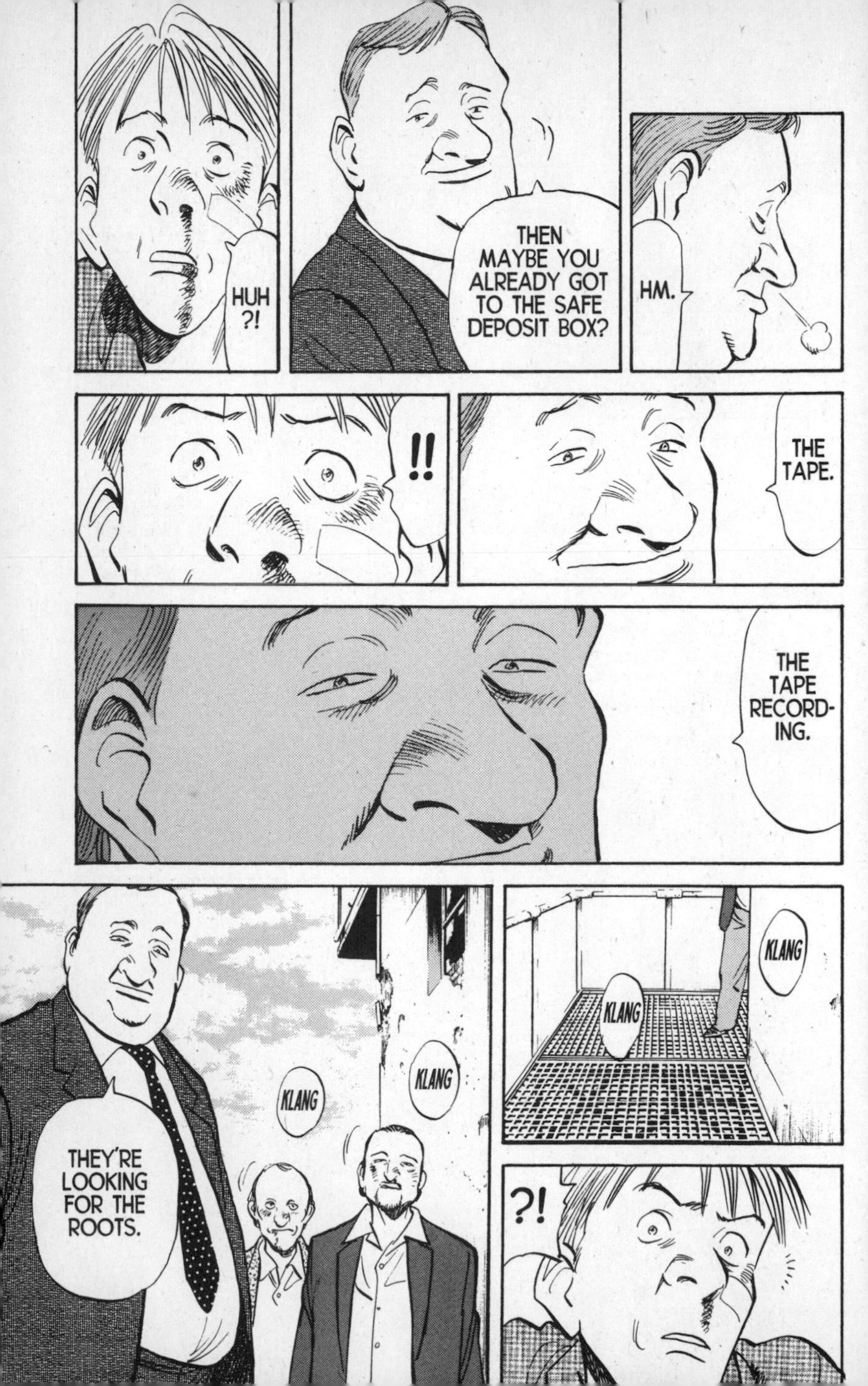
HM.
THEN MAYBE YOU ALREADY GOT TO THE SAFE DEPOSIT BOX?
HUH ?!
THE TAPE.
!!
THE TAPE RECORD- ING.
KLANG
KLANG
?!
KLANG
KLANG
THEY'RE LOOKING FOR THE ROOTS.

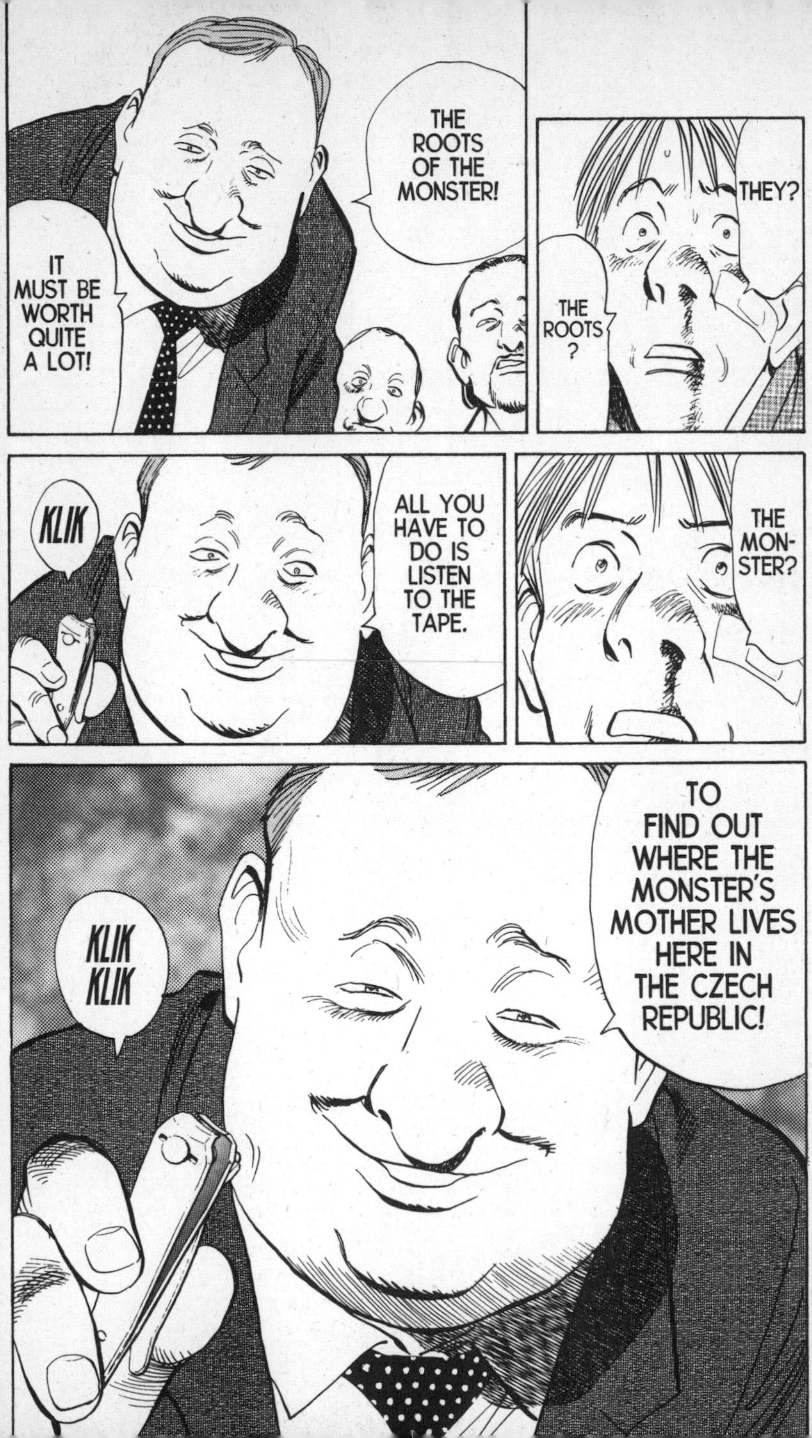
THEY?
THE ROOTS?
THE ROOTS OF THE MONSTER!
IT MUST BE WORTH QUITE A LOT!
THE MON-STER?
ALL YOU HAVE TO DO IS LISTEN TO THE TAPE.
KLIK
TO FIND OUT WHERE THE MONSTER'S MOTHER LIVES HERE IN THE CZECH REPUBLIC!
KLIK KLIK

Chapter 6 The Adventures of Magnificent Steiner

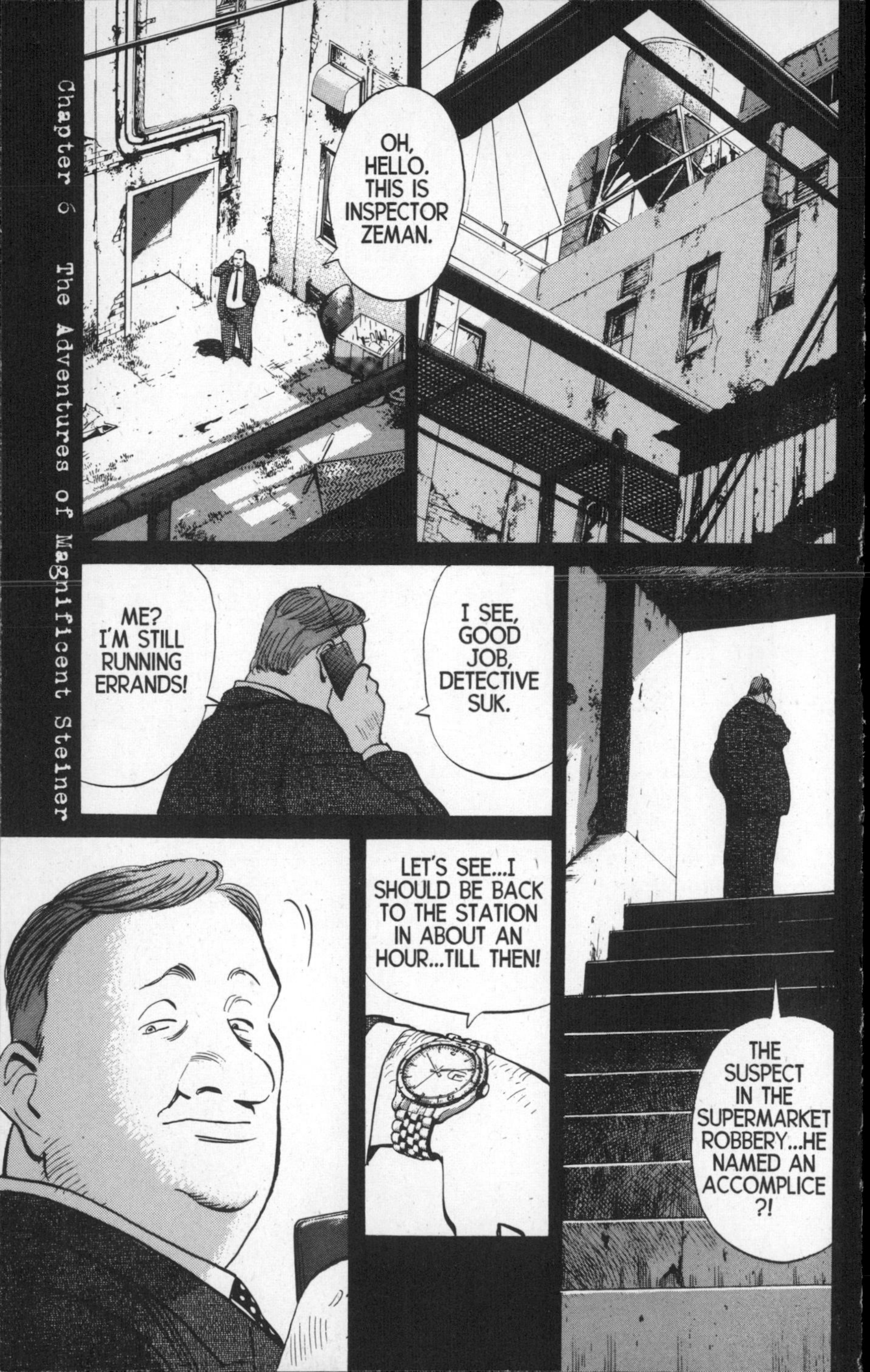
OH, HELLO. THIS IS INSPECTOR ZEMAN.
THE SUSPECT IN THE SUPERMARKET ROBBERY...HE NAMED AN ACCOMPLICE ?!
I SEE, GOOD JOB, DETECTIVE SUK.
ME? I'M STILL RUNNING ERRANDS!
LET'S SEE...I SHOULD BE BACK TO THE STATION IN ABOUT AN HOUR...TILL THEN!

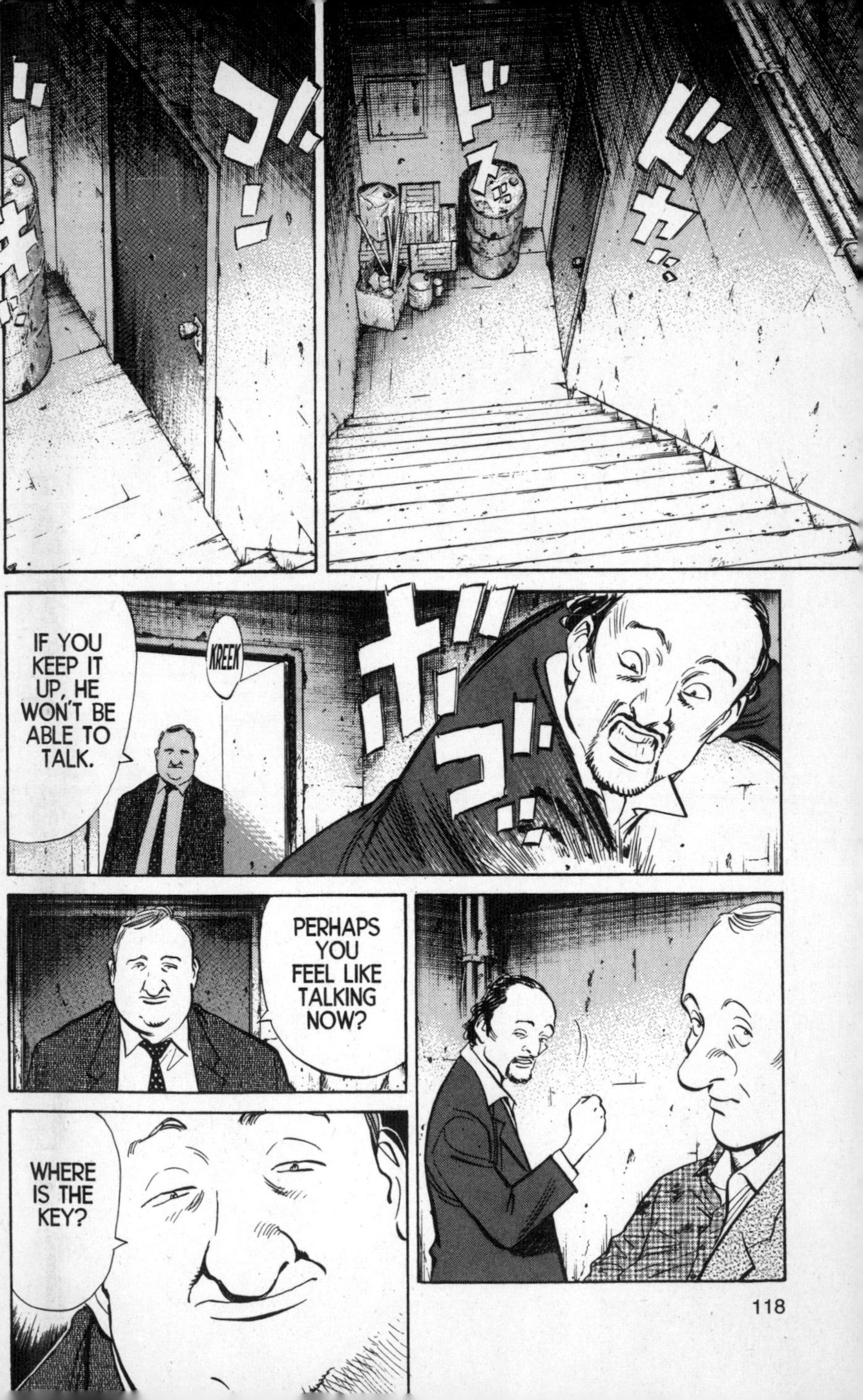
KREEK
IF YOU KEEP IT UP, HE WON'T BE ABLE TO TALK.
PERHAPS YOU FEEL LIKE TALKING NOW?
WHERE IS THE KEY?

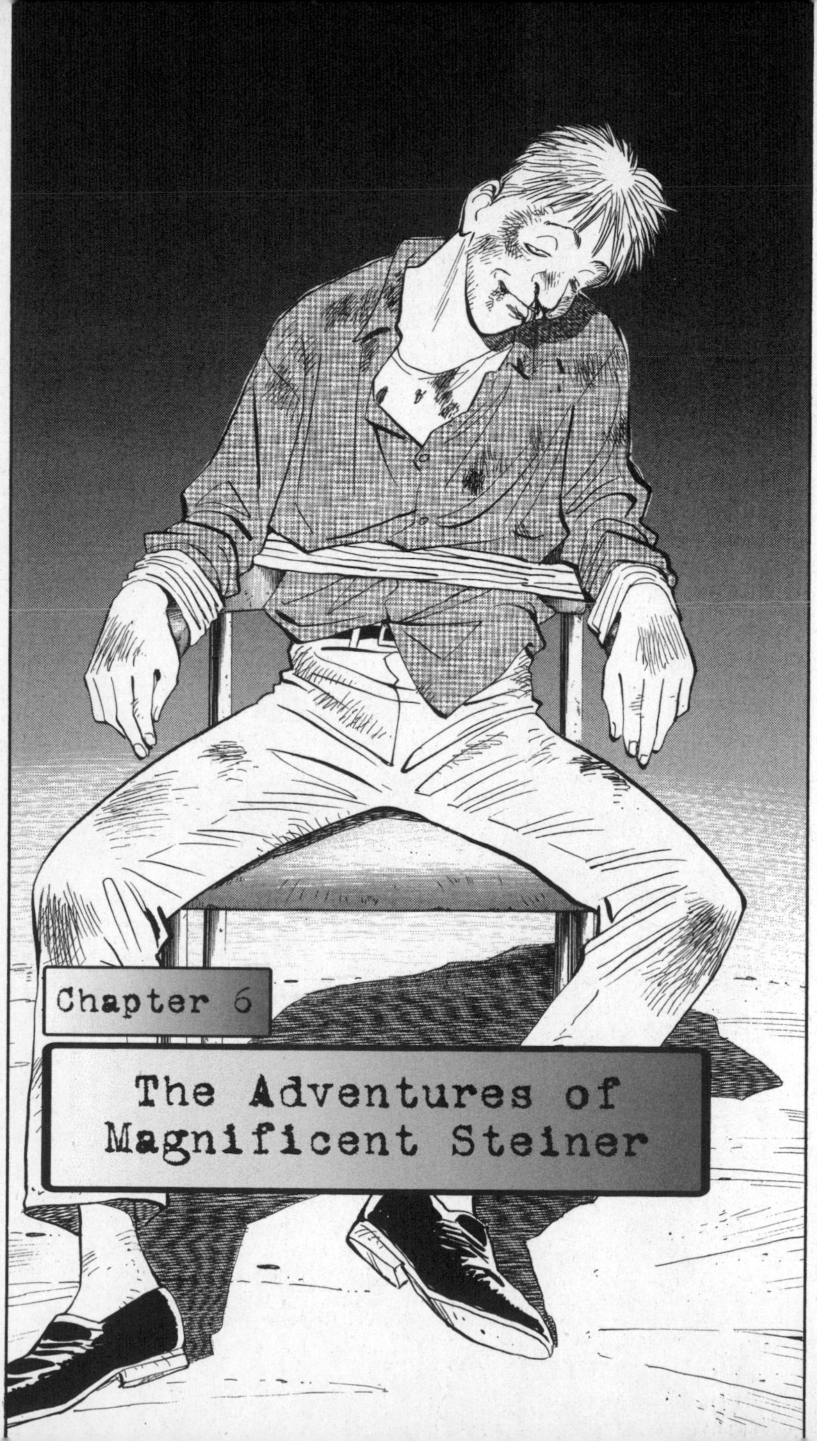
Chapter 6
The Adventures of Magnificent Steiner

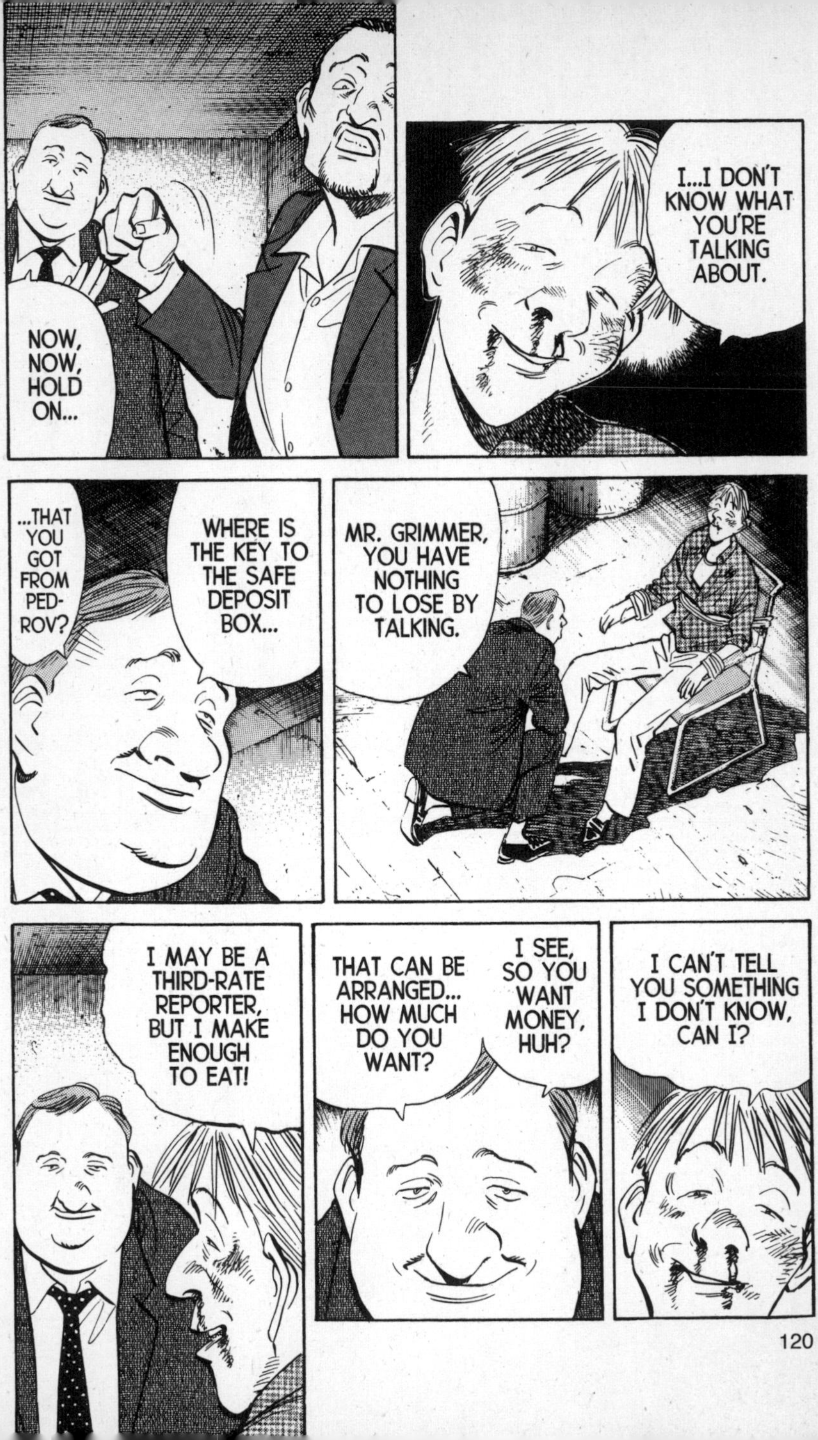
I...I DON'T KNOW WHAT YOU'RE TALKING ABOUT.
NOW, NOW, HOLD ON...
MR. GRIMMER, YOU HAVE NOTHING TO LOSE BY TALKING.
WHERE IS THE KEY TO THE SAFE DEPOSIT BOX...
...THAT YOU GOT FROM PED-ROV?
I CAN'T TELL YOU SOMETHING I DON'T KNOW, CAN I?
I SEE, SO YOU WANT MONEY, HUH?
THAT CAN BE ARRANGED... HOW MUCH DO YOU WANT?
I MAY BE A THIRD-RATE REPORTER, BUT I MAKE ENOUGH TO EAT!

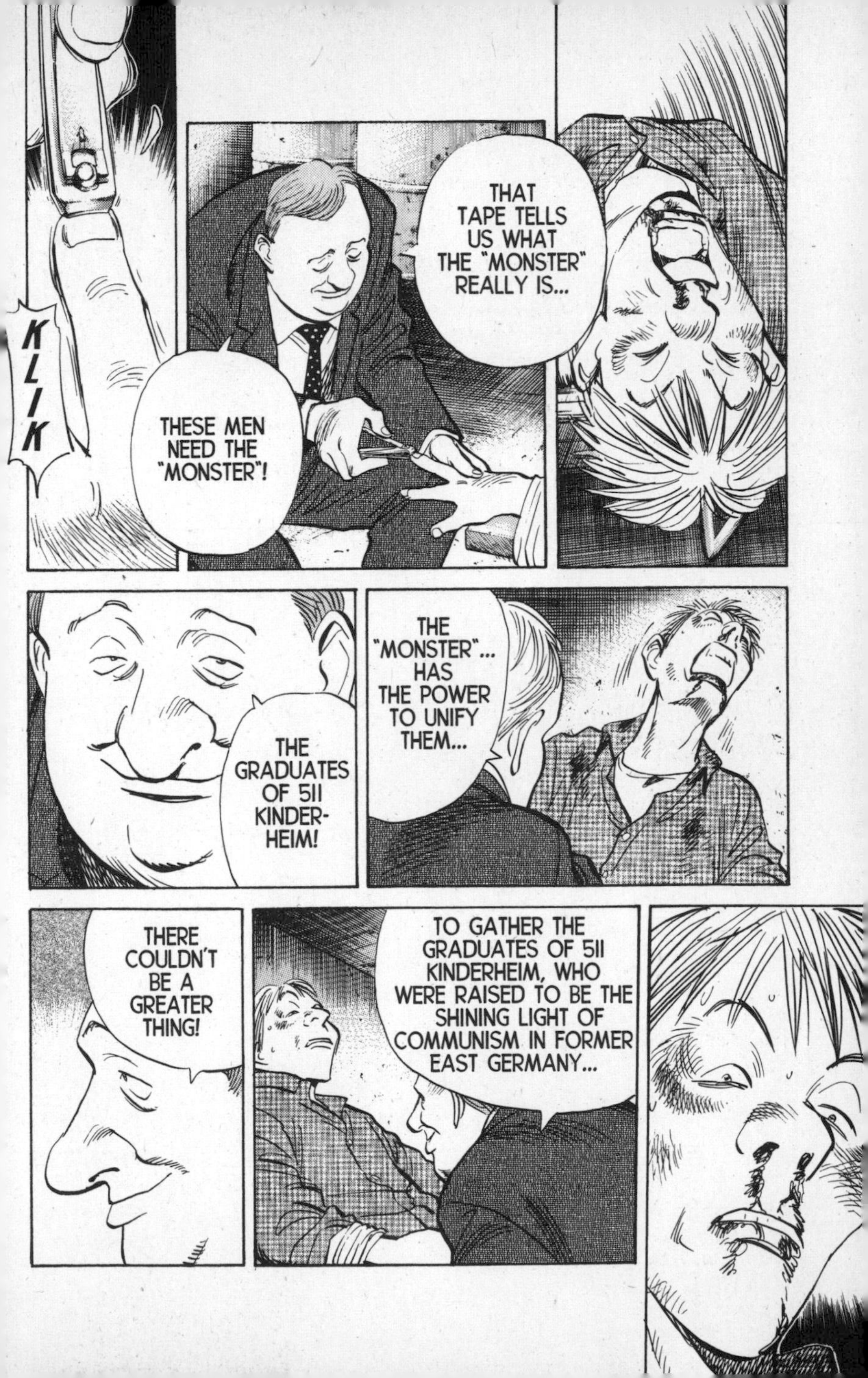
THAT TAPE TELLS US WHAT THE "MONSTER" REALLY IS...
THESE MEN NEED THE "MONSTER"!
KLIK
THE "MONSTER"... HAS THE POWER TO UNIFY THEM...
THE GRADUATES OF 511 KINDERHEIM!
TO GATHER THE GRADUATES OF 511 KINDERHEIM, WHO WERE RAISED TO BE THE SHINING LIGHT OF COMMUNISM IN FORMER EAST GERMANY...
THERE COULDN'T BE A GREATER THING!

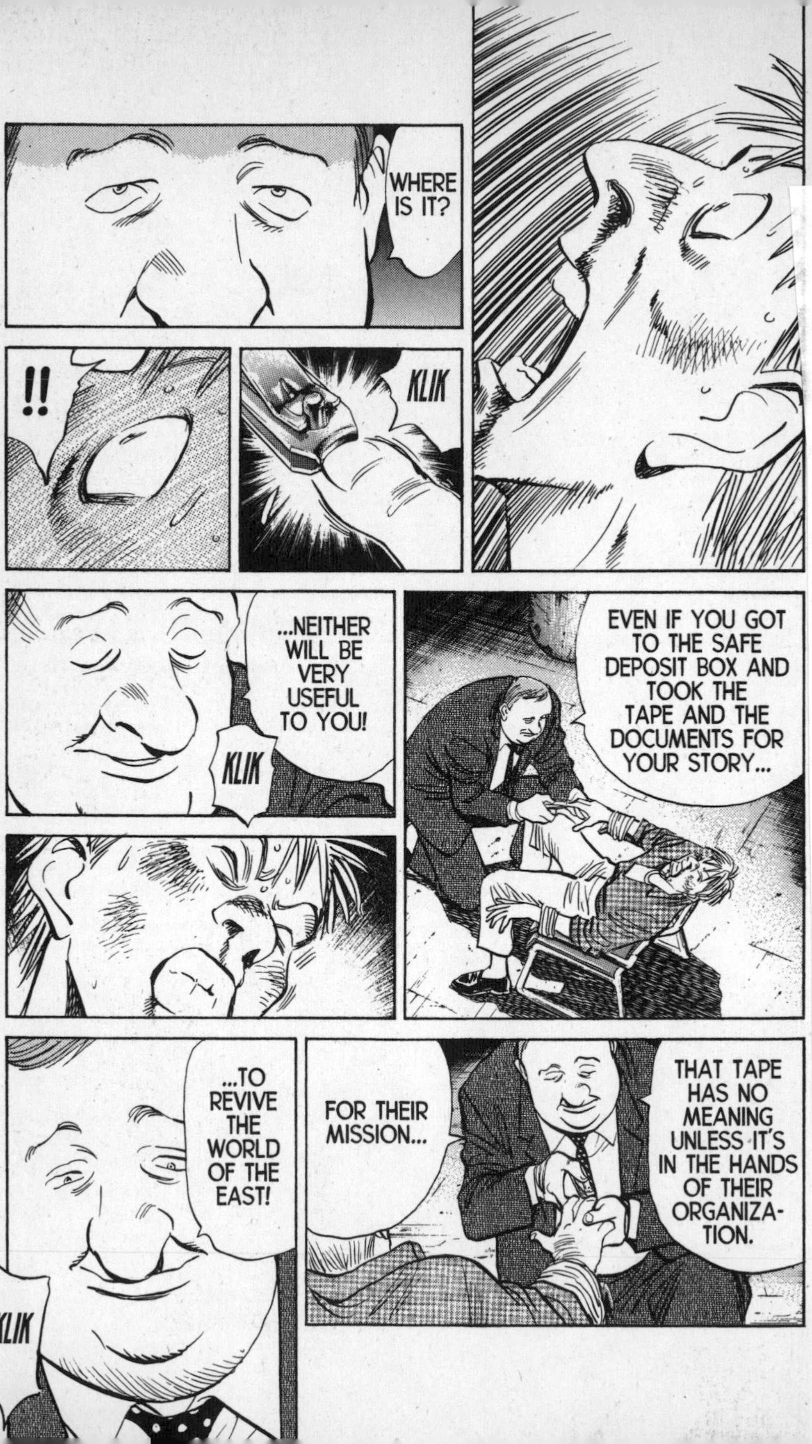
WHERE IS IT?
KLIK
!!
EVEN IF YOU GOT TO THE SAFE DEPOSIT BOX AND TOOK THE TAPE AND THE DOCUMENTS FOR YOUR STORY...
...NEITHER WILL BE VERY USEFUL TO YOU!
KLIK
THAT TAPE HAS NO MEANING UNLESS IT'S IN THE HANDS OF THEIR ORGANIZA-TION.
FOR THEIR MISSION...
...TO REVIVE THE WORLD OF THE EAST!
KLIK

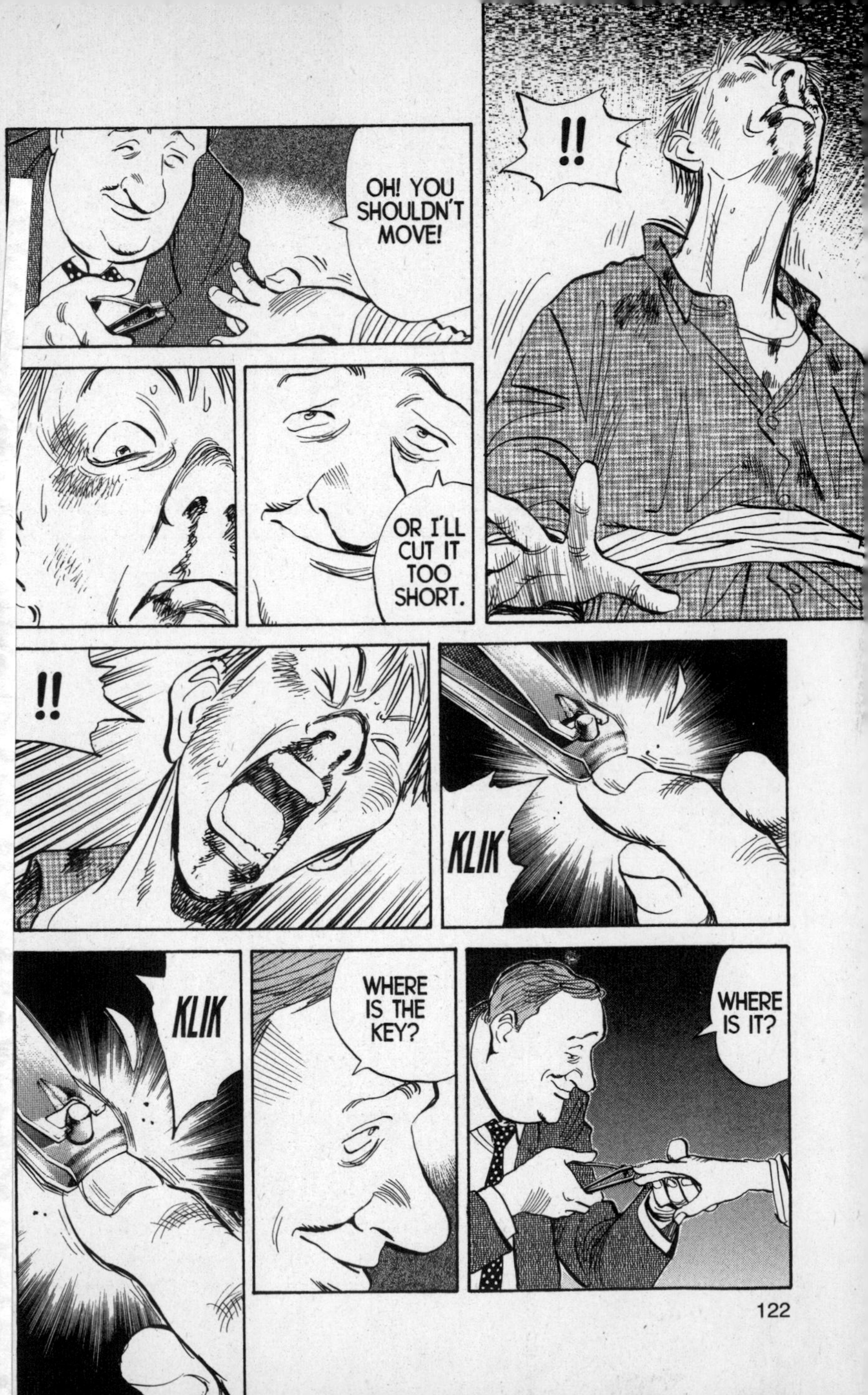
OH! YOU SHOULDN'T MOVE!
OR I'LL CUT IT TOO SHORT.
!!
!!
KLIK
KLIK
WHERE IS THE KEY?
WHERE IS IT?

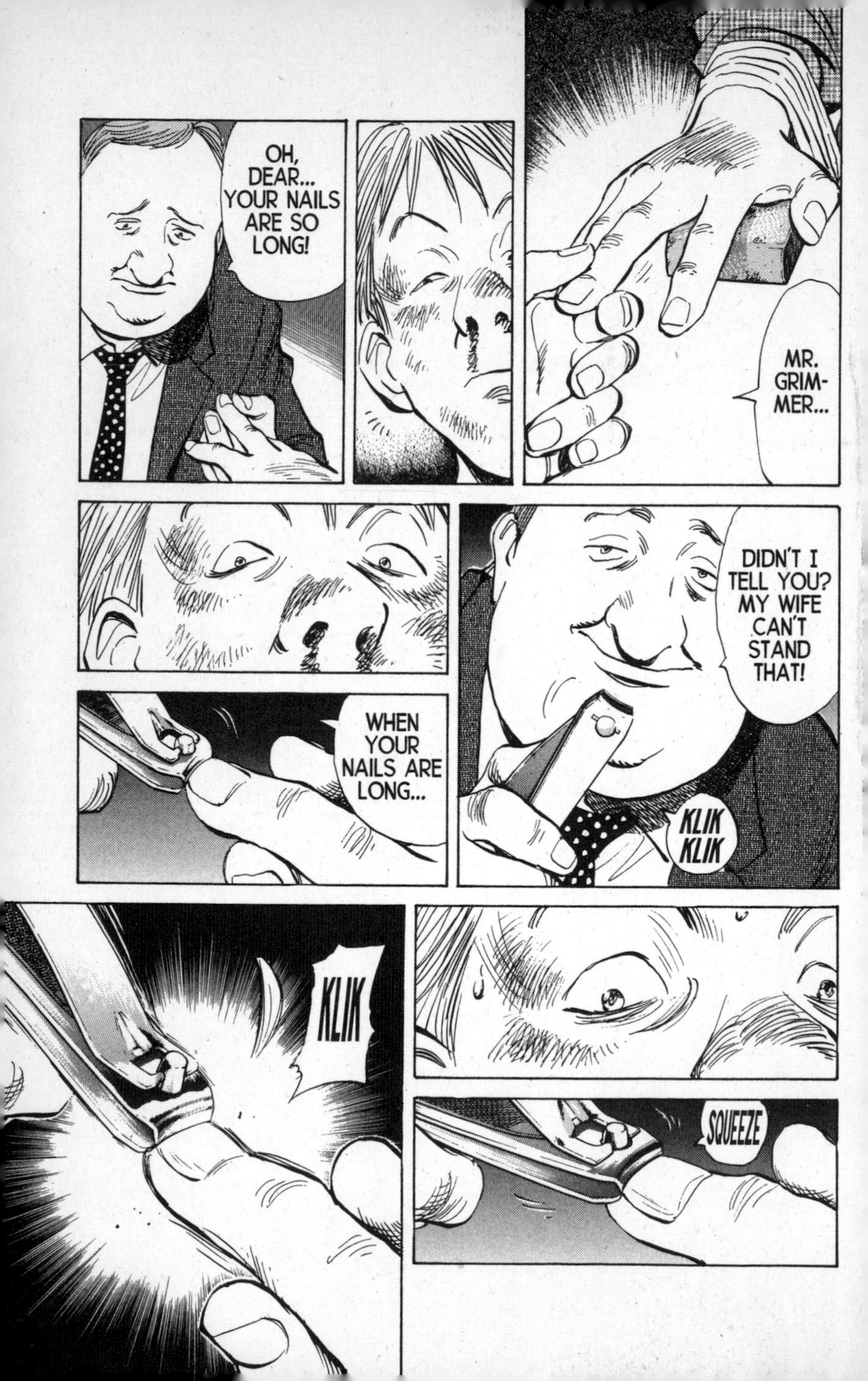
OH, DEAR... YOUR NAILS ARE SO LONG!
MR. GRIMMER...
WHEN YOUR NAILS ARE LONG...
DIDN'T I TELL YOU? MY WIFE CAN'T STAND THAT!
KLIK KLIK
KLIK
SQUEEZE

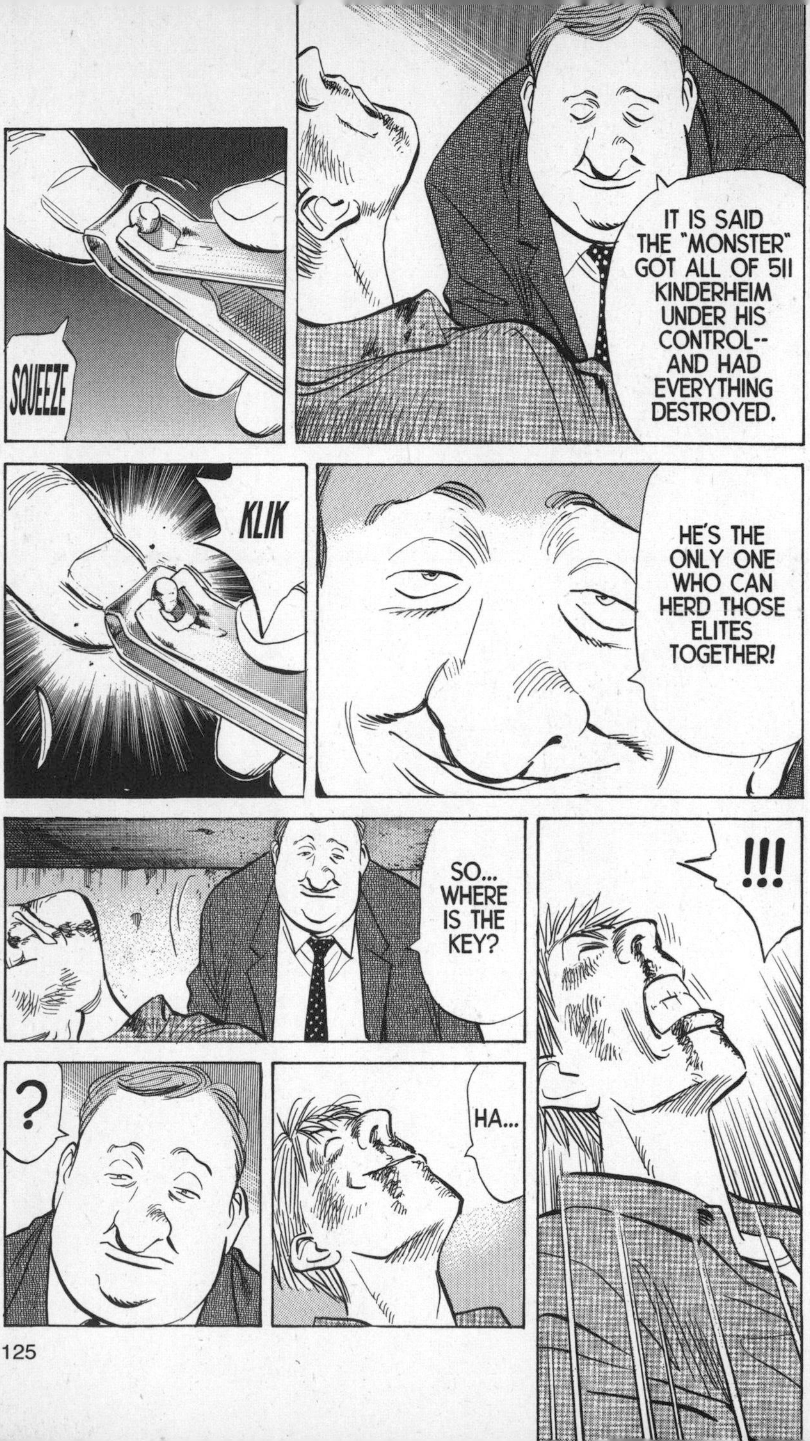
SQUEEZE
IT IS SAID THE "MONSTER" GOT ALL OF 511 KINDERHEIM UNDER HIS CONTROL-- AND HAD EVERYTHING DESTROYED.
KLIK
HE'S THE ONLY ONE WHO CAN HERD THOSE ELITES TOGETHER!
SO... WHERE IS THE KEY?
?
HA...
!!!

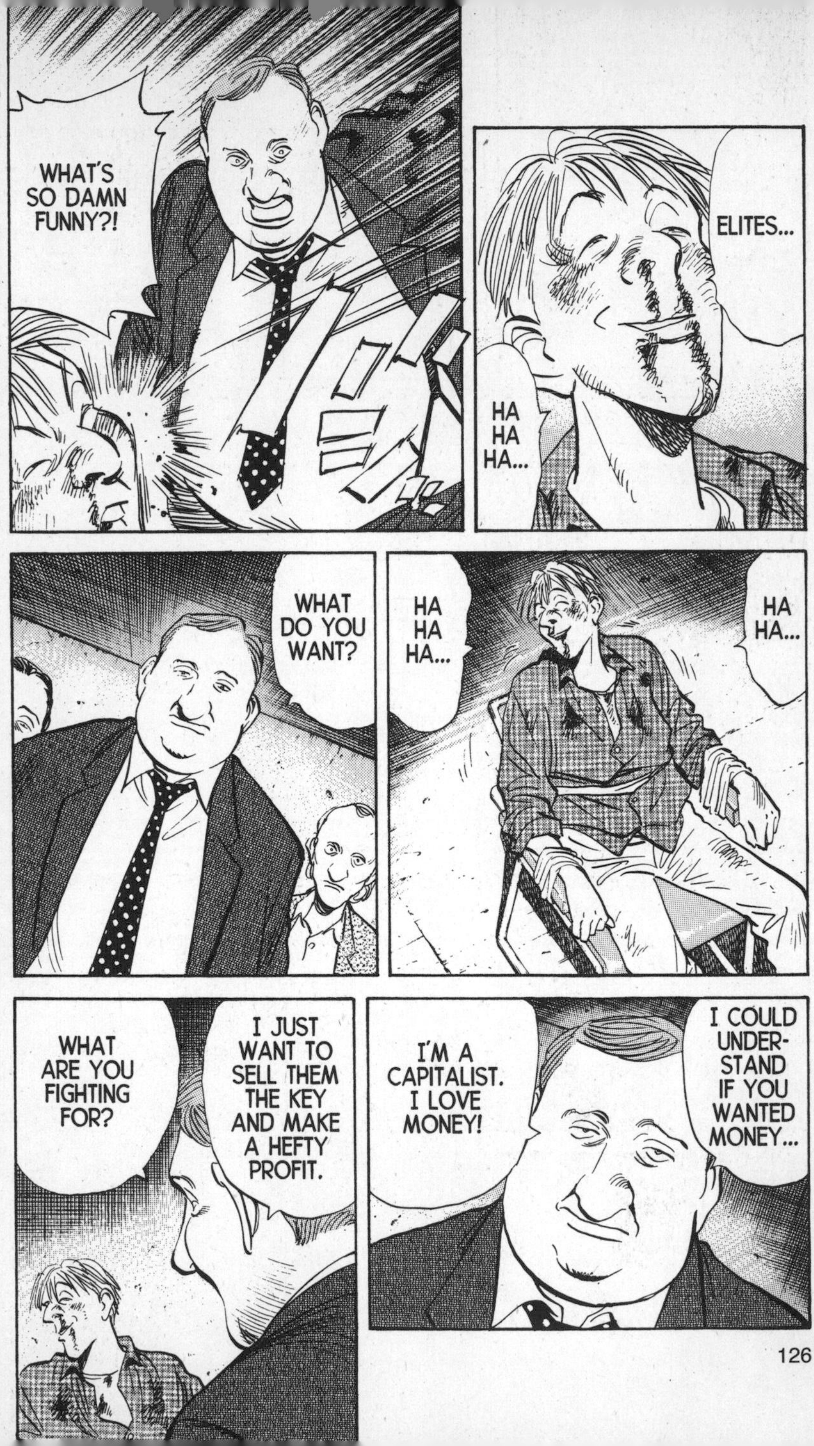
ELITES...
HA HA HA...
WHAT'S SO DAMN FUNNY?!
HA HA...
HA HA HA...
WHAT DO YOU WANT?
I COULD UNDER-STAND IF YOU WANTED MONEY...
I'M A CAPITALIST. I LOVE MONEY!
I JUST WANT TO SELL THEM THE KEY AND MAKE A HEFTY PROFIT.
WHAT ARE YOU FIGHTING FOR?

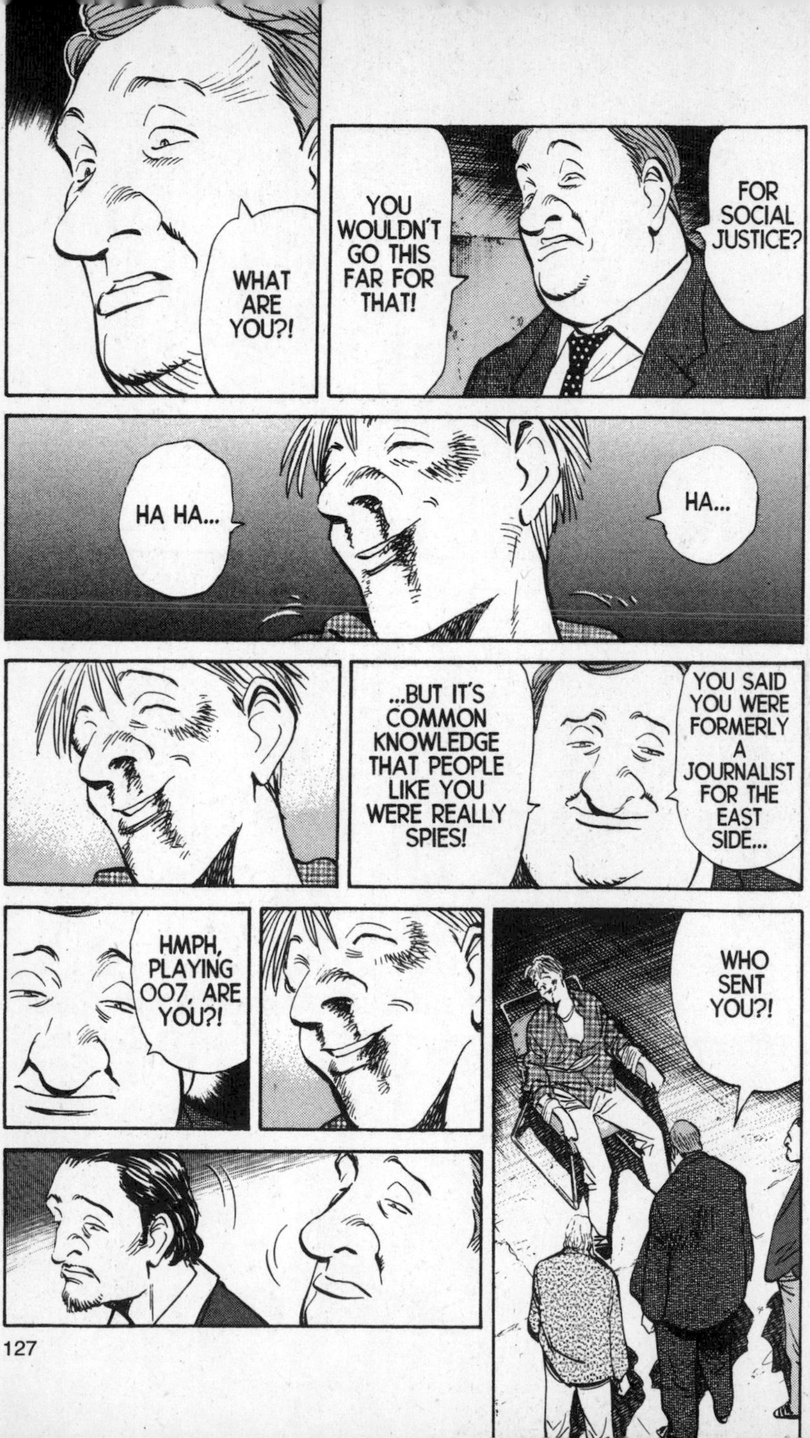
FOR SOCIAL JUSTICE?
YOU WOULDN'T GO THIS FAR FOR THAT!
WHAT ARE YOU?!
HA...
HA HA...
YOU SAID YOU WERE FORMERLY A JOURNALIST FOR THE EAST SIDE...
...BUT IT'S COMMON KNOWLEDGE THAT PEOPLE LIKE YOU WERE REALLY SPIES!
WHO SENT YOU?!
HMPH, PLAYING 007, ARE YOU?!

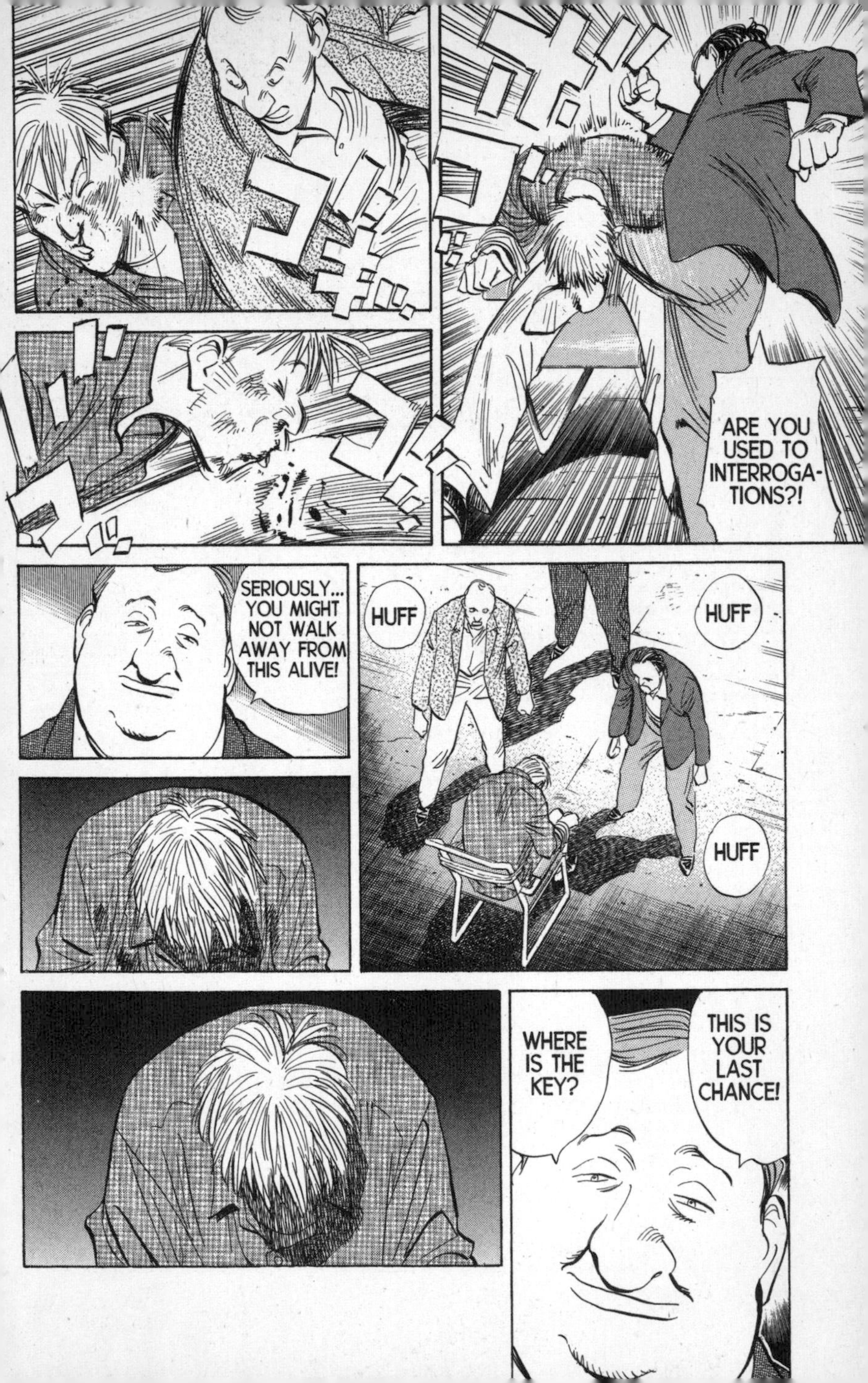
ARE YOU USED TO INTERROGA-TIONS?!
HUFF
HUFF
HUFF
SERIOUSLY... YOU MIGHT NOT WALK AWAY FROM THIS ALIVE!
THIS IS YOUR LAST CHANCE!
WHERE IS THE KEY?

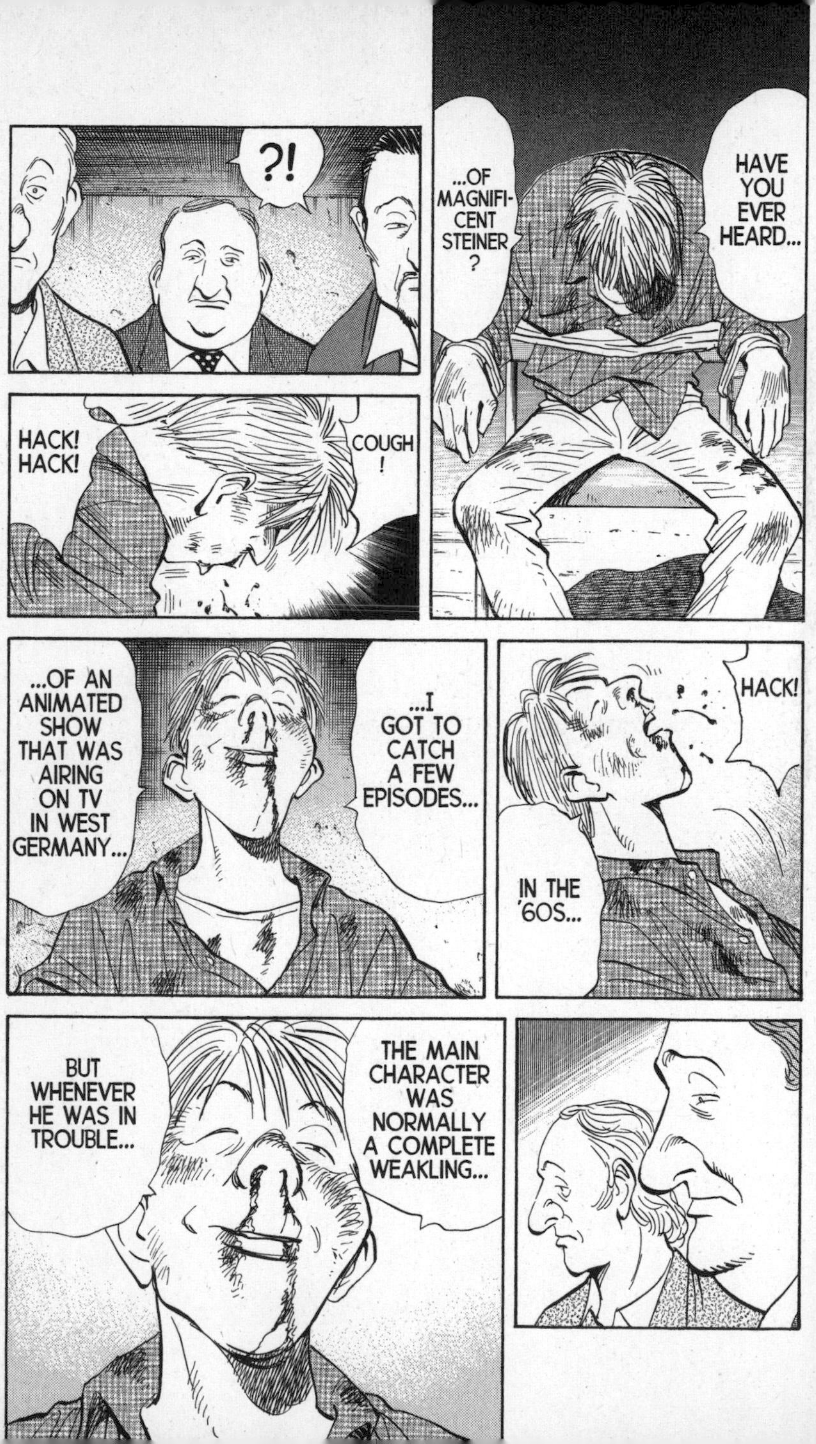
HAVE YOU EVER HEARD...
...OF MAGNIFICENT STEINER?
?!
COUGH!
HACK! HACK!
HACK!
IN THE '60S...
...I GOT TO CATCH A FEW EPISODES...
...OF AN ANIMATED SHOW THAT WAS AIRING ON TV IN WEST GERMANY...
THE MAIN CHARACTER WAS NORMALLY A COMPLETE WEAKLING...
BUT WHENEVER HE WAS IN TROUBLE...

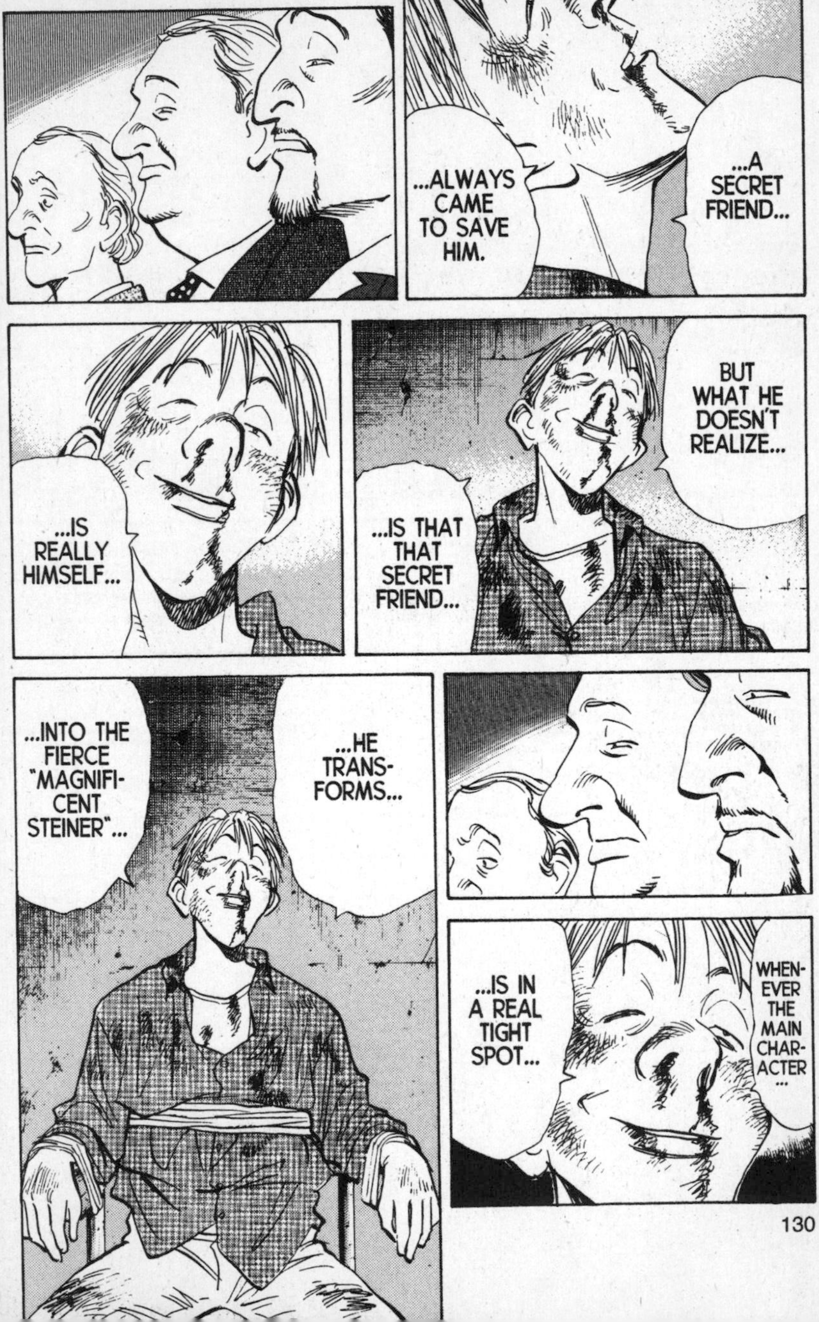
...A SECRET FRIEND...
...ALWAYS CAME TO SAVE HIM.
BUT WHAT HE DOESN'T REALIZE...
...IS THAT THAT SECRET FRIEND...
...IS REALLY HIMSELF...
WHEN-EVER THE MAIN CHAR-ACTER...
...IS IN A REAL TIGHT SPOT...
...HE TRANS-FORMS...
...INTO THE FIERCE "MAGNIFI-CENT STEINER"...

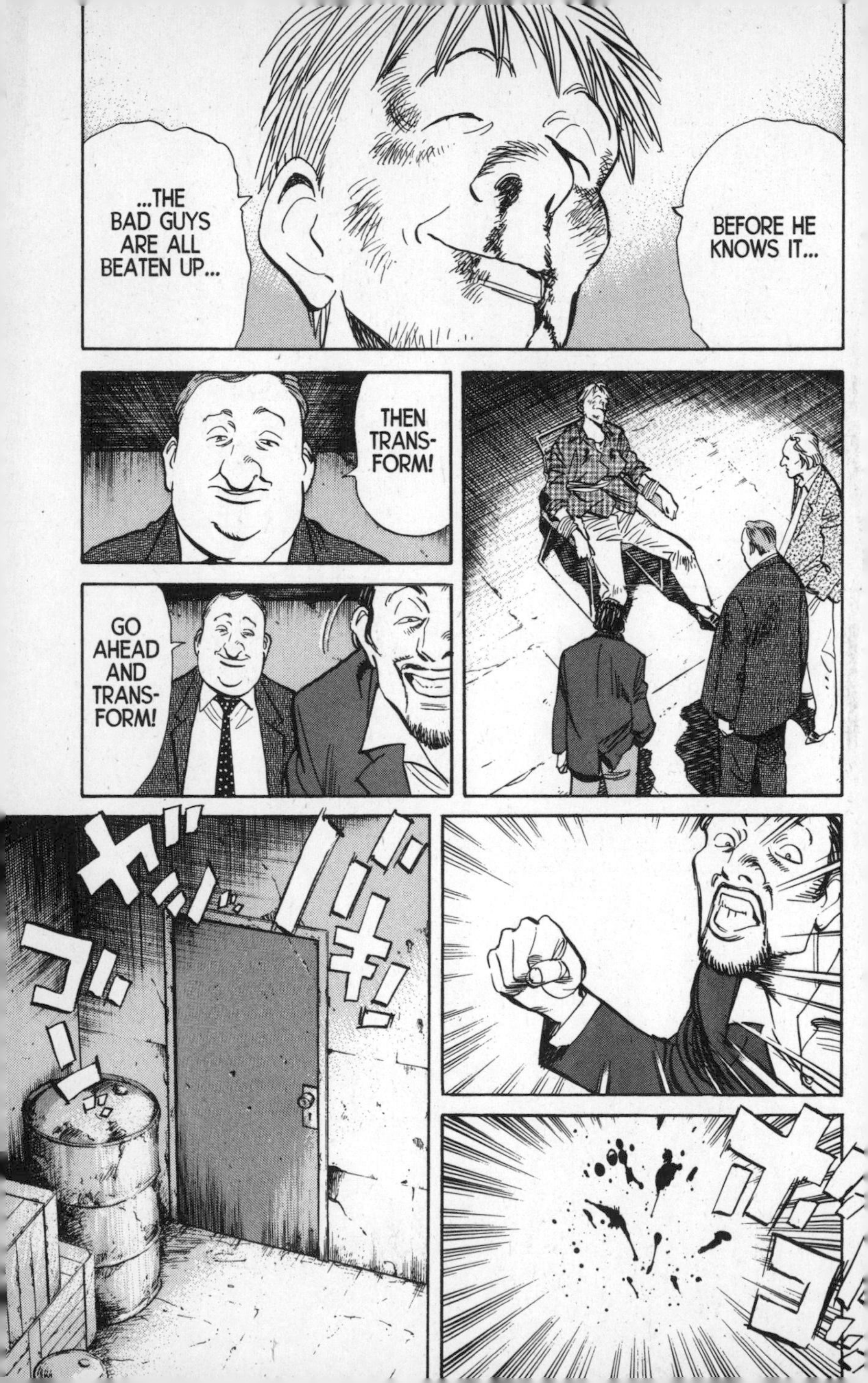
BEFORE HE KNOWS IT...
...THE BAD GUYS ARE ALL BEATEN UP...
THEN TRANS-FORM!
GO AHEAD AND TRANS-FORM!

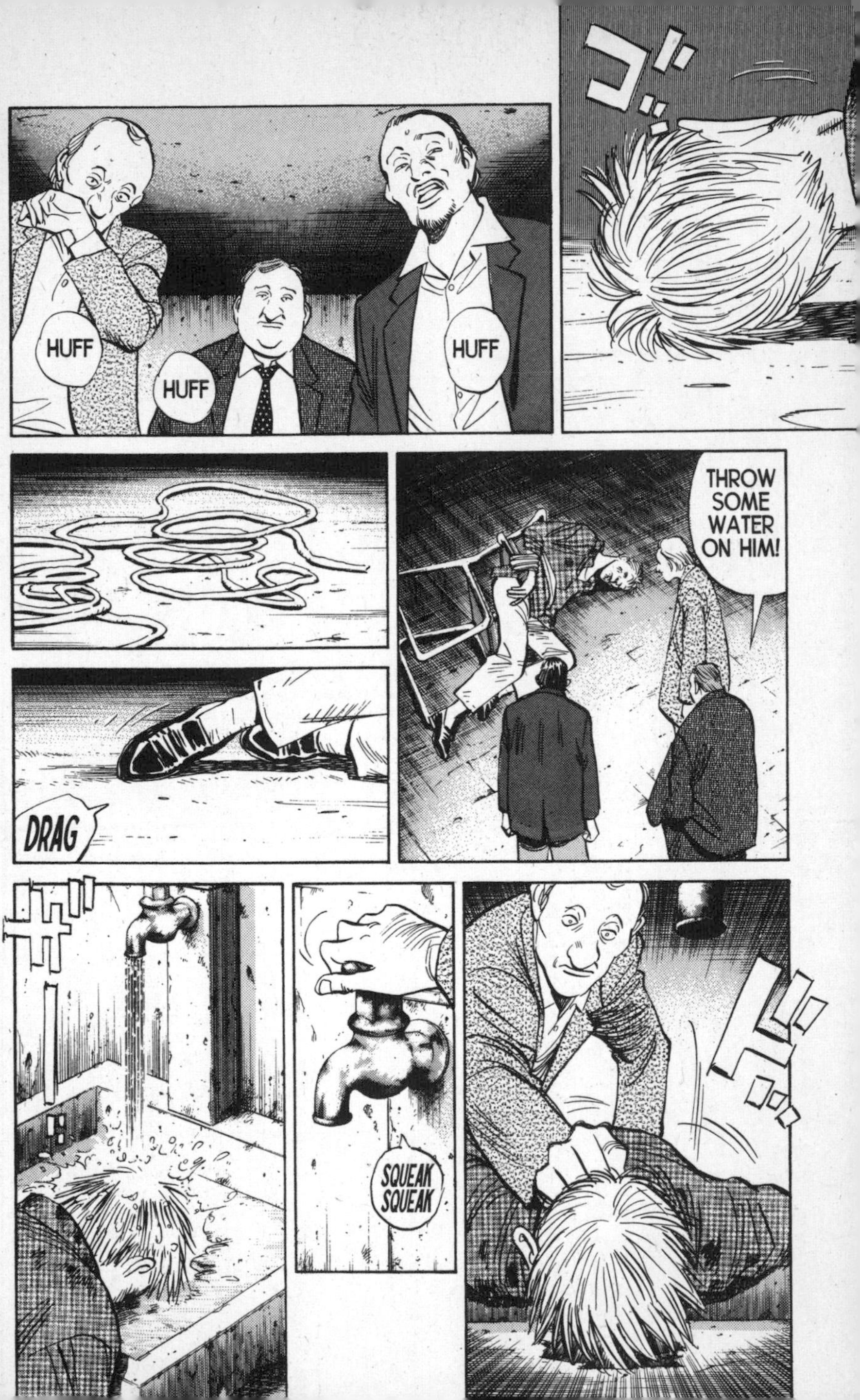
HUFF
HUFF
HUFF
THROW SOME WATER ON HIM!
DRAG
SQUEAK SQUEAK

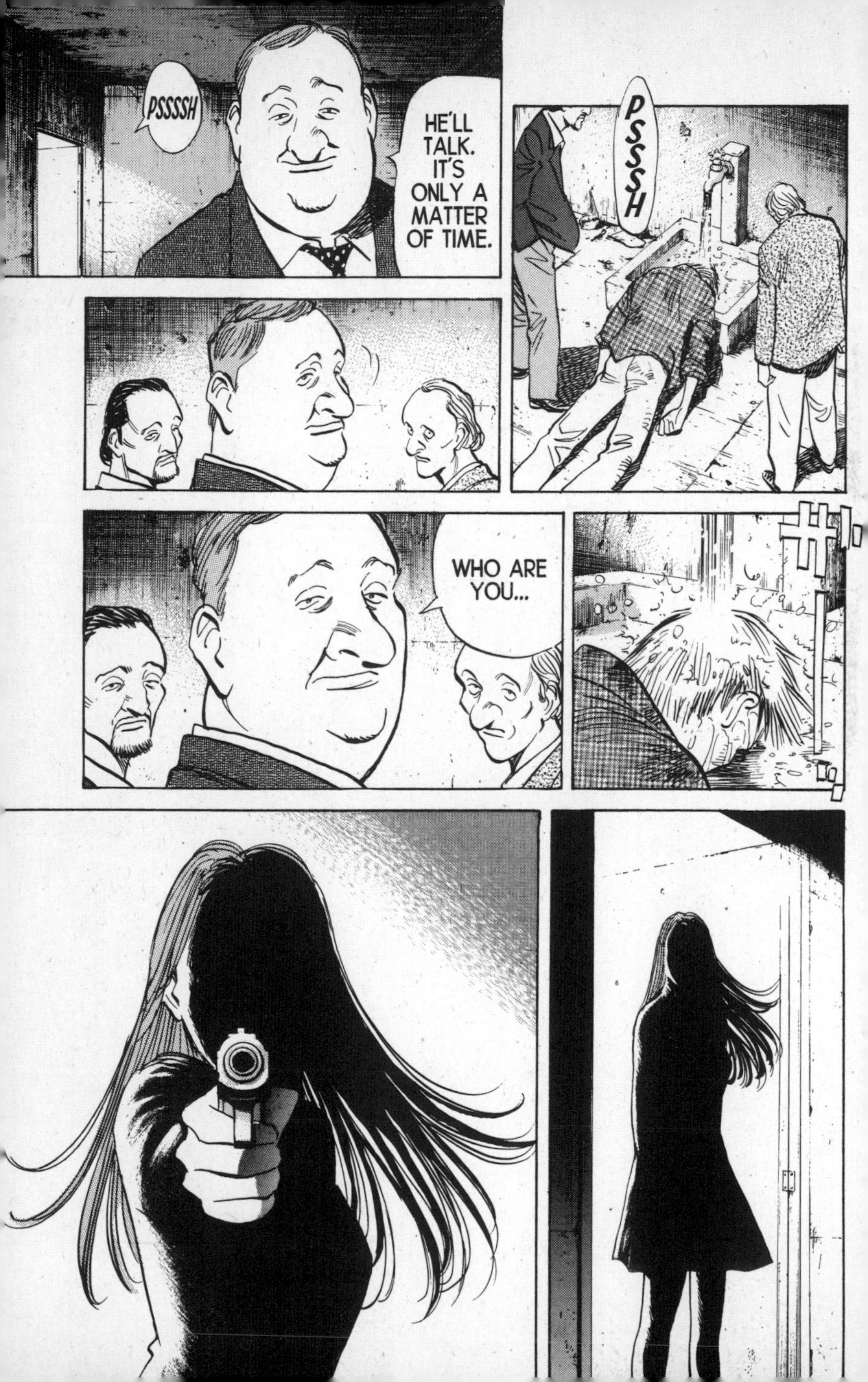
PSSSH
PSSSSH
HE'LL TALK. IT'S ONLY A MATTER OF TIME.
WHO ARE YOU...

UGH
...

UGHHH...

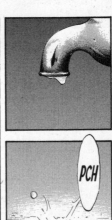

PCH

PCH

PCH

134

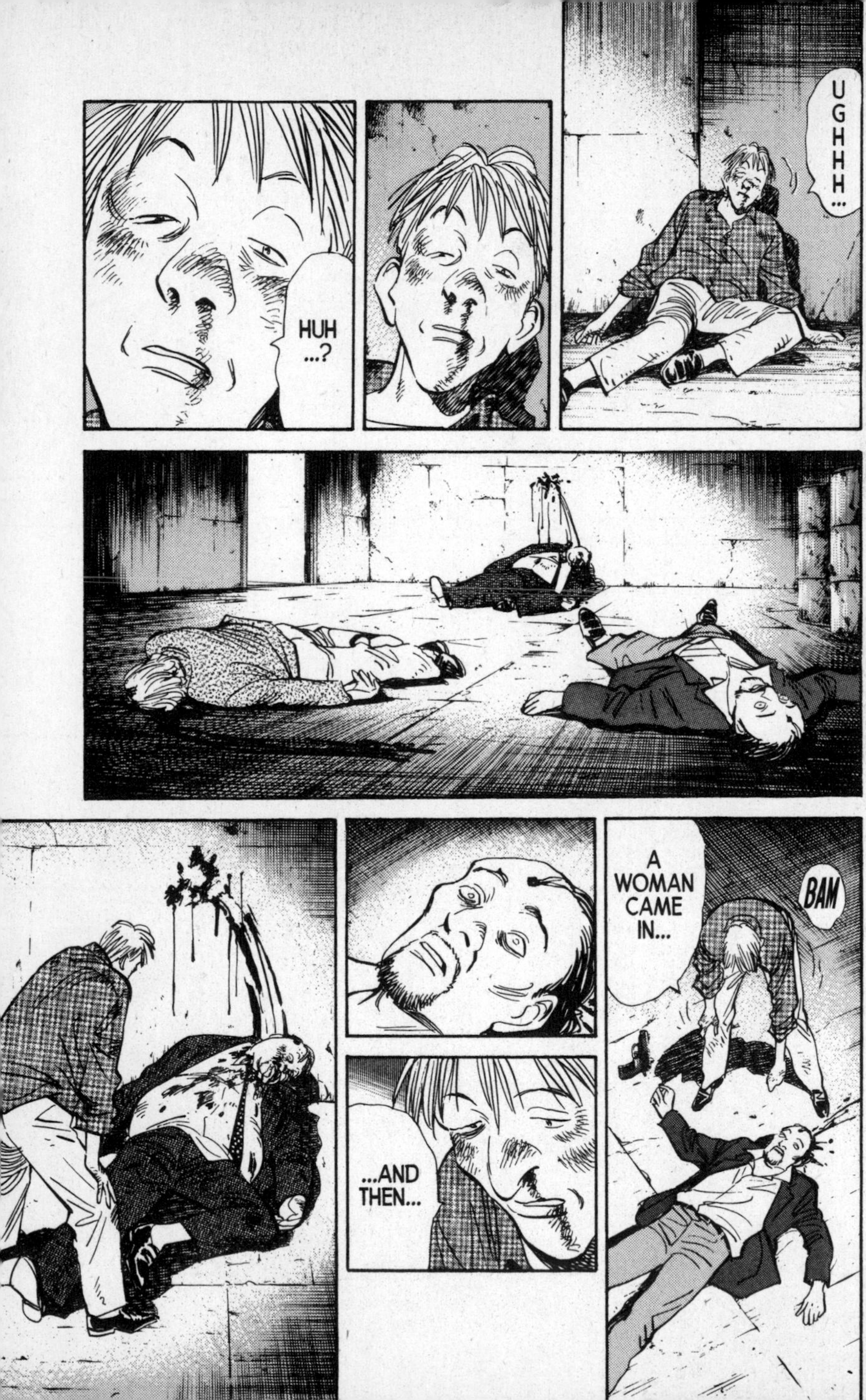
UGHHH...
HUH ...?
A WOMAN CAME IN...
BAM
...AND THEN...

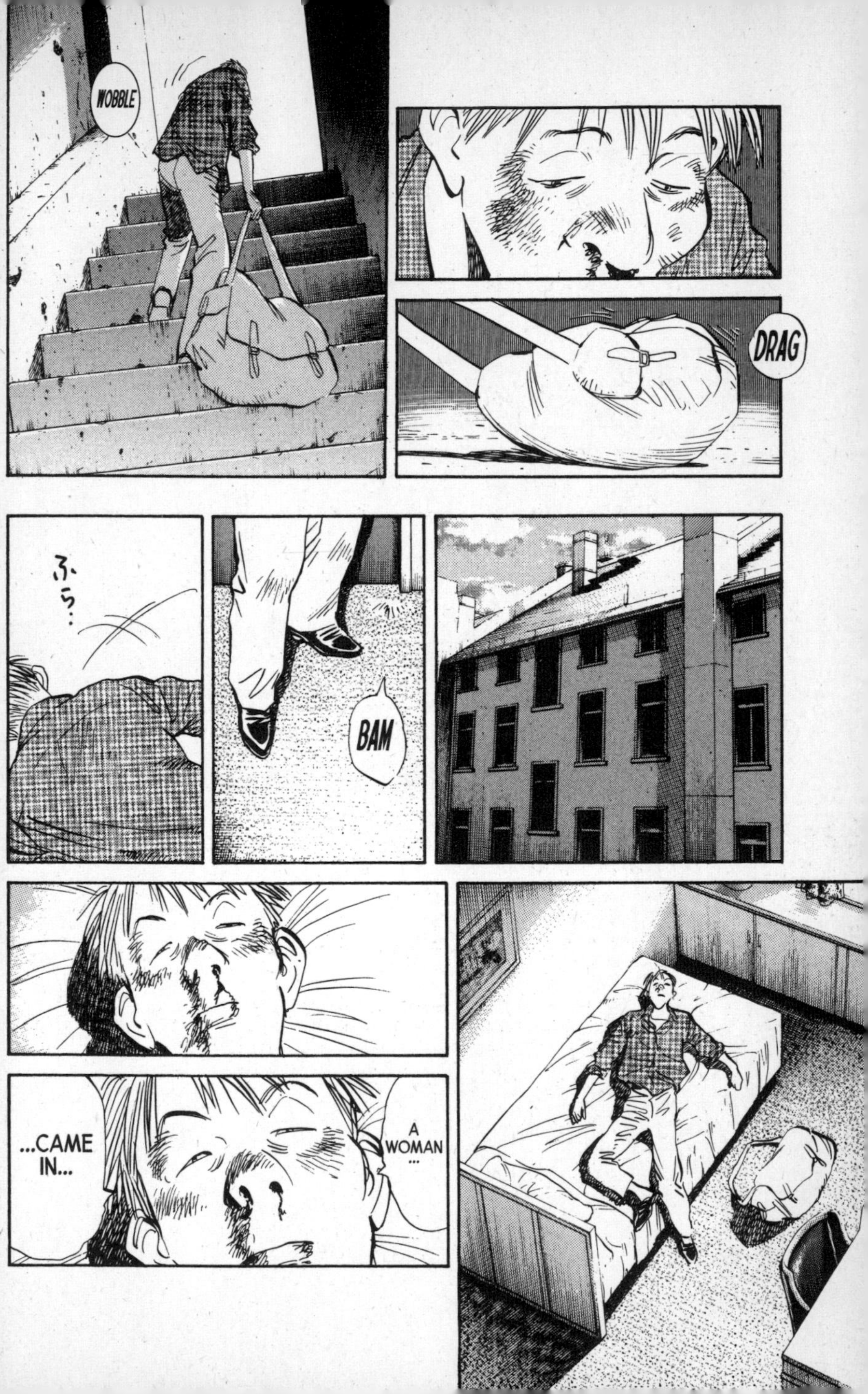
DRAG
WOBBLE
BAM
ふら…
A WOMAN ...
...CAME IN...

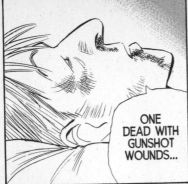

ONE GUNSHOT...
ONE DEAD WITH GUNSHOT WOUNDS...
THE OTHER TWO BODIES...
...WEREN'T SHOT...
...BUT WERE BEATEN TO DEATH...

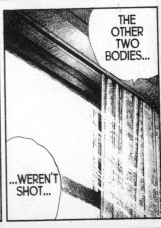

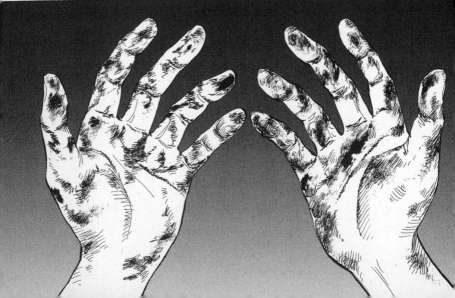

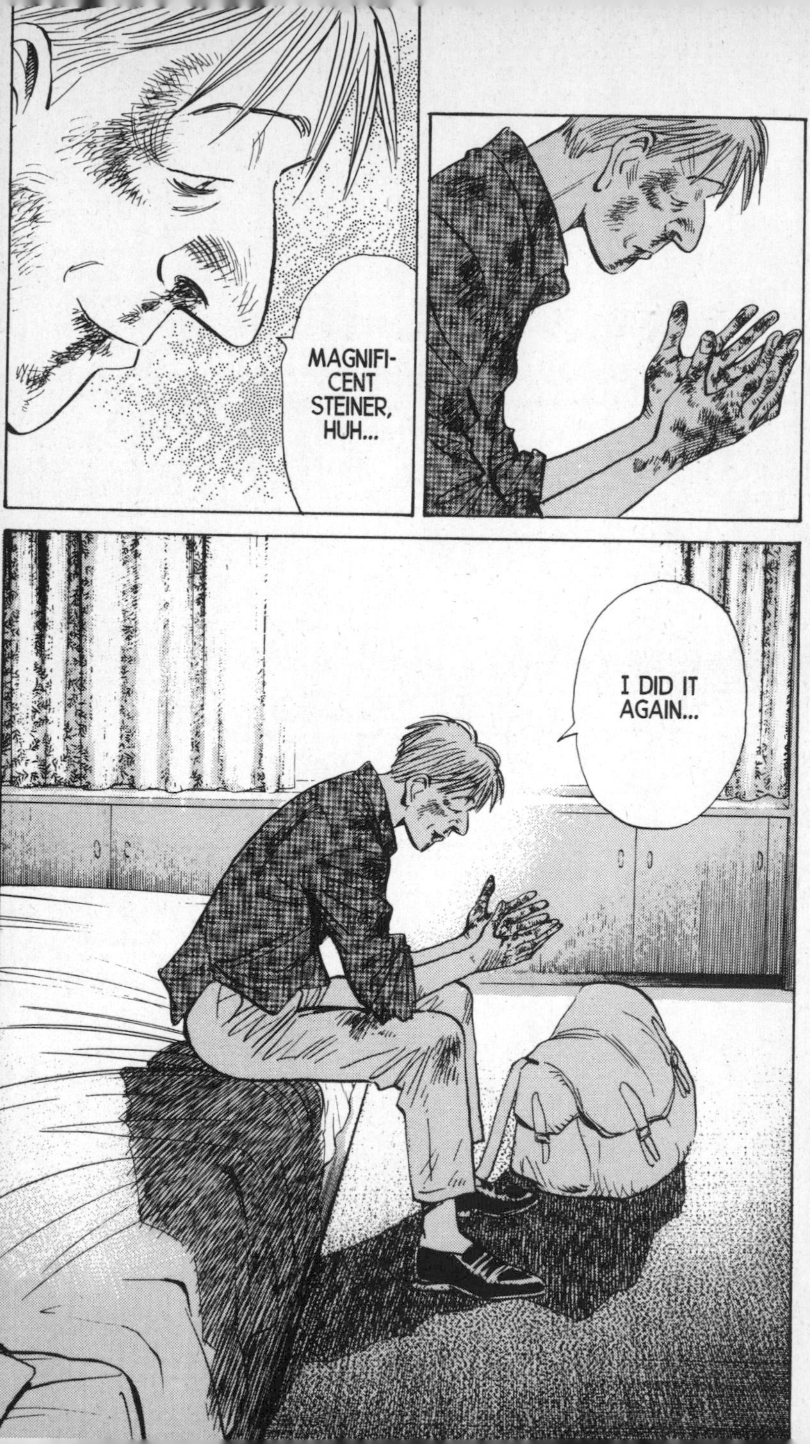
MAGNIFI-CENT STEINER, HUH...
I DID IT AGAIN...

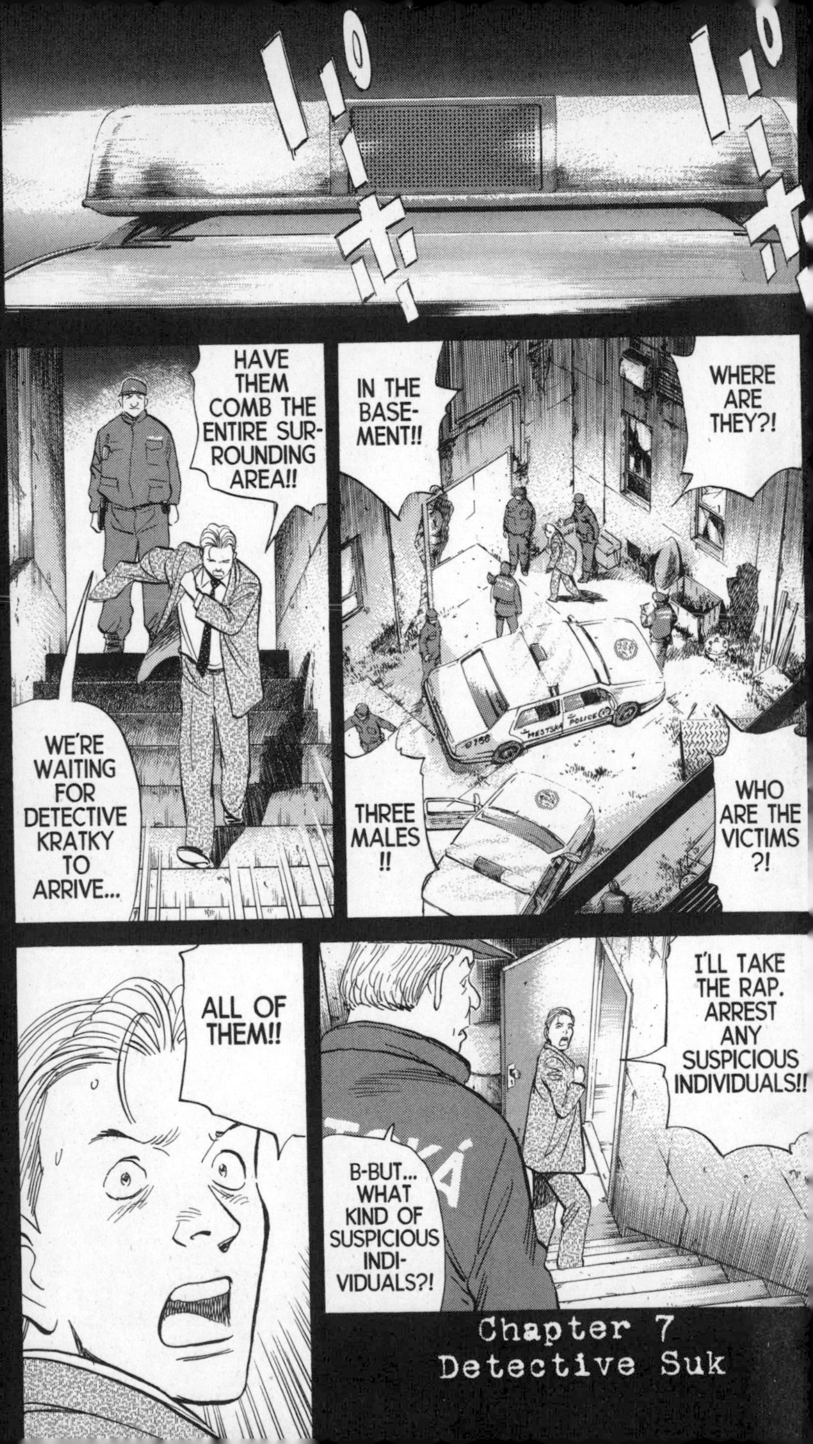
WHERE ARE THEY?!
IN THE BASEMENT!!
WHO ARE THE VICTIMS?!
THREE MALES!!
HAVE THEM COMB THE ENTIRE SURROUNDING AREA!!
WE'RE WAITING FOR DETECTIVE KRATKY TO ARRIVE...
I'LL TAKE THE RAP. ARREST ANY SUSPICIOUS INDIVIDUALS!!
B-BUT... WHAT KIND OF SUSPICIOUS INDIVIDUALS?!
ALL OF THEM!!

Chapter 7
Detective Suk

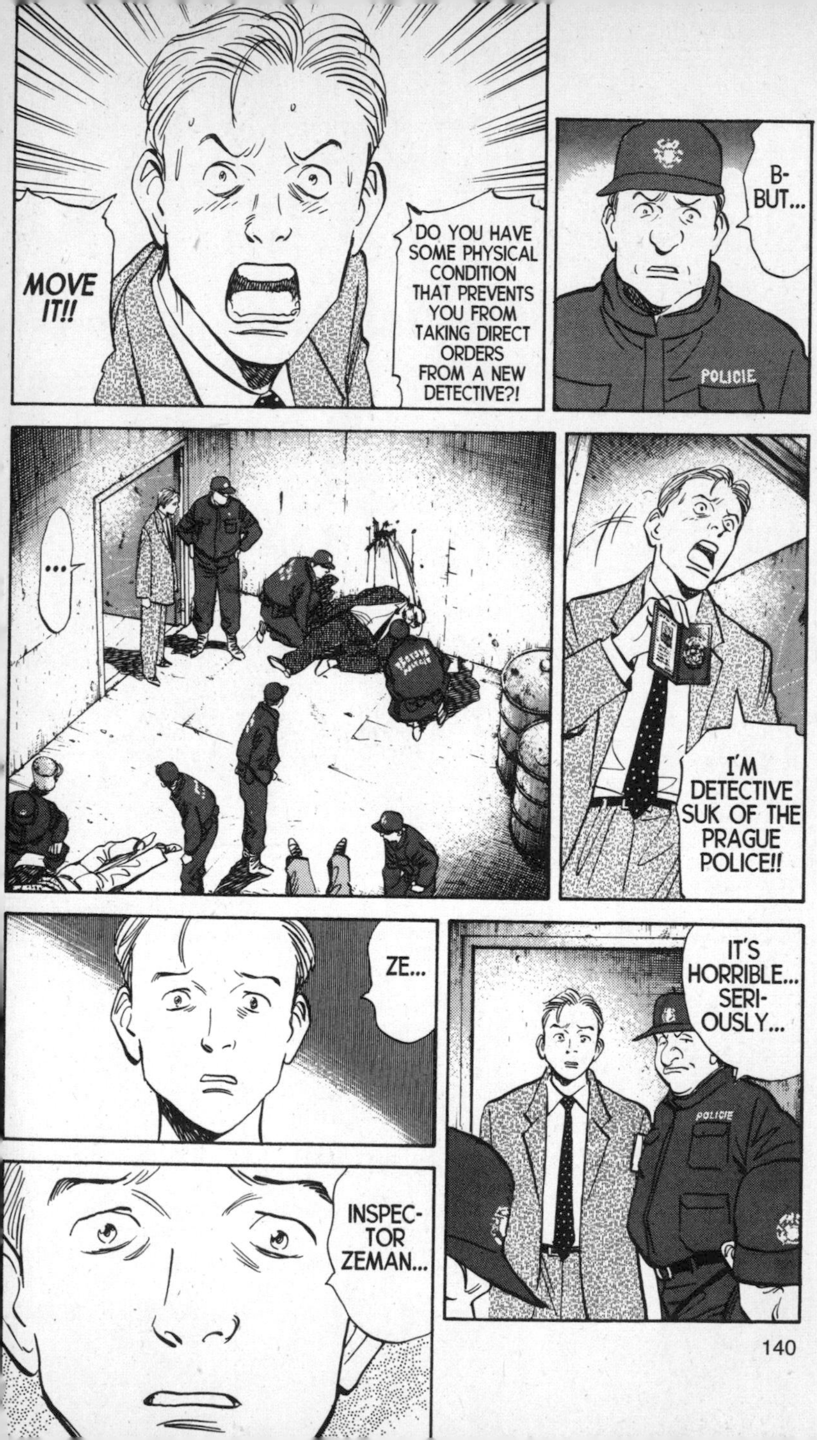
B- BUT...
DO YOU HAVE SOME PHYSICAL CONDITION THAT PREVENTS YOU FROM TAKING DIRECT ORDERS FROM A NEW DETECTIVE?!
MOVE IT!!
I'M DETECTIVE SUK OF THE PRAGUE POLICE!!
...
IT'S HORRIBLE... SERIOUSLY...
ZE...
INSPECTOR ZEMAN...

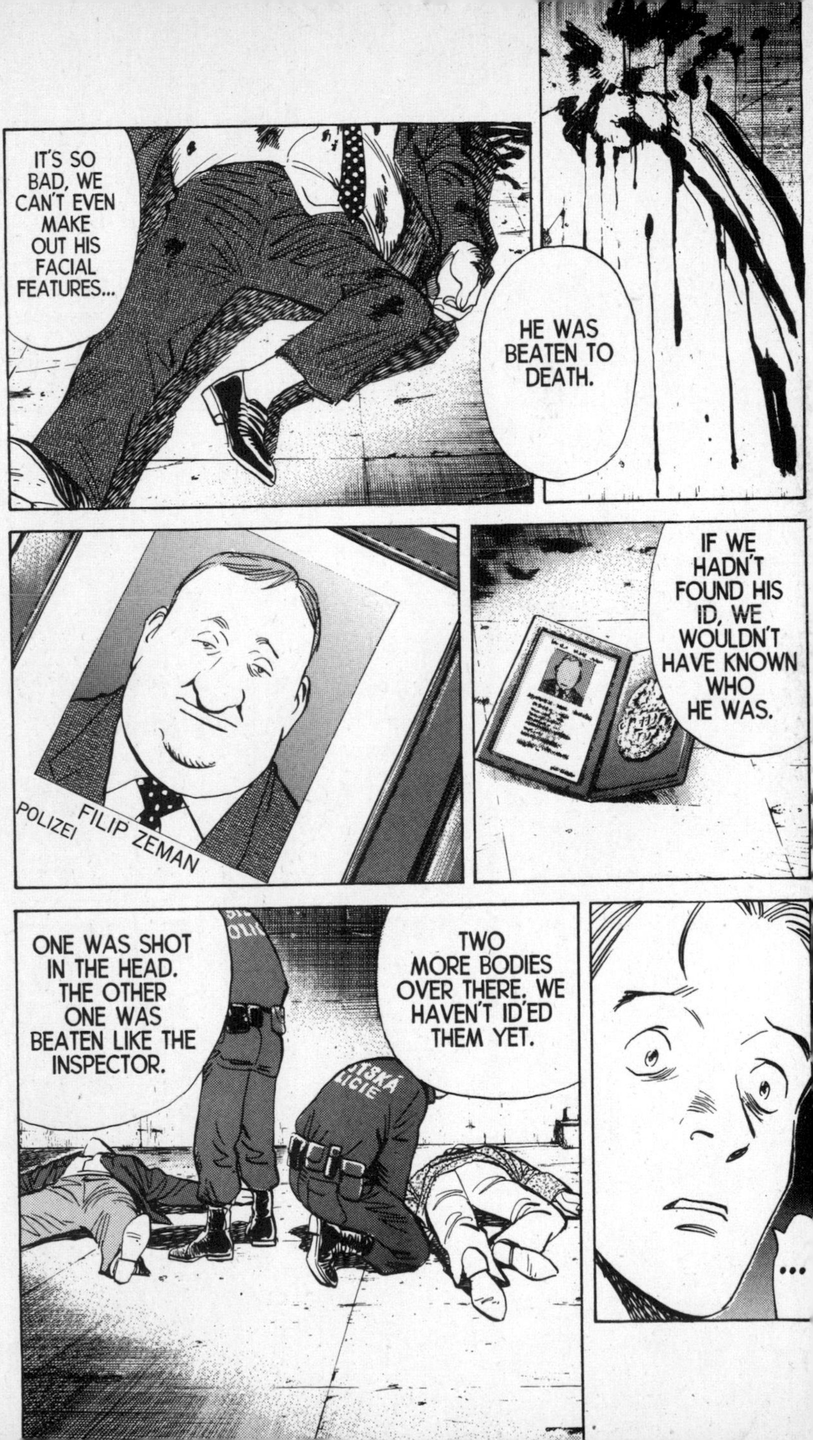
HE WAS BEATEN TO DEATH.
IT'S SO BAD, WE CAN'T EVEN MAKE OUT HIS FACIAL FEATURES...
IF WE HADN'T FOUND HIS ID, WE WOULDN'T HAVE KNOWN WHO HE WAS.
FILIP ZEMAN
POLIZEI
...
TWO MORE BODIES OVER THERE. WE HAVEN'T ID'ED THEM YET.
ONE WAS SHOT IN THE HEAD. THE OTHER ONE WAS BEATEN LIKE THE INSPECTOR.

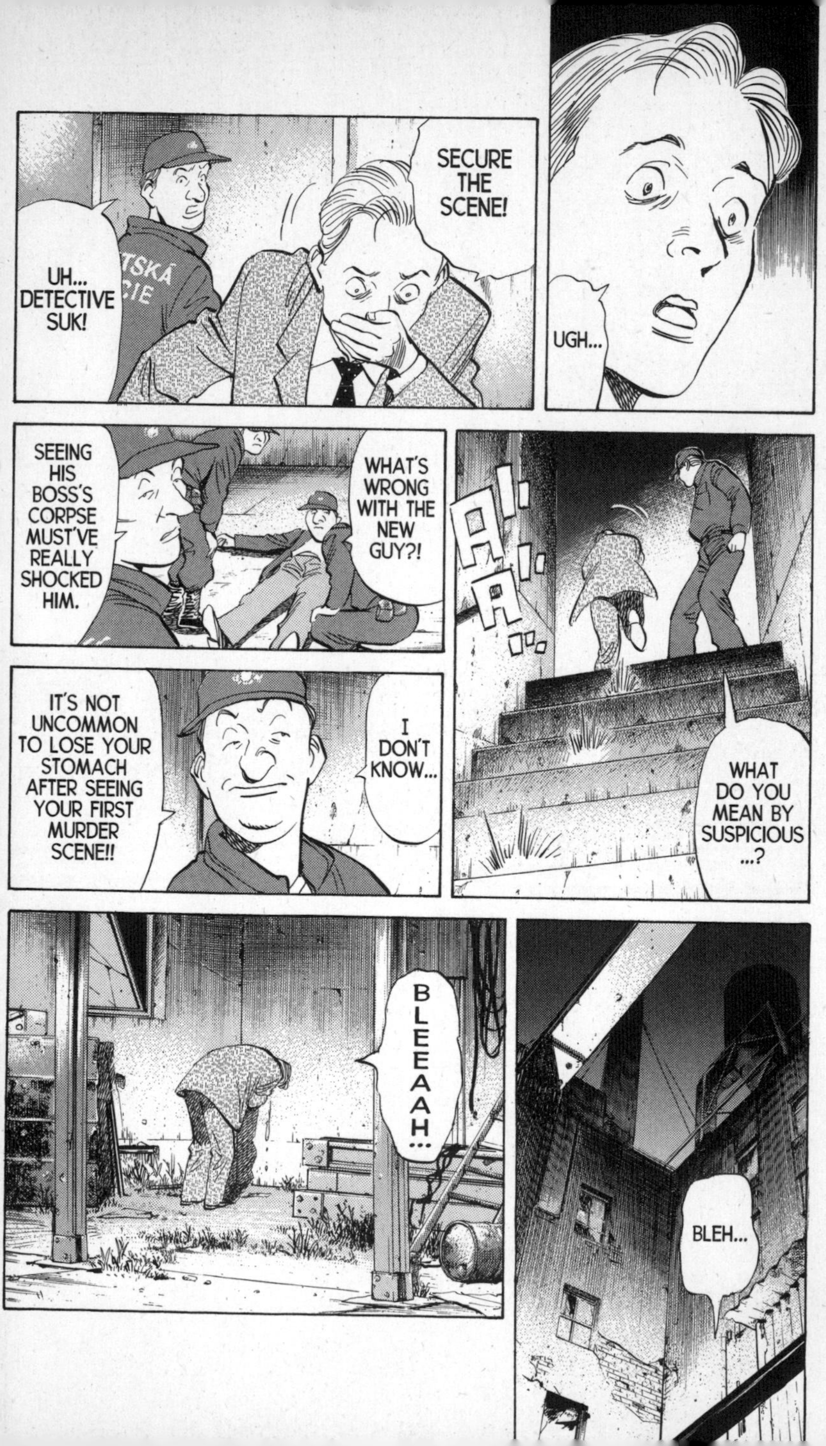
UGH...
SECURE THE SCENE!
UH... DETECTIVE SUK!
WHAT DO YOU MEAN BY SUSPICIOUS ...?
WHAT'S WRONG WITH THE NEW GUY?!
SEEING HIS BOSS'S CORPSE MUST'VE REALLY SHOCKED HIM.
I DON'T KNOW...
IT'S NOT UNCOMMON TO LOSE YOUR STOMACH AFTER SEEING YOUR FIRST MURDER SCENE!!
BLEH...
BLEEAAAH...

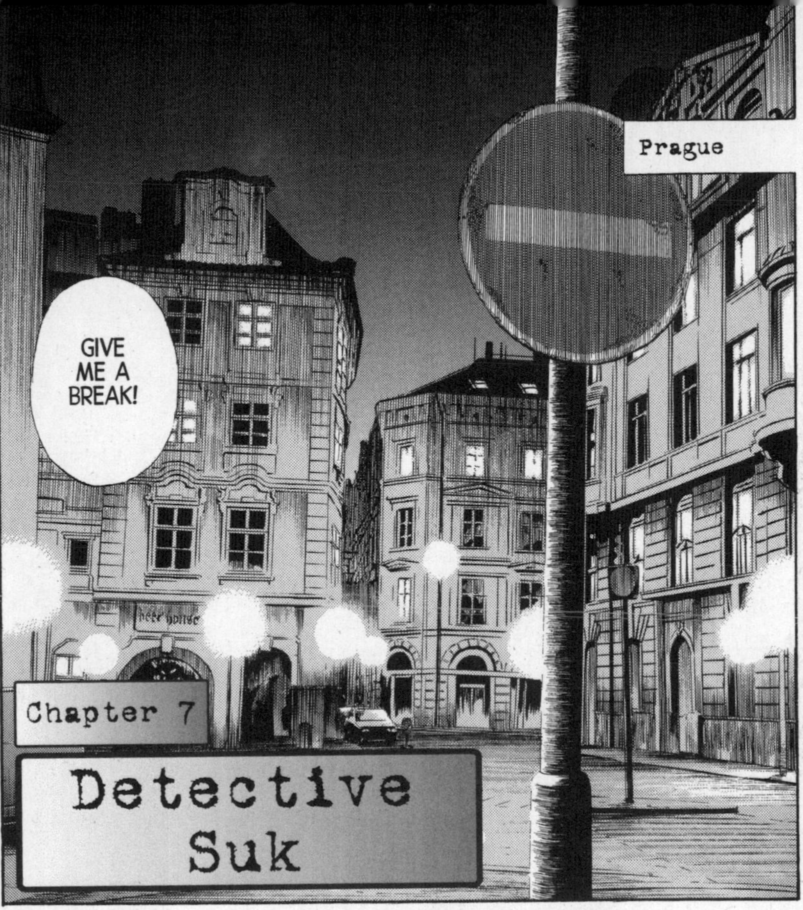
Prague
GIVE ME A BREAK!
Chapter 7
Detective Suk

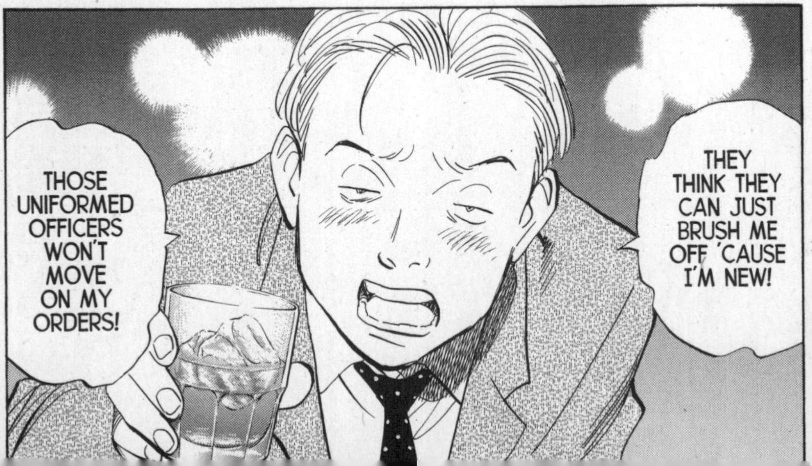
THOSE UNIFORMED OFFICERS WON'T MOVE ON MY ORDERS!
THEY THINK THEY CAN JUST BRUSH ME OFF 'CAUSE I'M NEW!

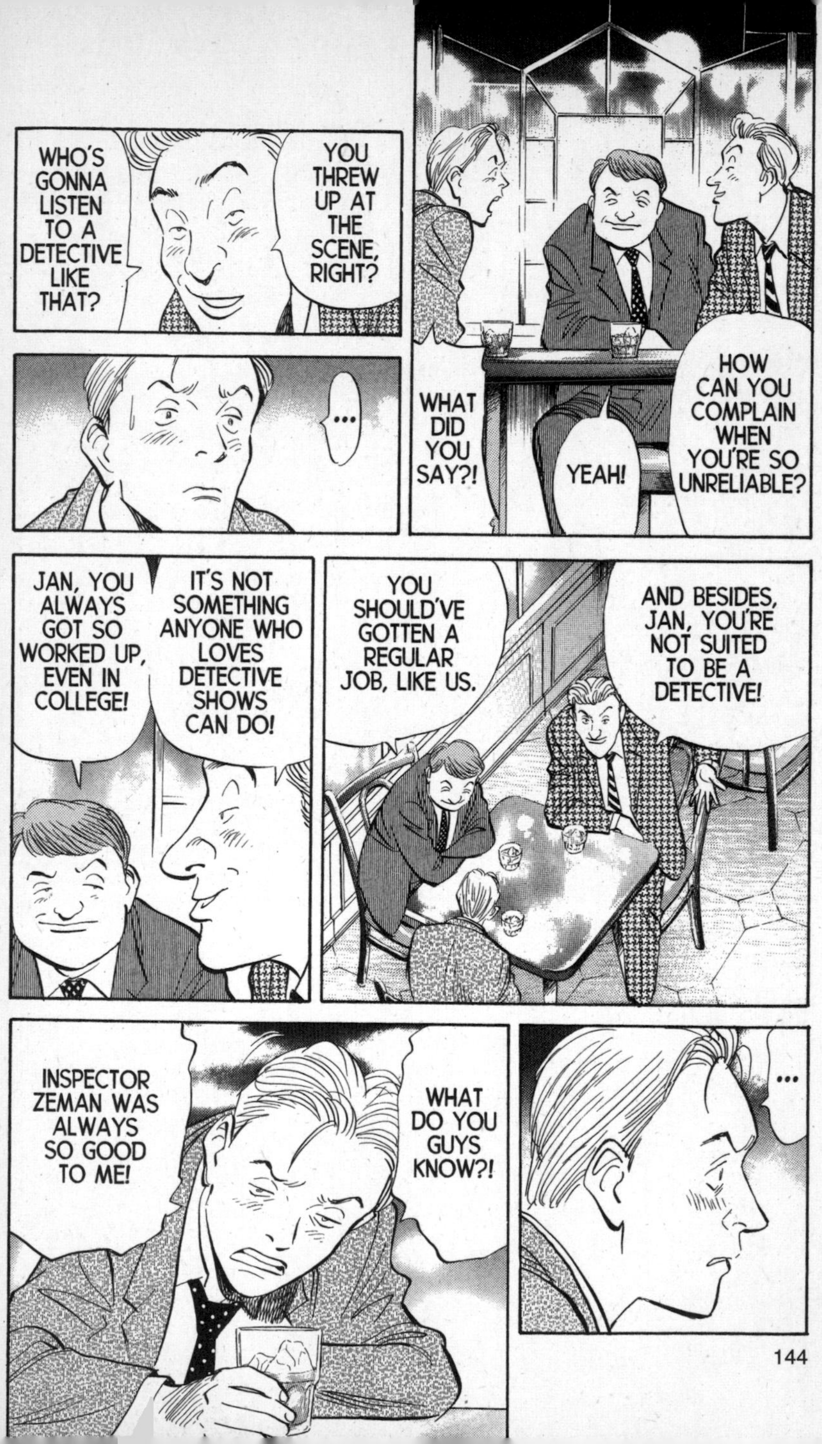
HOW CAN YOU COMPLAIN WHEN YOU'RE SO UNRELIABLE?
YEAH!
WHAT DID YOU SAY?!
YOU THREW UP AT THE SCENE, RIGHT?
WHO'S GONNA LISTEN TO A DETECTIVE LIKE THAT?
...
AND BESIDES, JAN, YOU'RE NOT SUITED TO BE A DETECTIVE!
YOU SHOULD'VE GOTTEN A REGULAR JOB, LIKE US.
IT'S NOT SOMETHING ANYONE WHO LOVES DETECTIVE SHOWS CAN DO!
JAN, YOU ALWAYS GOT SO WORKED UP, EVEN IN COLLEGE!
...
WHAT DO YOU GUYS KNOW?!
INSPECTOR ZEMAN WAS ALWAYS SO GOOD TO ME!

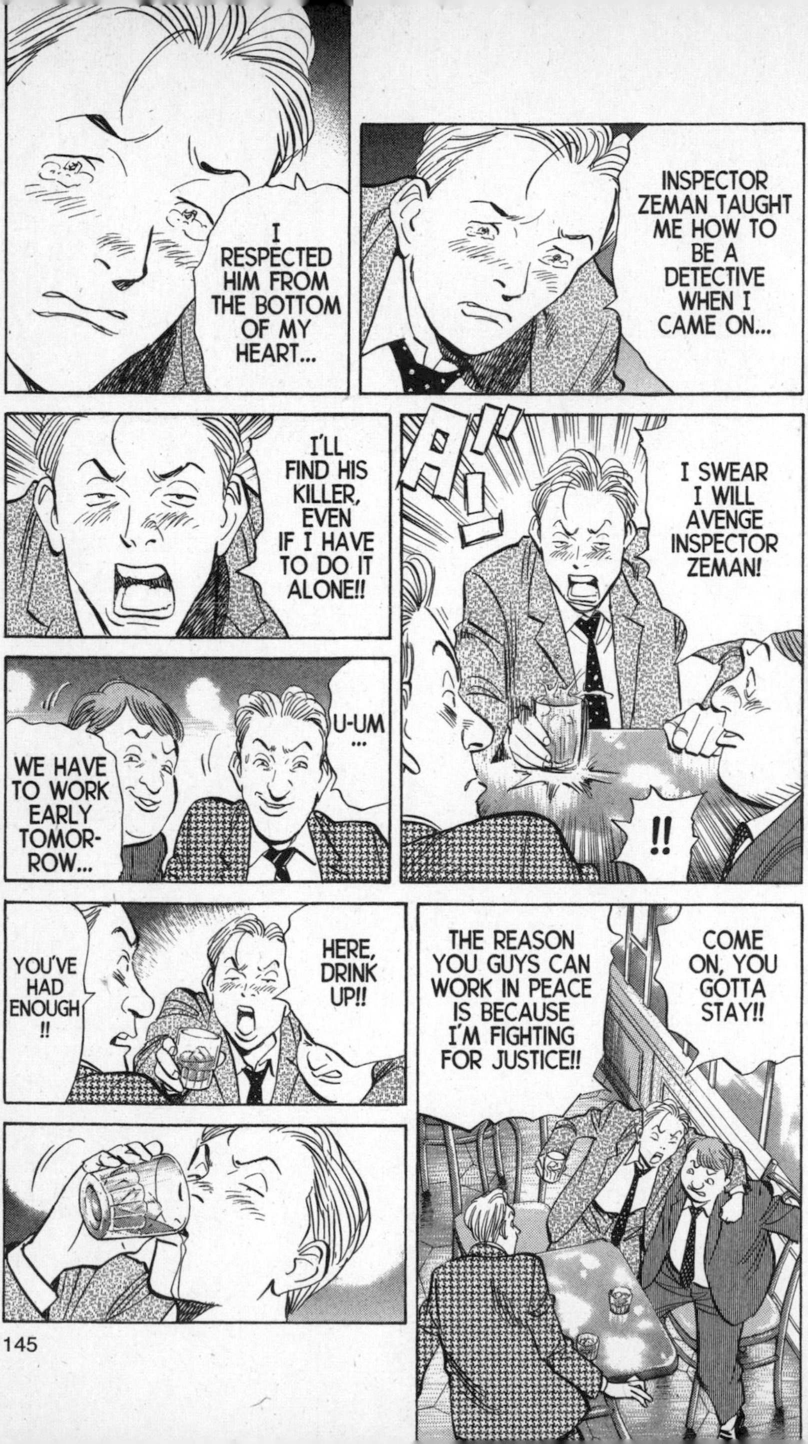
INSPECTOR ZEMAN TAUGHT ME HOW TO BE A DETECTIVE WHEN I CAME ON...
I RESPECTED HIM FROM THE BOTTOM OF MY HEART...
I SWEAR I WILL AVENGE INSPECTOR ZEMAN!
!!
I'LL FIND HIS KILLER, EVEN IF I HAVE TO DO IT ALONE!!
U-UM...
WE HAVE TO WORK EARLY TOMOR-ROW...
COME ON, YOU GOTTA STAY!!
THE REASON YOU GUYS CAN WORK IN PEACE IS BECAUSE I'M FIGHTING FOR JUSTICE!!
HERE, DRINK UP!!
YOU'VE HAD ENOUGH!!

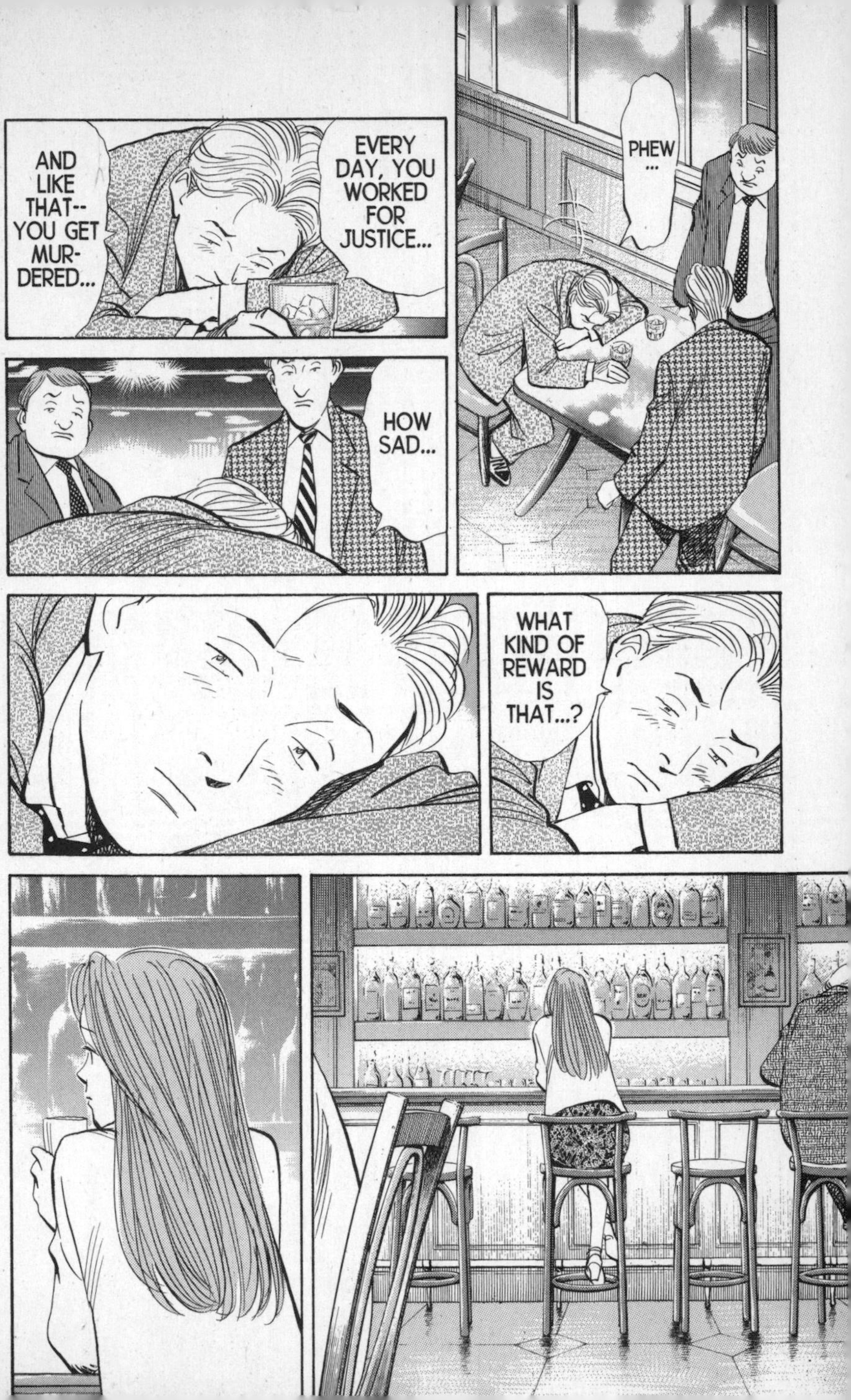
PHEW ...
EVERY DAY, YOU WORKED FOR JUSTICE...
AND LIKE THAT-- YOU GET MUR-DERED...
HOW SAD...
WHAT KIND OF REWARD IS THAT...?

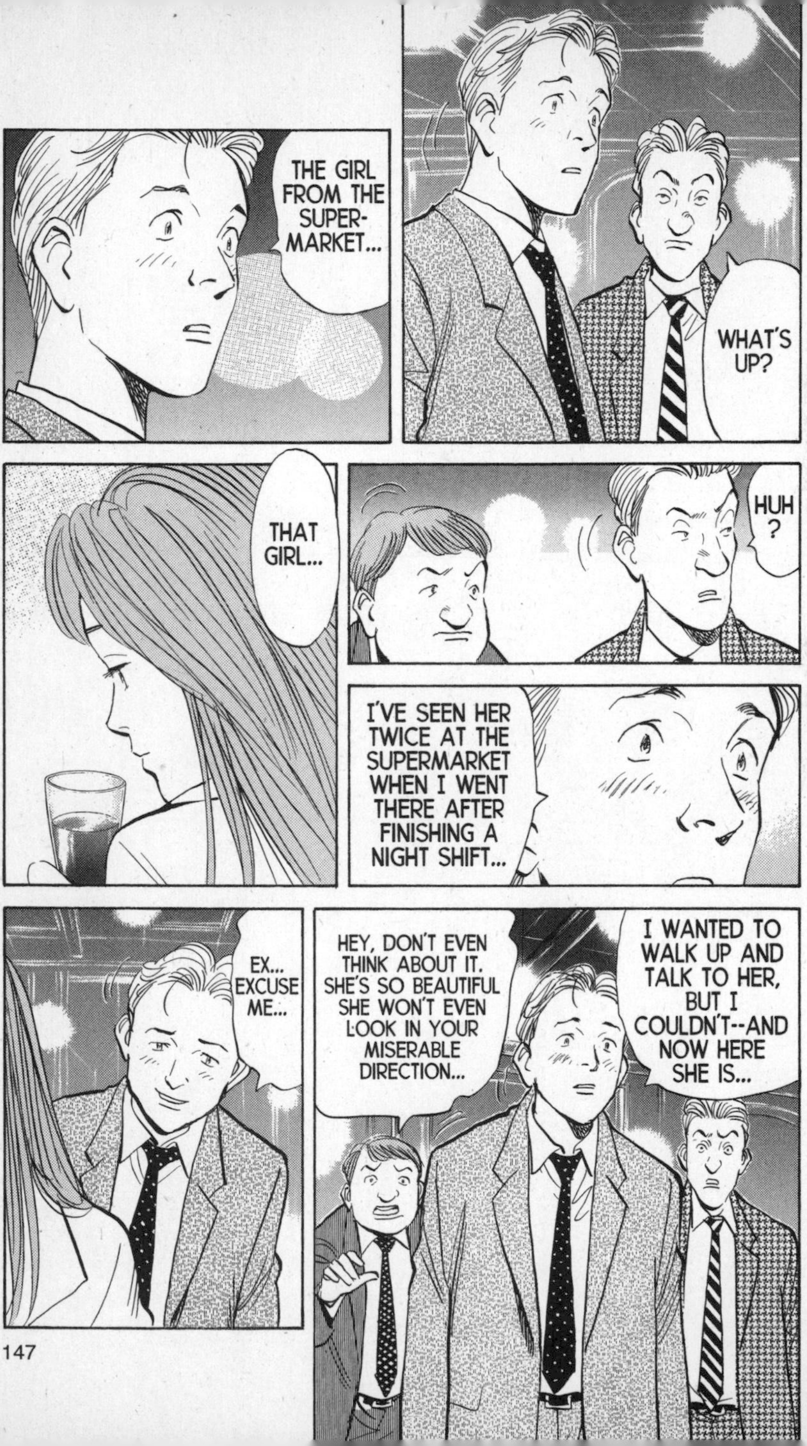
WHAT'S UP?
THE GIRL FROM THE SUPER-MARKET...
HUH?
I'VE SEEN HER TWICE AT THE SUPERMARKET WHEN I WENT THERE AFTER FINISHING A NIGHT SHIFT...
THAT GIRL...
I WANTED TO WALK UP AND TALK TO HER, BUT I COULDN'T--AND NOW HERE SHE IS...
HEY, DON'T EVEN THINK ABOUT IT. SHE'S SO BEAUTIFUL SHE WON'T EVEN LOOK IN YOUR MISERABLE DIRECTION...
EX... EXCUSE ME...

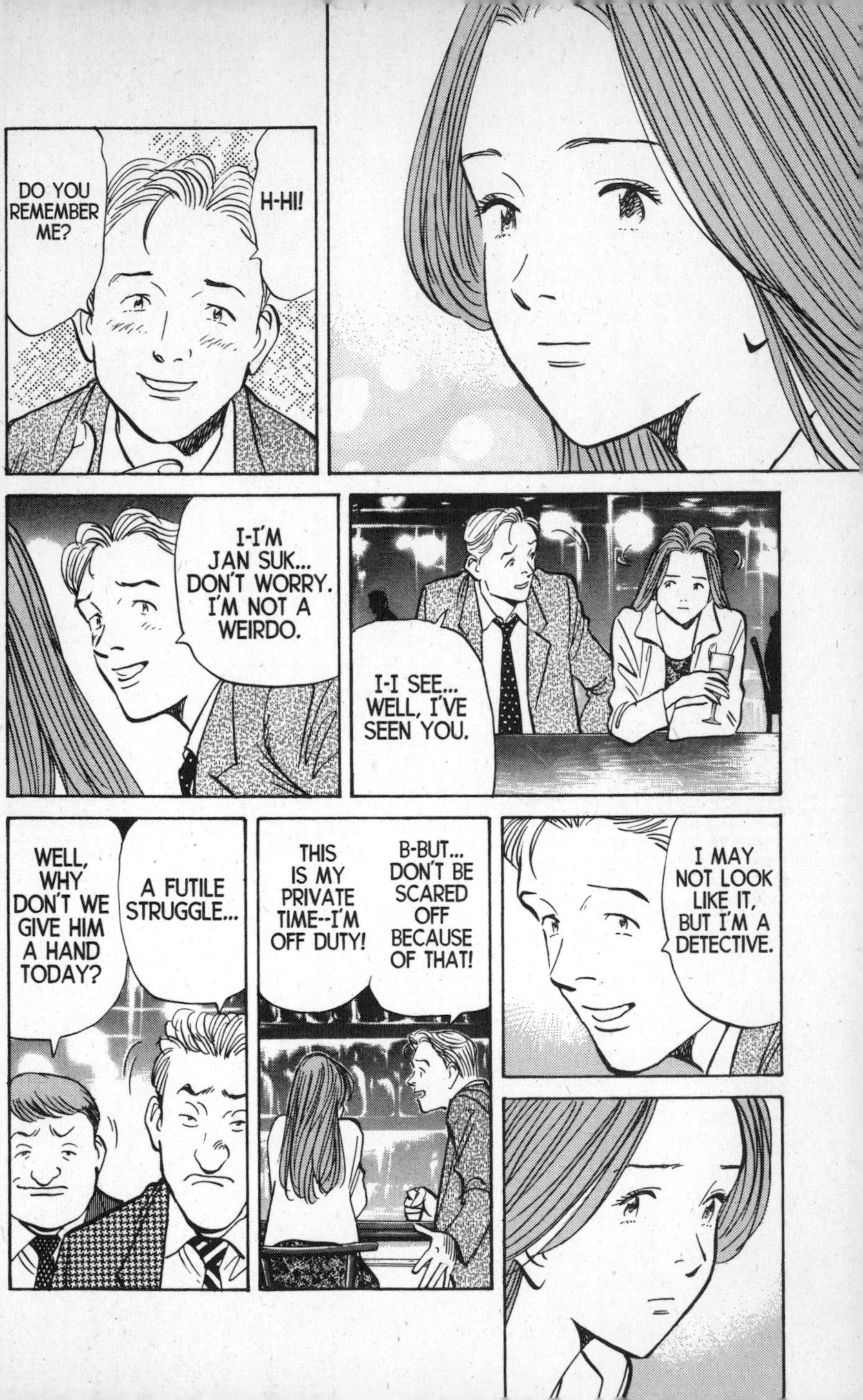
H-HI!
DO YOU REMEMBER ME?
I-I SEE... WELL, I'VE SEEN YOU.
I-I'M JAN SUK... DON'T WORRY. I'M NOT A WEIRDO.
I MAY NOT LOOK LIKE IT, BUT I'M A DETECTIVE.
B-BUT... DON'T BE SCARED OFF BECAUSE OF THAT!
THIS IS MY PRIVATE TIME--I'M OFF DUTY!
A FUTILE STRUGGLE...
WELL, WHY DON'T WE GIVE HIM A HAND TODAY?

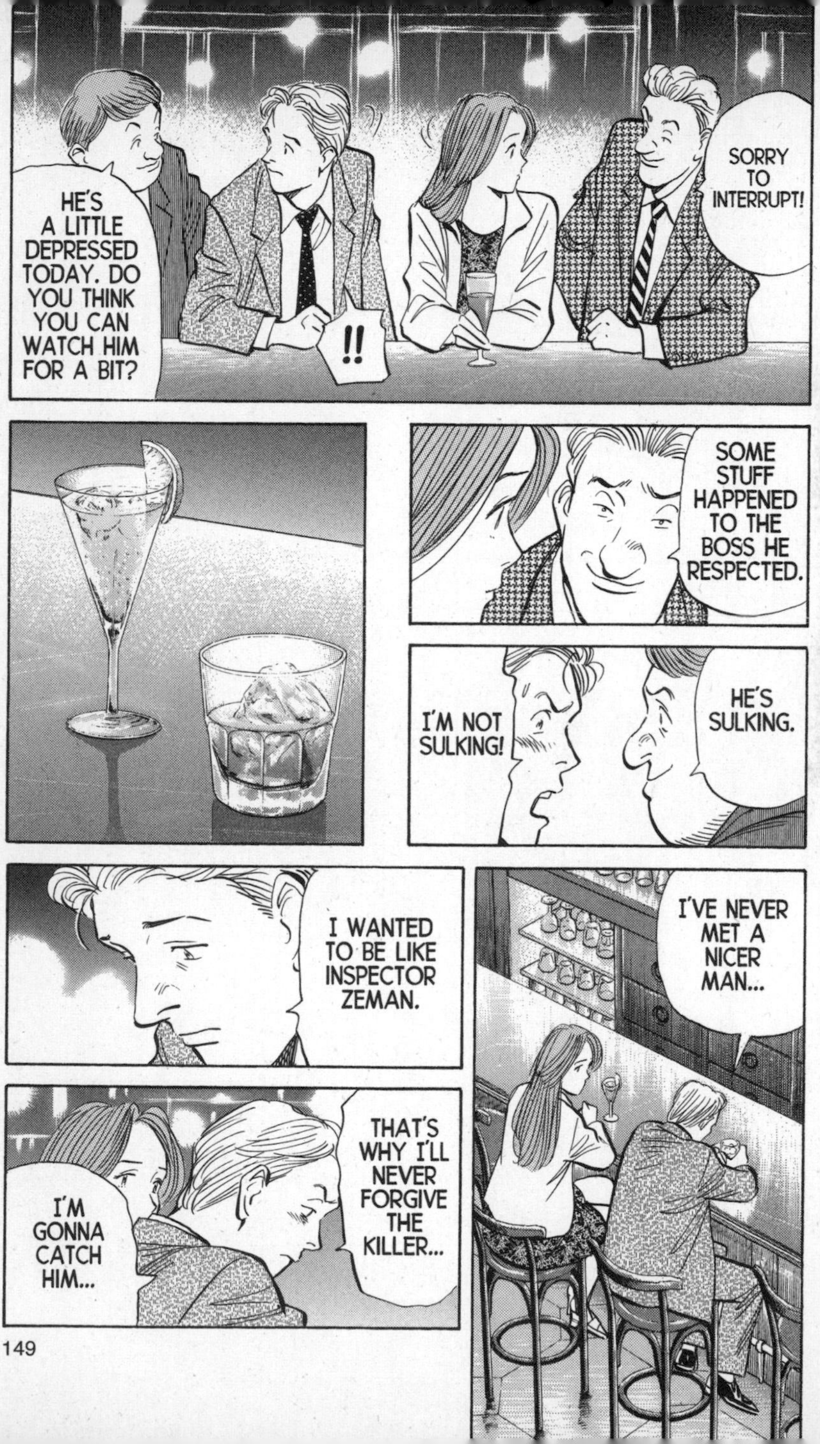

SORRY TO INTERRUPT!
!!
HE'S A LITTLE DEPRESSED TODAY. DO YOU THINK YOU CAN WATCH HIM FOR A BIT?
SOME STUFF HAPPENED TO THE BOSS HE RESPECTED.
HE'S SULKING.
I'M NOT SULKING!
I'VE NEVER MET A NICER MAN...
I WANTED TO BE LIKE INSPECTOR ZEMAN.
THAT'S WHY I'LL NEVER FORGIVE THE KILLER...
I'M GONNA CATCH HIM...

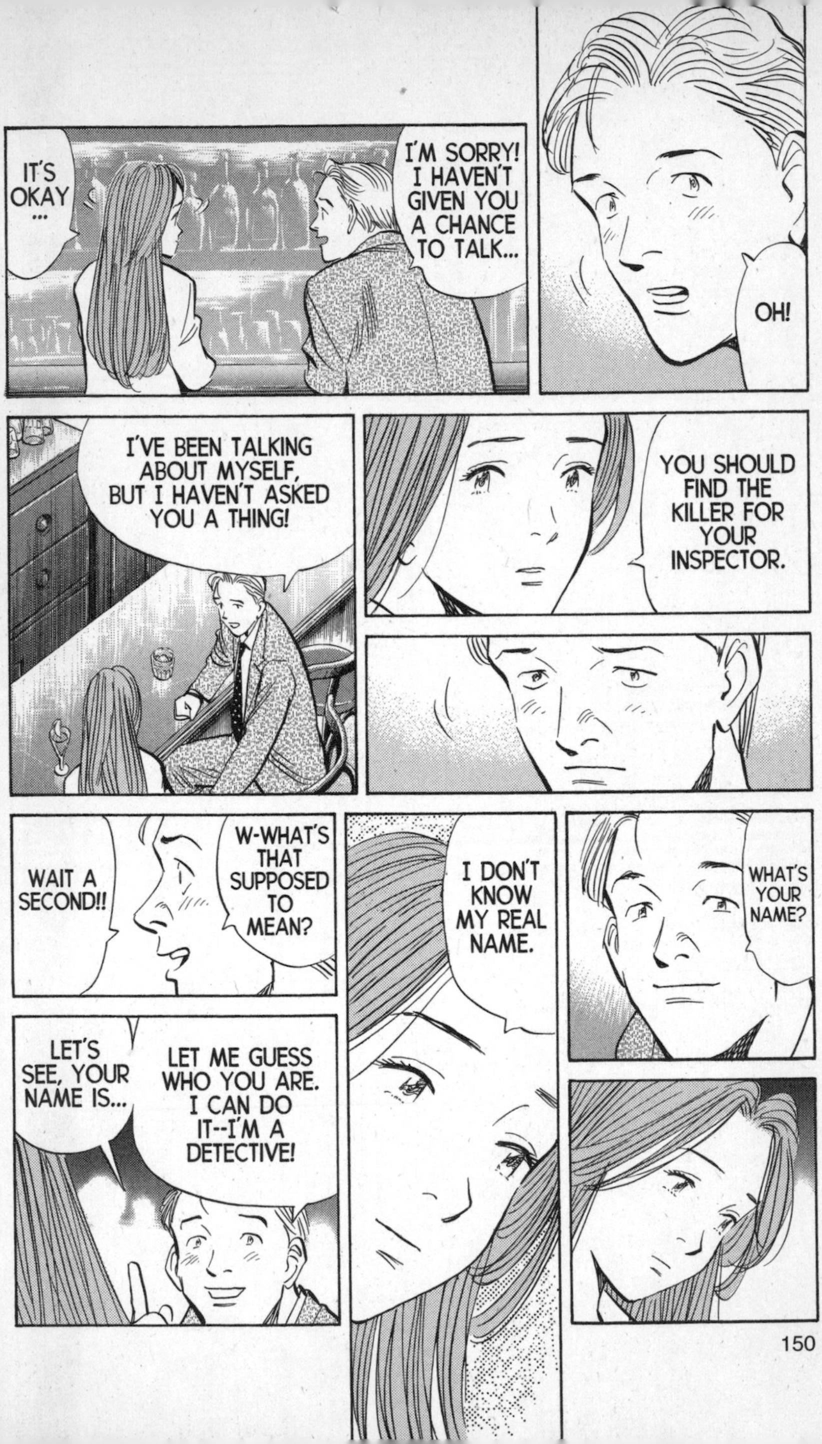
OH!
I'M SORRY! I HAVEN'T GIVEN YOU A CHANCE TO TALK...
IT'S OKAY ...
YOU SHOULD FIND THE KILLER FOR YOUR INSPECTOR.
I'VE BEEN TALKING ABOUT MYSELF, BUT I HAVEN'T ASKED YOU A THING!
WHAT'S YOUR NAME?
I DON'T KNOW MY REAL NAME.
W-WHAT'S THAT SUPPOSED TO MEAN?
WAIT A SECOND!!
LET ME GUESS WHO YOU ARE. I CAN DO IT--I'M A DETECTIVE!
LET'S SEE, YOUR NAME IS...

IF EVEN I DON'T KNOW, HOW COULD YOU POSSIBLY KNOW?

ALL I DO KNOW ABOUT MYSELF IS...

ALMA!

THEN... JITKA!

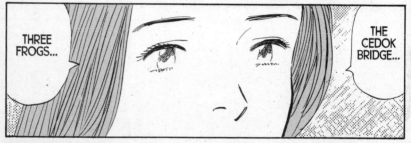

THREE FROGS...

THE CEDOK BRIDGE...

WAIT! WHEN CAN I SEE YOU AGA--

H-HEY!!

THAT'S ALL.

IT WAS ALL BUT A DREAM. BEST TO FORGET IT.

SEE, I TOLD YOU.

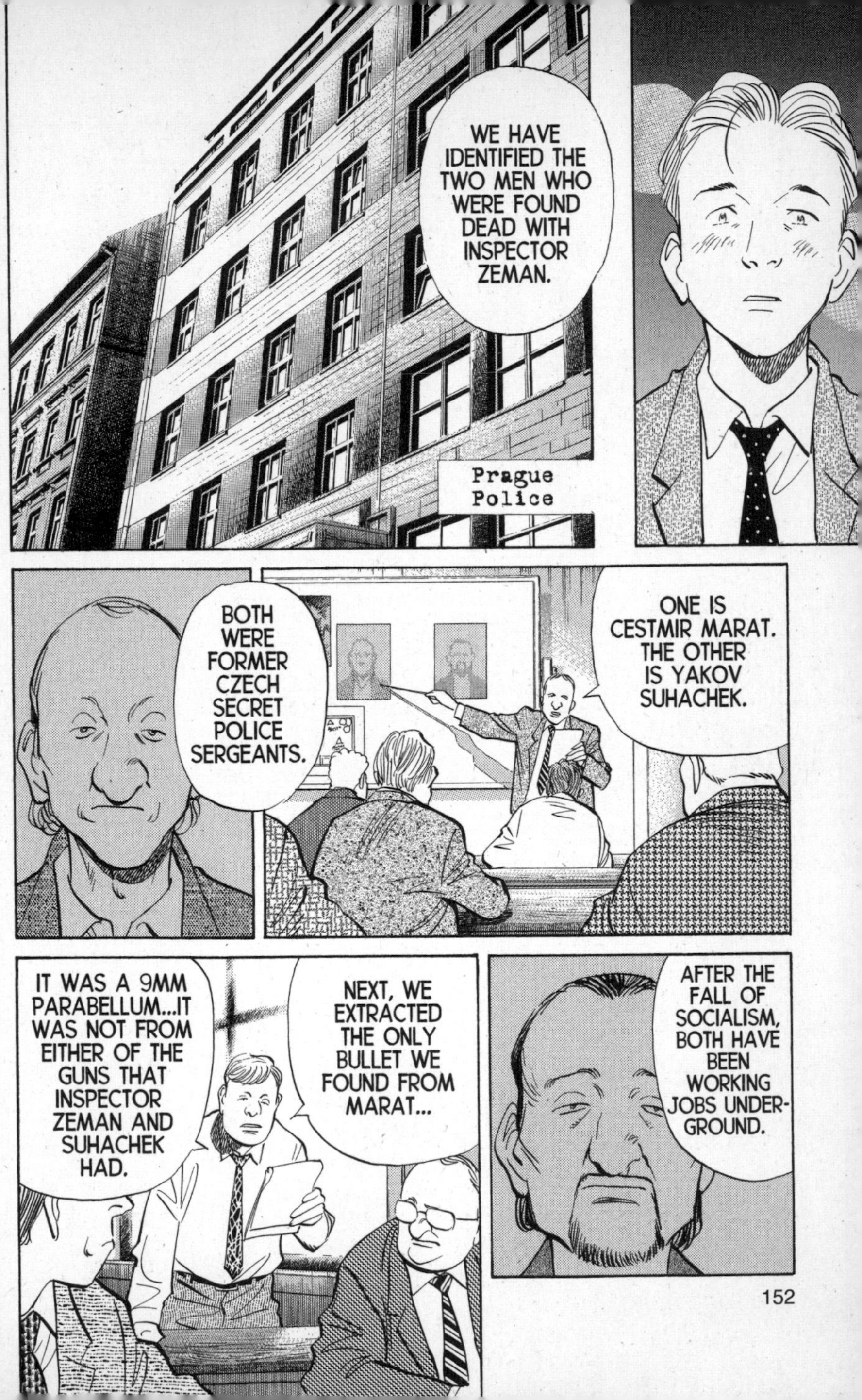
WE HAVE IDENTIFIED THE TWO MEN WHO WERE FOUND DEAD WITH INSPECTOR ZEMAN.
Prague Police
ONE IS CESTMIR MARAT. THE OTHER IS YAKOV SUHACHEK.
BOTH WERE FORMER CZECH SECRET POLICE SERGEANTS.
AFTER THE FALL OF SOCIALISM, BOTH HAVE BEEN WORKING JOBS UNDER-GROUND.
NEXT, WE EXTRACTED THE ONLY BULLET WE FOUND FROM MARAT...
IT WAS A 9MM PARABELLUM...IT WAS NOT FROM EITHER OF THE GUNS THAT INSPECTOR ZEMAN AND SUHACHEK HAD.

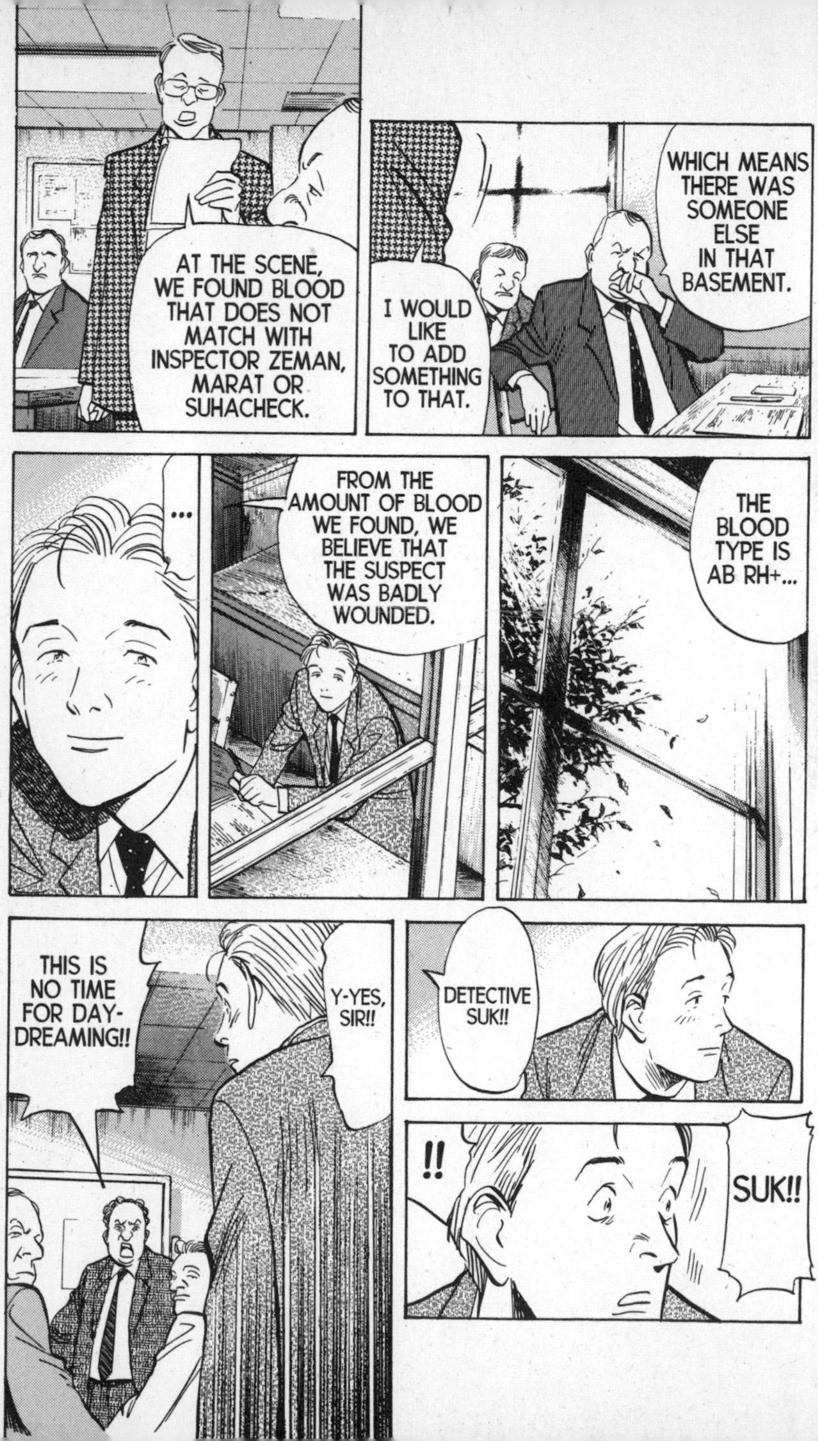
AT THE SCENE, WE FOUND BLOOD THAT DOES NOT MATCH WITH INSPECTOR ZEMAN, MARAT OR SUHACHECK.
I WOULD LIKE TO ADD SOMETHING TO THAT.
WHICH MEANS THERE WAS SOMEONE ELSE IN THAT BASEMENT.
...
FROM THE AMOUNT OF BLOOD WE FOUND, WE BELIEVE THAT THE SUSPECT WAS BADLY WOUNDED.
THE BLOOD TYPE IS AB RH+...
THIS IS NO TIME FOR DAY-DREAMING!!
Y-YES, SIR!!
DETECTIVE SUK!!
!!
SUK!!

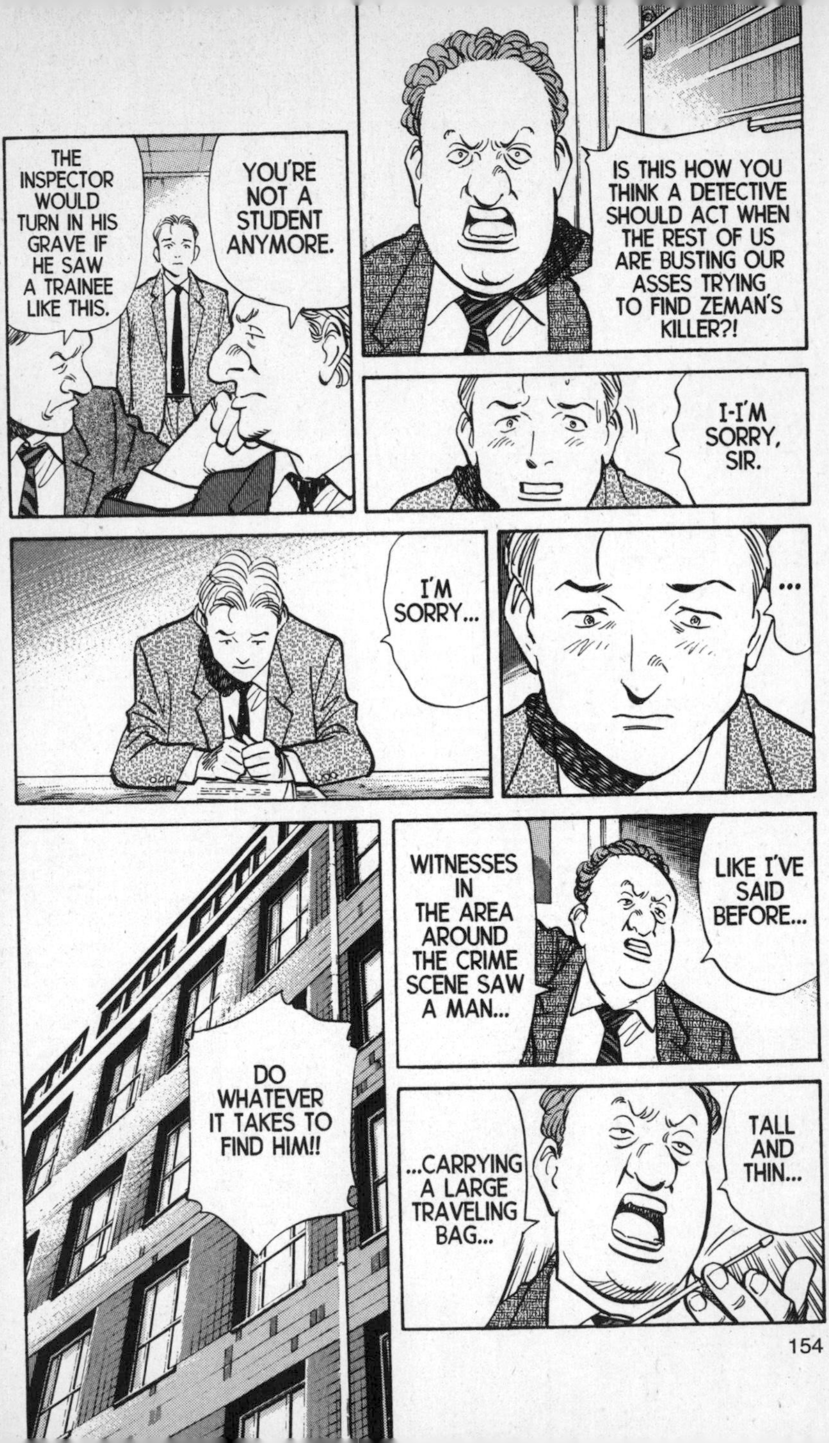
IS THIS HOW YOU THINK A DETECTIVE SHOULD ACT WHEN THE REST OF US ARE BUSTING OUR ASSES TRYING TO FIND ZEMAN'S KILLER?!
I-I'M SORRY, SIR.
YOU'RE NOT A STUDENT ANYMORE.
THE INSPECTOR WOULD TURN IN HIS GRAVE IF HE SAW A TRAINEE LIKE THIS.
...
I'M SORRY...
LIKE I'VE SAID BEFORE...
WITNESSES IN THE AREA AROUND THE CRIME SCENE SAW A MAN...
TALL AND THIN...
...CARRYING A LARGE TRAVELING BAG...
DO WHATEVER IT TAKES TO FIND HIM!!

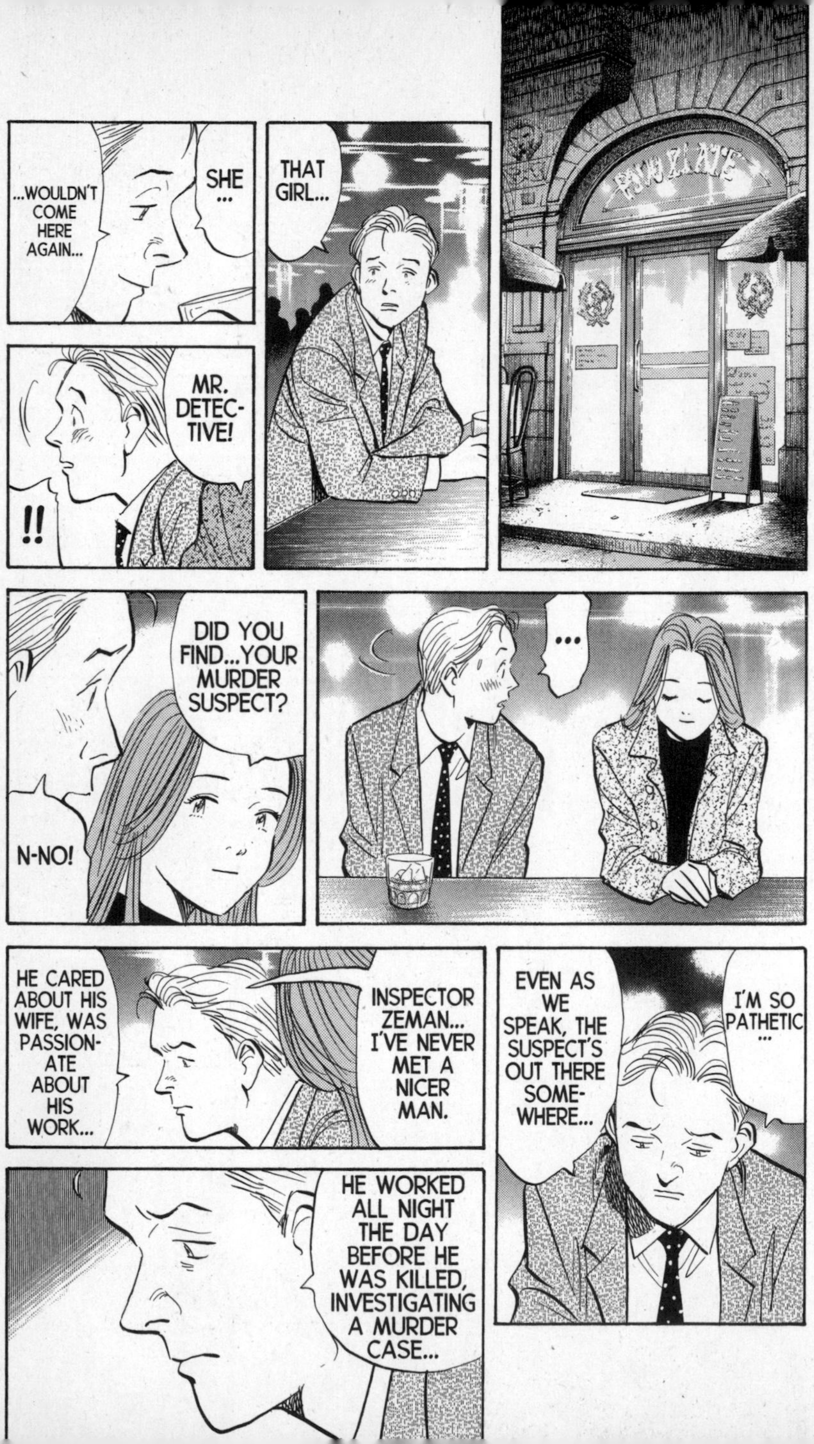
THAT GIRL...
SHE...
...WOULDN'T COME HERE AGAIN...
MR. DETECTIVE!
!!
...
DID YOU FIND...YOUR MURDER SUSPECT?
N-NO!
I'M SO PATHETIC...
EVEN AS WE SPEAK, THE SUSPECT'S OUT THERE SOME-WHERE...
INSPECTOR ZEMAN... I'VE NEVER MET A NICER MAN.
HE CARED ABOUT HIS WIFE, WAS PASSION-ATE ABOUT HIS WORK...
HE WORKED ALL NIGHT THE DAY BEFORE HE WAS KILLED, INVESTIGATING A MURDER CASE...

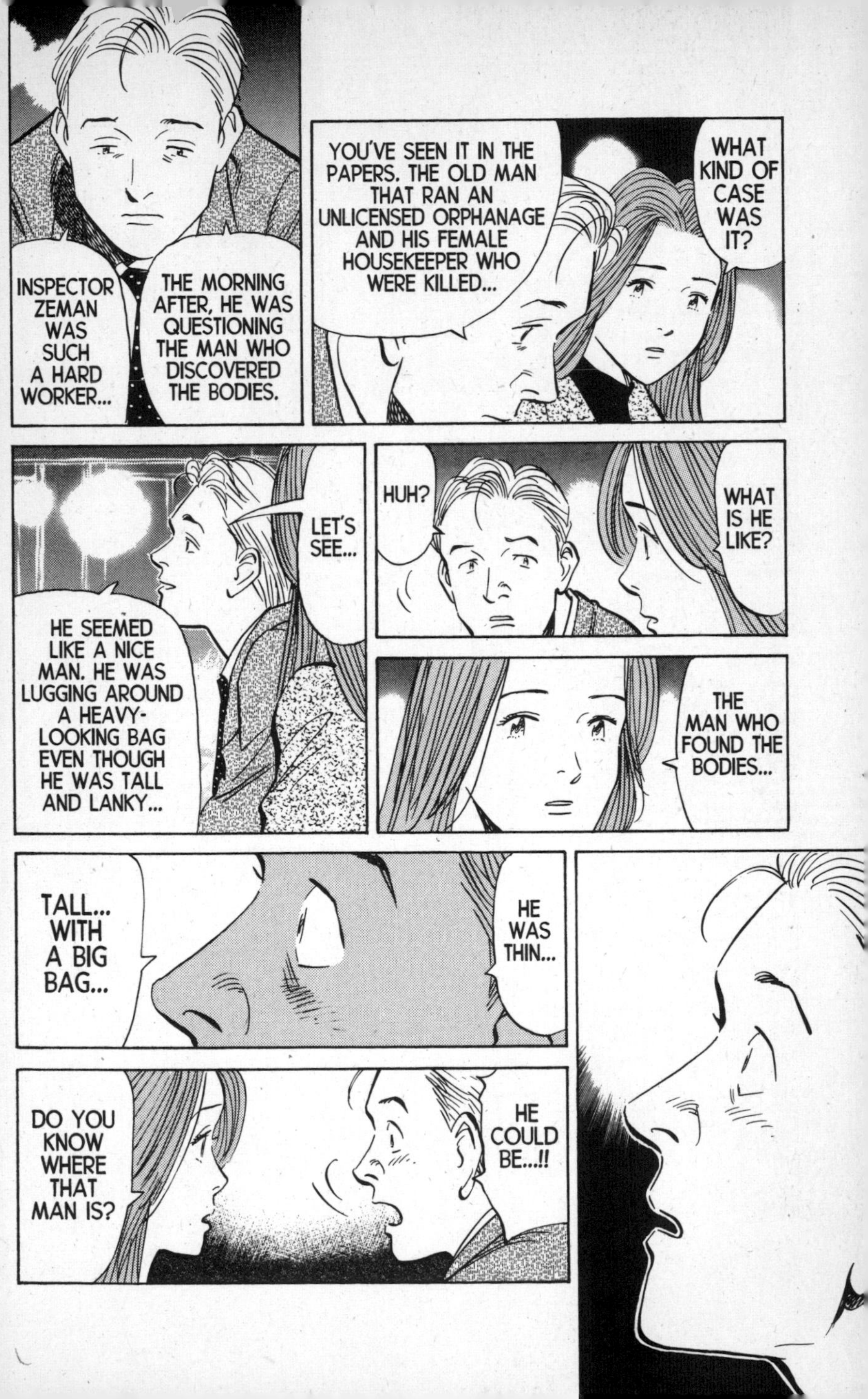
WHAT KIND OF CASE WAS IT?
YOU'VE SEEN IT IN THE PAPERS. THE OLD MAN THAT RAN AN UNLICENSED ORPHANAGE AND HIS FEMALE HOUSEKEEPER WHO WERE KILLED...
INSPECTOR ZEMAN WAS SUCH A HARD WORKER...
THE MORNING AFTER, HE WAS QUESTIONING THE MAN WHO DISCOVERED THE BODIES.
WHAT IS HE LIKE?
HUH?
THE MAN WHO FOUND THE BODIES...
LET'S SEE...
HE SEEMED LIKE A NICE MAN. HE WAS LUGGING AROUND A HEAVY-LOOKING BAG EVEN THOUGH HE WAS TALL AND LANKY...
HE WAS THIN...
TALL... WITH A BIG BAG...
HE COULD BE...!!
DO YOU KNOW WHERE THAT MAN IS?

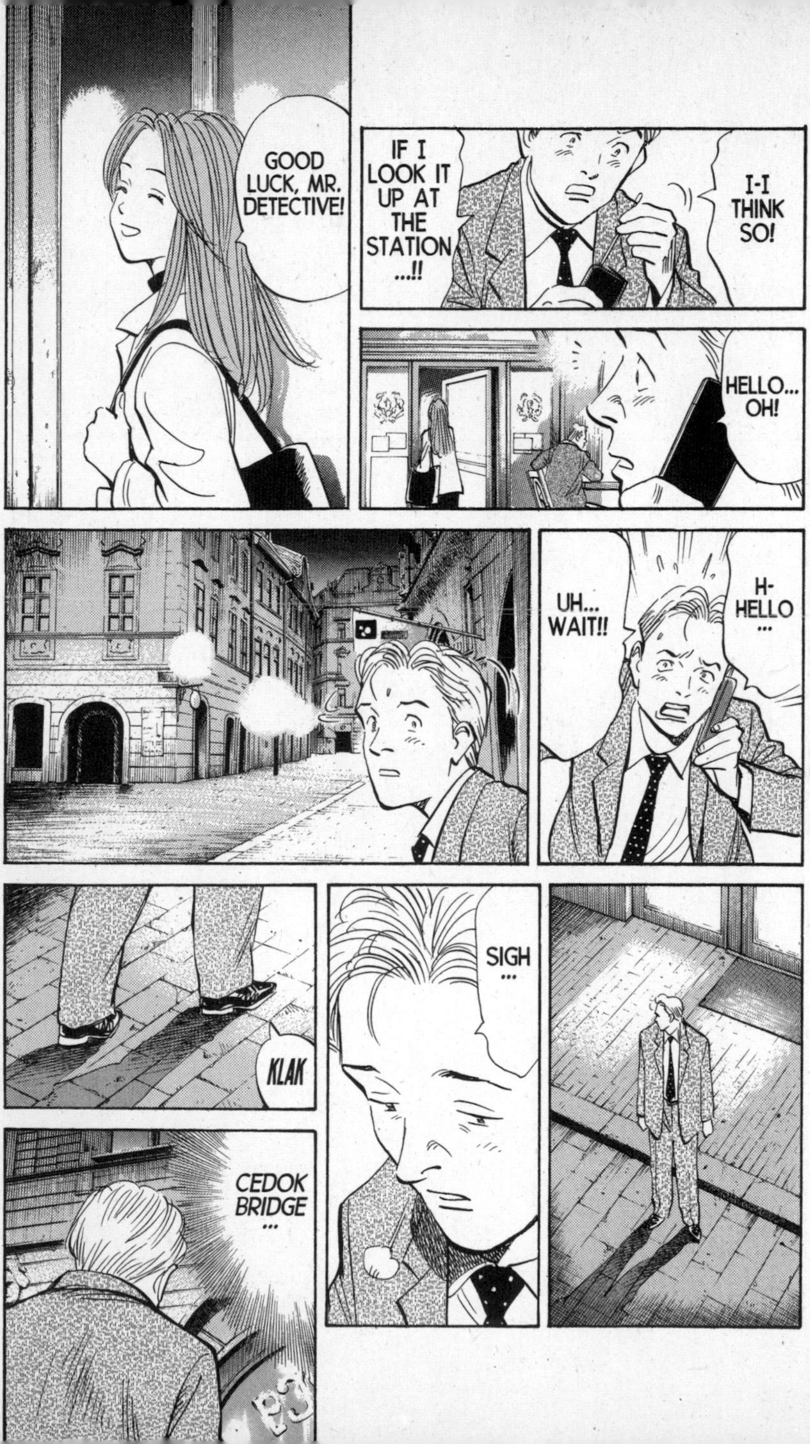
I-I THINK SO!
IF I LOOK IT UP AT THE STATION ...!!
HELLO... OH!
GOOD LUCK, MR. DETECTIVE!
H-HELLO ...
UH... WAIT!!
SIGH ...
KLAK
CEDOK BRIDGE ...

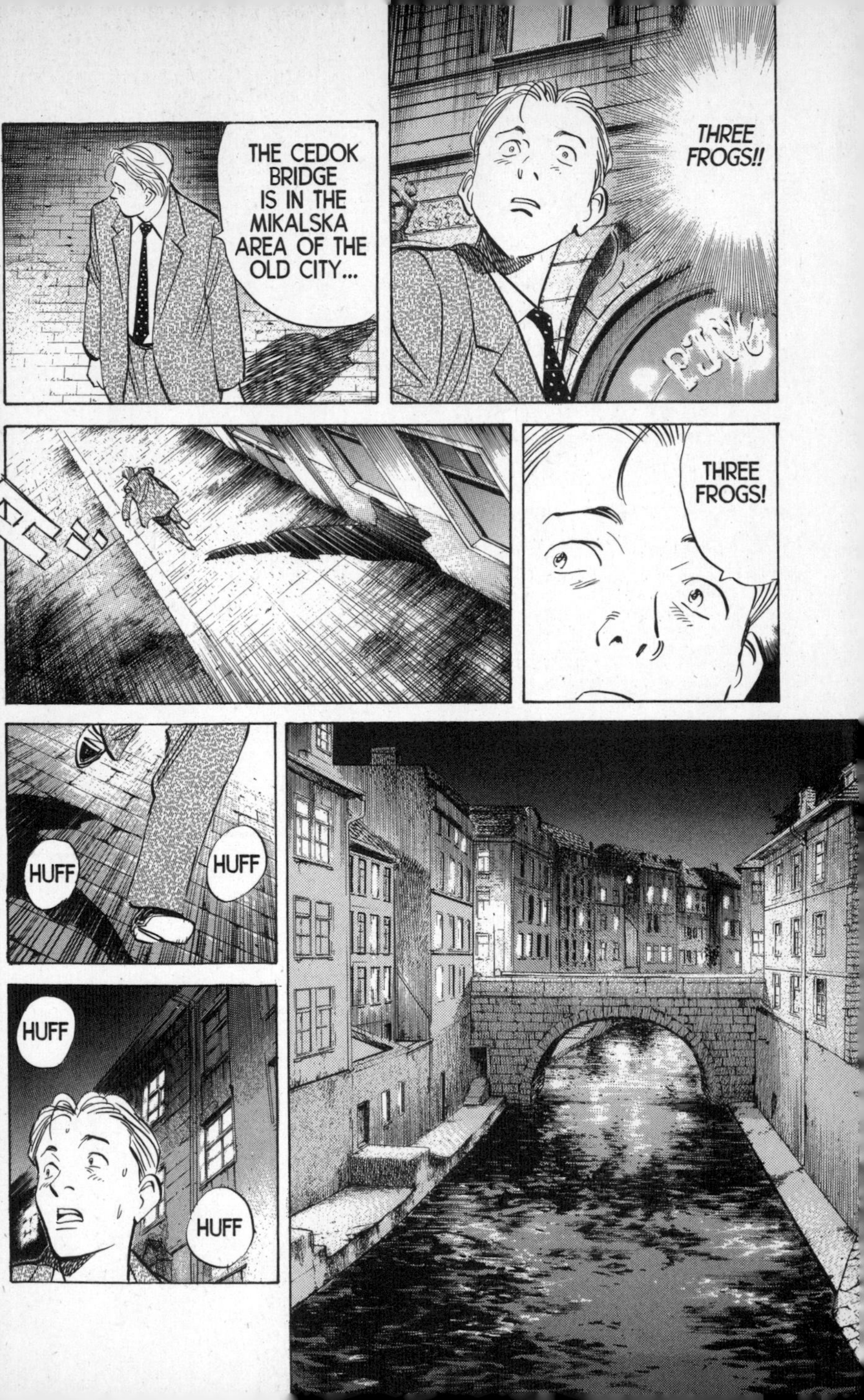
THREE FROGS!!
THE CEDOK BRIDGE IS IN THE MIKALSKA AREA OF THE OLD CITY...
THREE FROGS!
HUFF
HUFF
HUFF
HUFF

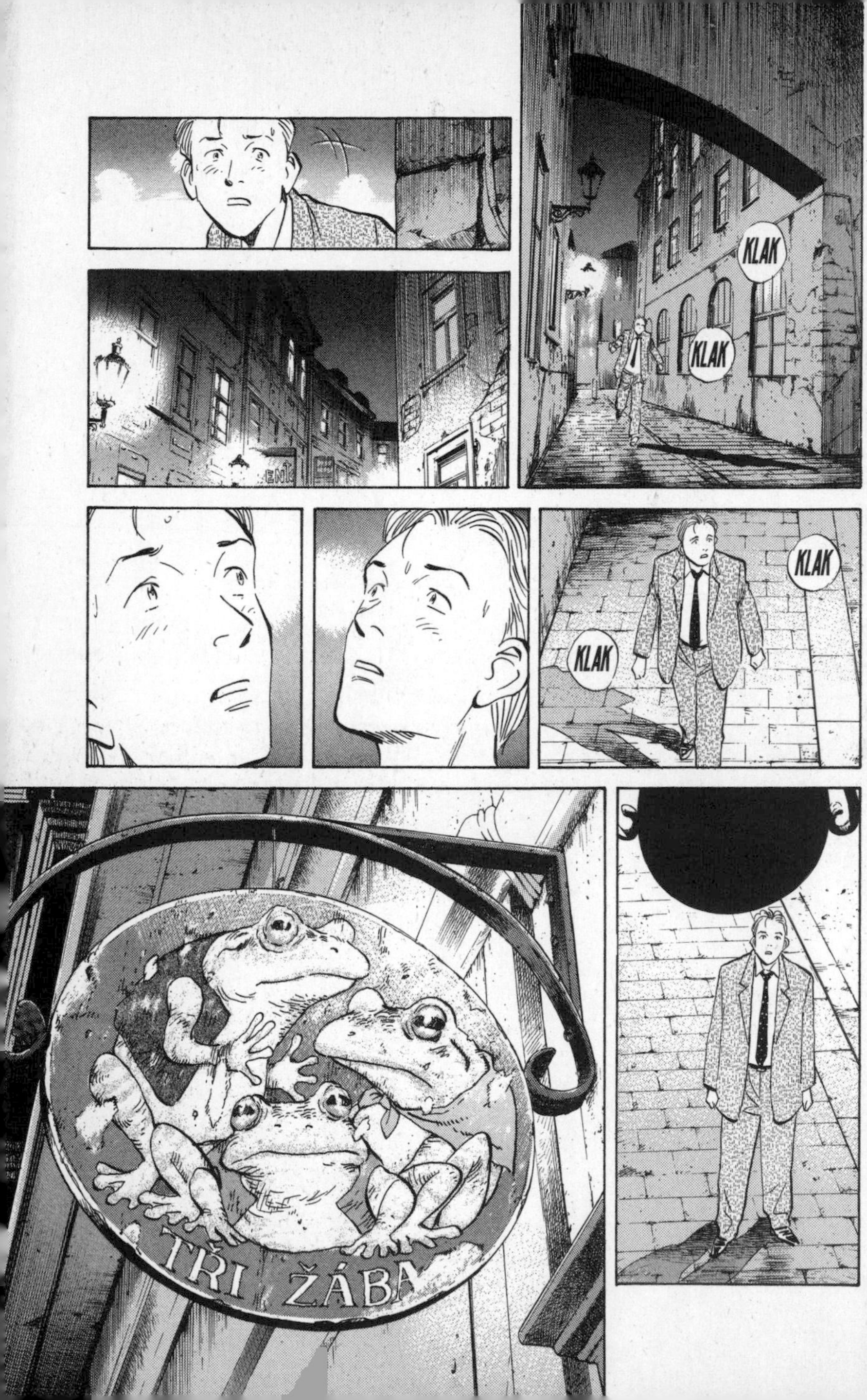
KLAK
KLAK
KLAK
KLAK
TŘI ŽÁBA

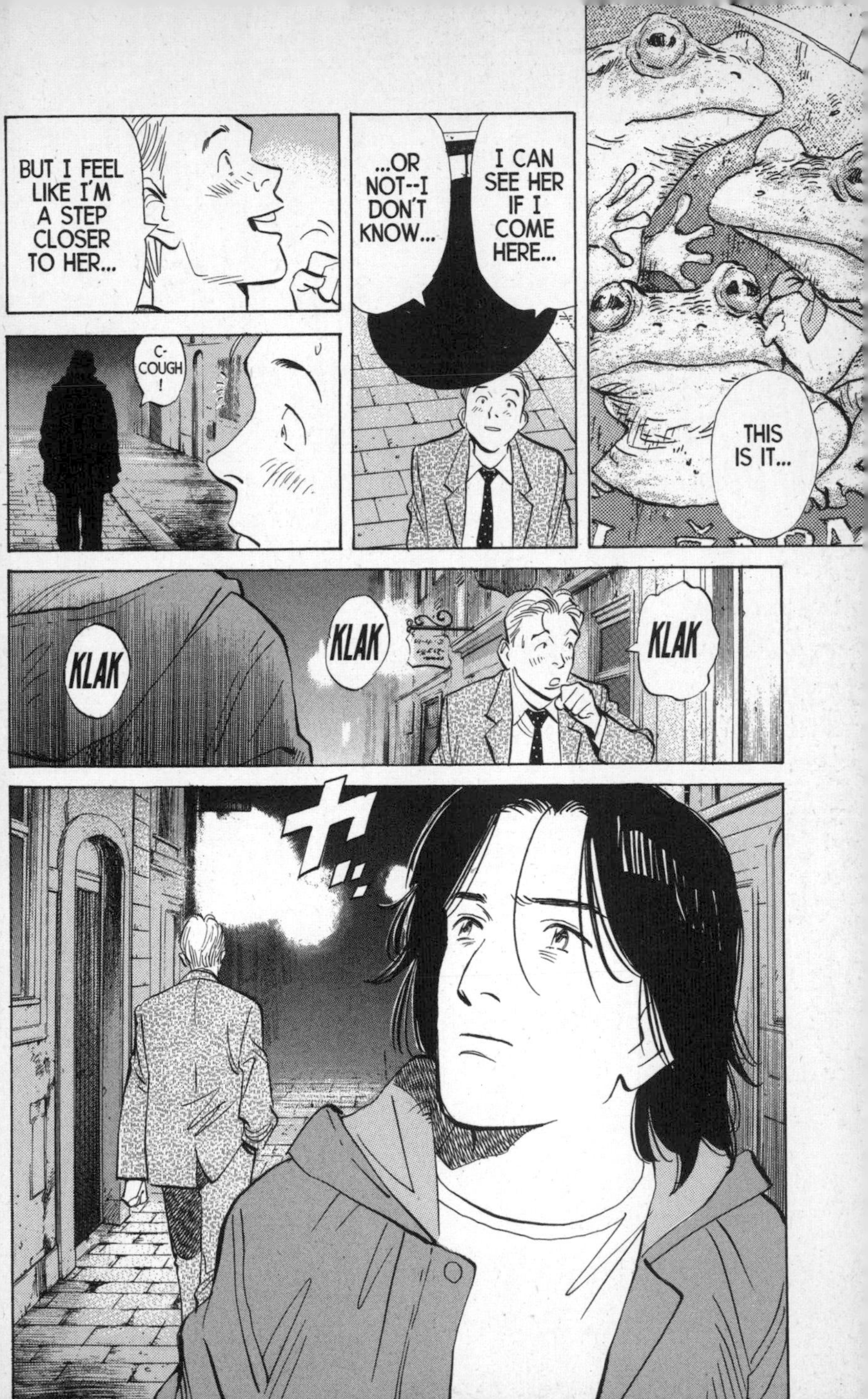
THIS IS IT...
I CAN SEE HER IF I COME HERE...
...OR NOT--I DON'T KNOW...
BUT I FEEL LIKE I'M A STEP CLOSER TO HER...
C-COUGH!
KLAK
KLAK
KLAK

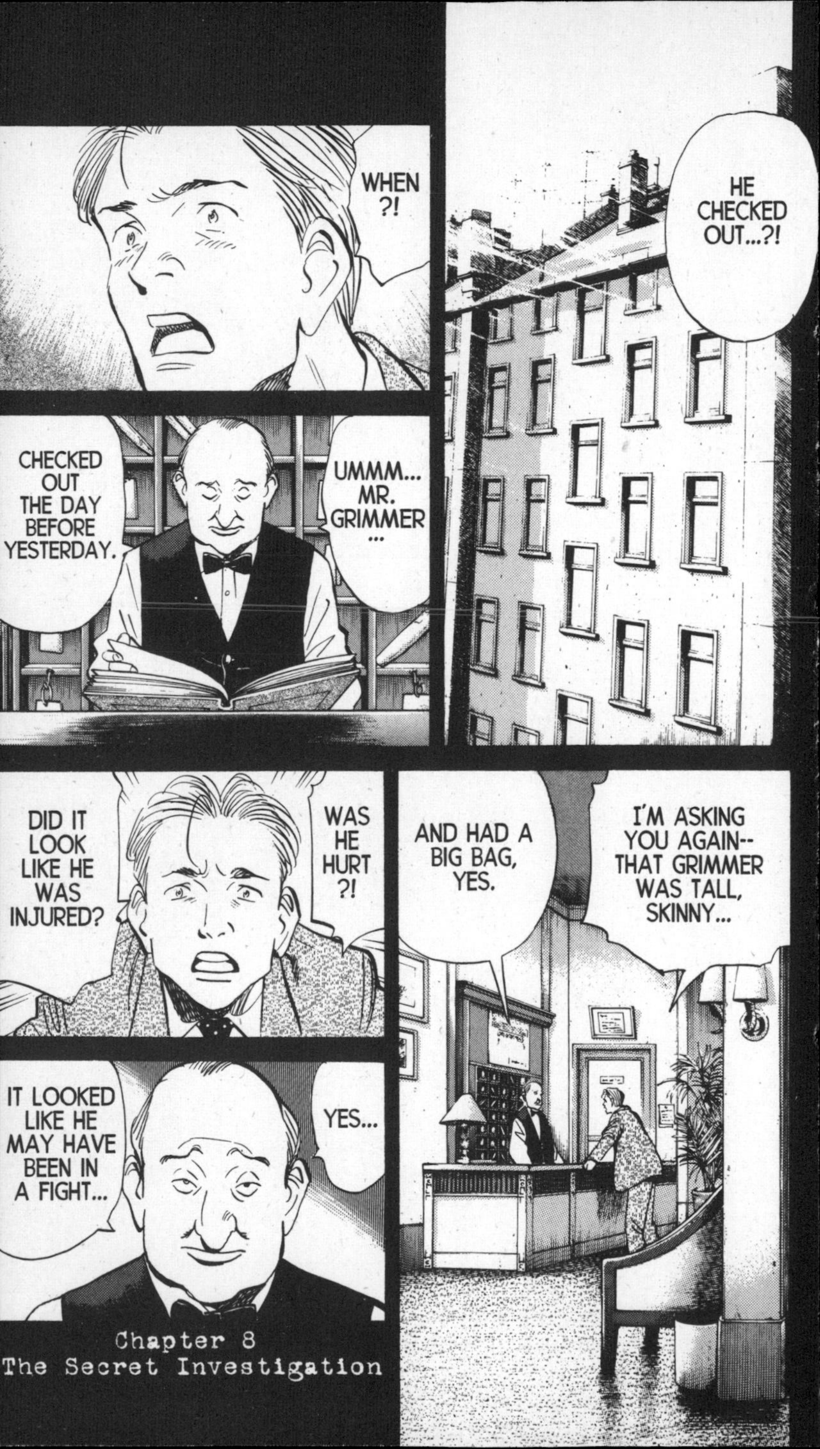
HE CHECKED OUT...?!
WHEN ?!
UMMM... MR. GRIMMER ...
CHECKED OUT THE DAY BEFORE YESTERDAY.
I'M ASKING YOU AGAIN-- THAT GRIMMER WAS TALL, SKINNY...
AND HAD A BIG BAG, YES.
WAS HE HURT ?!
DID IT LOOK LIKE HE WAS INJURED?
YES...
IT LOOKED LIKE HE MAY HAVE BEEN IN A FIGHT...

Chapter 8
The Secret Investigation

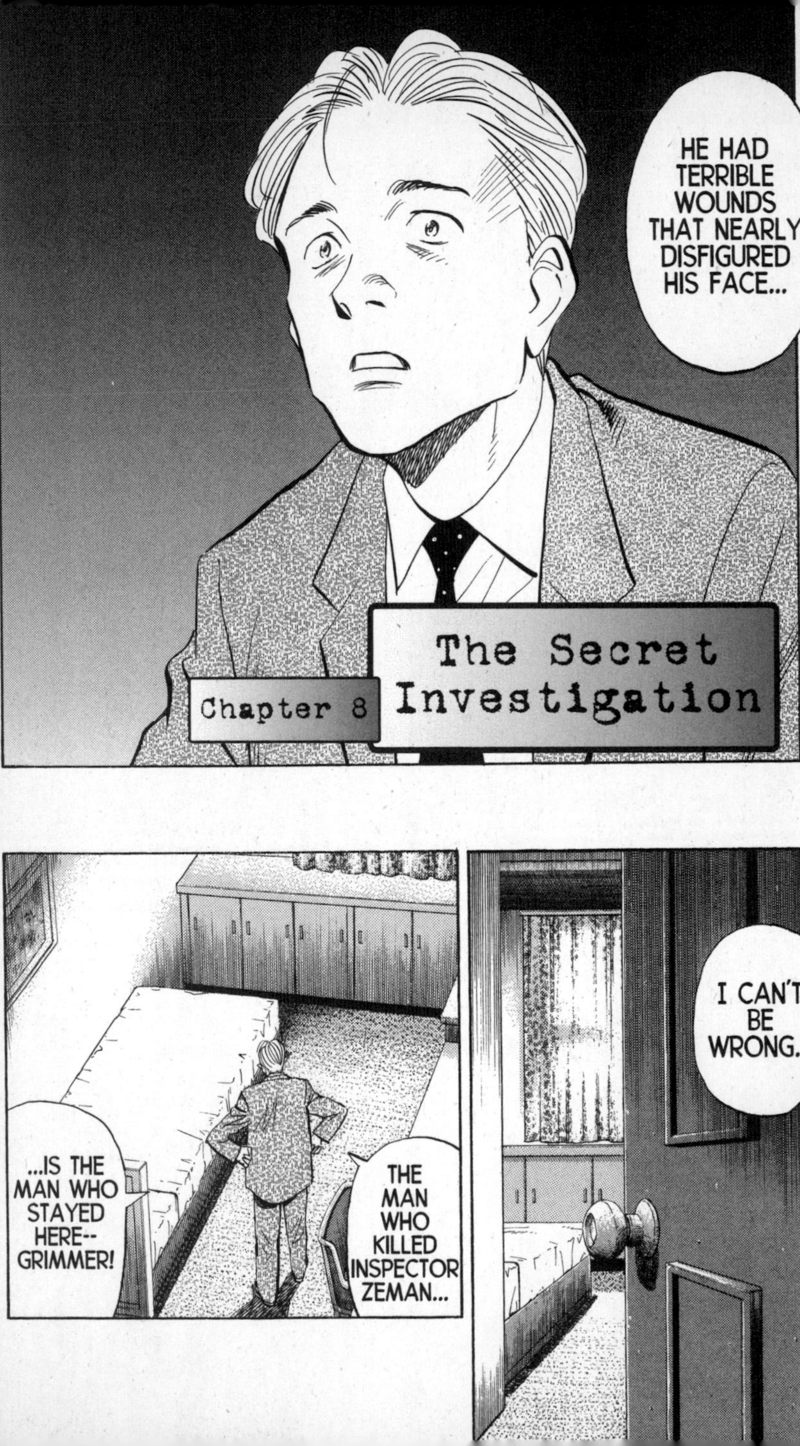
HE HAD TERRIBLE WOUNDS THAT NEARLY DISFIGURED HIS FACE...
Chapter 8 The Secret Investigation
I CAN'T BE WRONG...
THE MAN WHO KILLED INSPECTOR ZEMAN...
...IS THE MAN WHO STAYED HERE-- GRIMMER!

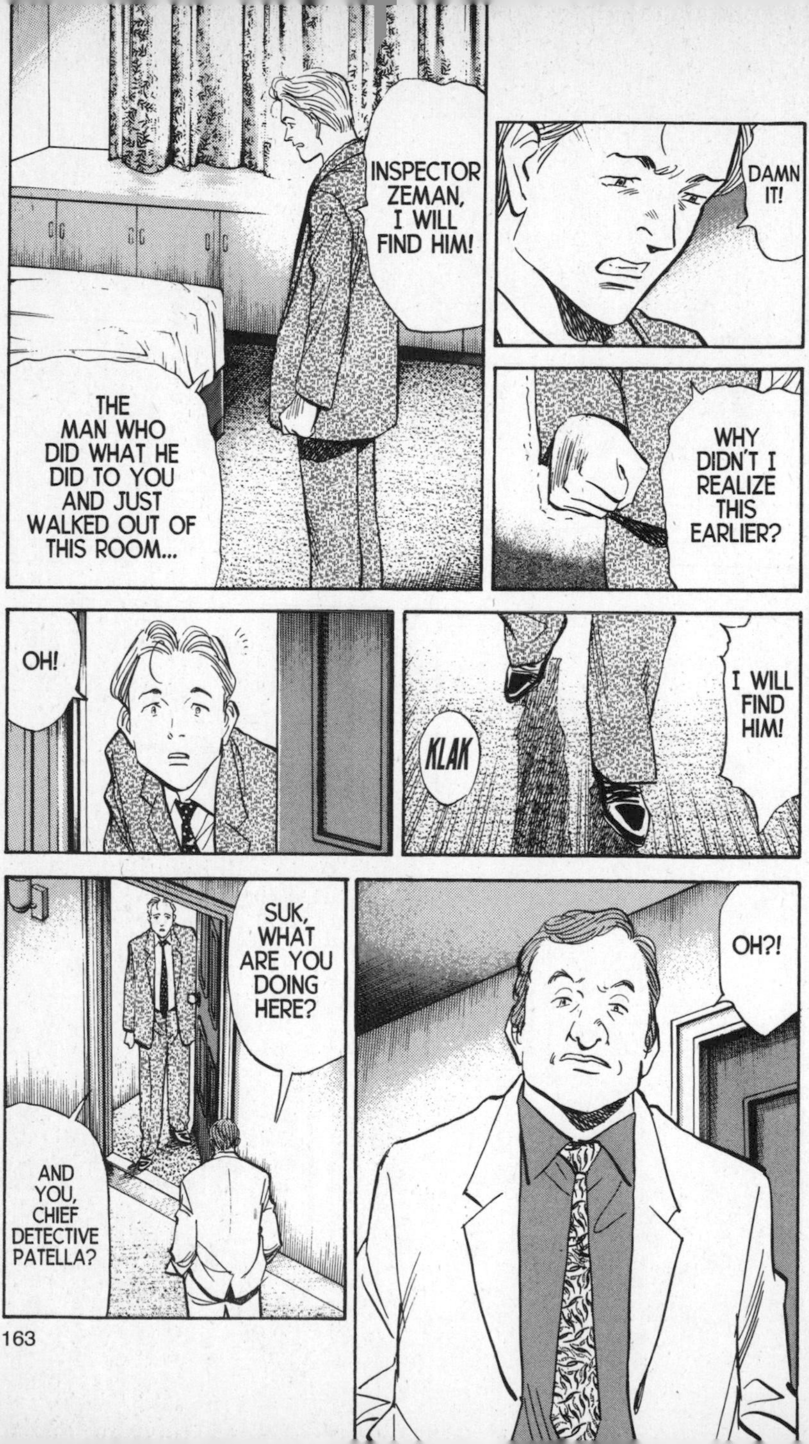
DAMN IT!
WHY DIDN'T I REALIZE THIS EARLIER?
INSPECTOR ZEMAN, I WILL FIND HIM!
THE MAN WHO DID WHAT HE DID TO YOU AND JUST WALKED OUT OF THIS ROOM...
I WILL FIND HIM!
KLAK
OH!
OH?!
SUK, WHAT ARE YOU DOING HERE?
AND YOU, CHIEF DETECTIVE PATELLA?

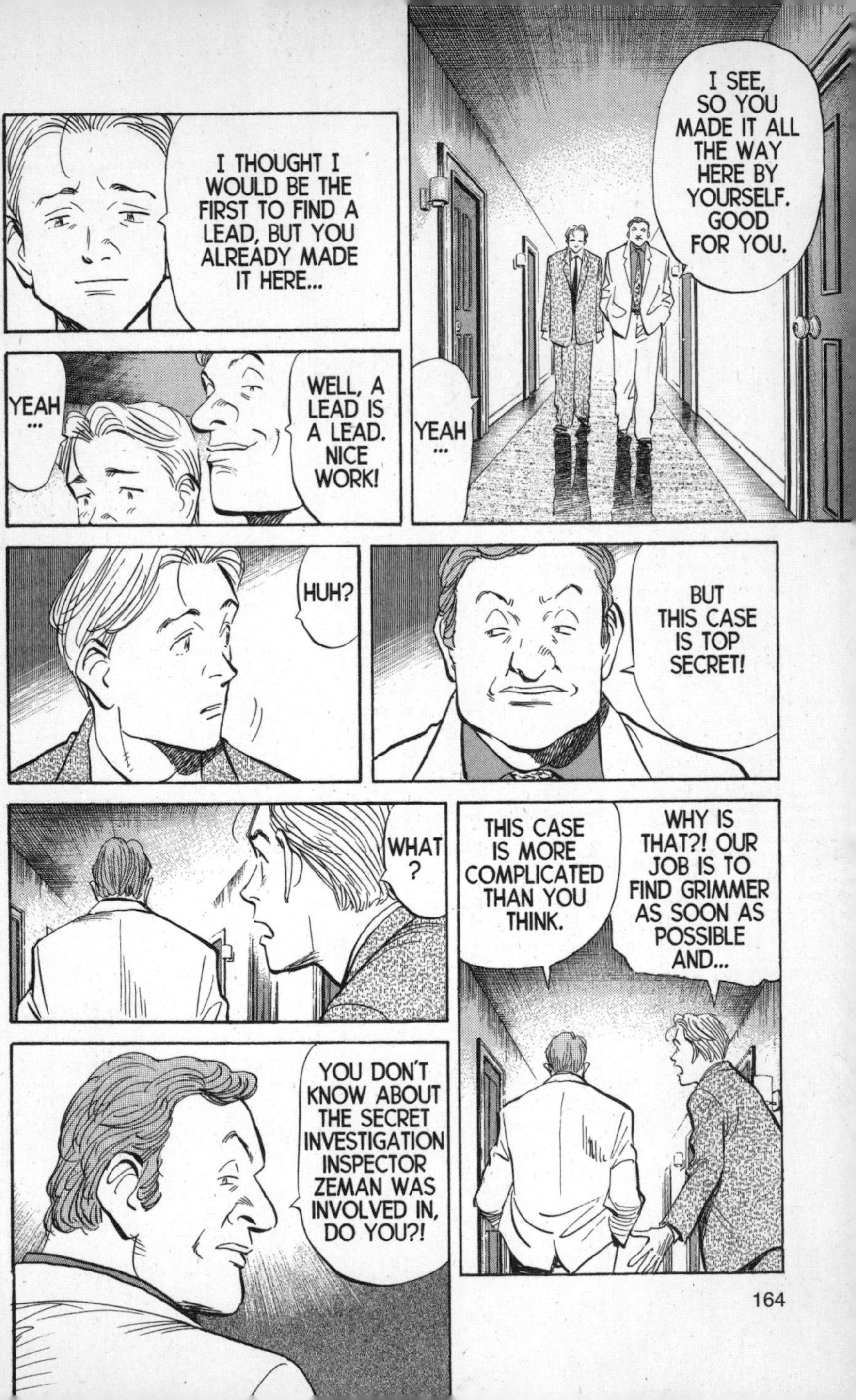
I SEE, SO YOU MADE IT ALL THE WAY HERE BY YOURSELF. GOOD FOR YOU.
YEAH...
I THOUGHT I WOULD BE THE FIRST TO FIND A LEAD, BUT YOU ALREADY MADE IT HERE...
WELL, A LEAD IS A LEAD. NICE WORK!
YEAH...
BUT THIS CASE IS TOP SECRET!
HUH?
WHY IS THAT?! OUR JOB IS TO FIND GRIMMER AS SOON AS POSSIBLE AND...
THIS CASE IS MORE COMPLICATED THAN YOU THINK.
WHAT?
YOU DON'T KNOW ABOUT THE SECRET INVESTIGATION INSPECTOR ZEMAN WAS INVOLVED IN, DO YOU?!

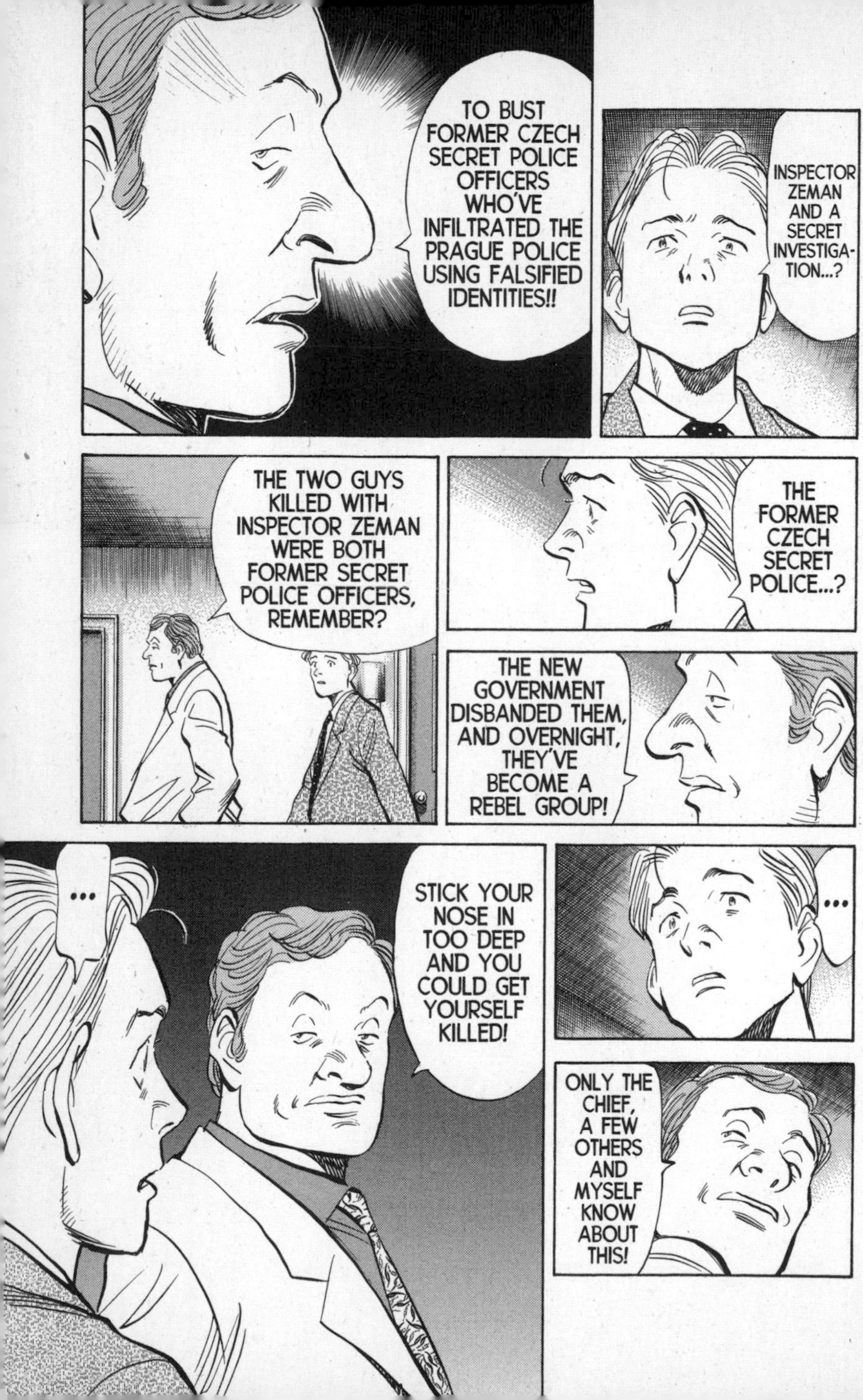
INSPECTOR ZEMAN AND A SECRET INVESTIGA-TION...?
TO BUST FORMER CZECH SECRET POLICE OFFICERS WHO'VE INFILTRATED THE PRAGUE POLICE USING FALSIFIED IDENTITIES!!
THE FORMER CZECH SECRET POLICE...?
THE NEW GOVERNMENT DISBANDED THEM, AND OVERNIGHT, THEY'VE BECOME A REBEL GROUP!
THE TWO GUYS KILLED WITH INSPECTOR ZEMAN WERE BOTH FORMER SECRET POLICE OFFICERS, REMEMBER?
...
ONLY THE CHIEF, A FEW OTHERS AND MYSELF KNOW ABOUT THIS!
STICK YOUR NOSE IN TOO DEEP AND YOU COULD GET YOURSELF KILLED!
...

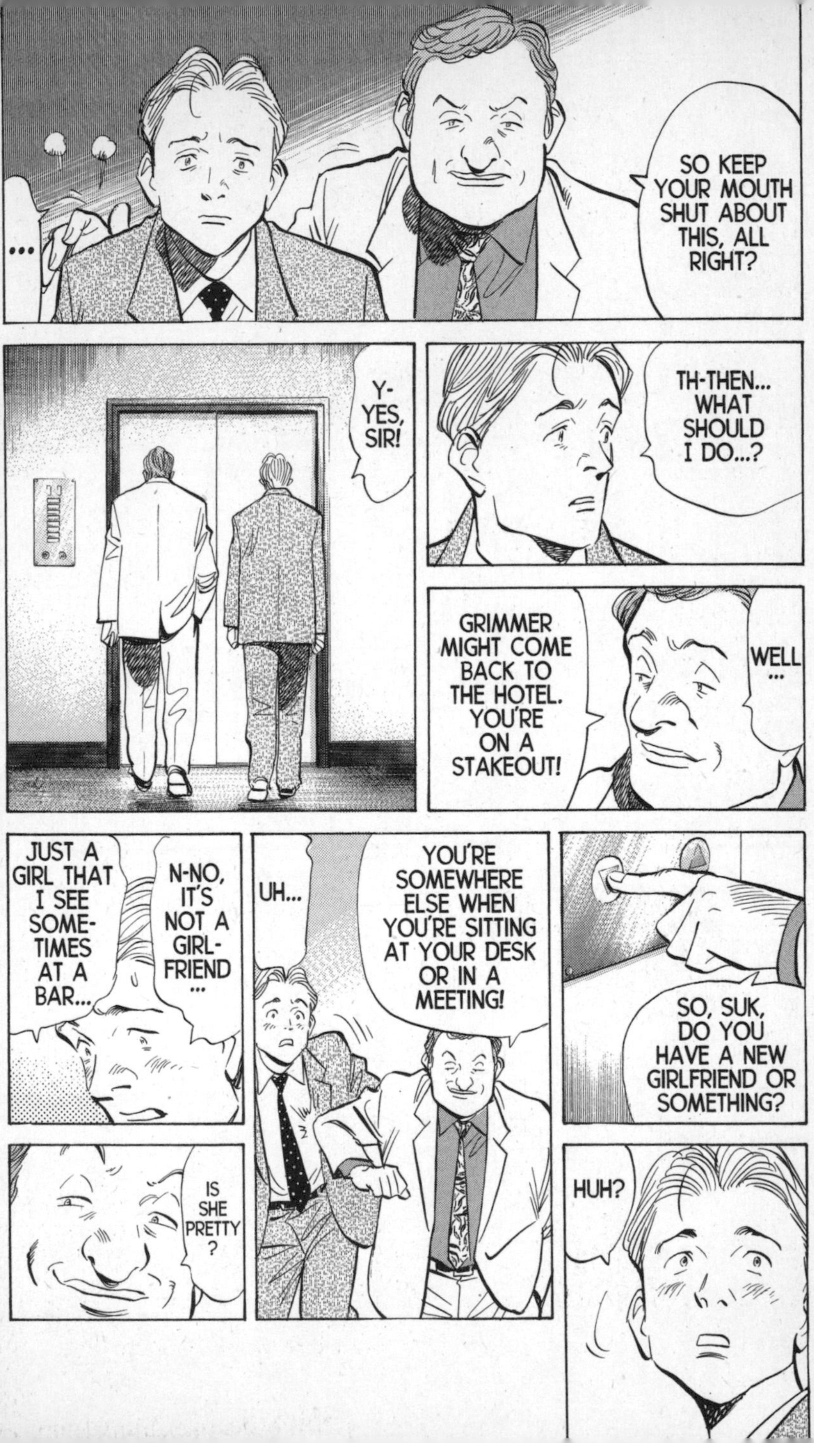
SO KEEP YOUR MOUTH SHUT ABOUT THIS, ALL RIGHT?
...
TH-THEN... WHAT SHOULD I DO...?
WELL...
GRIMMER MIGHT COME BACK TO THE HOTEL. YOU'RE ON A STAKEOUT!
Y-YES, SIR!
SO, SUK, DO YOU HAVE A NEW GIRLFRIEND OR SOMETHING?
HUH?
YOU'RE SOMEWHERE ELSE WHEN YOU'RE SITTING AT YOUR DESK OR IN A MEETING!
UH...
N-NO, IT'S NOT A GIRLFRIEND...
JUST A GIRL THAT I SEE SOMETIMES AT A BAR...
IS SHE PRETTY?

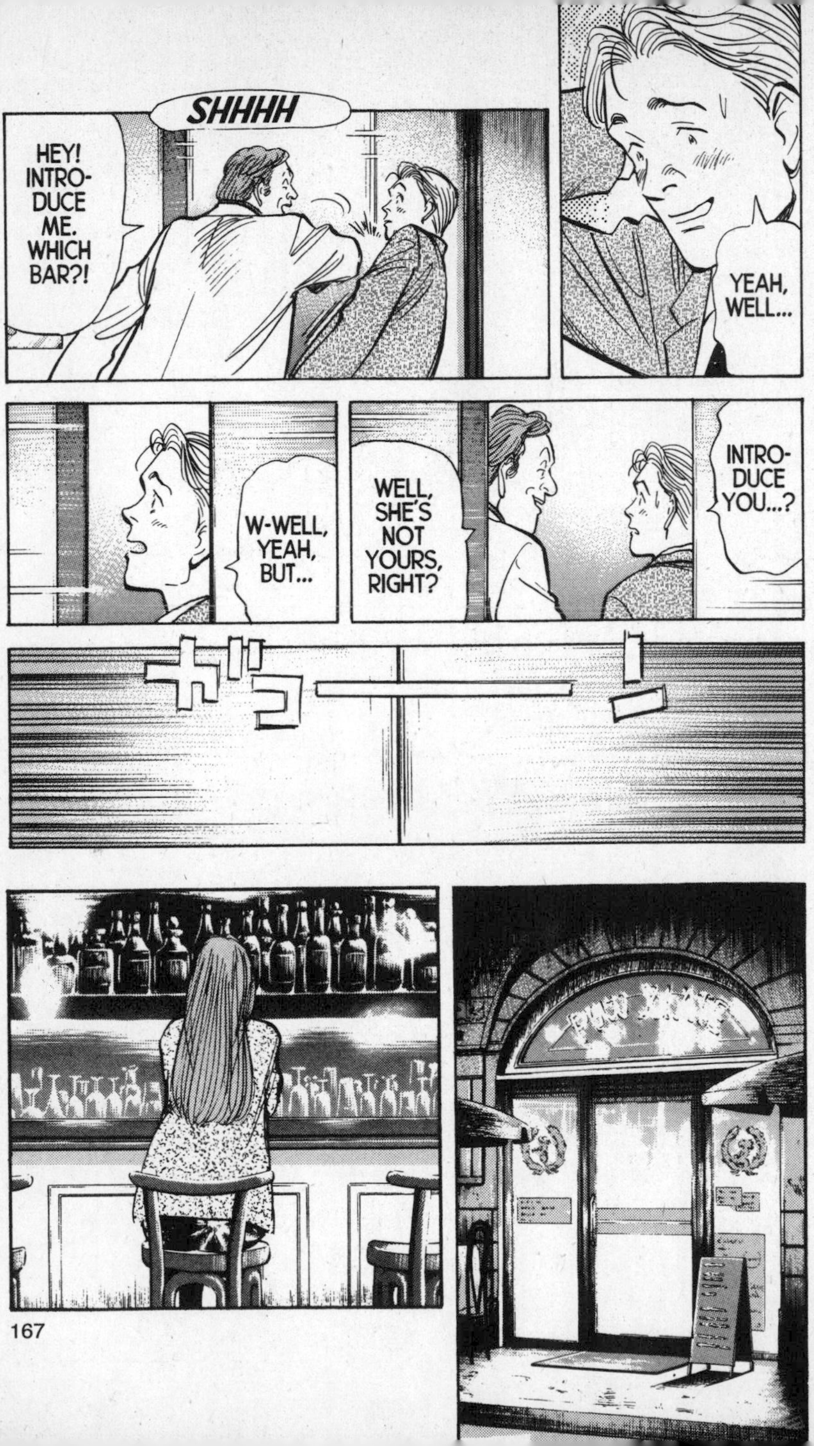
YEAH, WELL...
SHHHH
HEY! INTRODUCE ME. WHICH BAR?!
INTRO-DUCE YOU...?
WELL, SHE'S NOT YOURS, RIGHT?
W-WELL, YEAH, BUT...

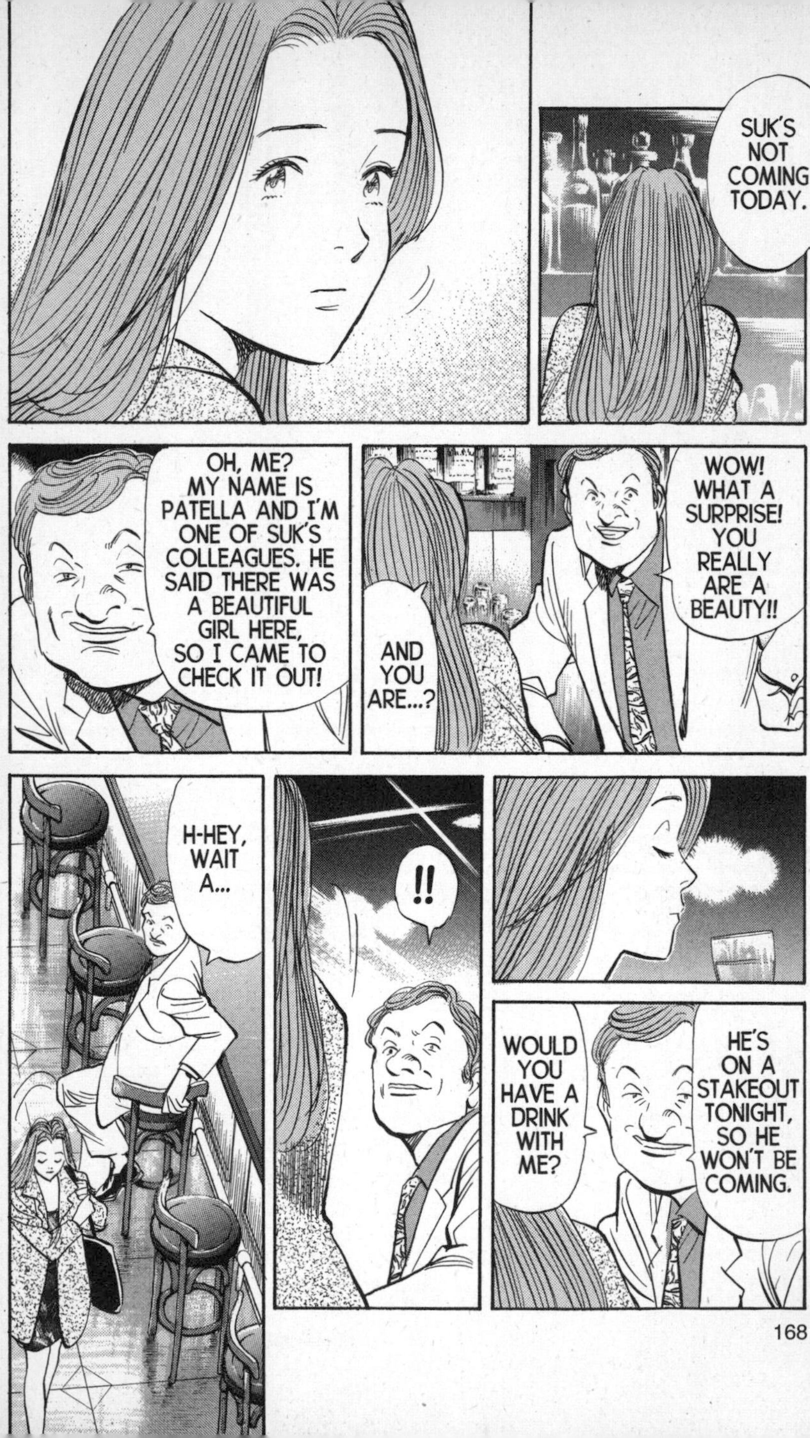
SUK'S NOT COMING TODAY.
WOW! WHAT A SURPRISE! YOU REALLY ARE A BEAUTY!!
AND YOU ARE...?
OH, ME? MY NAME IS PATELLA AND I'M ONE OF SUK'S COLLEAGUES. HE SAID THERE WAS A BEAUTIFUL GIRL HERE, SO I CAME TO CHECK IT OUT!
HE'S ON A STAKEOUT TONIGHT, SO HE WON'T BE COMING.
WOULD YOU HAVE A DRINK WITH ME?
!!
H-HEY, WAIT A...

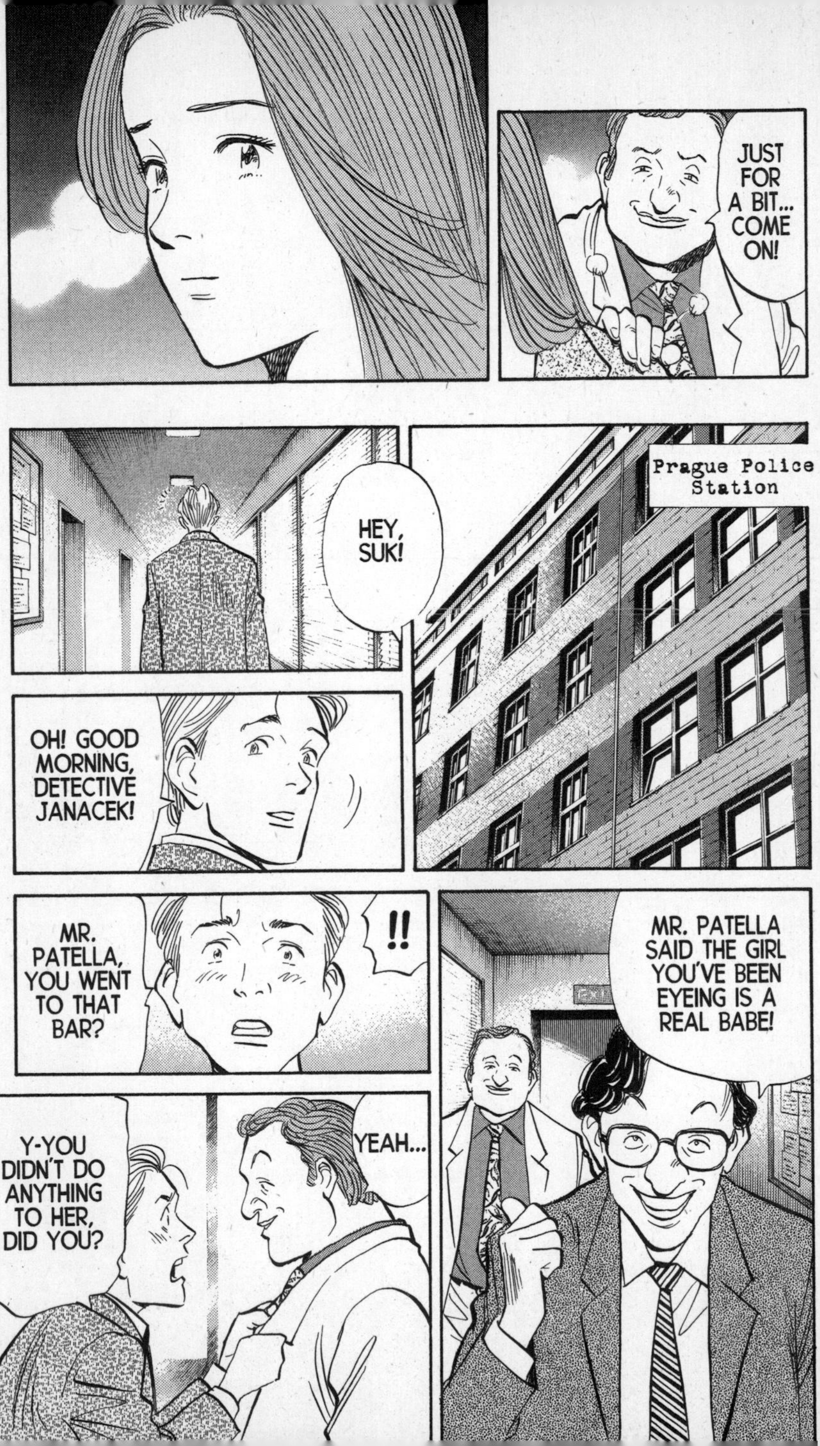
JUST FOR A BIT... COME ON!
Prague Police Station
HEY, SUK!
OH! GOOD MORNING, DETECTIVE JANACEK!
MR. PATELLA SAID THE GIRL YOU'VE BEEN EYEING IS A REAL BABE!
!!
MR. PATELLA, YOU WENT TO THAT BAR?
YEAH...
Y-YOU DIDN'T DO ANYTHING TO HER, DID YOU?

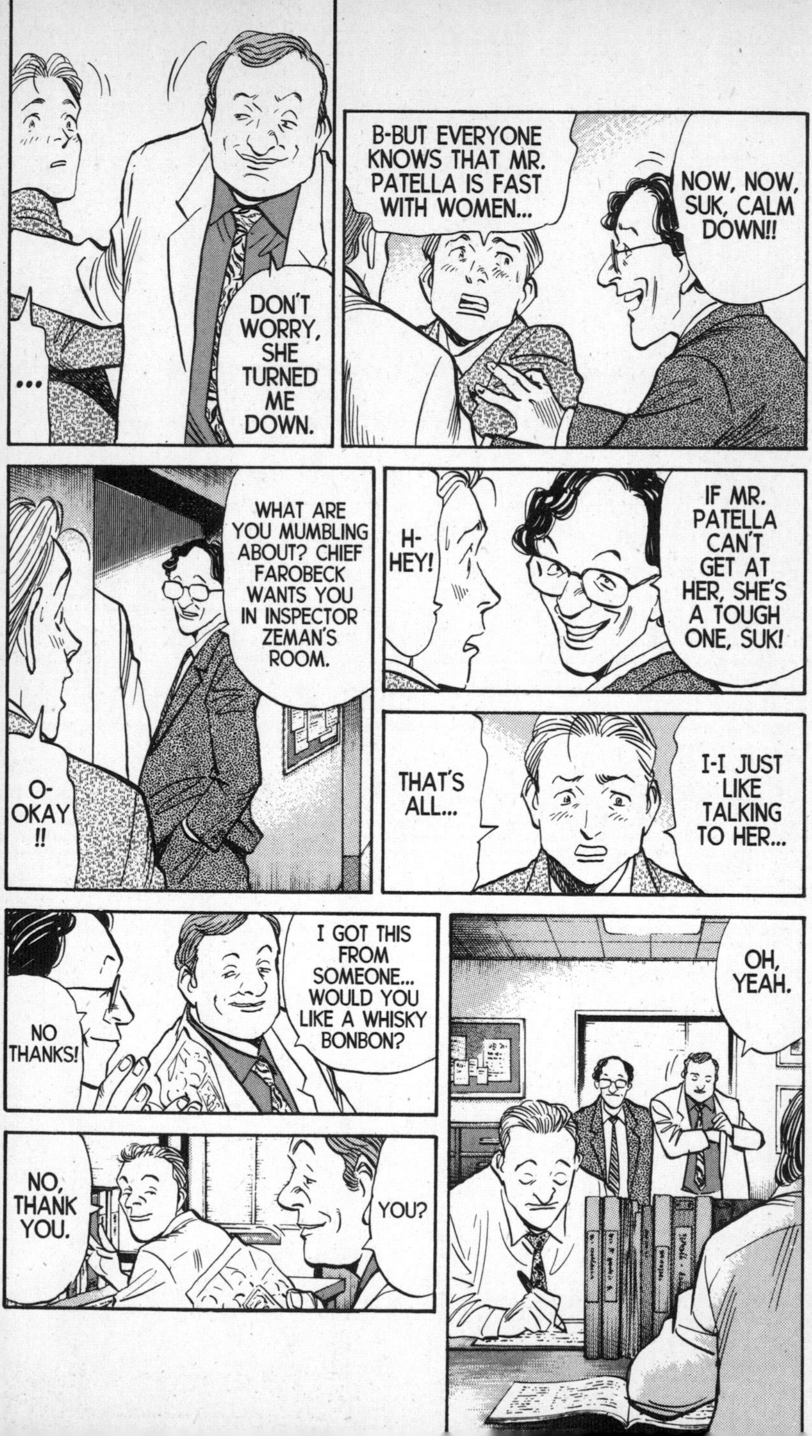
NOW, NOW, SUK, CALM DOWN!!
B-BUT EVERYONE KNOWS THAT MR. PATELLA IS FAST WITH WOMEN...
DON'T WORRY, SHE TURNED ME DOWN.
...
IF MR. PATELLA CAN'T GET AT HER, SHE'S A TOUGH ONE, SUK!
H-HEY!
I-I JUST LIKE TALKING TO HER...
THAT'S ALL...
WHAT ARE YOU MUMBLING ABOUT? CHIEF FAROBECK WANTS YOU IN INSPECTOR ZEMAN'S ROOM.
O-OKAY!!
OH, YEAH.
I GOT THIS FROM SOMEONE... WOULD YOU LIKE A WHISKY BONBON?
NO THANKS!
YOU?
NO, THANK YOU.

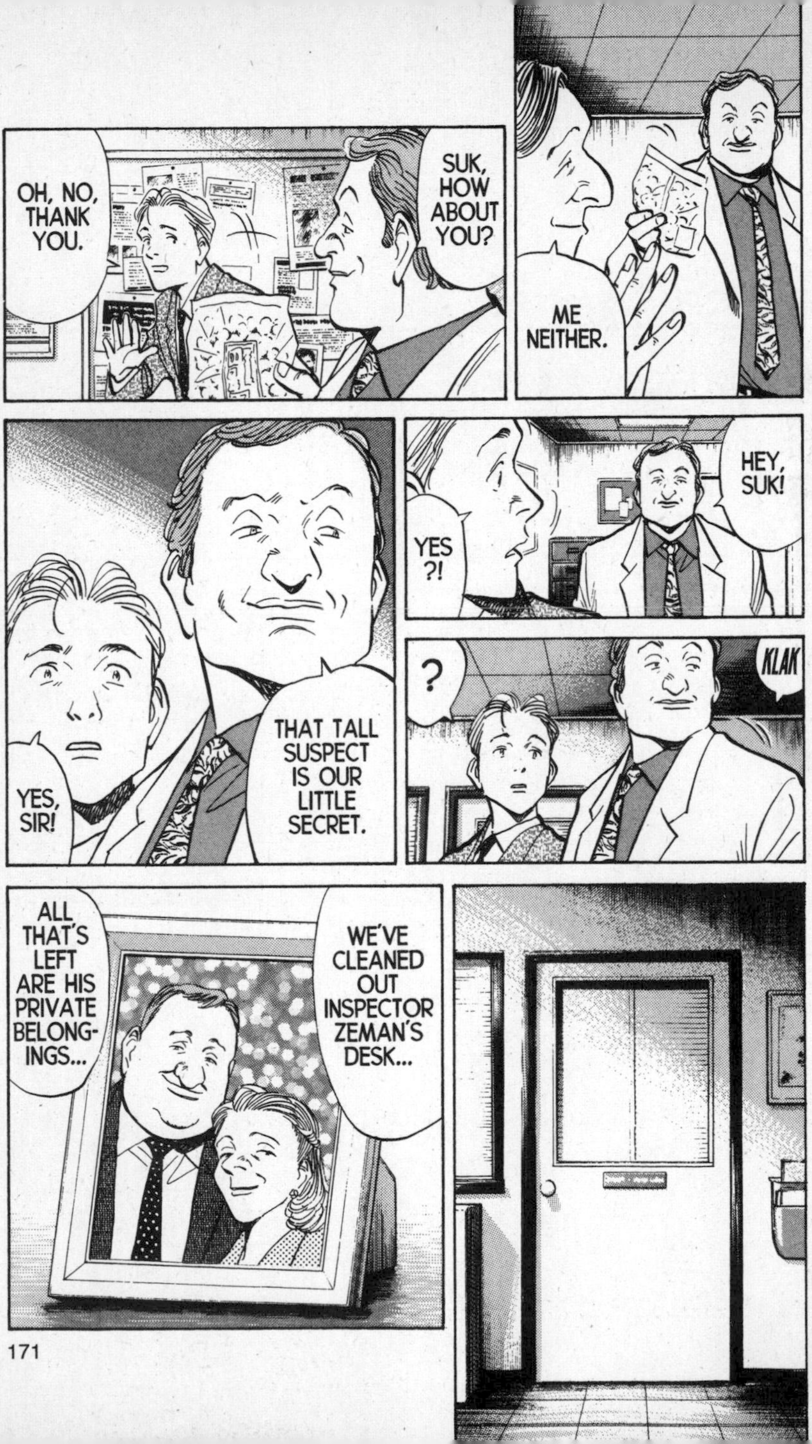
ME NEITHER.
SUK, HOW ABOUT YOU?
OH, NO, THANK YOU.
HEY, SUK!
YES ?!
THAT TALL SUSPECT IS OUR LITTLE SECRET.
YES, SIR!
?
KLAK
WE'VE CLEANED OUT INSPECTOR ZEMAN'S DESK...
ALL THAT'S LEFT ARE HIS PRIVATE BELONG-INGS...

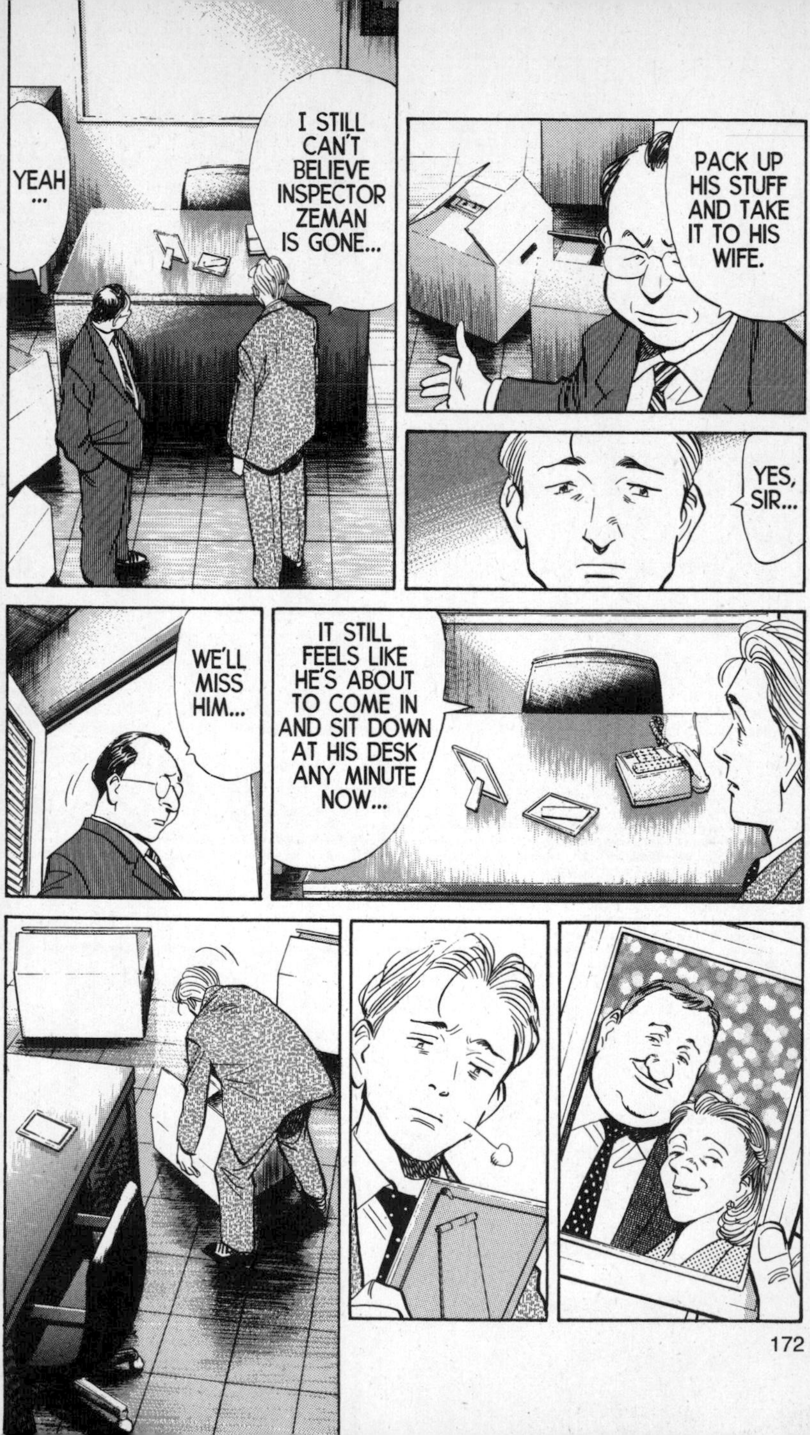
I STILL CAN'T BELIEVE INSPECTOR ZEMAN IS GONE...
YEAH ...
PACK UP HIS STUFF AND TAKE IT TO HIS WIFE.
YES, SIR...
WE'LL MISS HIM...
IT STILL FEELS LIKE HE'S ABOUT TO COME IN AND SIT DOWN AT HIS DESK ANY MINUTE NOW...

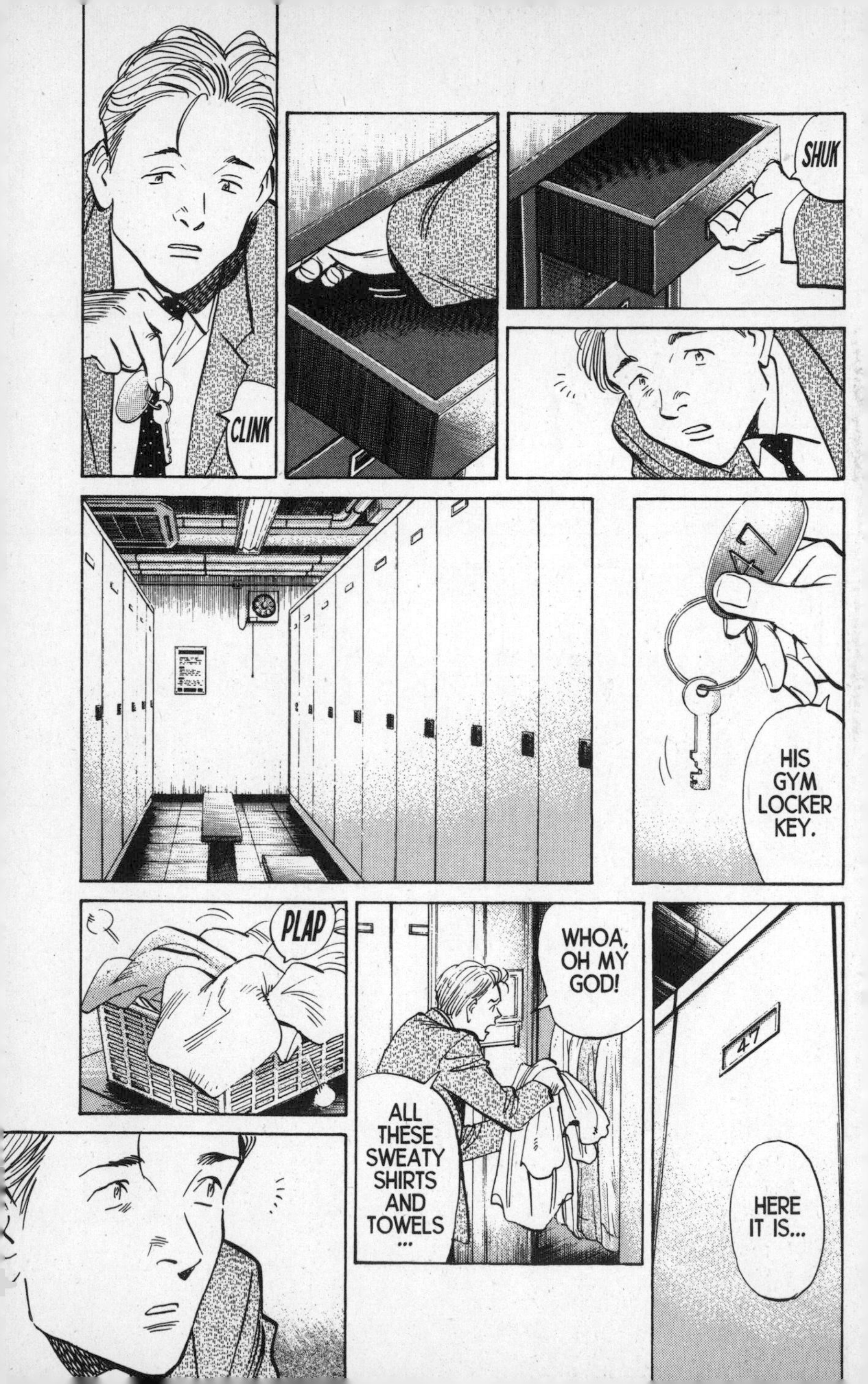
SHUK
CLINK
HIS GYM LOCKER KEY.
HERE IT IS...
WHOA, OH MY GOD!
ALL THESE SWEATY SHIRTS AND TOWELS...
PLAP

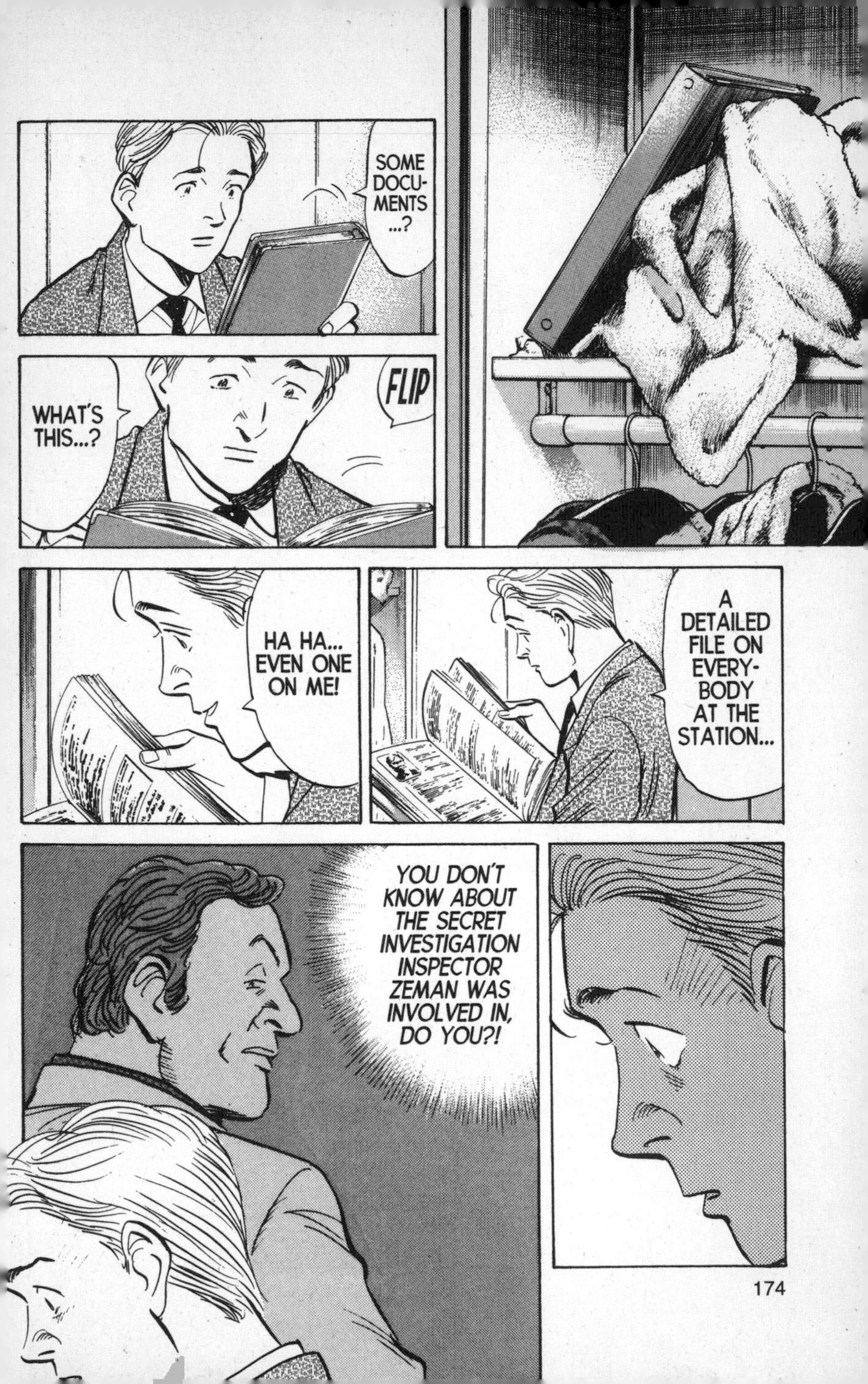
SOME DOCU-MENTS ...?
FLIP
WHAT'S THIS...?
A DETAILED FILE ON EVERY-BODY AT THE STATION...
HA HA... EVEN ONE ON ME!
YOU DON'T KNOW ABOUT THE SECRET INVESTIGATION INSPECTOR ZEMAN WAS INVOLVED IN, DO YOU?!

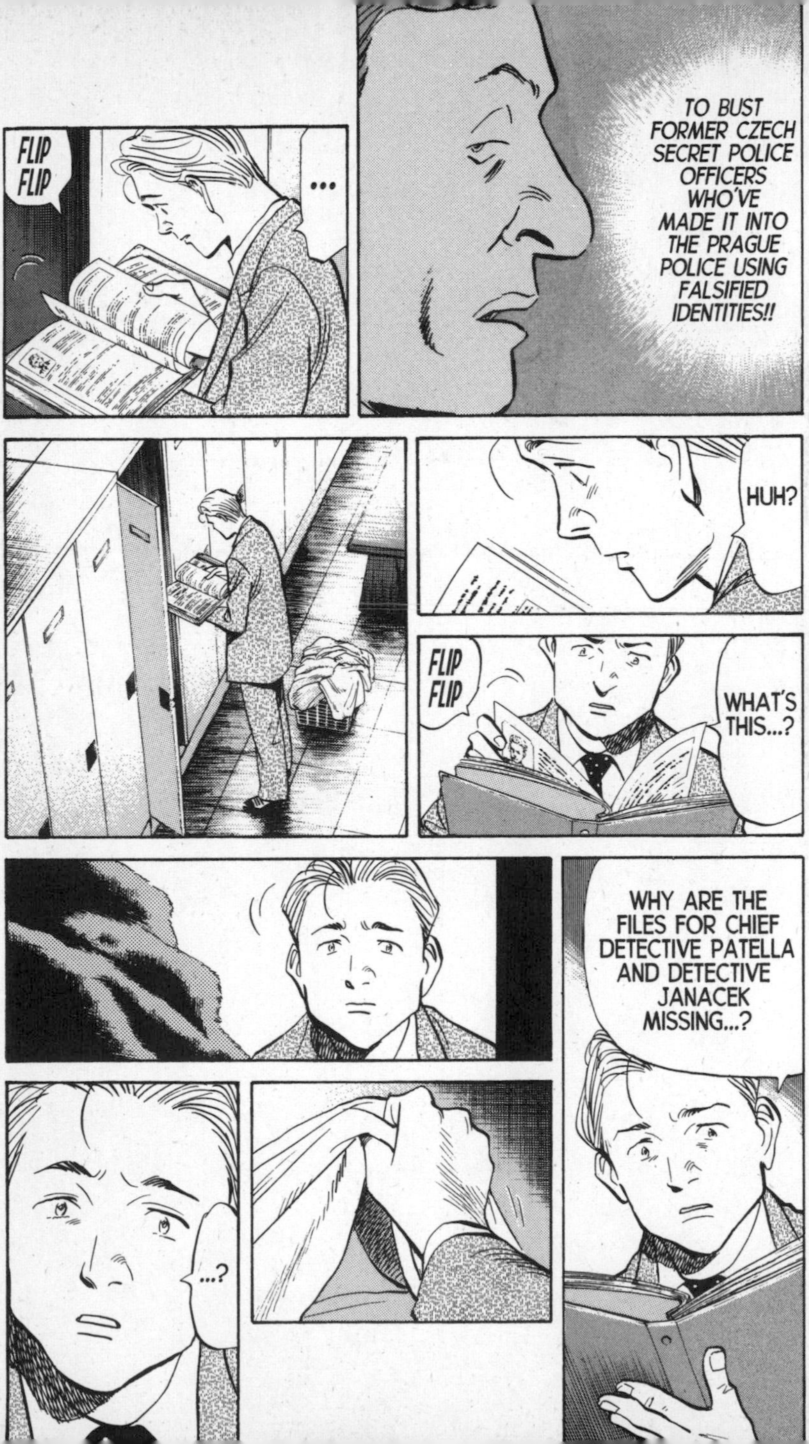
TO BUST FORMER CZECH SECRET POLICE OFFICERS WHO'VE MADE IT INTO THE PRAGUE POLICE USING FALSIFIED IDENTITIES!!
FLIP FLIP
...
HUH?
FLIP FLIP
WHAT'S THIS...?
WHY ARE THE FILES FOR CHIEF DETECTIVE PATELLA AND DETECTIVE JANACEK MISSING...?
...?

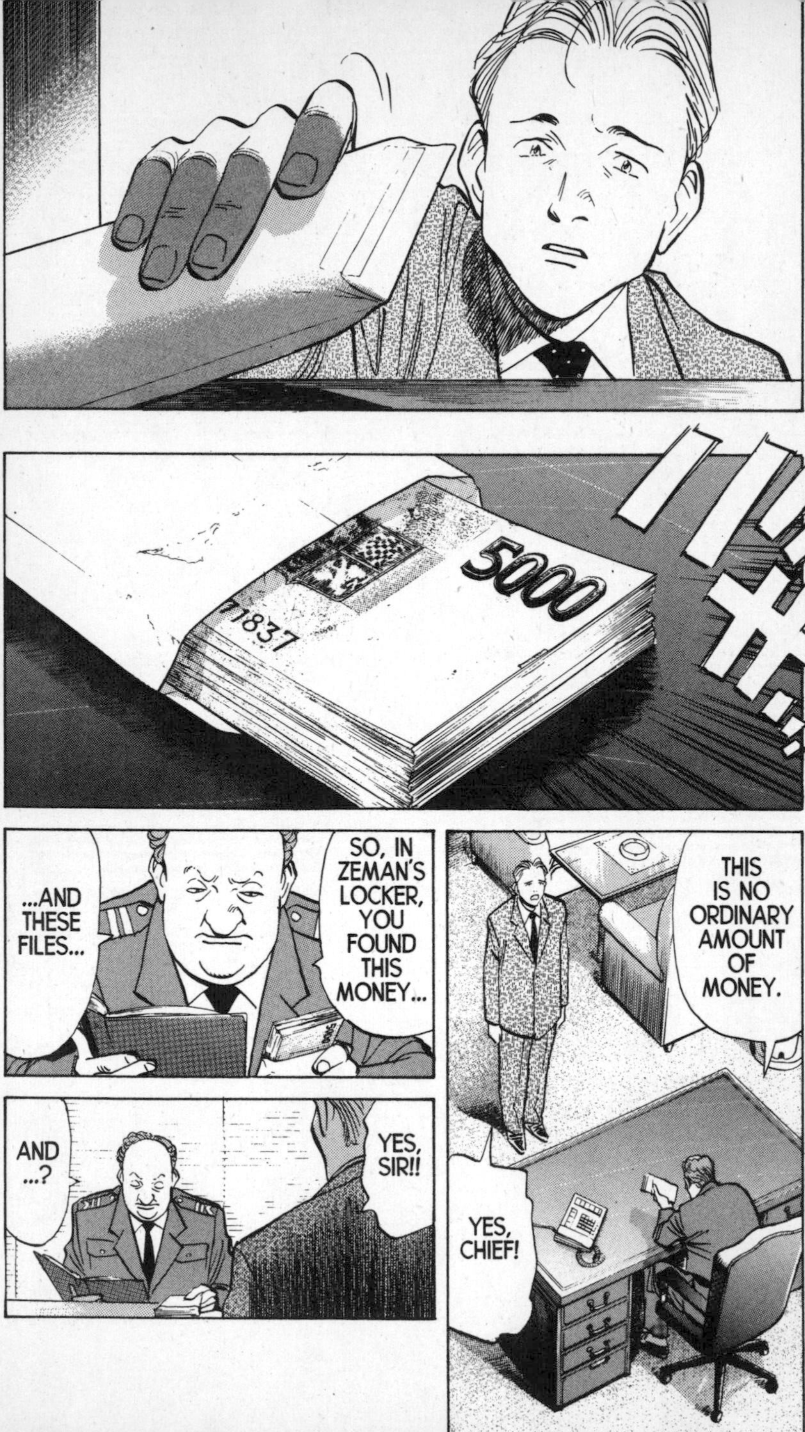
5000
71837
THIS IS NO ORDINARY AMOUNT OF MONEY.
YES, CHIEF!
SO, IN ZEMAN'S LOCKER, YOU FOUND THIS MONEY...
...AND THESE FILES...
YES, SIR!!
AND ...?

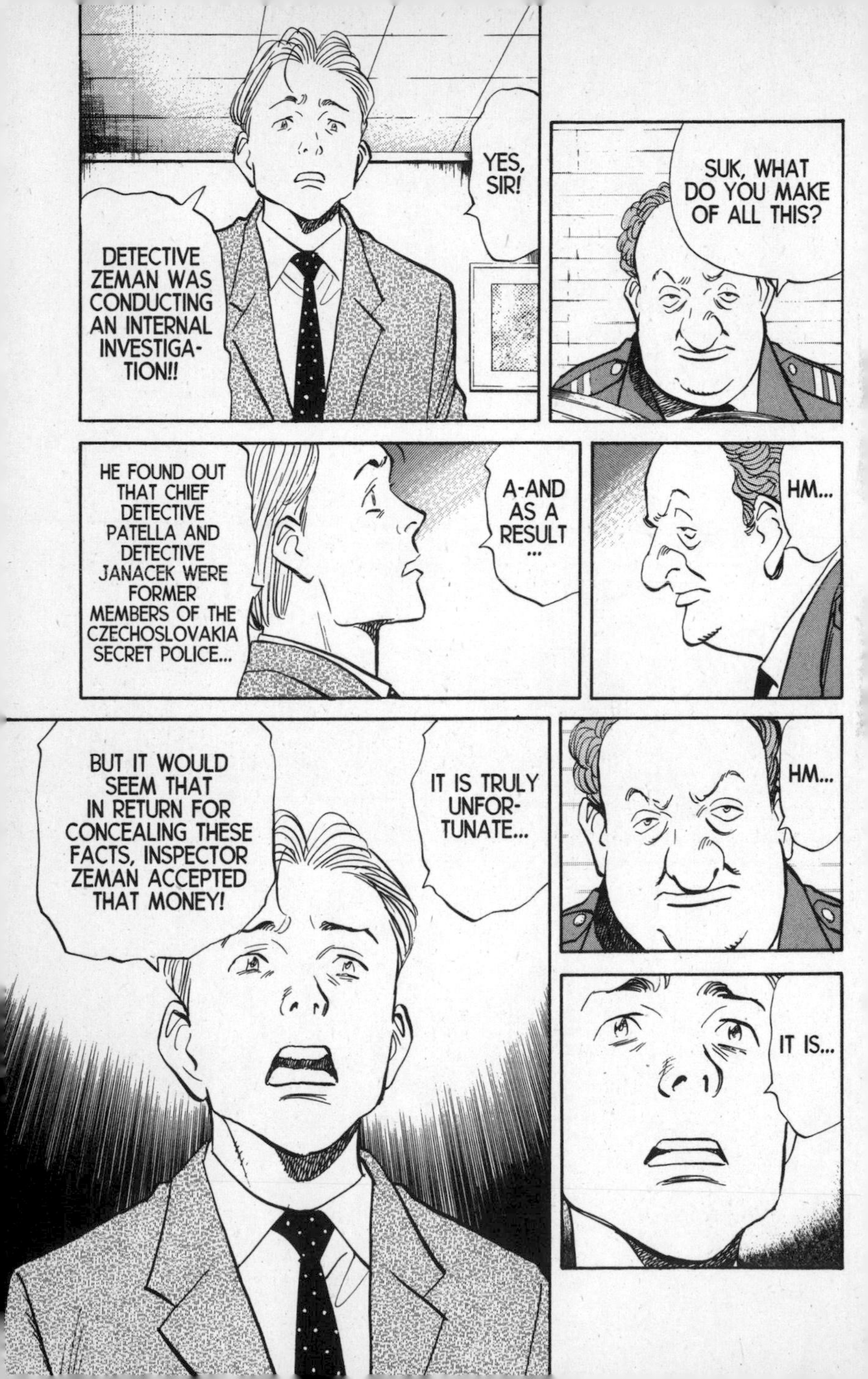
SUK, WHAT DO YOU MAKE OF ALL THIS?
YES, SIR!
DETECTIVE ZEMAN WAS CONDUCTING AN INTERNAL INVESTIGA-TION!!
HM...
A-AND AS A RESULT ...
HE FOUND OUT THAT CHIEF DETECTIVE PATELLA AND DETECTIVE JANACEK WERE FORMER MEMBERS OF THE CZECHOSLOVAKIA SECRET POLICE...
HM...
IT IS...
IT IS TRULY UNFOR-TUNATE...
BUT IT WOULD SEEM THAT IN RETURN FOR CONCEALING THESE FACTS, INSPECTOR ZEMAN ACCEPTED THAT MONEY!

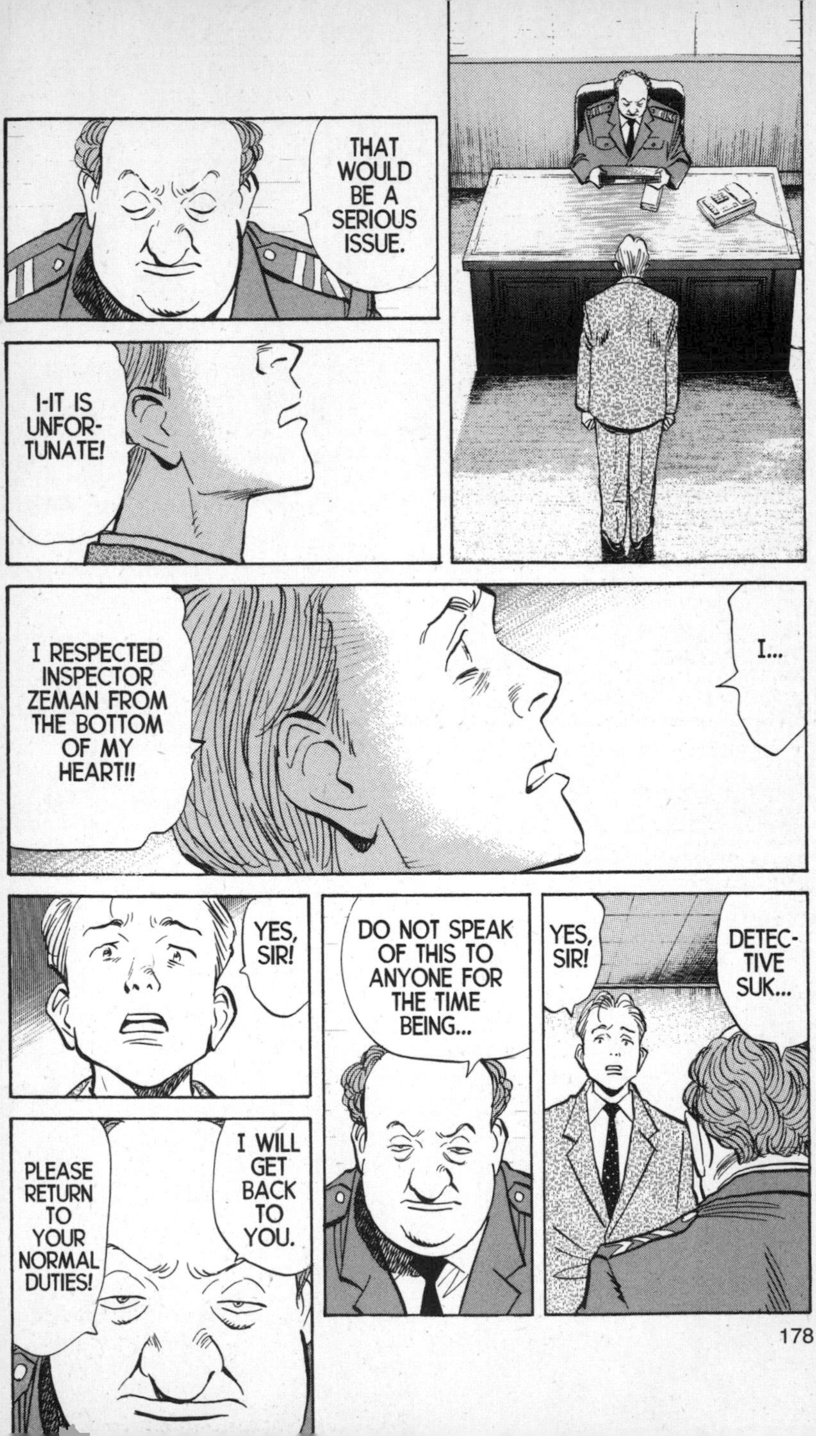
THAT WOULD BE A SERIOUS ISSUE.
I-IT IS UNFORTUNATE!
I...
I RESPECTED INSPECTOR ZEMAN FROM THE BOTTOM OF MY HEART!!
DETECTIVE SUK...
YES, SIR!
DO NOT SPEAK OF THIS TO ANYONE FOR THE TIME BEING...
YES, SIR!
I WILL GET BACK TO YOU.
PLEASE RETURN TO YOUR NORMAL DUTIES!

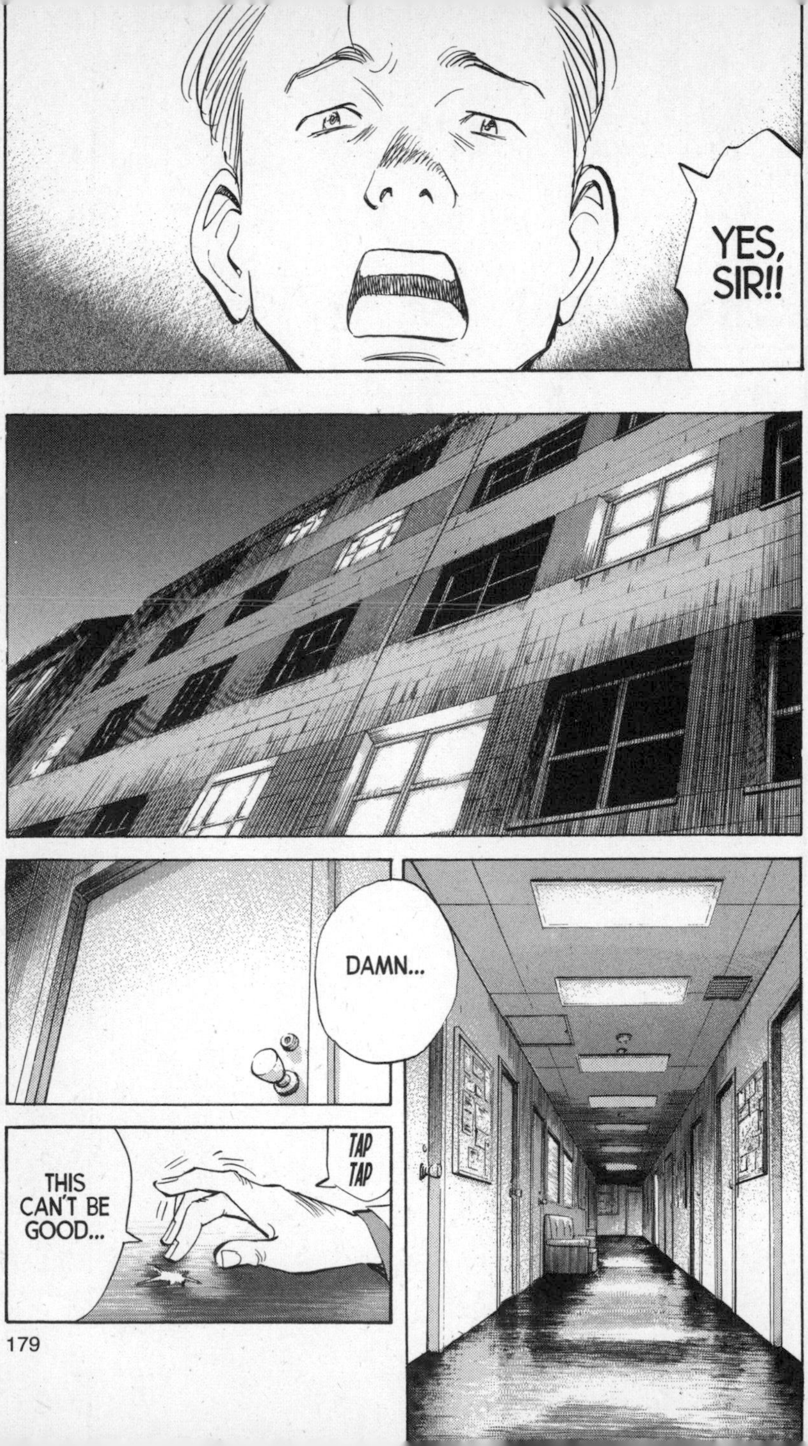
YES, SIR!!
DAMN...
TAP TAP
THIS CAN'T BE GOOD...

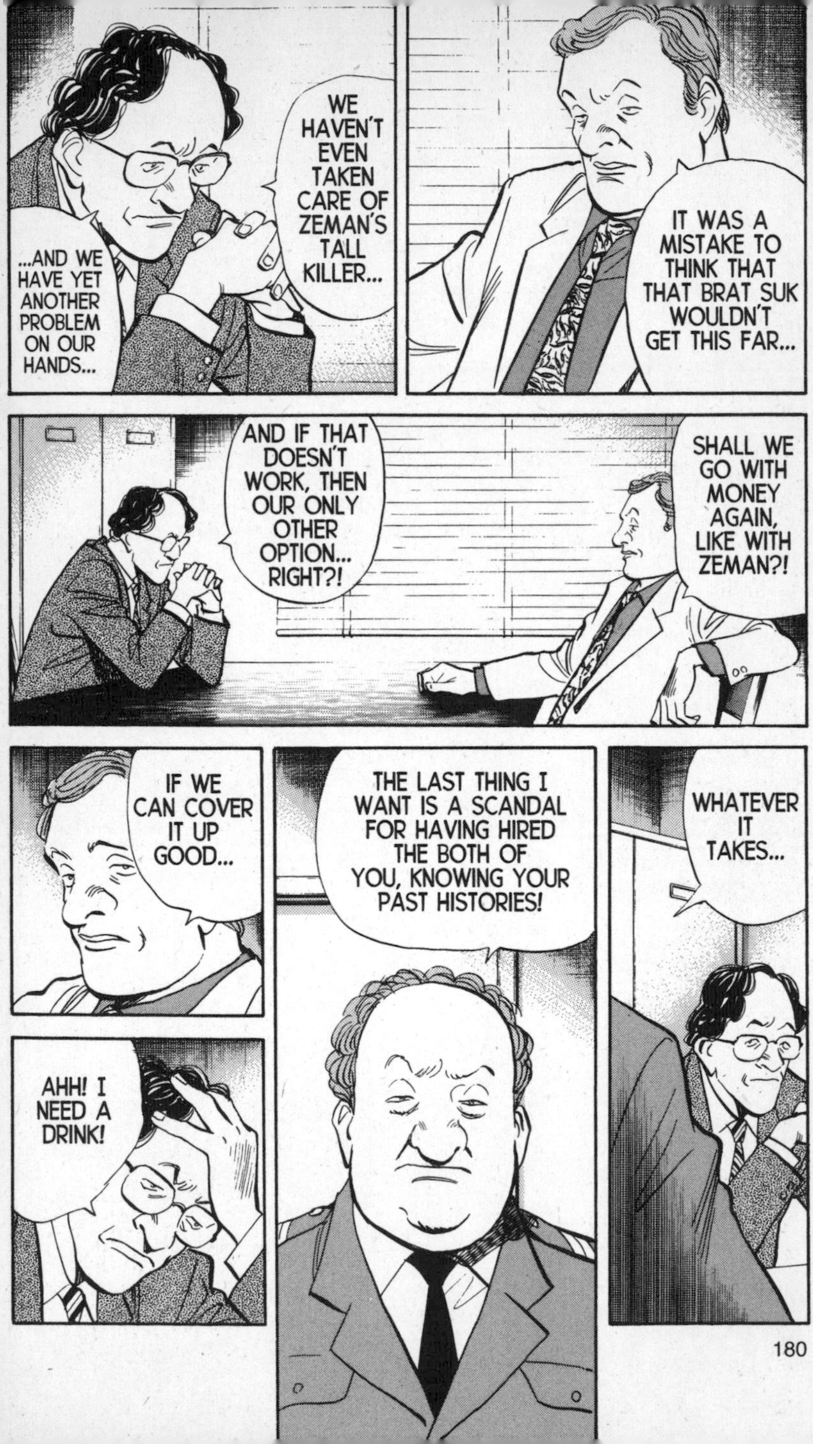
IT WAS A MISTAKE TO THINK THAT THAT BRAT SUK WOULDN'T GET THIS FAR...
WE HAVEN'T EVEN TAKEN CARE OF ZEMAN'S TALL KILLER...
...AND WE HAVE YET ANOTHER PROBLEM ON OUR HANDS...
SHALL WE GO WITH MONEY AGAIN, LIKE WITH ZEMAN?!
AND IF THAT DOESN'T WORK, THEN OUR ONLY OTHER OPTION... RIGHT?!
WHATEVER IT TAKES...
THE LAST THING I WANT IS A SCANDAL FOR HAVING HIRED THE BOTH OF YOU, KNOWING YOUR PAST HISTORIES!
IF WE CAN COVER IT UP GOOD...
AHH! I NEED A DRINK!

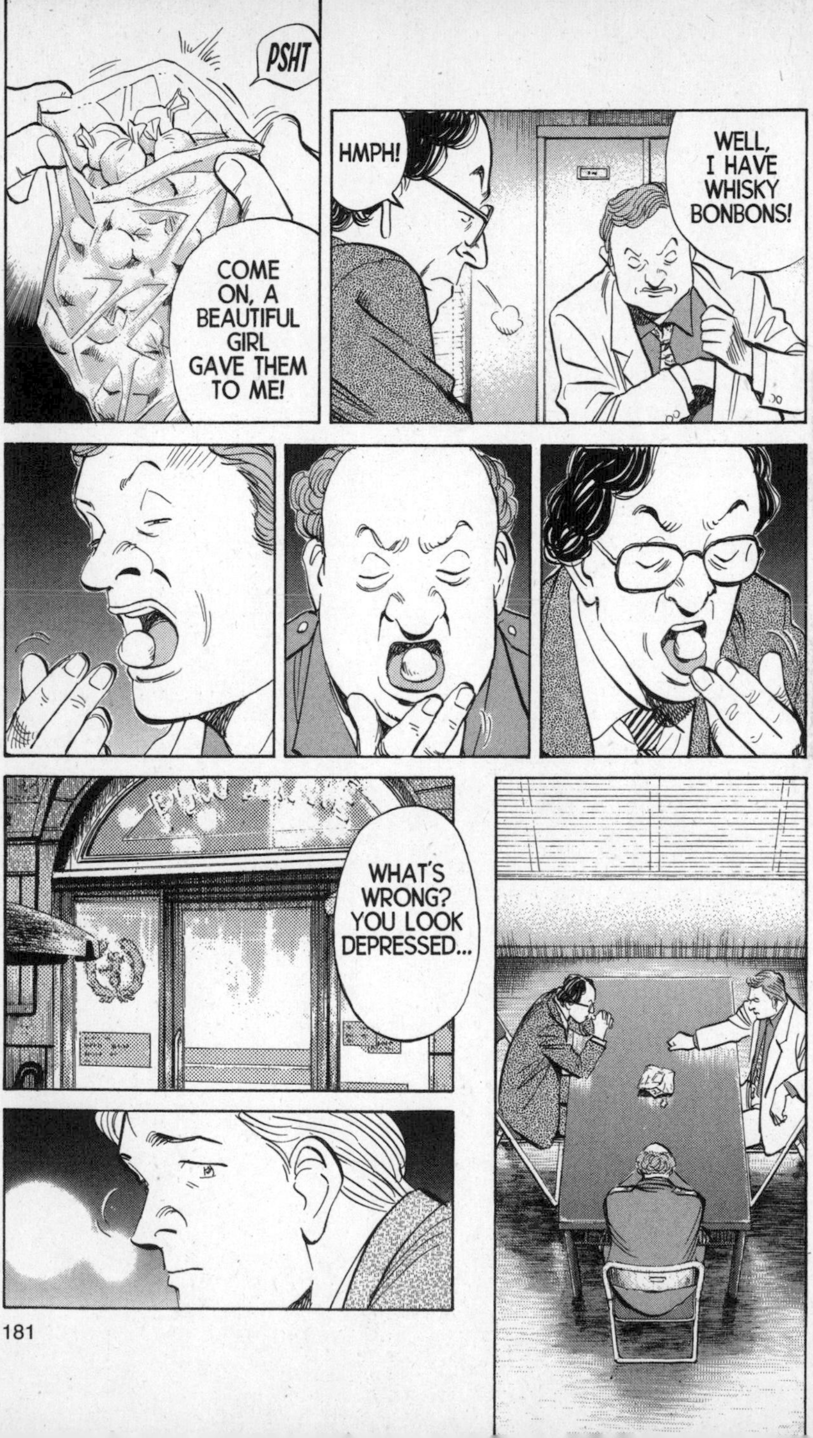
WELL, I HAVE WHISKY BONBONS!
HMPH!
PSHT
COME ON, A BEAUTIFUL GIRL GAVE THEM TO ME!
WHAT'S WRONG? YOU LOOK DEPRESSED...

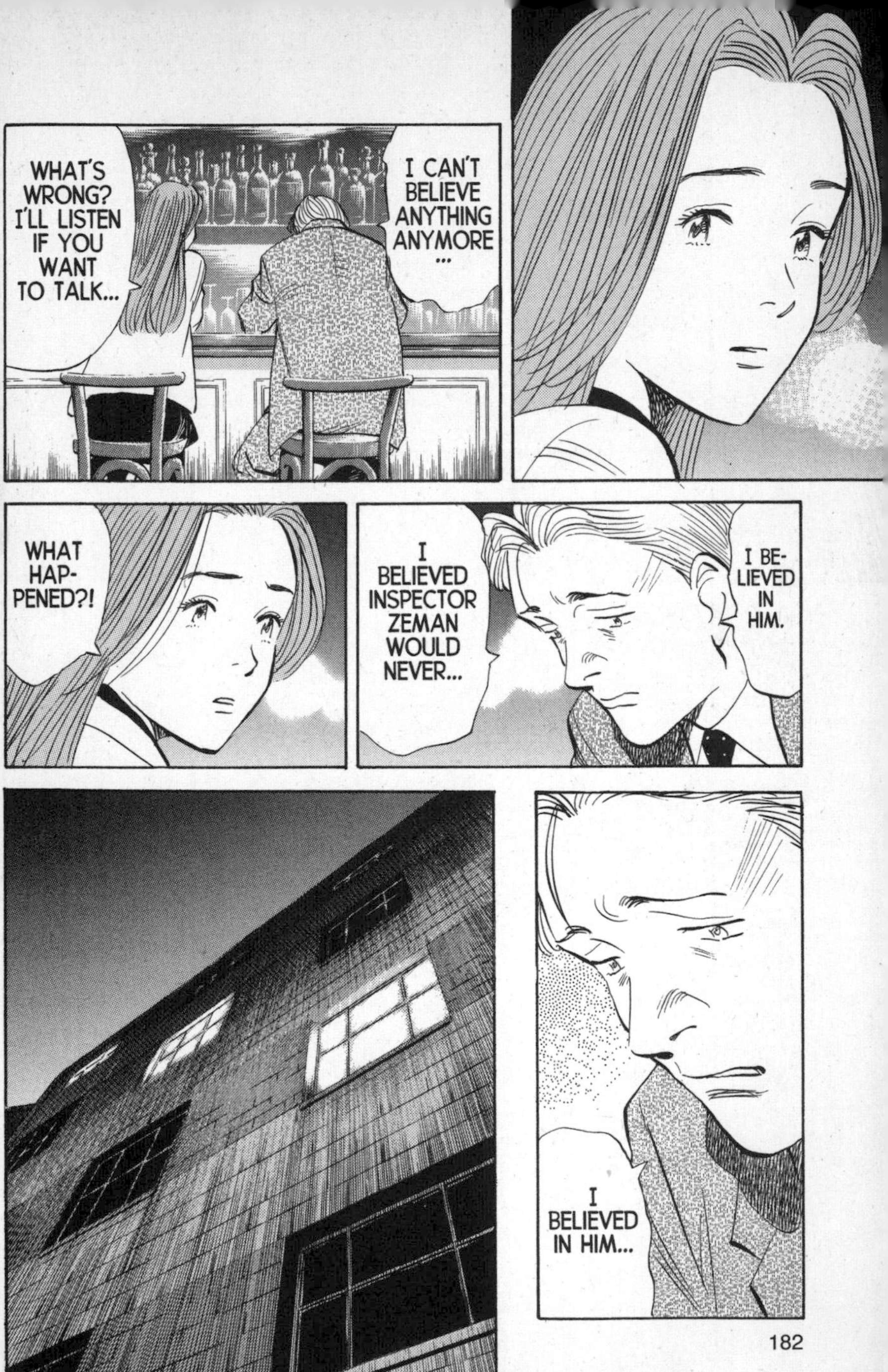
I CAN'T BELIEVE ANYTHING ANYMORE...
WHAT'S WRONG? I'LL LISTEN IF YOU WANT TO TALK...
I BELIEVED INSPECTOR ZEMAN WOULD NEVER...
I BE-LIEVED IN HIM.
WHAT HAP-PENED?!
I BELIEVED IN HIM...

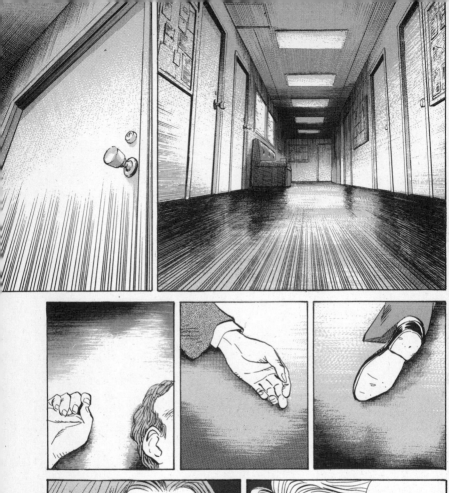

THE ONLY
PEACE
I FIND...

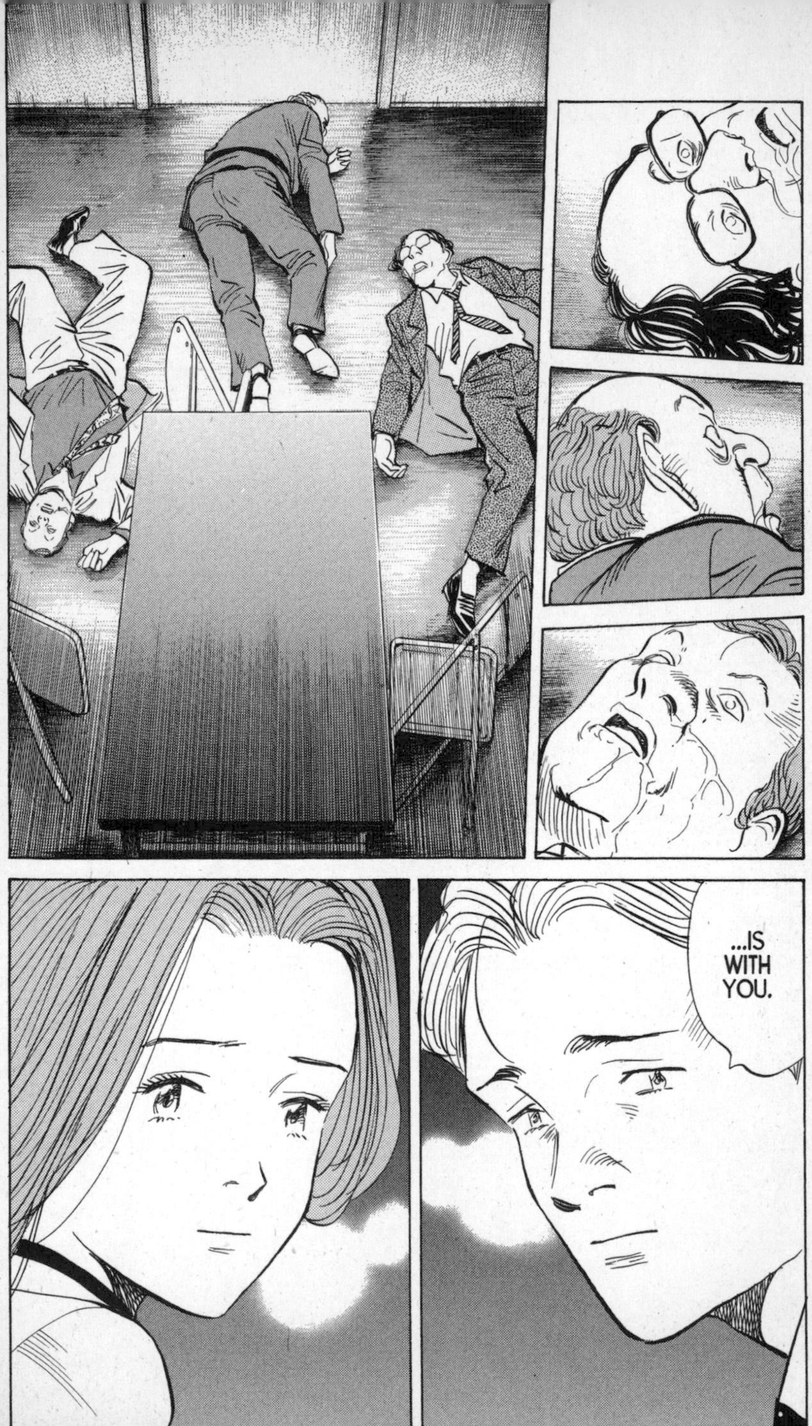
...IS
WITH
YOU.

Chapter 9 Something Important

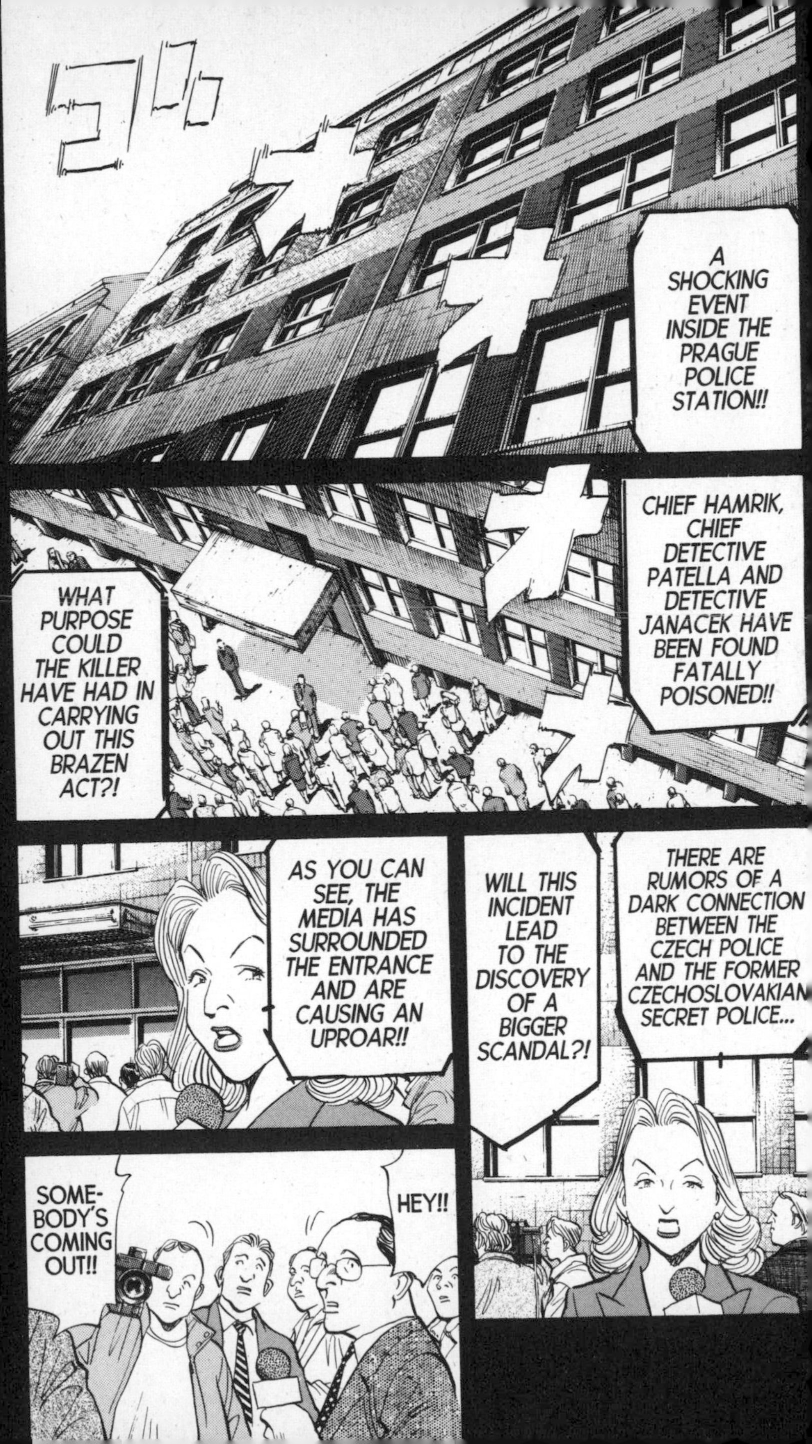
A SHOCKING EVENT INSIDE THE PRAGUE POLICE STATION!!
CHIEF HAMRIK, CHIEF DETECTIVE PATELLA AND DETECTIVE JANACEK HAVE BEEN FOUND FATALLY POISONED!!
WHAT PURPOSE COULD THE KILLER HAVE HAD IN CARRYING OUT THIS BRAZEN ACT?!
THERE ARE RUMORS OF A DARK CONNECTION BETWEEN THE CZECH POLICE AND THE FORMER CZECHOSLOVAKIAN SECRET POLICE...
WILL THIS INCIDENT LEAD TO THE DISCOVERY OF A BIGGER SCANDAL?!
AS YOU CAN SEE, THE MEDIA HAS SURROUNDED THE ENTRANCE AND ARE CAUSING AN UPROAR!!
HEY!!
SOME-BODY'S COMING OUT!!

IS IT TRUE THAT EVEN CHIEF HAMRIK WAS CONNECTED TO THE SECRET POLICE?!

CAN YOU CONFIRM THAT THE POISON USED IN THIS KILLING WAS A MUSCLE RELAXANT?!

DO YOU HAVE A SUSPECT?!

W-WE ARE CURRENTLY STILL INVESTIGATING THOSE CASES...

SO THE POLICE HAVE CONNECTED THESE CASES TO EACH OTHER?

UH... NO...

IS THERE A CONNECTION TO THE MURDER OF INSPECTOR ZEHMAN LAST WEEK?

THE RESPONSE IS TOO SLOW!!

AS SOON AS WE HAVE GATHERED ALL THE INFORMATION THAT WE'RE ABLE TO RELEASE.

WHEN ARE YOU HOLDING THE OFFICIAL PRESS CONFERENCE?!

I'M SORRY. HE'S NOT ON THIS CASE...

NO...LIKE I SAID, WE ARE CONTINUING THE INVESTIGATIONS AND LOOKING INTO THE POSSIBILITY THAT...

QUIT BLATHERING AND GO!

Y-YES, SIR!

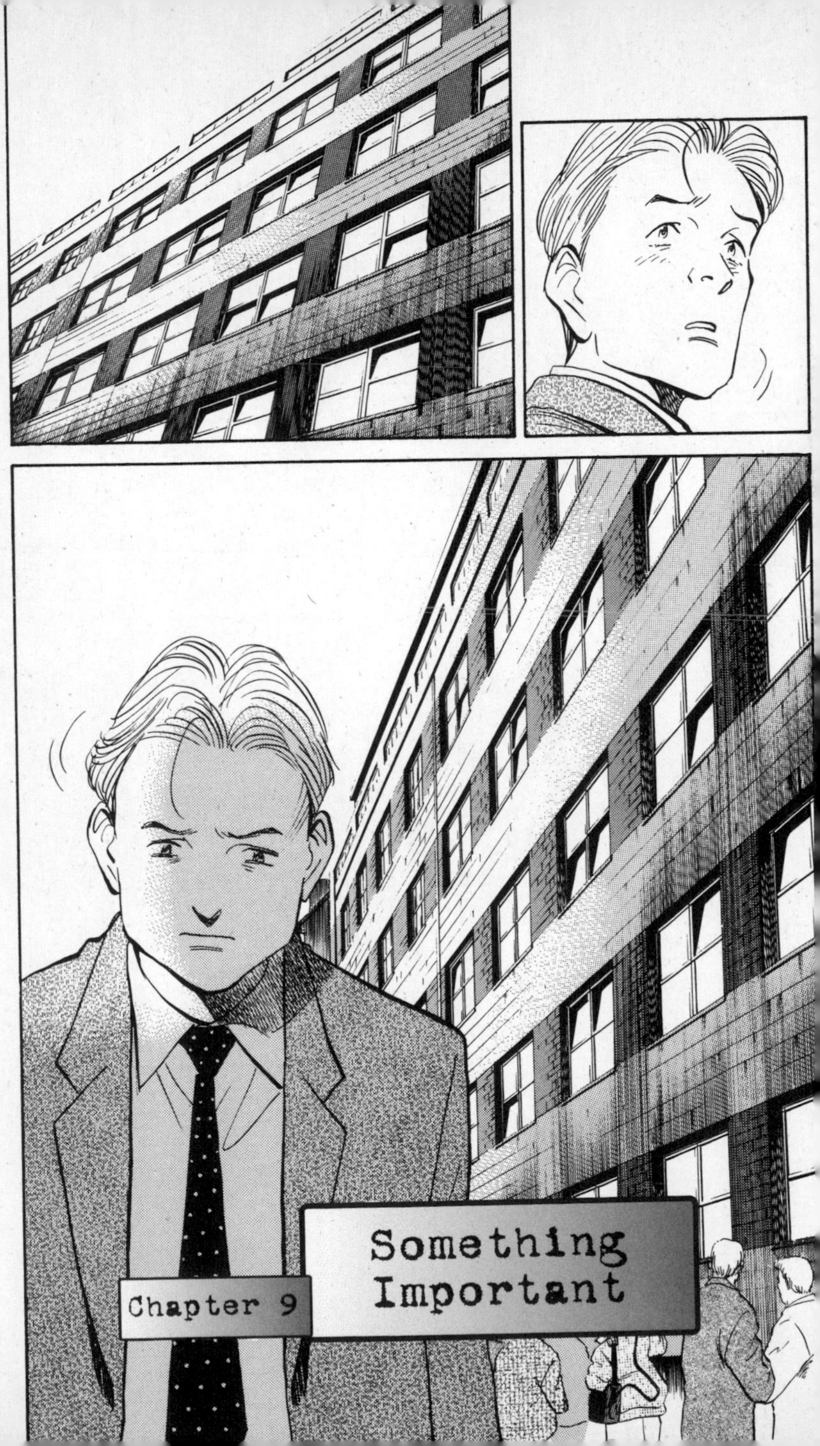
Something Important
Chapter 9

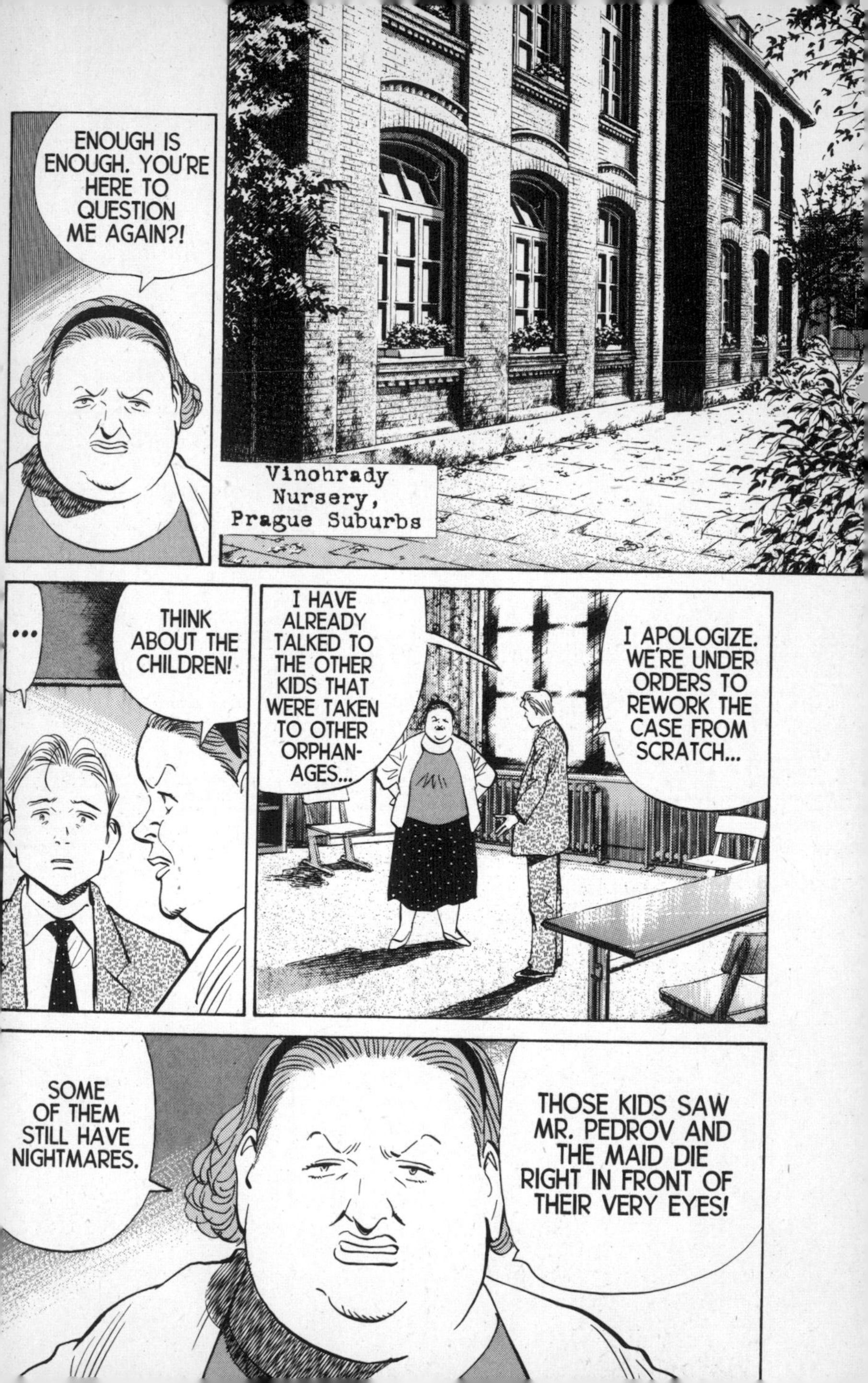
Vinohrady Nursery, Prague Suburbs
ENOUGH IS ENOUGH. YOU'RE HERE TO QUESTION ME AGAIN?!
I APOLOGIZE. WE'RE UNDER ORDERS TO REWORK THE CASE FROM SCRATCH...
I HAVE ALREADY TALKED TO THE OTHER KIDS THAT WERE TAKEN TO OTHER ORPHAN-AGES...
THINK ABOUT THE CHILDREN!
...
THOSE KIDS SAW MR. PEDROV AND THE MAID DIE RIGHT IN FRONT OF THEIR VERY EYES!
SOME OF THEM STILL HAVE NIGHTMARES.

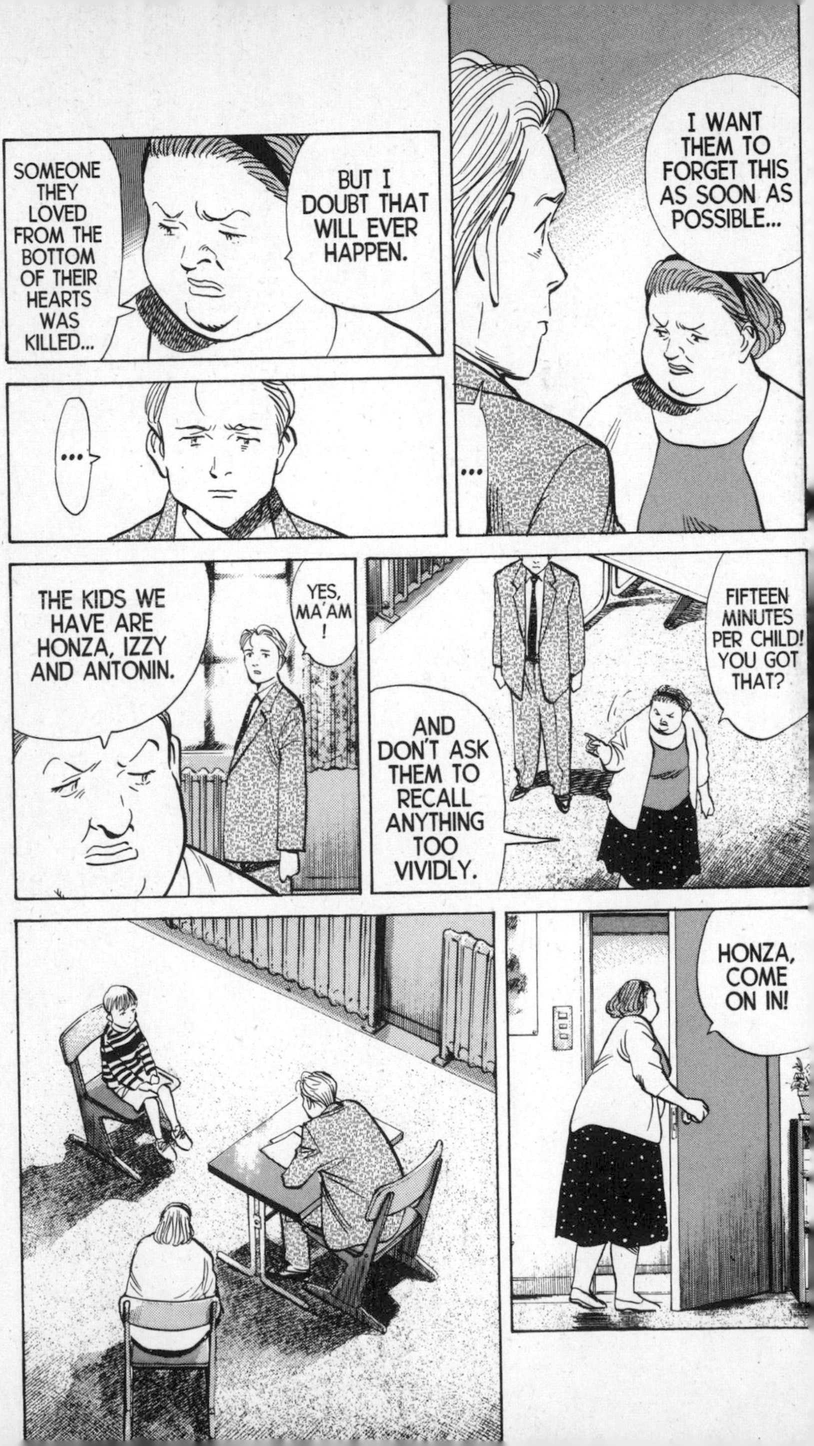
I WANT THEM TO FORGET THIS AS SOON AS POSSIBLE...
...
SOMEONE THEY LOVED FROM THE BOTTOM OF THEIR HEARTS WAS KILLED...
BUT I DOUBT THAT WILL EVER HAPPEN.
...
FIFTEEN MINUTES PER CHILD! YOU GOT THAT?
AND DON'T ASK THEM TO RECALL ANYTHING TOO VIVIDLY.
THE KIDS WE HAVE ARE HONZA, IZZY AND ANTONIN.
YES, MA'AM!
HONZA, COME ON IN!

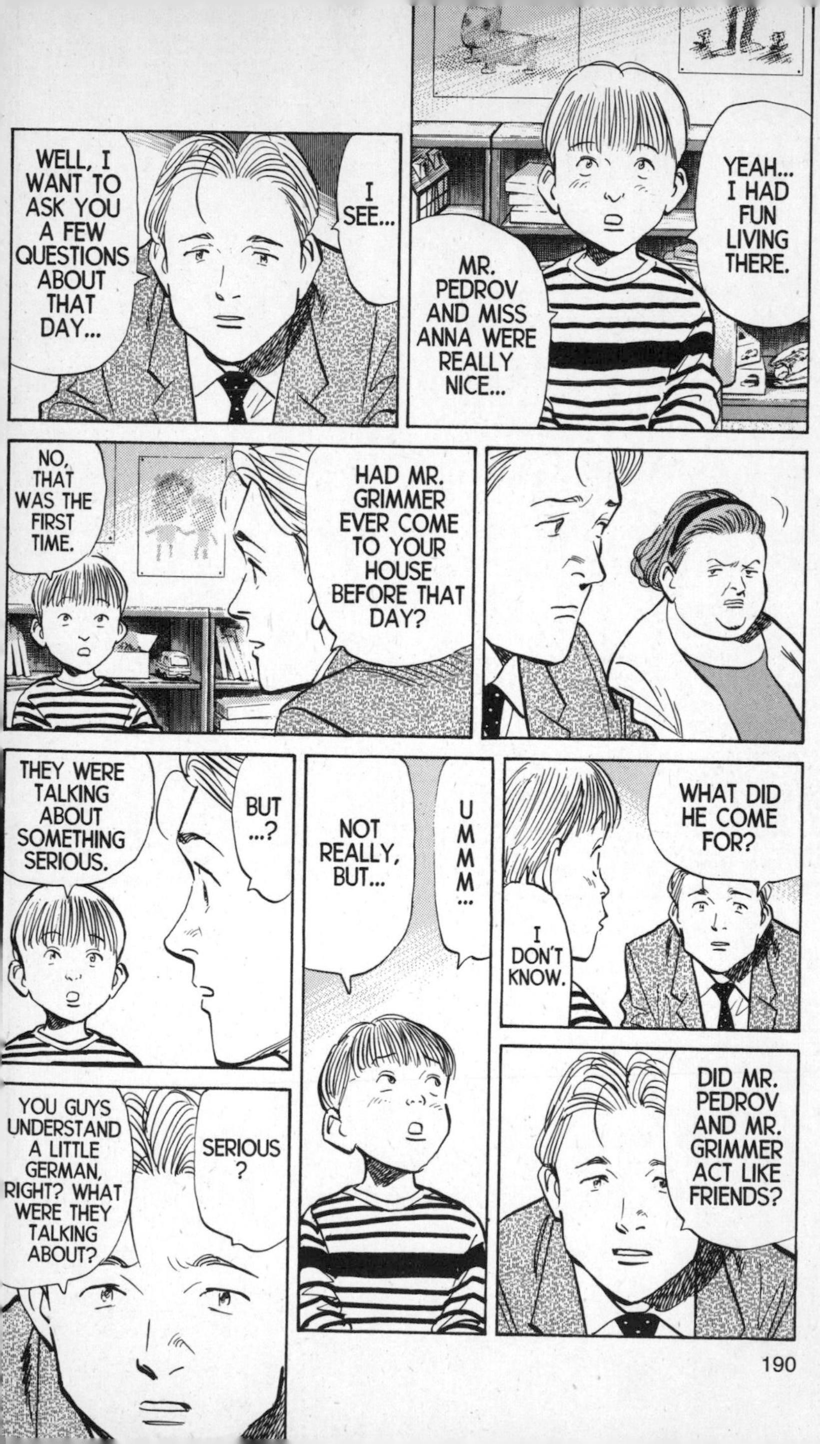
YEAH... I HAD FUN LIVING THERE.
MR. PEDROV AND MISS ANNA WERE REALLY NICE...
I SEE...
WELL, I WANT TO ASK YOU A FEW QUESTIONS ABOUT THAT DAY...
HAD MR. GRIMMER EVER COME TO YOUR HOUSE BEFORE THAT DAY?
NO, THAT WAS THE FIRST TIME.
WHAT DID HE COME FOR?
I DON'T KNOW.
DID MR. PEDROV AND MR. GRIMMER ACT LIKE FRIENDS?
UMMM...
NOT REALLY, BUT...
BUT ...?
THEY WERE TALKING ABOUT SOMETHING SERIOUS.
SERIOUS ?
YOU GUYS UNDERSTAND A LITTLE GERMAN, RIGHT? WHAT WERE THEY TALKING ABOUT?

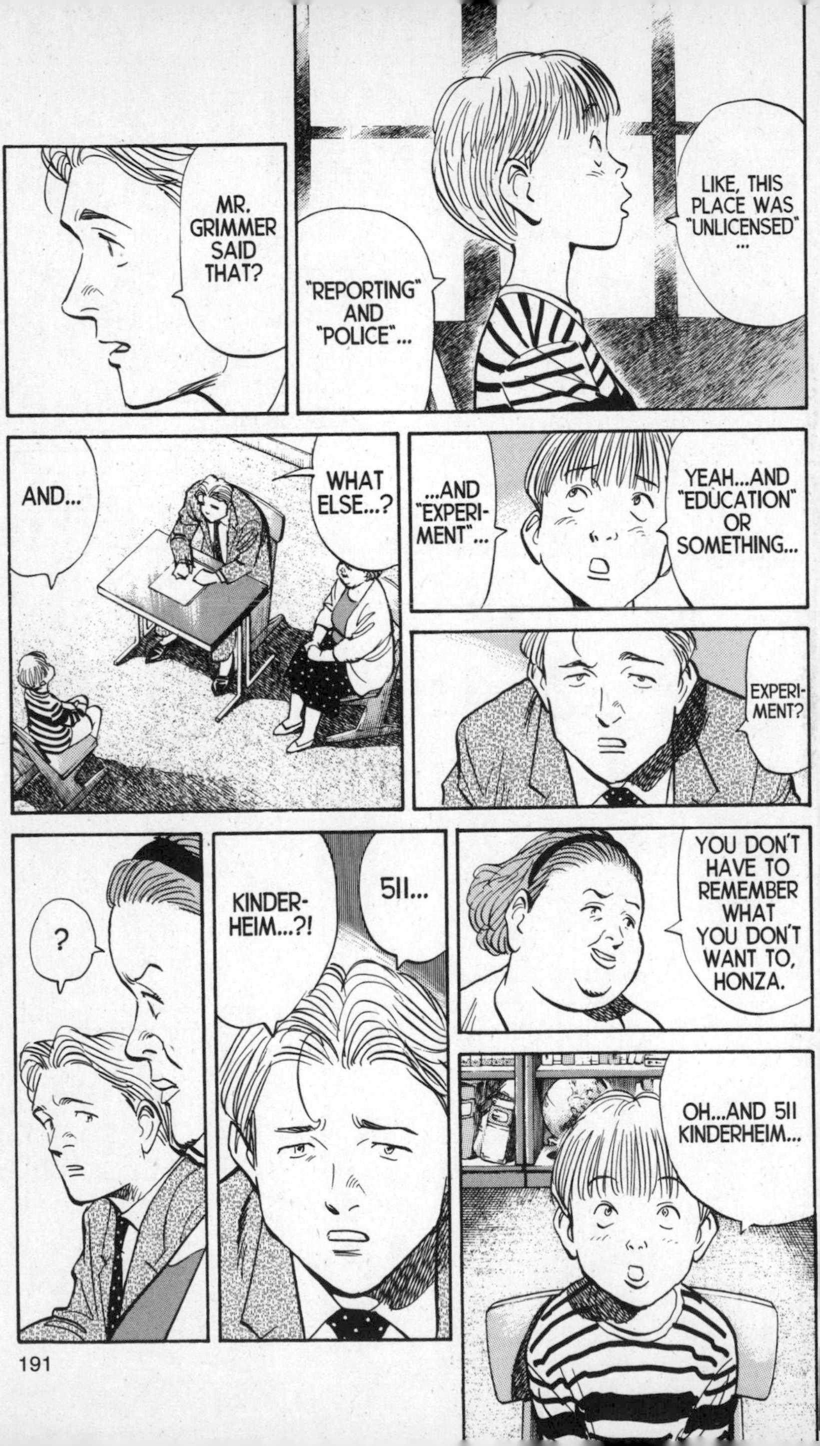
LIKE, THIS PLACE WAS "UNLICENSED"...
"REPORTING" AND "POLICE"...
MR. GRIMMER SAID THAT?
YEAH...AND "EDUCATION" OR SOMETHING...
...AND "EXPERI-MENT"...
EXPERI-MENT?
WHAT ELSE...?
AND...
YOU DON'T HAVE TO REMEMBER WHAT YOU DON'T WANT TO, HONZA.
OH...AND 511 KINDERHEIM...
511...
KINDER-HEIM...?!
?

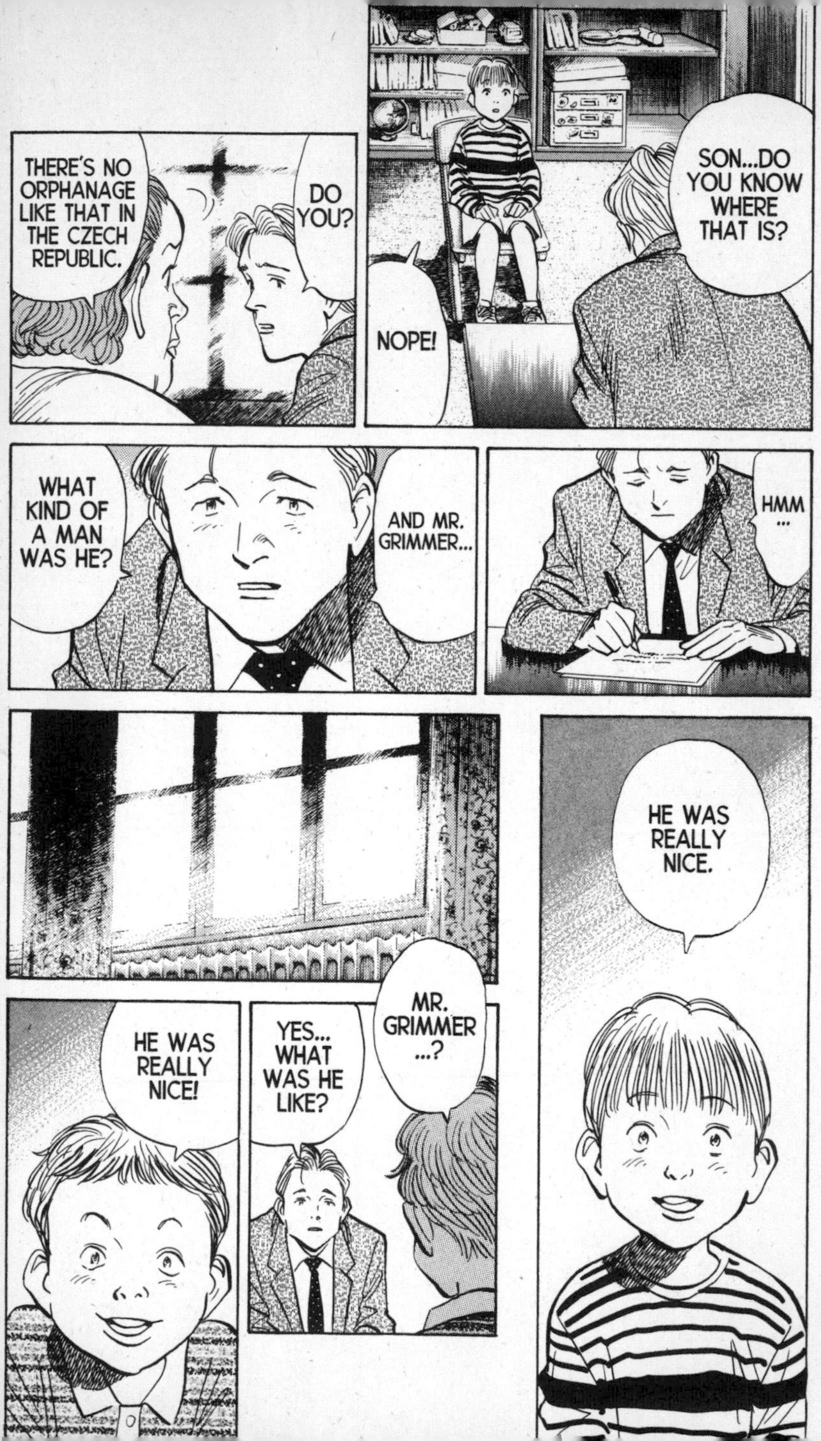
SON...DO YOU KNOW WHERE THAT IS?
NOPE!
DO YOU?
THERE'S NO ORPHANAGE LIKE THAT IN THE CZECH REPUBLIC.
HMM ...
AND MR. GRIMMER...
WHAT KIND OF A MAN WAS HE?
HE WAS REALLY NICE.
MR. GRIMMER ...?
YES... WHAT WAS HE LIKE?
HE WAS REALLY NICE!

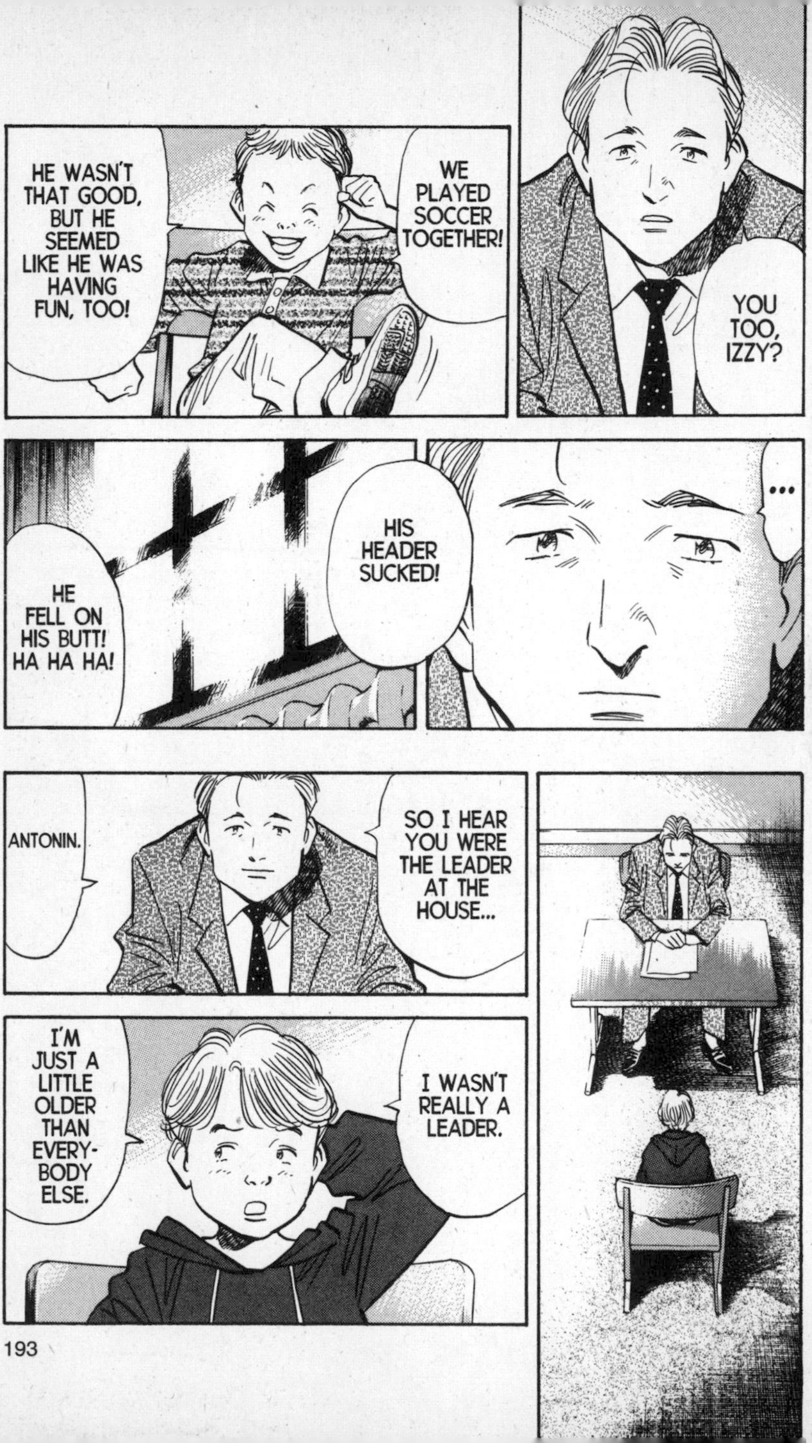
YOU TOO, IZZY?
WE PLAYED SOCCER TOGETHER!
HE WASN'T THAT GOOD, BUT HE SEEMED LIKE HE WAS HAVING FUN, TOO!
...
HIS HEADER SUCKED!
HE FELL ON HIS BUTT! HA HA HA!
SO I HEAR YOU WERE THE LEADER AT THE HOUSE...
ANTONIN.
I WASN'T REALLY A LEADER.
I'M JUST A LITTLE OLDER THAN EVERY-BODY ELSE.

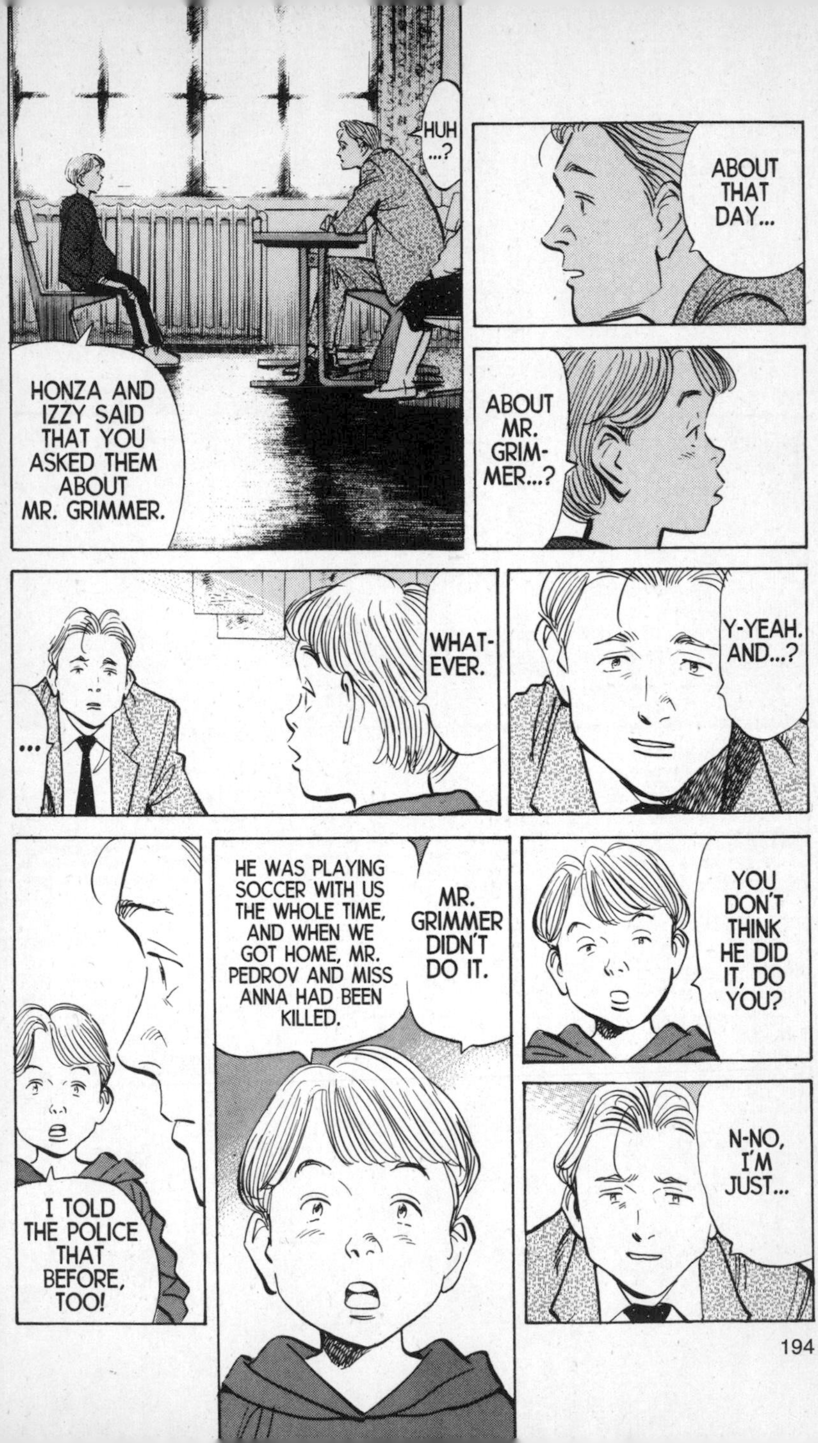
HONZA AND IZZY SAID THAT YOU ASKED THEM ABOUT MR. GRIMMER.
HUH ...?
ABOUT THAT DAY...
ABOUT MR. GRIM-MER...?
...
WHAT-EVER.
Y-YEAH. AND...?
I TOLD THE POLICE THAT BEFORE, TOO!
HE WAS PLAYING SOCCER WITH US THE WHOLE TIME, AND WHEN WE GOT HOME, MR. PEDROV AND MISS ANNA HAD BEEN KILLED.
MR. GRIMMER DIDN'T DO IT.
YOU DON'T THINK HE DID IT, DO YOU?
N-NO, I'M JUST...

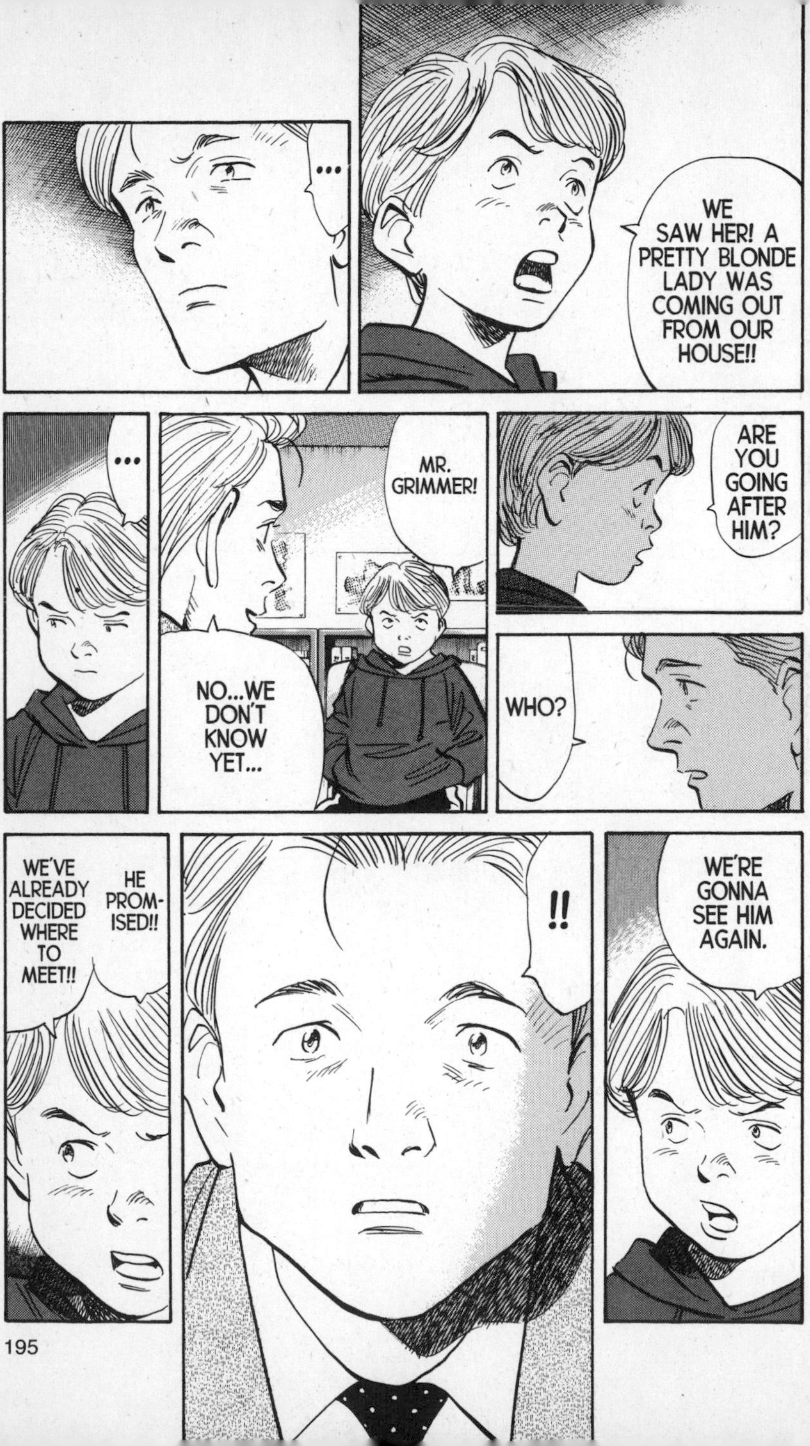
WE SAW HER! A PRETTY BLONDE LADY WAS COMING OUT FROM OUR HOUSE!!
...
ARE YOU GOING AFTER HIM?
WHO?
MR. GRIMMER!
NO...WE DON'T KNOW YET...
...
WE'RE GONNA SEE HIM AGAIN.
!!
HE PROMISED!!
WE'VE ALREADY DECIDED WHERE TO MEET!!

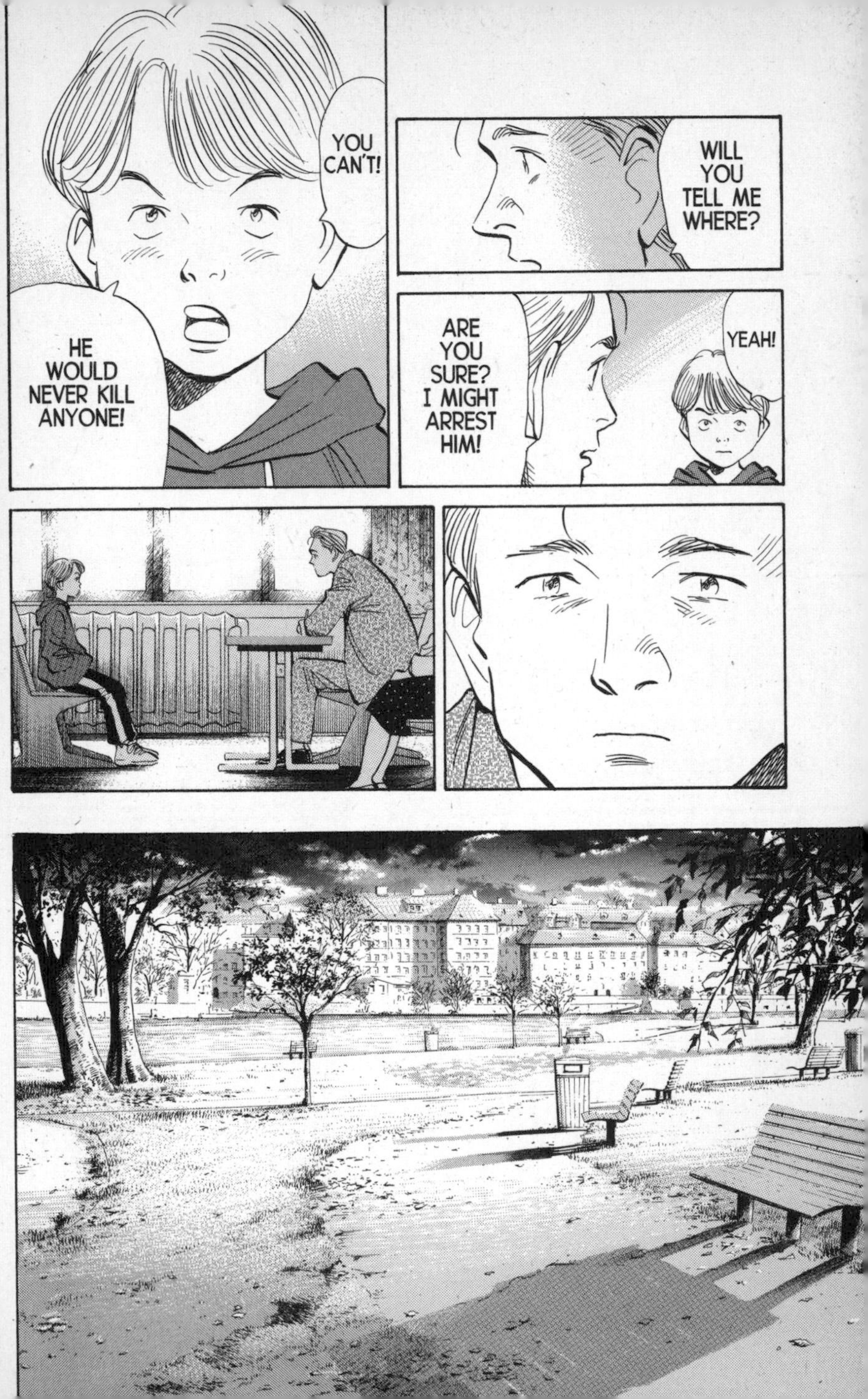
WILL YOU TELL ME WHERE?
ARE YOU SURE? I MIGHT ARREST HIM!
YEAH!
YOU CAN'T!
HE WOULD NEVER KILL ANYONE!

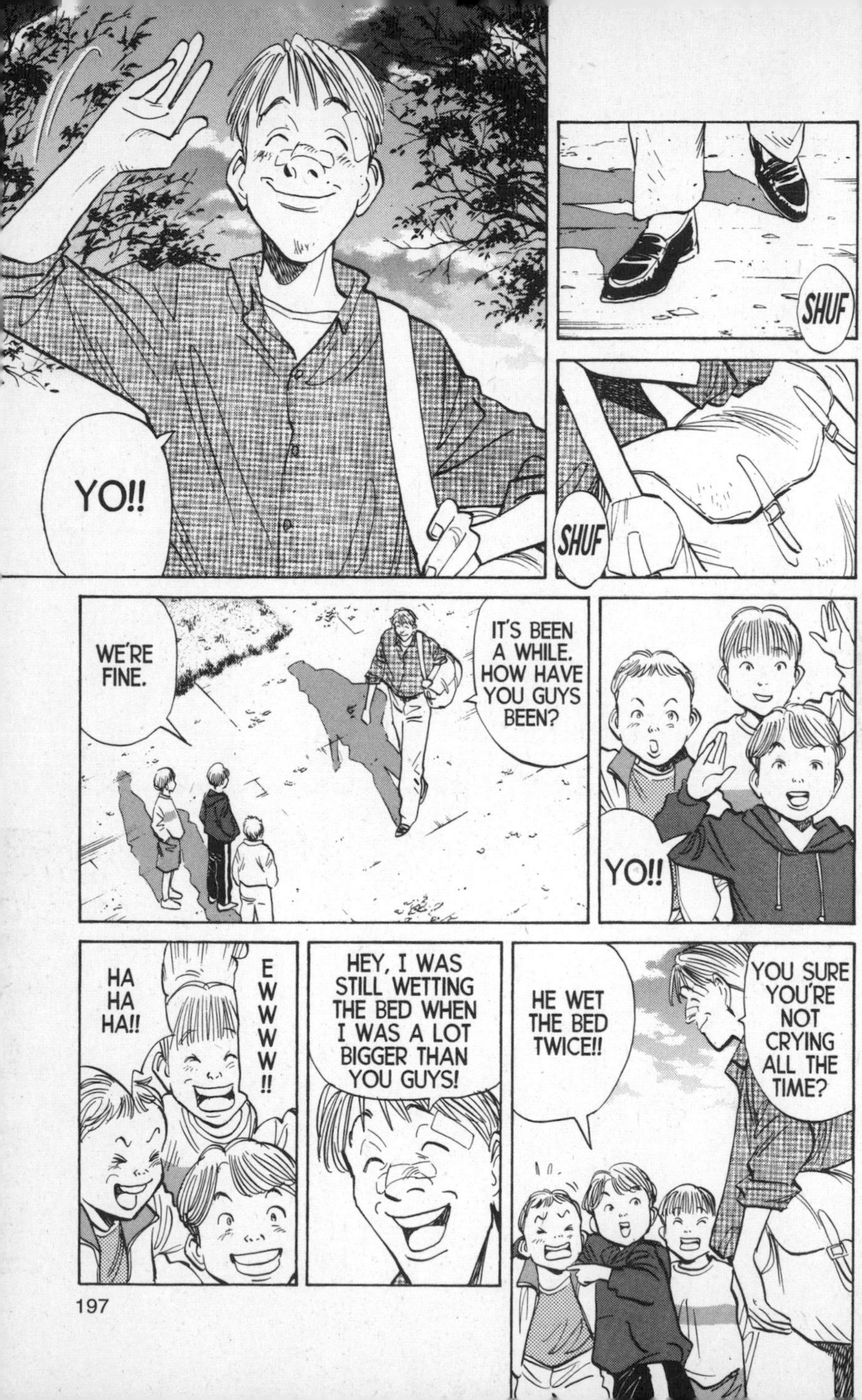
SHUF
SHUF
YO!!
YO!!
IT'S BEEN A WHILE. HOW HAVE YOU GUYS BEEN?
WE'RE FINE.
YOU SURE YOU'RE NOT CRYING ALL THE TIME?
HE WET THE BED TWICE!!
HEY, I WAS STILL WETTING THE BED WHEN I WAS A LOT BIGGER THAN YOU GUYS!
EWWWWW!!
HA HA HA!!

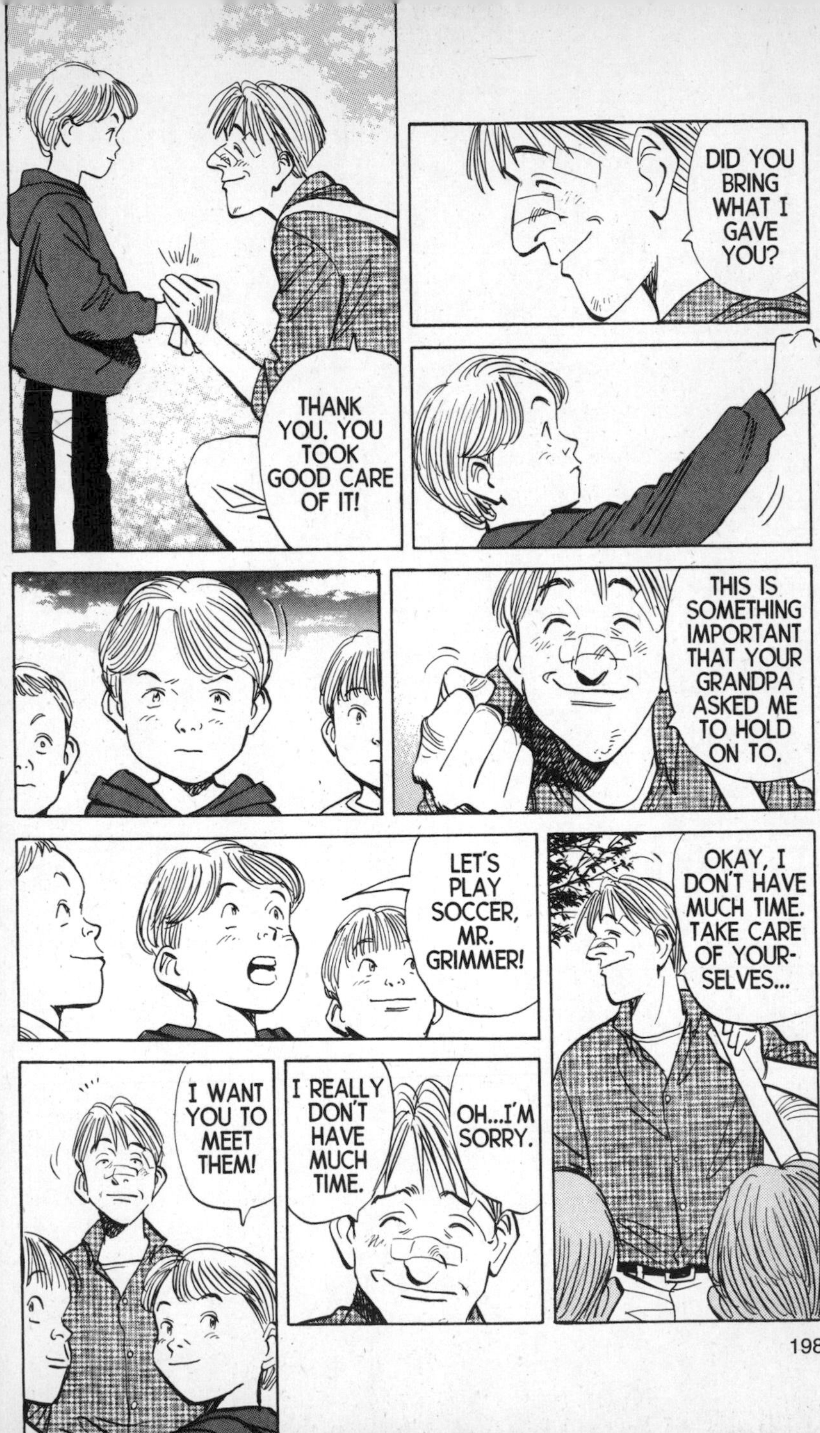
DID YOU BRING WHAT I GAVE YOU?
THANK YOU. YOU TOOK GOOD CARE OF IT!
THIS IS SOMETHING IMPORTANT THAT YOUR GRANDPA ASKED ME TO HOLD ON TO.
OKAY, I DON'T HAVE MUCH TIME. TAKE CARE OF YOUR-SELVES...
LET'S PLAY SOCCER, MR. GRIMMER!
OH...I'M SORRY.
I REALLY DON'T HAVE MUCH TIME.
I WANT YOU TO MEET THEM!

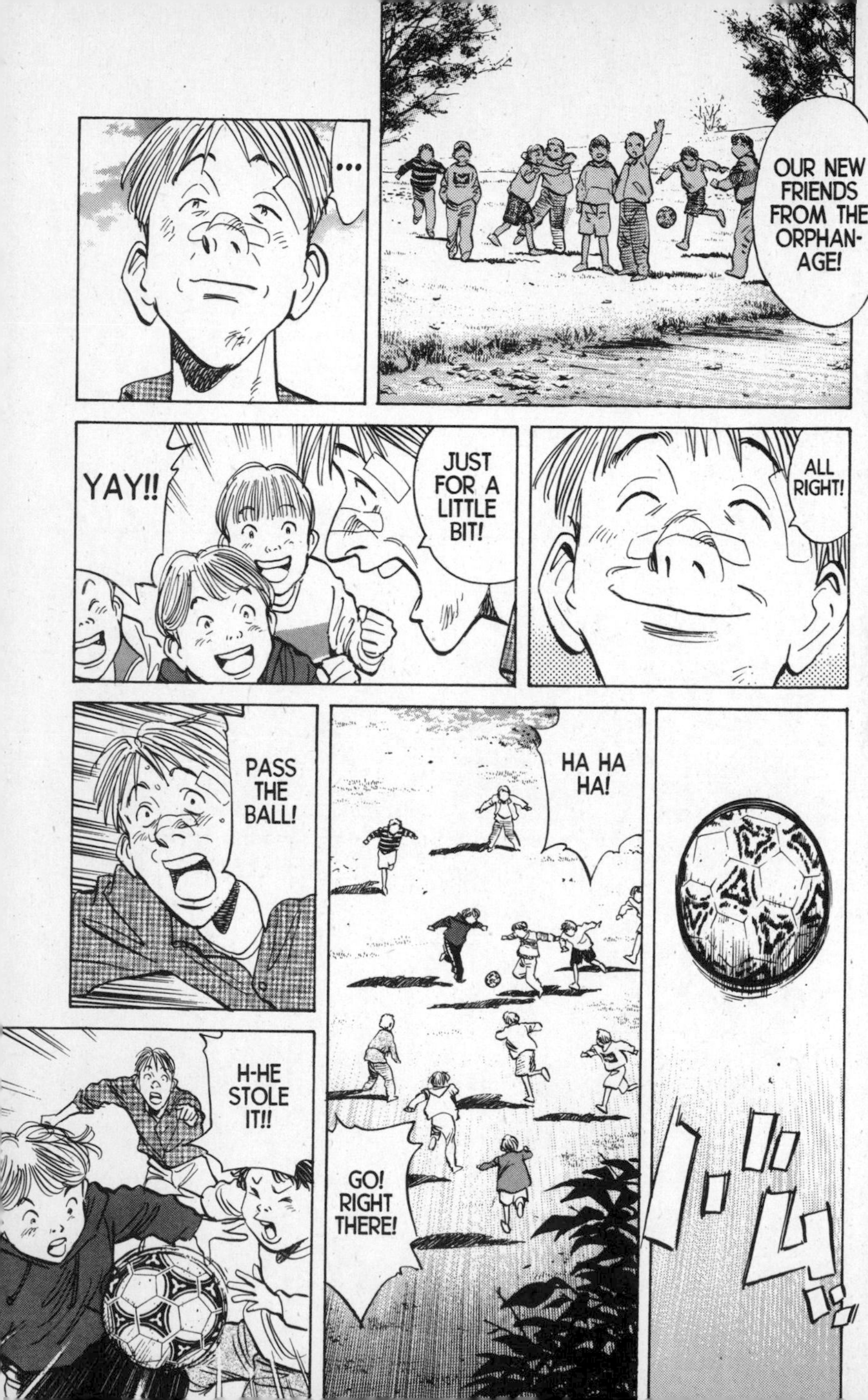
OUR NEW FRIENDS FROM THE ORPHAN-AGE!
...
ALL RIGHT!
JUST FOR A LITTLE BIT!
YAY!!
HA HA HA!
GO! RIGHT THERE!
PASS THE BALL!
H-HE STOLE IT!!

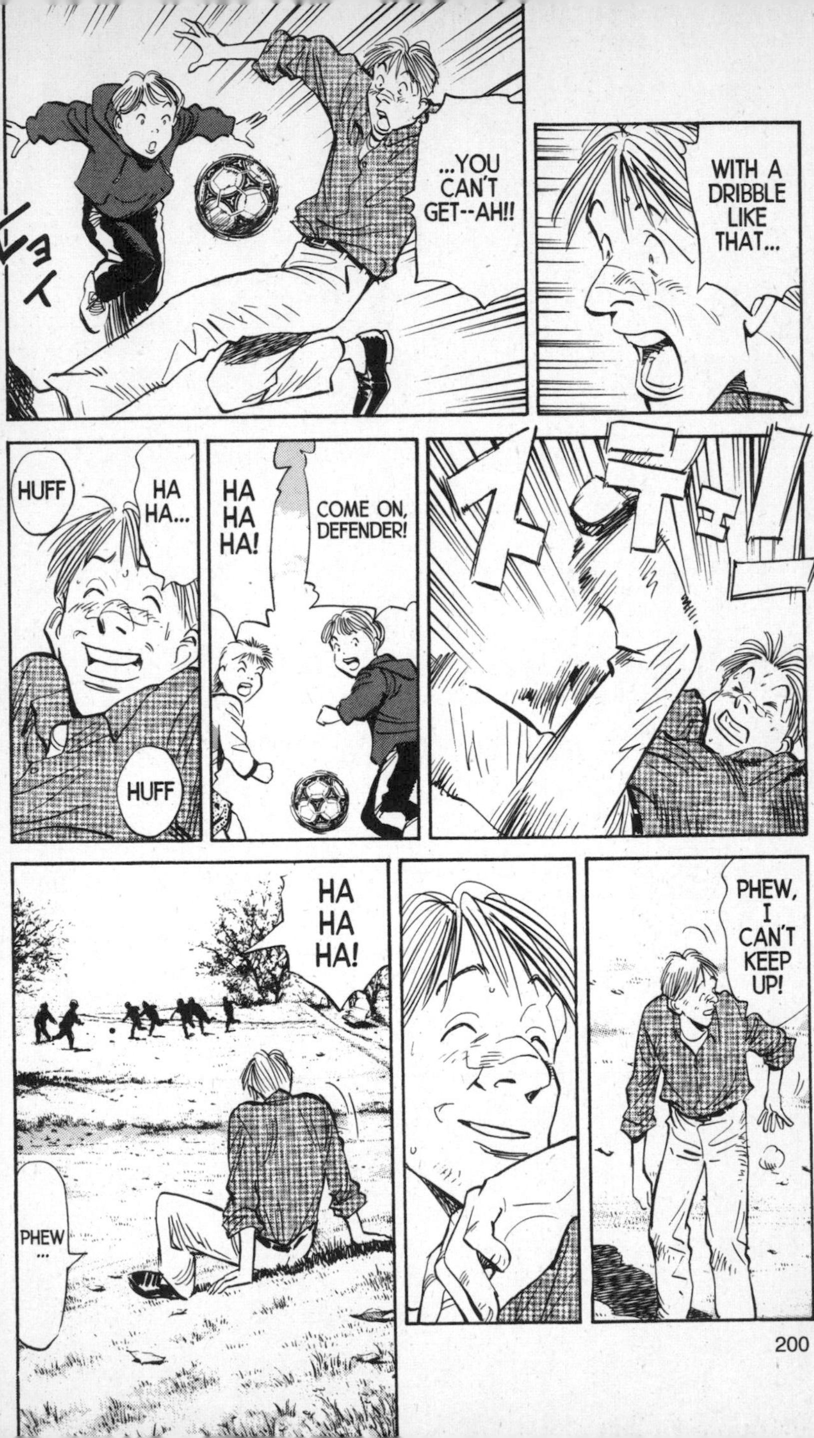
WITH A DRIBBLE LIKE THAT...
...YOU CAN'T GET--AH!!
ヒョイ
ズデェー!
COME ON, DEFENDER!
HA HA HA!
HA HA...
HUFF
HUFF
PHEW, I CAN'T KEEP UP!
HA HA HA!
PHEW ...

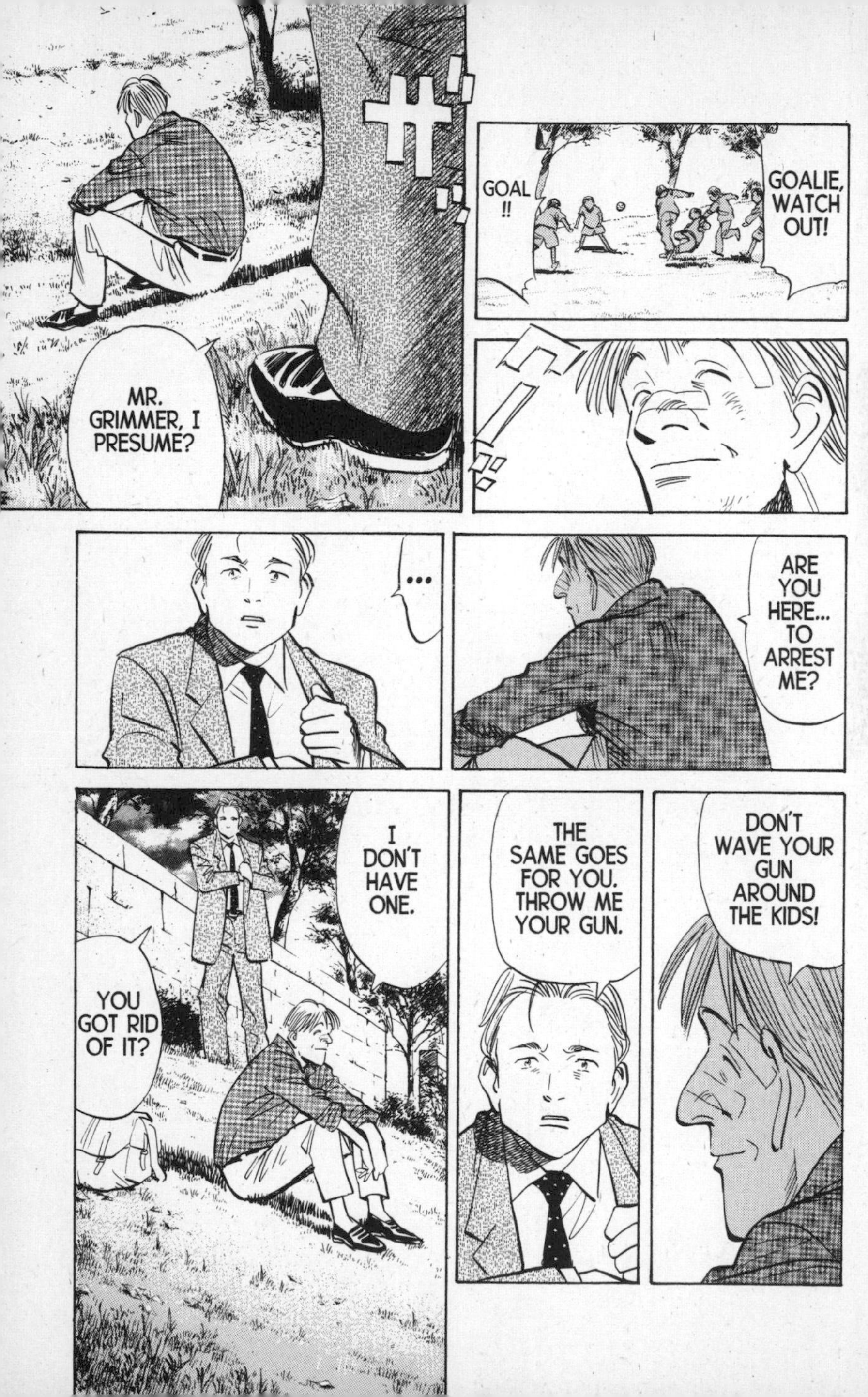
GOALIE, WATCH OUT!
GOAL !!
MR. GRIMMER, I PRESUME?
ARE YOU HERE... TO ARREST ME?
...
DON'T WAVE YOUR GUN AROUND THE KIDS!
THE SAME GOES FOR YOU. THROW ME YOUR GUN.
I DON'T HAVE ONE.
YOU GOT RID OF IT?

SHUF

....

...HAVE I EVER CARRIED A GUN IN MY LIFE!

NOT ONCE...

?

I DON'T KNOW...

DID YOU KILL INSPECTOR ZEMAN...?

I WAS BEING INTERROGATED AND BEATEN SENSELESS...

YOUR NAILS...

....

I DIDN'T FIRE THE GUN.

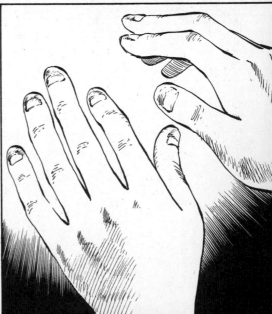

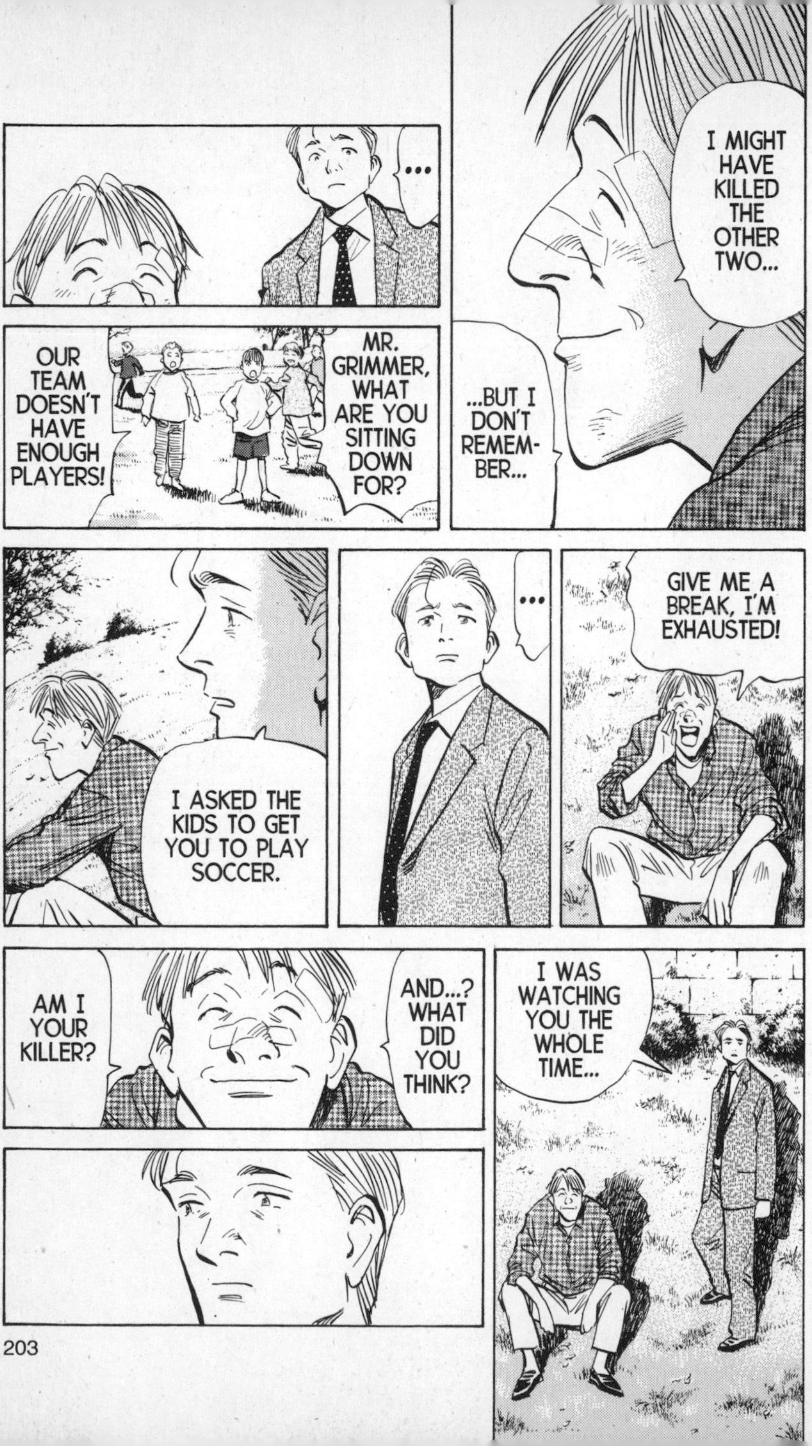
I MIGHT HAVE KILLED THE OTHER TWO...
...BUT I DON'T REMEMBER...
...
MR. GRIMMER, WHAT ARE YOU SITTING DOWN FOR?
OUR TEAM DOESN'T HAVE ENOUGH PLAYERS!
GIVE ME A BREAK, I'M EXHAUSTED!
...
I ASKED THE KIDS TO GET YOU TO PLAY SOCCER.
I WAS WATCHING YOU THE WHOLE TIME...
AND...? WHAT DID YOU THINK?
AM I YOUR KILLER?

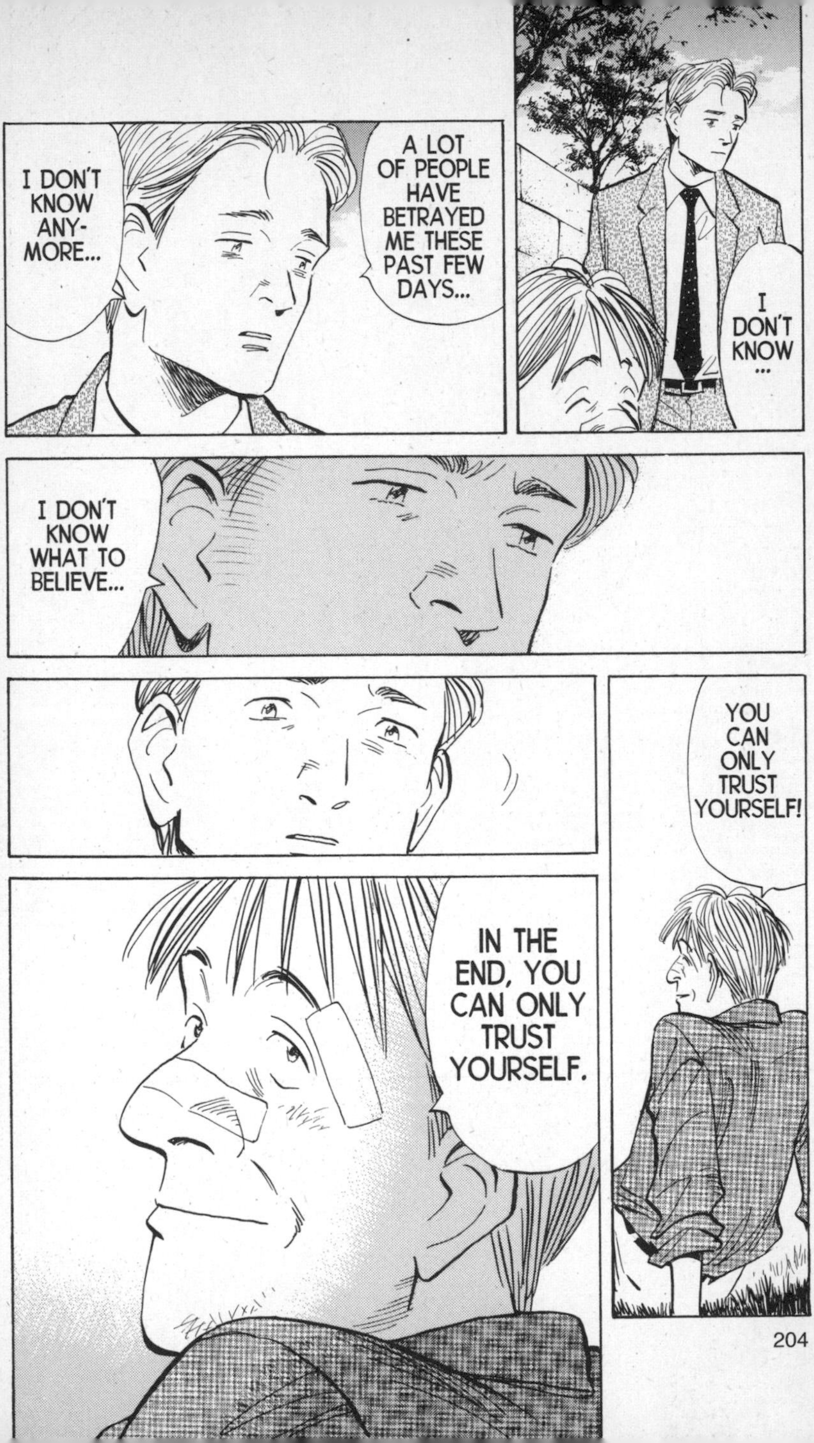
I DON'T KNOW ...
A LOT OF PEOPLE HAVE BETRAYED ME THESE PAST FEW DAYS...
I DON'T KNOW ANY-MORE...
I DON'T KNOW WHAT TO BELIEVE...
YOU CAN ONLY TRUST YOURSELF!
IN THE END, YOU CAN ONLY TRUST YOURSELF.

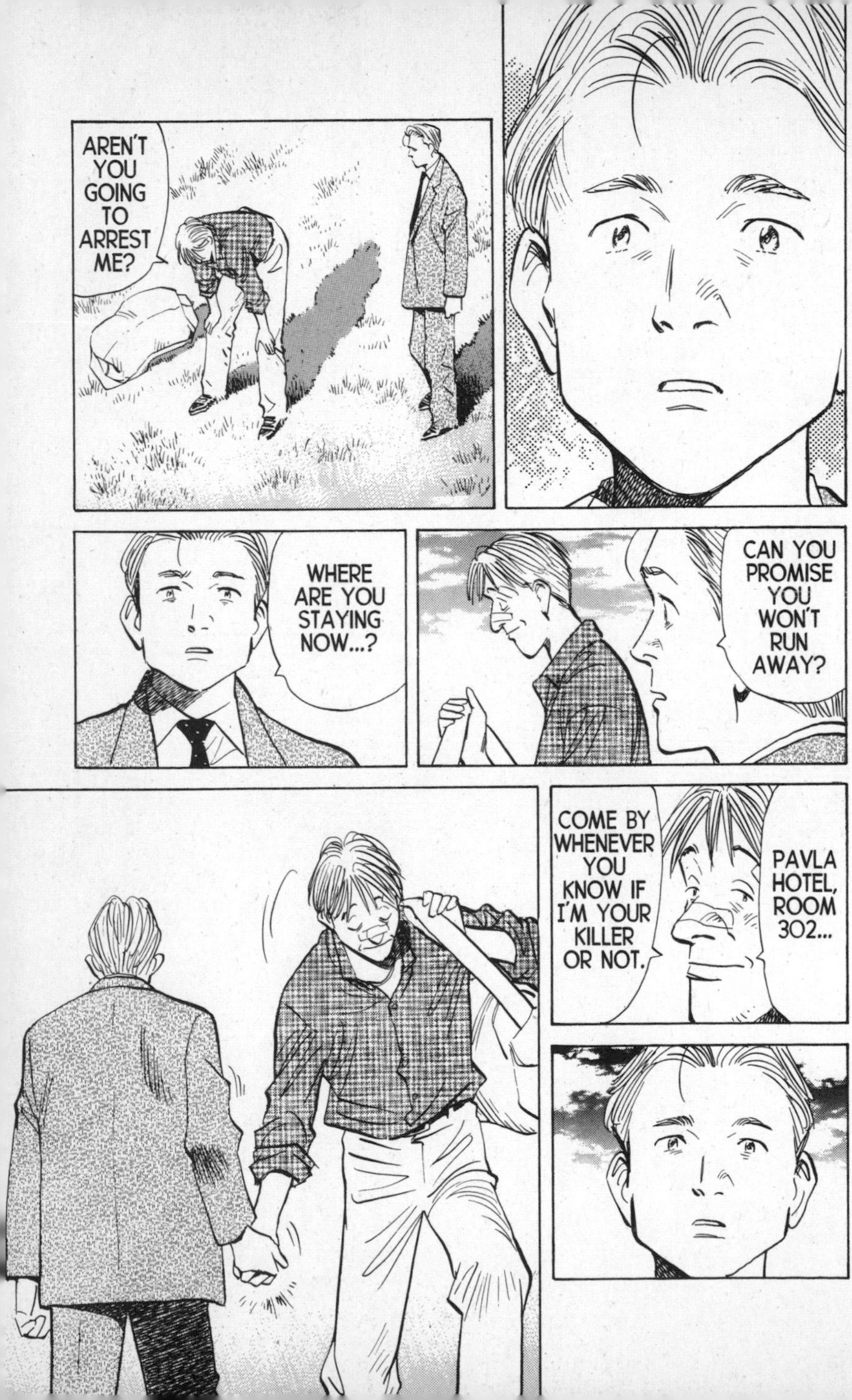
AREN'T YOU GOING TO ARREST ME?
CAN YOU PROMISE YOU WON'T RUN AWAY?
WHERE ARE YOU STAYING NOW...?
PAVLA HOTEL, ROOM 302...
COME BY WHENEVER YOU KNOW IF I'M YOUR KILLER OR NOT.

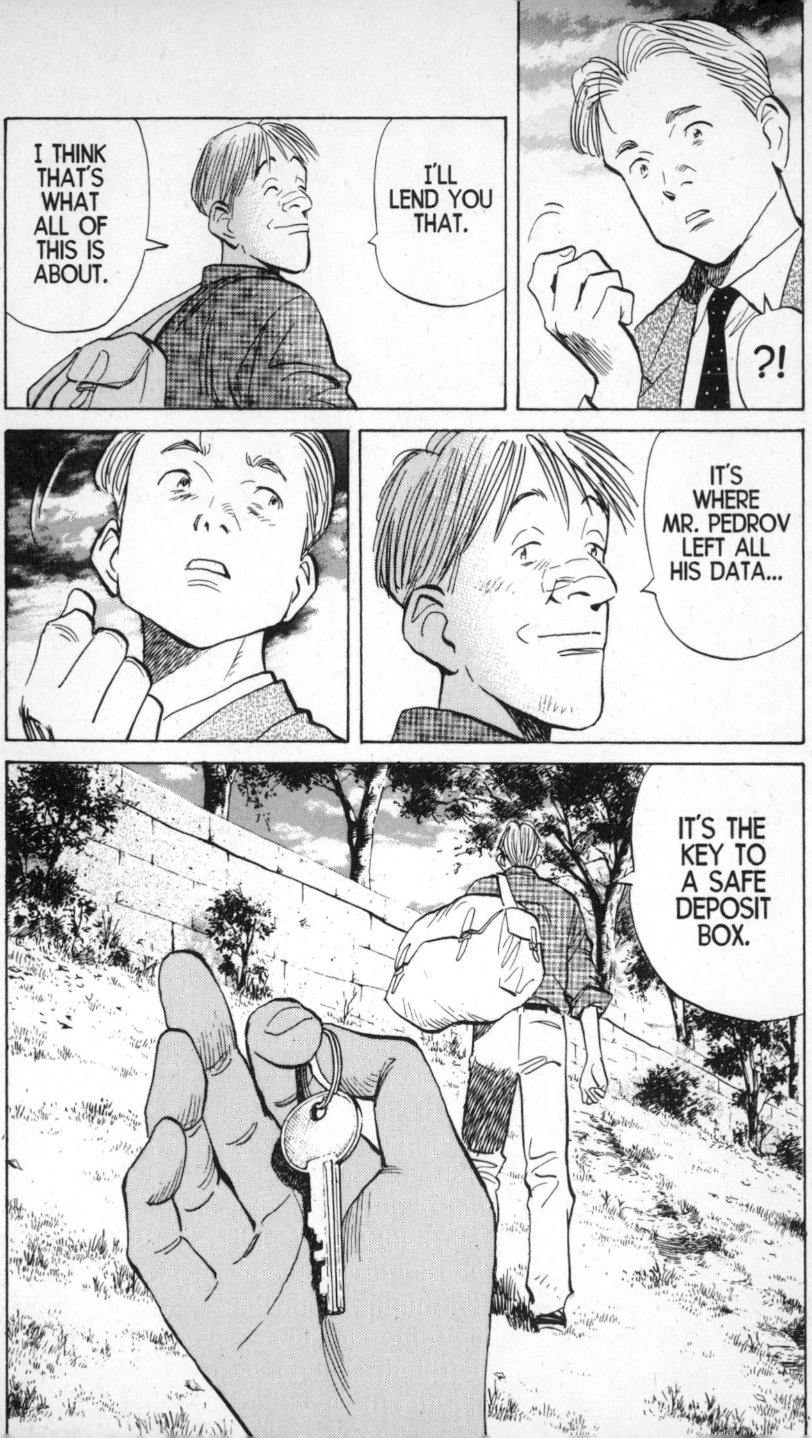
?!
I'LL LEND YOU THAT.
I THINK THAT'S WHAT ALL OF THIS IS ABOUT.
IT'S WHERE MR. PEDROV LEFT ALL HIS DATA...
IT'S THE KEY TO A SAFE DEPOSIT BOX.

about the author

Naoki Urasawa, born in Tokyo in 1960, is Japan's manga master of the suspense thriller. Critically acclaimed and immensely popular, his award-winning works include *20th Century Boys*, *Master Keaton*, *Pineapple Army*, and *Yawara*.

158.4—FX: Da (dash)

160.6—FX: Ka (klak)

Chapter 8

167.5—FX: Gakooon (slam)

176.2—FX: Basa (bam)

Chapter 9

185.2—FX: Gooo (roar)

186.1—FX: Wai wai wai (crowd noises)

186.7—FX: Wai wai wai (crowd noises)

199.5—FX: Bamu (bomp)

200.2—FX: Hyoi (jump)

200.3—FX: Suten (thud)

201.2—FX: Waaa (yay)

201.3—FX: Za (shuf)

glossary

Chapter 1

20.4—FX: Dosa (thud)

20.5—FX: So (thud)

21.1—FX: Paaan (train)

23.7—FX: Gatan

(door opening)

25.7—FX: Batan (bam)

Chapter 2

28.1—FX: Za za za

(shuf shuf shuf)

29.4—FX: Zu (shove)

29.6—FX: Za za (shuf shuf)

31.2—FX: Gatan gatan

(kdunk kdunk)

31.4—FX: Za za za

(shuf shuf shuf)

32.2—FX: Za (rustle)

46.4—FX: Dosa (thud)

Chapter 3

56.3—FX: Bashi (bash)

60.7—FX: Batan (bam)

61.1—FX: Ba (bam)

61.3—FX: Da (dash)

67.5—FX: Da (dash)

70.1—FX: Da (dash)

Chapter 4

84.1—FX: Bamu (bomp)

86.4—FX: Yotata (staggering)

86.5—FX: Doden (thud)

88.2—FX: Da (dash)

89.2—FX: Ba (shuf)

89.3—FX: Don don

(bam bam)

89.4—FX: Gi (kreek)

90.3—FX: Ba (bam)

Chapter 5

97.4—FX: Gon (bam)

105.4—FX: Buoo (vroom)

106.7—FX: Gu (grip)

107.6—FX: Buoo (vroom)

107.10—FX: Oon (vroom)

108.1—FX: Oon (vroom)

108.8—FX: Kikii (squeeek)

110.6—FX: Go (bash)

111.1—FX: Baga gasu dogo

(slam bash punch)

111.2—FX: Dodo (thud)

111.4—FX: Ba (bam)

111.7—FX: Da (dash)

113.4—FX: Don don

(bang bang)

Chapter 6

118.1—FX: Doka dosu

(bash bash)

118.2—FX: Gon bakin

(bam crack)

118.3—FX: Bogo (bash)

126.2—FX: Bashu (bash)

128.1—FX: Bogo (bash)

128.2—FX: Goki (smash)

128.3—FX: Go (punch)

128.3—FX: Bako (bam)

131.6—FX: Bogo (bash)

131.7—FX: Bakin (crack)

131.7—FX: Gashi (bam)

131.7—FX: Gon (crash)

132.1—FX: Go (thud)

132.6—FX: Do (thud)

132.8—FX: Zaaaa (pssssh)

133.4—FX: Zaaaa (psssssh)

134.1—FX: Zaaaaaa (pssssssh)

134.3—FX: Don (bang)

136.6—FX: Fura (wobble)

Chapter 7

139.1—FX: Paahoo paahoo

(weeeooo weeeooo)

142.2—FX: Dada (dash)

145.3—FX: Dan (bam)

151.7—FX: Batan (Bam)

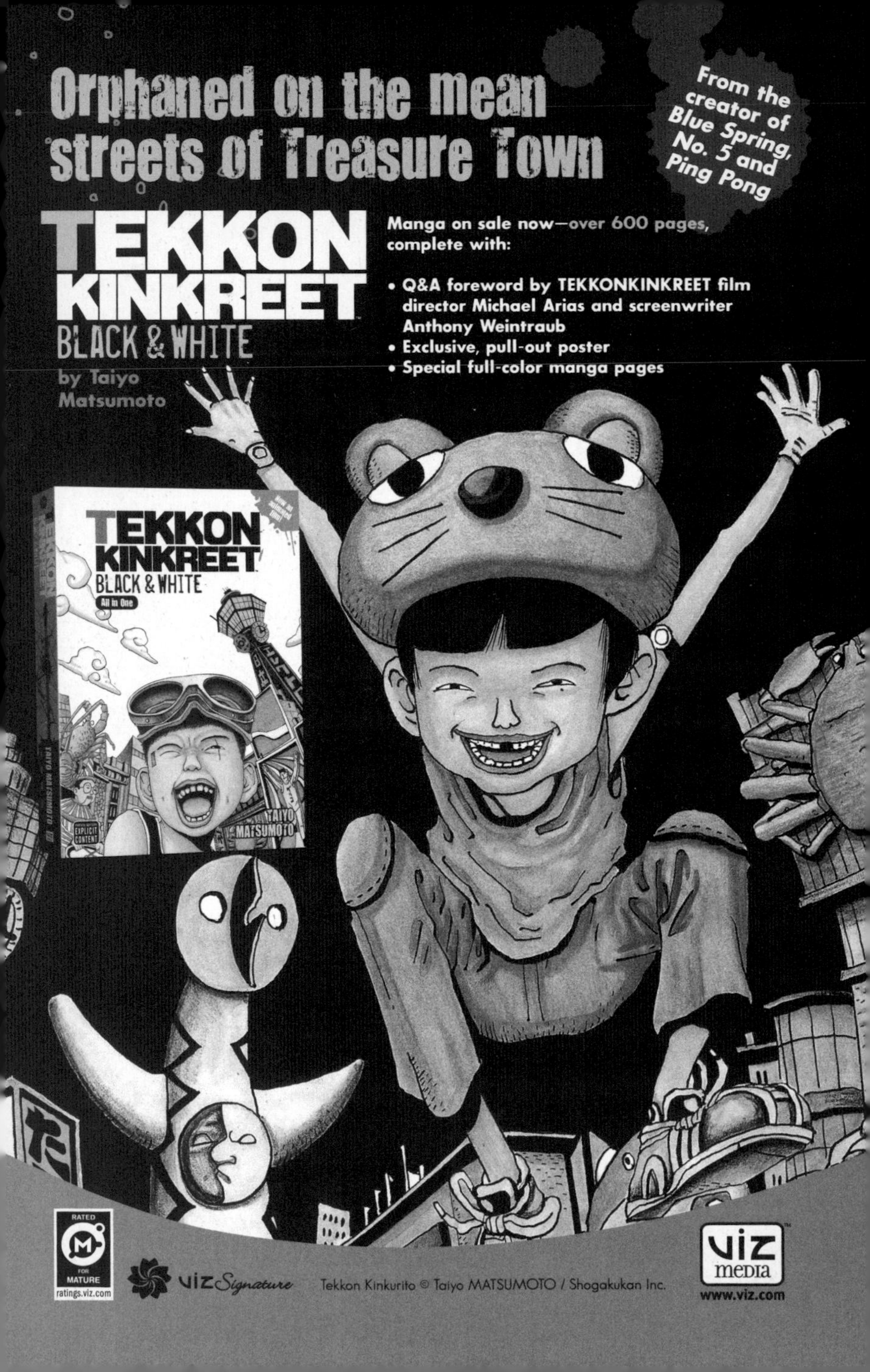
Orphaned on the mean streets of Treasure Town
From the creator of Blue Spring, No. 5 and Ping Pong
TEKKON KINKREET
BLACK & WHITE
by Taiyo Matsumoto
Manga on sale now—over 600 pages, complete with:
• Q&A foreword by TEKKONKINKREET film director Michael Arias and screenwriter Anthony Weintraub
• Exclusive, pull-out poster
• Special full-color manga pages
TEKKON KINKREET
BLACK & WHITE
All in One
TAIYO MATSUMOTO
EXPLICIT CONTENT
RATED M FOR MATURE
ratings.viz.com
VIZ Signature
Tekkon Kinkurito © Taiyo MATSUMOTO / Shogakukan Inc.
VIZ media
www.viz.com

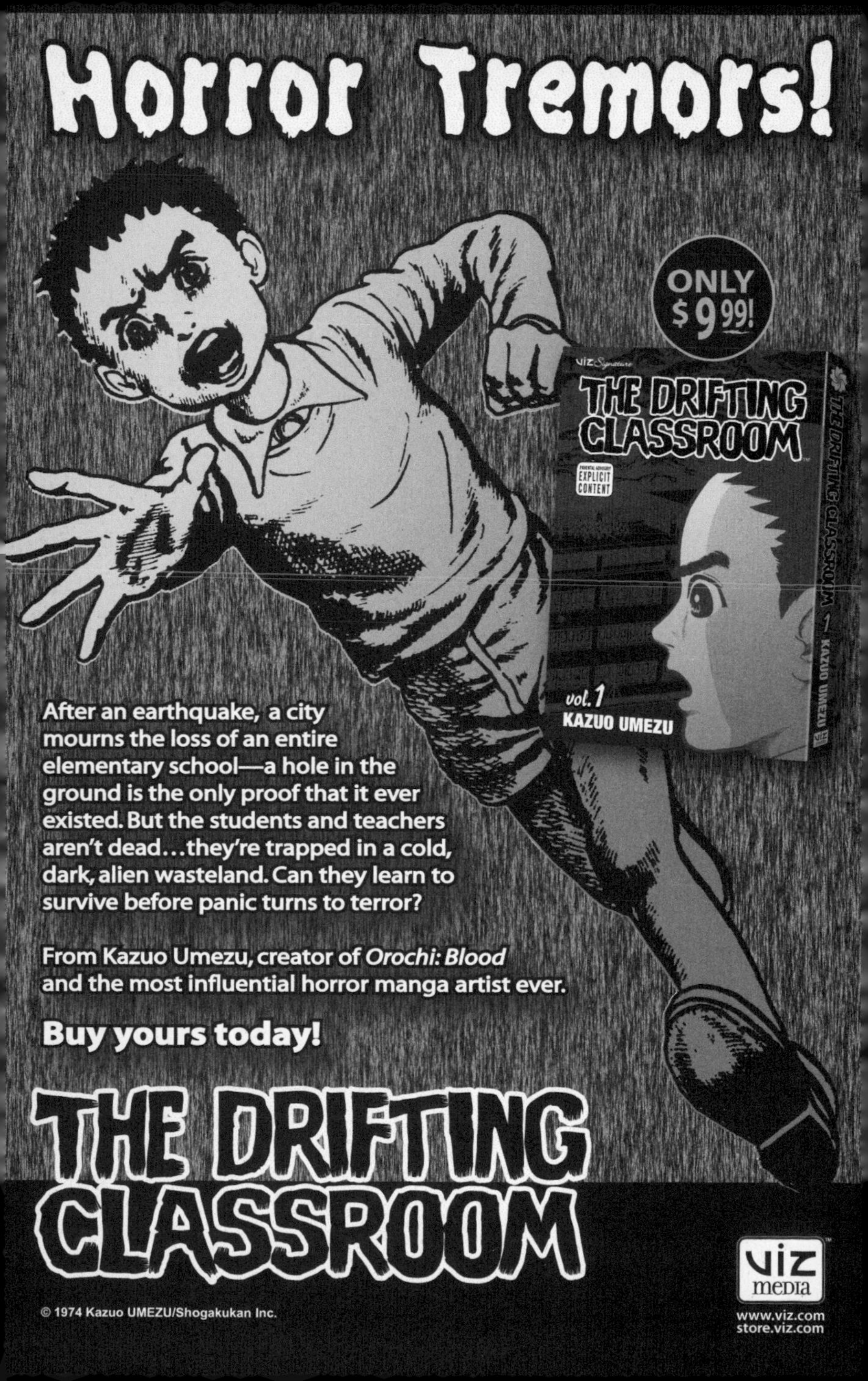
Horror Tremors!
ONLY $9.99!
VIZ Signature
THE DRIFTING CLASSROOM
PARENTAL ADVISORY EXPLICIT CONTENT
vol.1
KAZUO UMEZU
After an earthquake, a city mourns the loss of an entire elementary school—a hole in the ground is the only proof that it ever existed. But the students and teachers aren't dead...they're trapped in a cold, dark, alien wasteland. Can they learn to survive before panic turns to terror?
From Kazuo Umezu, creator of Orochi: Blood and the most influential horror manga artist ever.
Buy yours today!
THE DRIFTING CLASSROOM
VIZ media
© 1974 Kazuo UMEZU/Shogakukan Inc.
www.viz.com
store.viz.com

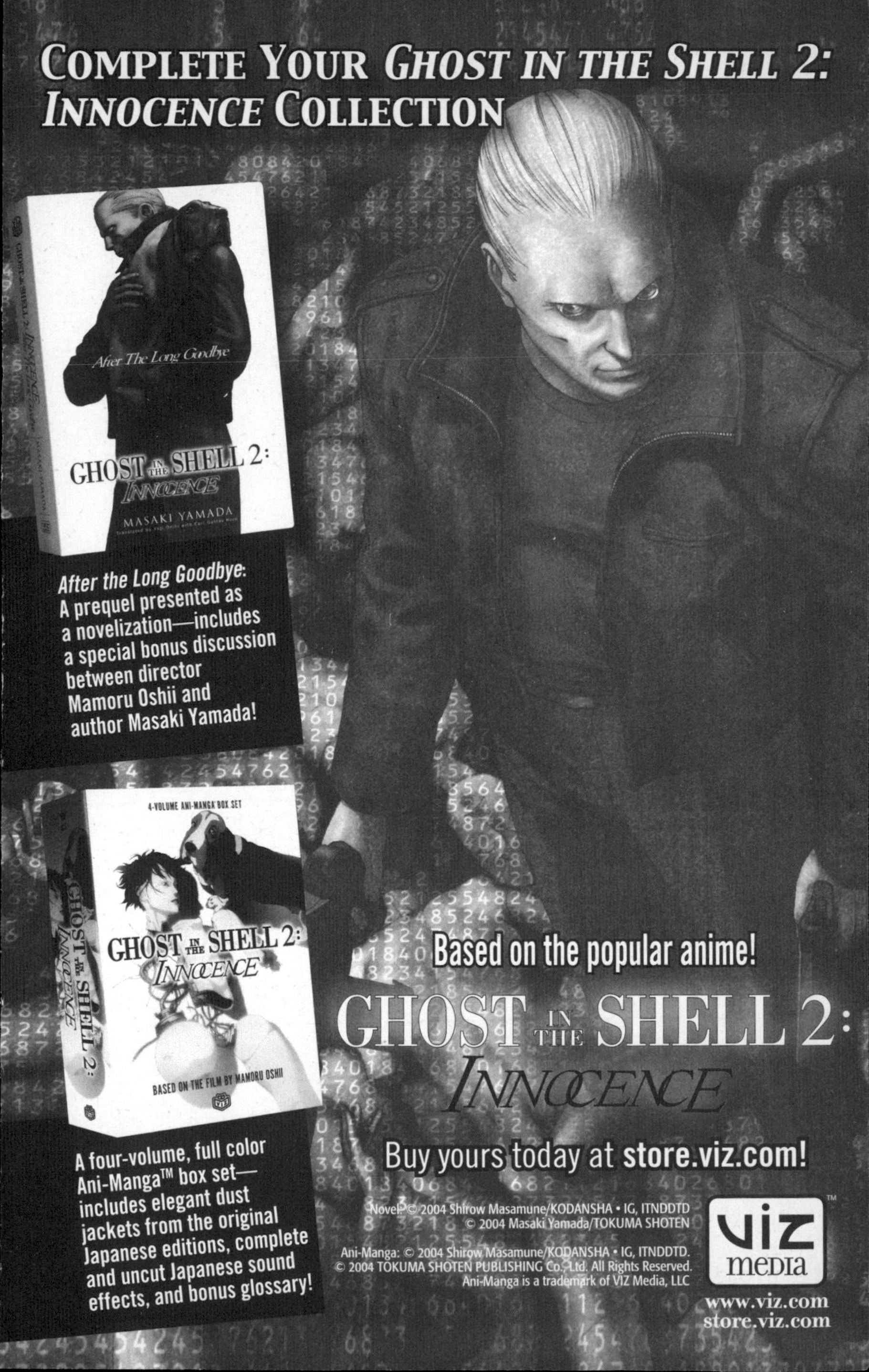

COMPLETE YOUR GHOST IN THE SHELL 2: INNOCENCE COLLECTION
After The Long Goodbye
GHOST IN THE SHELL 2: INNOCENCE
MASAKI YAMADA
After the Long Goodbye: A prequel presented as a novelization—includes a special bonus discussion between director Mamoru Oshii and author Masaki Yamada!
4-VOLUME ANI-MANGA BOX SET
GHOST IN THE SHELL 2: INNOCENCE
BASED ON THE FILM BY MAMORU OSHII
A four-volume, full color Ani-Manga™ box set—includes elegant dust jackets from the original Japanese editions, complete and uncut Japanese sound effects, and bonus glossary!
Based on the popular anime!
GHOST IN THE SHELL 2: INNOCENCE
Buy yours today at store.viz.com!
Novel: © 2004 Shirow Masamune/KODANSHA • IG, ITNDDTD
© 2004 Masaki Yamada/TOKUMA SHOTEN
Ani-Manga: © 2004 Shirow Masamune/KODANSHA • IG, ITNDDTD.
© 2004 TOKUMA SHOTEN PUBLISHING Co., Ltd. All Rights Reserved.
Ani-Manga is a trademark of VIZ Media, LLC
viz media
www.viz.com
store.viz.com

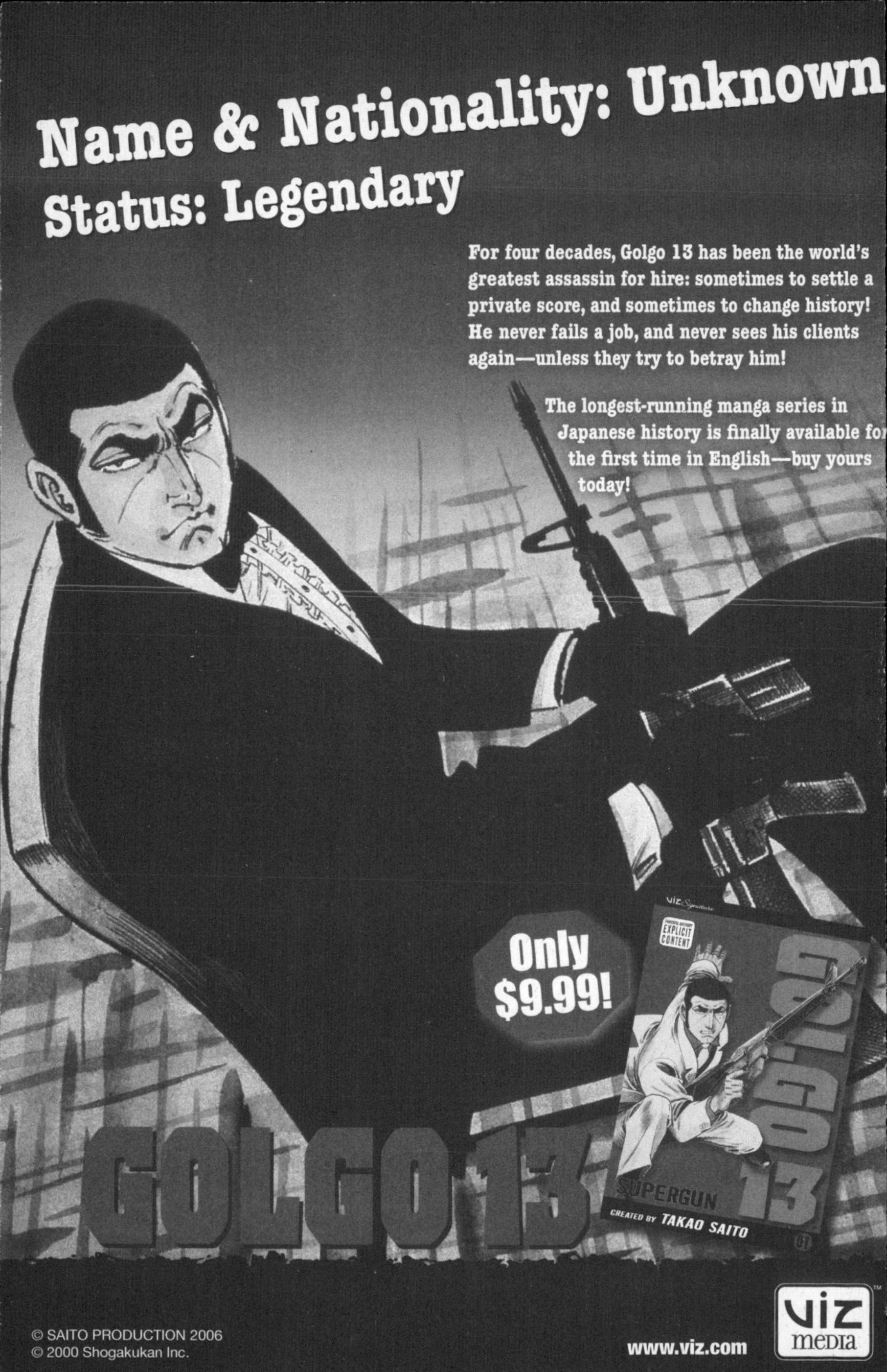
Name & Nationality: Unknown
Status: Legendary
For four decades, Golgo 13 has been the world's greatest assassin for hire: sometimes to settle a private score, and sometimes to change history! He never fails a job, and never sees his clients again—unless they try to betray him!
The longest-running manga series in Japanese history is finally available for the first time in English—buy yours today!
Only $9.99!
EXPLICIT CONTENT
GOLGO 13
SUPERGUN
CREATED BY TAKAO SAITO
GOLGO 13
viz media
www.viz.com
© SAITO PRODUCTION 2006
© 2000 Shogakukan Inc.

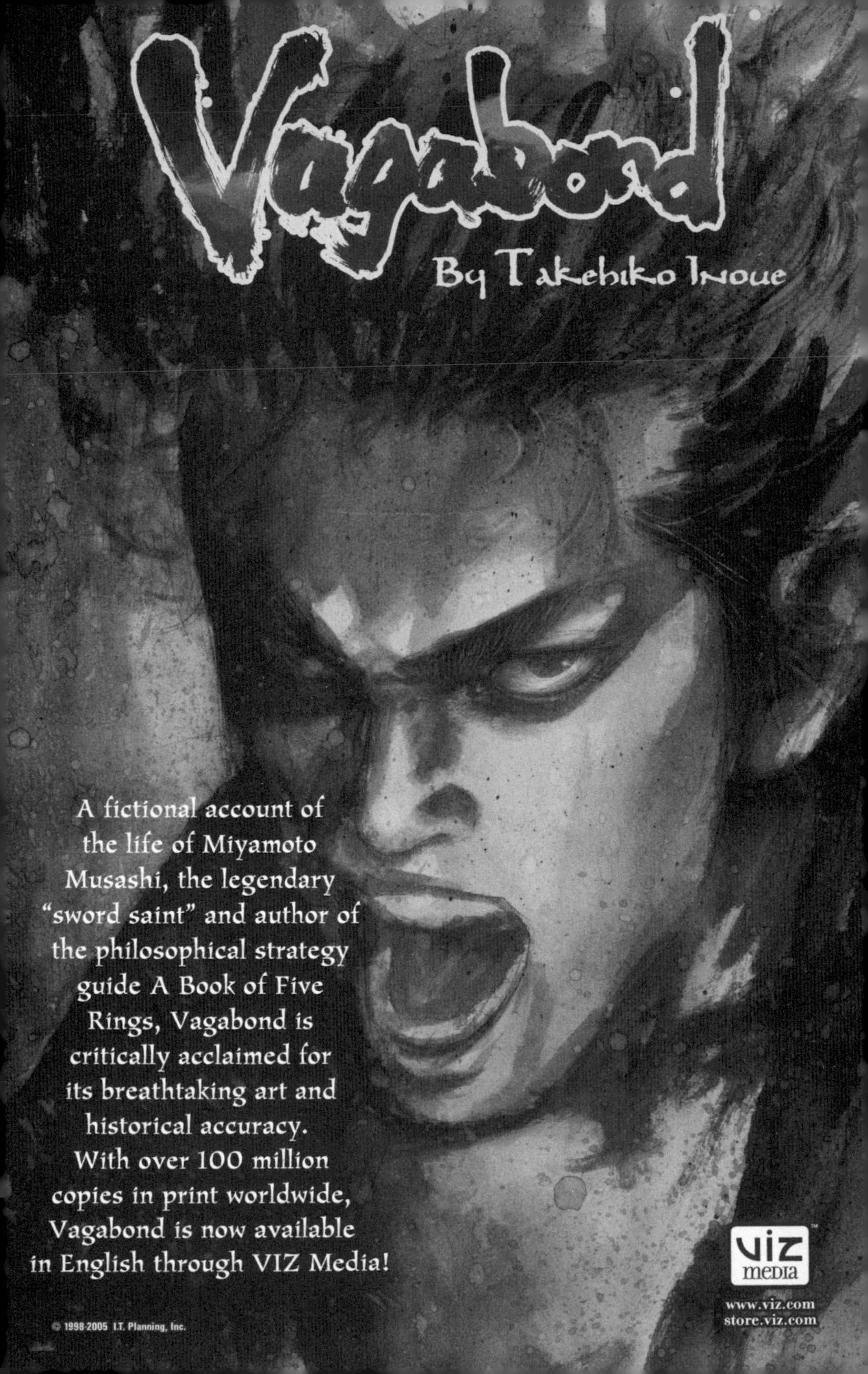
Vagabond
By Takehiko Inoue
A fictional account of the life of Miyamoto Musashi, the legendary "sword saint" and author of the philosophical strategy guide A Book of Five Rings, Vagabond is critically acclaimed for its breathtaking art and historical accuracy. With over 100 million copies in print worldwide, Vagabond is now available in English through VIZ Media!
VIZ media
www.viz.com
store.viz.com
© 1998-2005 I.T. Planning, Inc.

The Quest for the Ultimate Menu

The Challenge
Create a model meal that embodies the pinnacle of Japanese cuisine.

The Chef
A cynical journalist with no initiative, but an incredibly refined palate and an encyclopedic knowledge of food.

The Result
Find out in *Oishinbo a La Carte* manga—Buy yours today!

O!SHINBO
A La Carte

Story by Tetsu Kariya | Art by Akira Hanasaki

On sale at store.viz.com
Also available at your local bookstore and comic store.